# THE NATURAL HISTORY OF WALNEY ISLAND

*Dedicated to my parents,*
*Jack and Marian Dean*

0 948558 04 0

Published by
Faust Publications,
Thorneyholme Hall, Roughlee, Burnley, Lancashire.

Printed by
Turner and Earnshaw Limited,
Westway House, Sycamore Avenue, Burnley, Lancashire.

# The Natural History of Walney Island

Tim Dean

# Contents

# Preface and Acknowledgements

It has been a long illness. The germ germinated in 1980; it's now late 1990 — so how come the long delay? Hiccups began at the very outset — the sources of information were not as straightforward as perhaps they should have been. Prior to 1974 Walney Island was in Lancashire; since then it has been in Cumbria, and in addition has always been tacked on as a worthwhile natural history appendage to the Lake District region. Consequently, records relating to the island had to be gathered from numerous journals, bulletins and reports assembled by natural history societies in these three areas. A relapse occurred when the bird records from Walney Bird Observatory were studied. Here was a vast amount of data set out month by month for at least fifteen years but with one vital omission — there were no species' names! The first task therefore was to allot species to the plethora of numbers, a task which could have proved nigh impossible but for the fact that the patterns and sequences of numbers seemed to confirm that the Observatory was using the rather out of fashion Wetmore order of species for its log books. However, despite this breakthrough of decoding, the work still necessitated a fair amount of skilful deduction and much cross-referencing using individuals' notes and county natural history reports to verify some records. No sooner had that ailment been treated than further complications arose — the absence of any records or log books for AD 1974. Now it is true that the fortunes of the Observatory at this period had hit rock bottom, but was it really necessary to commit 1974 to the incinerator just because a certain Observatory stalwart's back door could not be opened fully to permit his bike into the kitchen? Consequently the whole year had to be rerun with resource to county reports and observers' notebooks. At last the patient seemed to be on the mend and recuperation took place in Birmingham. Here the barebones of twenty-plus years were united by my father, John Dean, who devoted almost two years tabulating figures in his own inimitable and precise manner. Many first-class stamps were used during that period (1982 to 1984) as we sorted out the idiosyncratic methods used by the idiosyncratic recorders at the Observatory — the various meanings of ticks, question marks, asterisks and all sorts of codes in columns that were really meant for just a plain, standard, regular number. By late 1984, the Observatory records had been pummelled into a shape that could be used without too much hesitation, and so began the "book proper". Since 1985, the book has been ready for publication, but only in 1988 was a publisher game enough to take it on, and the intervening two years has seen the updating of statistics and facts to the end of 1989.

I am indebted wholeheartedly to all the people who allowed my grubby paws and prying eyes access to their notebooks, most especially Jack Sheldon, Howard Tickle and Richard Wimpress who not only helped piece together 1974, but also contributed to shaping the years immediately preceding the Observatory. I am grateful for the personal notes loaned by John Barnes and Bob Benson which have assisted in putting together breeding information for both ends of the island in the 1940s and 1950s; Bob was also of enormous help with other aspects of the island's natural history. Records from North Walney have been well-documented since the Cumbria Wildlife Trust took on the wardening of this superb site in late 1983. Prior to this, the bulk of available bird data has come from Bob Treen who has counted the wildfowl and waders each month since the mid-1970s. Without his diligent observations there would be very little substance to the North Walney species list. Likewise I must give enormous thanks to Peter Zaltowski, Lew Sanderson and Shaun Lawson who regularly work the area between the two nature reserves.

This volume is the work of many people and organisations who have helped in a variety of ways — everything from contributing records to giving me encouragement. If it was not for the Cumbria Wildlife Trust, I would not be here (somebody else would have done the volume in quicker time and made a better job as well). Thank you to them for providing me with more than just a job and access to their files. And the Observatory, without which there would be no members, records, personality clashes or ringing; their upkeep of data, no matter how indisciplined is the backbone of the last twenty five years of bird records (let's hope they've got their figures in the correct columns and we'll forget about the Pallas's Grasshopper Warbler which featured in the systematic list of 1970 as follows: "One possible on 27th September. Not caught but seen to be fairly large and had the characteristic of flying some way before seeking cover". Ah well, I suppose we all have skeletons . . . . .). In fact if you ever visit the Observatory on an extremely wet day when the tide is out, see if you can bribe the warden to let you have a peek at the 'Old Chatty Log' and you can thrill to the flock of 25 Little Ringed Plovers in July 1967, marvel at the enormous grey warblers that frequented the central marsh in October 1968, and be entertained by the Andalusian Hemipode/Quail/young Grey Partridge of September 1969, the Wilson's Phalarope of 1975, the Hobby of . . . . . etc. You may even stumble across an account of the Observatory on walkabout in Argyll ringing young Lapwings! Ah, Walney Bird Observatory, home of the finest and usually the emptiest Heligoland traps in the western Palearctic, and if you linger too long you'll be coerced into building one.

So thank you to the following: Bolton Institute of Higher Education and Bolton Metropolitan College steered by Geoff Hosey, Frank Goodridge, Peter Cutting, Paul Rees and Marie Jacques — for all their gull colony counts, no matter how disparate; Mike Rogers, John Wilson and Eric Hardy for providing data and literature; Ian Kinley, Keith Parkes and Malcolm Hutcheson for keeping me up to date with records; Ian Spence for his valuable work on the LBBGs; Julian Clokie for identifying seaweeds (and demonstrating how to cook them); Kelsey Thompson and Ray Castell who have spent time becoming familiar with phytoplanktons; the late Fred Robinson for his intertidal work; Ernie Emmett, Bill Kydd, Richard Warren, Ted Hancock and Neville Birkett who have at times been up to their necks in moths' genitalia; David Clarke and Dorothy Blezard for identifying our snails; Paul Kirkland, Chris McCarty, Howard Avery and the NCC for North Walney records; Mike Mulgrew and Peggy Braithwaite for insights into the past; Kathleen Atkinson, Jean Scott, Helga Frankland, Geoffrey Halliday, Mike Isherwood and John Horne for their valuable help pre-publication; the South Walney sub-committee for their support; George Higginbotham for his superb photographs; and to Julia, my wife, for her unstinting patience and tolerance of all this volume involved.

# The Illustrators

This volume is graced with the work of Chris Butler and Christine Isherwood who have captured pictorially the genuine natural history of Walney Island. The reader will notice for example that the pictures are not merely illustrations of Jackdaws or Sea-holly; the Jackdaws are Walney Jackdaws nesting in the crumbling 'offices' at South Walney, and the Sea-holly is Walney Sea-holly, North Walney in fact, growing against a background of the Duddon Estuary and Black Combe. There are over one hundred drawings and amongst them, my particular favourites are CAB's 'Tawny Pipit at the oyster farm' and CMI's 'Grey Seal at Bar Buoy'.

*Tim Dean*
*(September 1990)*

***Chris Butler,*** *who has drawn most of the birds, is an undergraduate at the University of Aberystwyth. He is a freelance artist and has illustrated 'Birds in Cumbria', the county natural history report, for the last two years.*

***Christine Isherwood,*** *who has drawn some of the birds and everything else, is the Cumbria Wildlife Trust's art editor and has also illustrated for the Woodland Trust. A freelance artist, she lives in Kirkby-in-Furness.*

# An Introduction to the Island

The journey from the mainland at Barrow-in-Furness to Walney, unlike that to other islands on which bird observatories are situated, has none of the jutting rocks, rafts of auks or basking seals that are typical in the accounts of intrepid voyagers to Skokholm, Cape Clear or Bardsey. The entrance to Walney is tamer by far; the A590 being carried a quarter of a mile across Walney Channel by Jubilee Bridge, built in the early years of the 20th. century and only rarely seen in the 'up' position. At the Walney end of the bridge, a set of traffic lights and St. Mary's church over-looking the newsagent, florist, turf-accountant and mini-cab establishments greet the island visitor. Only at 16.30 hours on weekdays is one asked to employ navigational skills equal to any west coast ferryman, when negotiating the hordes of workers emanating from Vicker's shipyard as the hooter sounds.

Walney Island, with its southern tip representing the most southerly part of Cumbria, is by far the largest of a group of low islands lying off the southwest corner of English Lakeland, which is known as Furness. Of the other islands, Barrow and Ramsey are virtually unrecognisable as such, having been swallowed up in the Vickers and dockyard complex; Foulney and Roa are connected to mainland Britain by causeways; and both Sheep and Piel are also accessible by foot and adventurous vehicles at low tide.

Sixteen kilometres in length and no more than 1,500 metres wide, Walney, lying on a north-northwest and south-southeast axis, forms a barrier against the westerly gales from the Irish Sea, giving protection to the port of Barrow-in-Furness. The island was formed during the recession of the last glaciation, and as the ice melted, depositions of rock, clay and sand were left behind. Exposures of the red boulder clay can be seen along the west shore of the island, a region which is being constantly eroded. Beneath this boulder clay, the island is composed almost entirely of three Mercian mudstones, Hambleton, Singleton and Kirkham.

The forces of erosion that act on the western shore can be seen at work daily. The combination of wave action and westerly winds has had a considerable effect upon the island over the centuries, and recent land-infilling operations at Thorneynook Lane and Honeypot Lane have been effected in order to combat the breaching of the island, which happened last in February 1983. Studies by Phillips and Rollinson (1971) have shown that a great deal of the south end of the island has been eroded away and subsequently deposited on the spit at South Walney. Even the construction of groynes and placement of breakwaters has not stopped the continual erosion, and within the last 250 years, Walney has been narrowed by as much as 300 metres in parts. Wind erosion compounds the problem, and the dunes at either end of the island have been formed by this process.

The topography of the eastern side of Walney has been formed in a different manner. The bays and salt marshes are the result of the combined action of the ebb and flow of the tides and the slow seepage of water off the land.

Altitude and cliffs are at a premium on Walney, but Hare Hill at the southern end combines both, albeit a heady 16 metres (above mean sea-level) of boulder clay and a face that in recent years held a Sand Martin colony. Yet Hare Hill is dwarfed by Walney's 'Everest', Beacon Brow at 23 metres, just east of the Coastguard Station.

Walney is now essentially a suburb of Barrow-in-Furness. There are upwards of 11,000 people on the island and the great increase has occurred since the 19th. century. The community of Vickerstown was established to house the shipyard workers and since then, residential and council estates have sprung up around the 'marine garden city'. Prior to the growth of Barrow-in-Furness, which so complements the growth of Walney, the island was made up of the townships of North Scale and Biggar village, each consisting of some 16 tenements, and an additional four tenements at North End and eight at South End, the total population exceeding no more than 300 people. The rapid change in Walney's demographic history can be linked with the arrival of Vickers and the opening of Jubilee Bridge in 1908.

Evidence in the form of pottery, middens and tool artefacts, has been found on the island which indicates that Walney had been populated since the retreat of the last glaciation. The west shore has yielded middens composed of various shellfish, and the presumption is that hunters and gatherers, using flint nodules, which are common on the beaches, subsisted on the shellfish that were exposed at low tides. Barnes (1968) suggests that the "thinness of the midden deposits suggests a series of seasonal camps, not prolonged habitation". Trough Head and Central Drive have yielded Mesolithic microliths, perhaps more than 5,000 years old, while the aforementioned locality and North Walney have given up pottery and arrowheads from the Neolithic and Bronze Ages. It is probable that these peoples made use of the seabird colonies.

There is little evidence that the Roman occupation of Britain touched the island, but surely some Latins must have visited on their way by sea from Chester (Deva) to Ravenglass (Glannaventa)? The finding by J. Jackson of a gaming board crudely scored on a flat pebble, may indicate that South Walney was used or visited by Roman mariners.

Definite traces of the Norse influence can be found in some of the island's place names, notably Biggar (barley field: "bygg", "gar") and Earnse (Eagle island: infering the presence of Ernes otherwise known as Sea-Eagles). Trescathric (1984) is of the opinion that the Norsemen arrived in the area during the late 9th. century and were probably civil war refugees from settlements in Ireland and the Isle of Man.

With the coming of the Normans and the Domesday Book in the late 11th. century, the Manor of Hougon, which contained much of Furness, also controlled Hougenai (Walney). Trescathric (1984) begins his book with an entertaining study of the many and various names that the island has been blessed with; Hveneay (the island of bent grass); Vognay (Killer Whale or grampus island); Wagenay (island of quicksands); Gwaun's island; Hougenai 1086; Wagneia 1127; Wannegai 1246; Waghenay 1336; Wawenay 1404; Waynow 1537; Wauay 1577. Trescathric considers Wagenay the most credible: the least plausible, Thomas West's "the walled island", a combination of 'wall' and 'eau', literally a wall in the water (1774).

Agriculture became increasingly important on the island as can be seen from the ledgers and documents of Furness Abbey. During the 12th. century, the Manor of Hougun, was given to the Abbey of Savigny and as such, remained in their control until 1536 and Henry VIII's 'Dissolution of the Monasteries'. The village of North Scale and the settlements at North End and South End are first listed in an inventory of 1247, while Biggar, referred to as a grange, is mentioned in 1292. Trescathric (1984) considers the South End to have been farmed by Lay Bretheren. Perhaps this accounts for the herbalists' paradise at South Walney, and may well account for the abundance of Henbane (Hyoscyamus niger), a friend to the monks in more ways than one, having medicinal, narcotic and hallucinogenic properties.

The ridge and furrow lines that can still be seen in some of the Walney fields, are a legacy of medieval times. However, the increase in wool prices in the late 15th. century, meant that some arable land was turned over to sheep pasture.

With the dissolution of the monasteries, the control that Furness Abbey had exerted over the island vanished. St. Mary's church was built towards the end of the 16th. century and as Trescathric (1984) remarks, "spiritual comfort was needed" when the plague took the lives of approximately 120 people in 1631, almost half the island's population. This was not the only misfortune that befell the island in this period for in 1644, during the Civil War, a group of Royalists burnt down all but two houses in North Scale. Eight years later, the Quaker, George Fox, visited Walney and was set upon by "forty men with staves, clubs and fishing poles". A fuller account of this episode can be found in Barnes (1968).

In 1872, the island became part of the Borough of Barrow-in-Furness, and though not immediately changing the parochial existence of the islanders, one can sense that change was not far around the corner. Barrow's rapid development in the late 19th. century and its subsequent increase in population has had far-reaching consequences. Initially, Barrow workers saw the island and Biggar Bank in particular, as a 'lung' to resort to after the working week, and the locality's popularity was increased with the introduction of a regular ferry service. There were even grandiose plans to make Walney into a large holiday resort, and similar schemes have been promoted since, most notably in the years immediately before and after the Second World War. Alderman Ellison favoured a layout akin to Blackpool, with a pleasure park at the south end, entertainment and sporting facilities between Biggar Bank and Earnse Point, and residential buildings in the sand dunes at the north end.

The island as an industrial centre was also not dismissed. The search for coal in the late 19th. century, resulted in the discovery of salt just south of Biggar village. Production began in 1897: brine was brought to the surface and pumped to reservoirs and filter beds at Hillock Whins. An evaporating plant, with six chimneys and 24 pans, was constructed at the south end and there were even plans for 40 houses with streets and shops. However, no more than a few cottages were built, and pressure from the Cheshire salt interests, caused the closure of the plant in 1909. Commercially, the sand and gravel industry has been far more successful. Extraction has occurred, certainly since the 1870s, when the pier at South Walney was built in order to carry the minerals by flat-bottomed barges and coasters to Preston and Liverpool. Production was probably at its height post Second World War with the rebuilding of the Liverpool docks, and more recently, with the construction of the Trident complex in Barrow. Additionally, McLung's gravel works operated at North Walney into the early 1970s.

The arrival of Vickers in Barrow brought an end to the conservative life of the island. The company needed housing for its skilled workmen, brought into the area from Scotland and the Northeast: hence Vickerstown. From a population of a few hundred in the late 1890s, by 1902 there were over 3,000, and the building of a bridge was only a few years away.

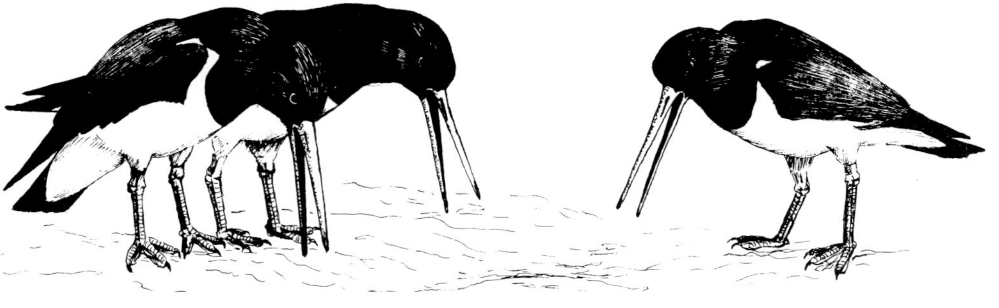

***Oystercatchers***

***References:***


Barnes, F. 1968, Barrow and District. Barrow-in-Furness Corporation.

Phillips, A. and Rollinson, W. 1971, Coastal changes on Walney Island, North Lancashire. Department of Geography, University of Liverpool.

Trescathric, B. 1984, Walney: a wall in the sea. Hougenai Press, Barrow.

# THE BIRDS OF WALNEY

# The Principal Areas

## URBAN WALNEY

The residential population of the island is condensed into an area bounded by the airfield to the north, Walney Channel to the east, Tummer Hill Marsh to the south and the Irish Sea to the west. It is a mix of council estates, terraced rows and more opulent dwellings which house the itinerant work force. Bird species and numbers are probably not typical of most urban areas in the north of England which display a similar pattern of close-knit houses with small regularly shaped gardens. Climatic conditions (strong winds and salt-laden air) mean that shrubbery is sparser and more stunted than in inland regions. Walney gardens do boast their Robins, Wrens, Dunnocks, Blackbirds, Song Thrushes, Blue Tits, Starlings and House Sparrows, but a dearth of tall trees does preclude some breeding species. Swifts and House Martins are nowhere common, but a few still favour some of the older houses.

Within urban Walney's boundaries, the allotments at Water Garth Nook and Central Drive, and the area around North End Farm are relative oases where typical garden birds can breed in the thicker, richer hedgerows and hawthorn stands, accompanied by the more wary Greenfinches, Chaffinches, Magpies and Blue Tits. James Dunn Park and the playing fields to the west hold Mistle Thrushes on the manicured lawns, Whitethroats and Goldfinches in the more unkempt areas, and at times, less common visitors, which have included Pied Flycatcher and Hawfinch. Close by, at Chairman's Walk, a worthwhile stand of tall (by island standards) sycamores is a regular site for Chiffchaffs, Willow Warblers, Collared Doves and less regular for Bonelli's Warbler, one of which trilled lustily in May 1984.

A large strip of recreational land extending from Thorneynook Lane, through Biggar Bank and the golf course to Earnse Bay caravan site, has largely been left underdeveloped, although the passage of feet is heavy. However, Meadow Pipits and Skylarks still use the less trampled places; the few remaining gorse patches support Linnets, perhaps a Stonechat pair and once in 1980, a wayward Melodious Warbler. The fairways of the golf course are temporary feeding grounds for Wheatears, more so in spring than in autumn.

***Linnet***

The central blot of residential Walney is increasing north and south and now comprises three council estates and five private housing schemes. The population in 1891 was 474; it is now more than 11,000 and the once isolated village of North Scale is engulfed in the sprawl. However, between Biggar and Walney Lighthouse, the island is very much unpopulated, and apart from the summer dwellers at South End caravan site, can muster only a score of residents. Rural Walney is vanishing and can no longer be called "the granary of Furness". Agriculture is chiefly pastoral and the fields around Biggar and North End Farm are largely left to grazing and silage pastures for a few cattle and the equine fraternity. The island has three caravan sites, an airfield, a pitch-and-putt and a golf course, a cricket ground, bowling club, a large recreational park, sports complex and numerous allotments. As a consequence, the island has gained many urban breeding birds at the expense of more specialised species that formerly nested such as Corncrake, and a lessening population of rough farmland and wetland birds such as Skylarks, Meadow Pipits, Mallards and Snipe. To the island's credit, in such a small area, over 300 hectares are protected as nature reserves at both the north and south ends.

## AGRICULTURAL WALNEY

To the south of Ocean Road and bordered by Tummer Hill, Sandy Nook, Creephaw and Wylock Marshes in the east, and to the north of South Walney Nature Reserve, and fringed by the Irish Sea in the west, is the major part of what is left of agricultural Walney. Around the Biggar area, thick hawthorn hedges still stand, probably a remnant of when they protected Walney's crops from the raging westerlies. Now they protect the existing livestock and also support hedge-nesting species and provide cover to migrant passerines. The number of fields has been reduced over the last century and it is sad to see two or three fields knocked into one, with resultant loss of hedgerow. However, many of the 150 or so enclosures are mostly undrained and virtually each of the larger ones hold breeding pairs of Lapwings with a scattering of Mallards and Shelducks, and a handful of Redshanks. Rakes Lane to the southwest of Biggar, thankfully almost prohibitive to traffic, can give a glimpse of pre-urban Walney. On either side of the lane are meadows and rough grazing with breeding wetland waders, wintering Curlews and spring Whimbrels, paired Mallards and Shelducks, while the thick hedgerows are home to Reed Buntings and Chaffinches, and havens for passage Whitethroats, Sedge Warblers and the occasional Grasshopper Warblers. Towards the end of the lane, the island wildfowlers have created a pond for the advancement of their Mallard ducklings, but this little site attracts Grey Herons, Shovelers, Snipe, passing chats and warblers. Hillock Whins, one of the last extensive gorse areas on the island, is vanishing due to the depredations caused by the scrambler motor bikes, which have carved unsightly ever-widening furrows between the stands of furze.

The fields on the Channel side of Biggar towards Long Rein Point hold the standard hedgerow species but being one of the most sheltered areas of the island, tends to support a variable collection of winter birds which may include healthy flocks of Linnets, Greenfinches, Reed Buntings, Tree Sparrows, winter thrushes, Short-eared Owls, and once a Firecrest. Magpies are now common and each hawthorn hedge appears to hold a pair, whereas 20 years ago, they were particularly scarce as an island bird. The village of Biggar itself displays a stand of tall sycamore trees which, if coming under the same sort of scrutiny that is heaped upon the parsonage at St. Agnes in the Isles of Scilly or Kilnsea Churchyard near Spurn, could easily harbour a rare passerine.

*Lapwing and chicks*

Across the road Lapwings and Redshanks nest on Biggar marsh, and in winter this rather damp area can yield good numbers of Snipe, sometimes Jack, and both Greenshank and Water Rail have been recorded.

The large open fields edged by turf and boulder bankings around the South End Farm and Hare Hill area hold few breeding passerines except for Meadow Pipits and Skylarks, but are prime sites for wintering Curlews, Lapwings, Redshanks, Golden Plovers and sometimes hard-weather geese. The thousands of fence posts atop the banks provide perches for spring and autumn Wheatears and Whinchats.

To the south of Rakes Lane, the infilled refuse tip provides a probable temporary barrier to the seas. The more mature grassed over areas are fairly sterile other than for mushrooms, but unfinished sections, not yet levelled and holding water, can be attractive to migrant waders. Additionally, this locality is a regular loafing ground and feeding spot for gulls and corvids, (often Hooded Crow), and roosting site for Oystercatchers, while finch flocks buzz around in winter.

## INTER-TIDAL WALNEY

The east side of the island boasts six crescentic bays with saltmarsh plants and varying amounts of choking spartina. To the north of Jubilee Bridge is North End marsh while to the south, the marshes of Tummer Hill, Sandy Nook, Wylock, Haws Bed and Lighthouse Bay maintain varying populations of wildfowl and waders. On the largest of these, North End, Tummer Hill and Haws Bed, large gatherings of Shelducks, Wigeon and Curlews assemble with Tummer Hill holding a sizeable Black-headed Gull roost. The other saltmarshes support smaller numbers of these species and also include Mallards, Teal and Snipe, with Wylock being a favoured haunt of Jack Snipe. As high tide approaches, the tip of each crèscent is dotted with waders forced to wait patiently until the waters ebb.

***Shelducks***

On the west side, shingle and sand beaches with occasional patches of largish boulders, stretch the entire length of the island and at high tide, roosting wader flocks are a regular feature. Prime sites include South Walney Nature Reserve, Hillock Whins and Biggar Bank where, during spring and autumn passage large concentrations of Turnstones, Ringed Plovers, Dunlin, Knot and Sanderlings assemble, while in winter, Grey Plovers and Oystercatchers join the throng. Mill Scar, near the golf course, is a traditional site for Purple Sandpipers and of course along the length of the west coast, Ringed Plovers and Oystercatchers set up their breeding territories.

## WILLOW WOODS

On the east side of the island, below Lenny Hill, is a comparatively sheltered area dominated by willow, ash and oak of an unprepossessing height. It has developed and matured since the Second World War and now supports a typical range of woodland and scrubland birds amongst which are Woodpigeons, Willow Warblers, Whitethroats, Chiffchaff and the only site on Walney for Bullfinch and

Lesser Whitethroat. Regular watching and less regular mist-netting commenced in 1983 and has produced in a short space of time Golden Oriole, Firecrest, two Red-backed Shrikes and a Woodchat, Hawfinch, Wood Warbler, Tawny and Long-eared Owl and Ortolan Bunting. Overwintering flocks of tits with occasional Treecreepers and Goldcrests have also occurred.

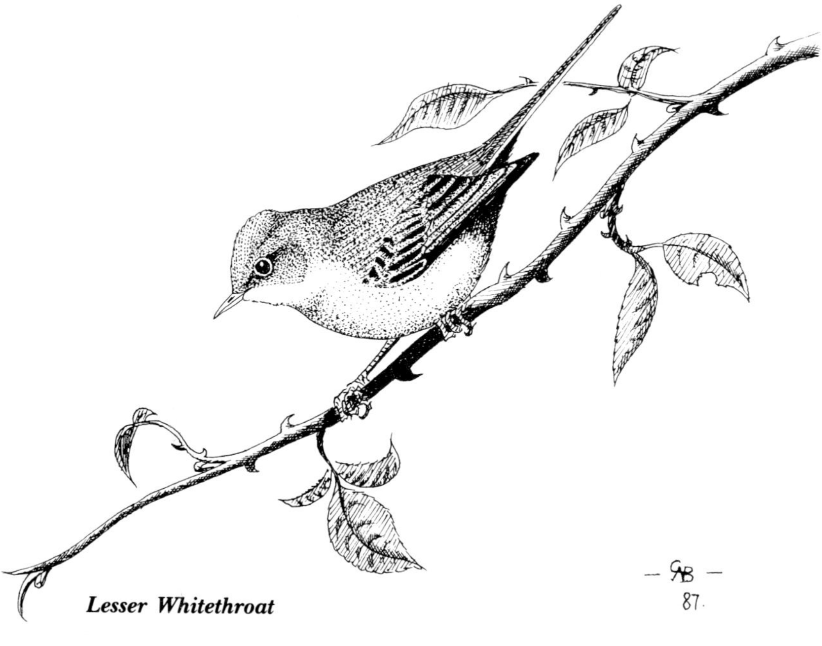

***Lesser Whitethroat***

# South Walney Nature Reserve

***Eiders***

A change in ownership, form the Buccleughs to the Cavendishes in 1963 resulted in the establishment of South Walney as a wardened nature reserve administered jointly by the Lake District Naturalists' Trust and the Lancashire Naturalists' Trust. This was not the first time that the area had been looked after. Harper Gaythorpe's article on the Walney Gulleries (Vol.XII Barrow Naturalists' Field Club and Literary and Scientific Associations. Annual reports 1913) refers to the protection afforded to the gulls at the south end in the early part of the 19th century by the tenant farmers Messrs. Hunter and Simpson, while William Postlethwaite tried vainly to protect those at the north end from the ever-growing Barrow populace. In 1878, when a far-sighted Duke of Buccleugh became the sole proprietor of South Walney, a watcher was appointed not only to guard against trespass during the breeding season, but also to direct small groups "to the best places for seeing the birds". Despite this, Barrow pirates still landed at the south end and shipped the gull and tern eggs off to the markets in the Midlands and sold as plover's eggs. W. A. Durnford's concern about the lack of protection on the island was conveyed to Harper Gaythorpe and the Barrow Naturalists' Field Club who made direct communication with the Home Secretary in 1896 prior to successfully petitioning Barrow County Council. Subsequently the act of 7th May 1897 prohibited the destruction of the eggs of wild birds on the island. However, Gaythorpe sadly reflects that illegal practices were still prevalent on the island after the passing of the act, additionally commending the protection afforded by the Duke of Buccleugh's agents at the south end, Messrs. Wadham and Hunter, and Mr. James Penny at the north end.

The fortunes of the breeding terns and gulls varied considerably in the 20th century; suffering due to wartime billeting of troops at the south end, but flourishing in the intervening years when continual human presence was at its least. The larger gulls began to establish themselves by the mid 1930s, but after the Second World War, there were still healthy Black-headed Gull and tern numbers supplemented by the surprising instance of breeding Eider duck. This was the catalyst perhaps that encouraged the Nature Conservancy to declare South Walney a Site of Special Scientific Interest in 1951. The importance of the area ornithologically was not the only consideration. With so many types of habitat in its 93 hectares, South Walney holds a very variable flora, not only with typical dune and saltmarsh plants, but also with species that thrive on the disturbed areas created by the sand and gravel extractions.

The first warden, Walter Shepherd, remembered for his weather-beaten face and guano bespattered trilby was, prior to his appointment, an employee of the sand and gravel concern. During his period of office, 1963 to 1975, South Walney and the gulleries, received increased publicity and many natural history societies benefitted from Walter's guided tours. In those same years, under the guidance of Professor Niko Tinbergen, the Animal Behaviour Research Group from Oxford University, conducted a series of studies into gull behaviour resulting in a Nobel prize for Niko (shared with Konrad Lorenz) and the seminal film "Signals for Survival". Ensuing educational cutbacks in the early 1980s have meant that the links with Oxford University have all but vanished, which does leave the way open for other establishments to make use of the Walney resources but as yet, only Bolton Metropolitan College and Bolton Institute of Higher Education have taken up the offer with serious residential studies.

Visitors have always come to South Walney to view the gulleries — individuals, school parties and natural history societies. In recent years virtually all the local schools have been escorted around the nature trails. Additionally there has been an encouraging increase in the number of out-of-season visitors, lured to South Walney by the prospects of high tide wader roosts, winter wildfowl, migrating passerines and the possibility of an oddity. This increase is due, in no small way, to the efforts of the Cumbria Wildlife Trust, who have erected three bird-watching hides for the benefit of the binocular fraternity. With these mod cons, no excuses can be made during inclement weather and consequently coverage has improved and recording (perhaps mis-recording !) has improved.

***Great Black-backed Gulls***

To many visitors during the breeding season, South Walney seems to be populated by Herring Gulls and Lesser Black-backed Gulls and nothing else. Admittedly there are a few (!), but a day's sojourn at the reserve should notch up most of the 35 or so breeding species. Most obvious should be the Oystercatchers, approaching 80 pairs in all, and except for a quite considerable concentration of nests on the spit, noticeably, regularly spaced out all over the reserve, with for example, ten nests along the channel side at intervals of between 100 and 200 metres. The breeding Shelducks are far more discrete in the location of their nest sites, but the adult birds are hardly difficult to see. It comes as a great surprise to many visitors that South Walney supports such a huge Eider colony. A walk along the nature trail may yield only a handful of devoutly sitting females, but abundant they are, with over 1,200 nests in 1988, and virtually all are found within the gull colony. Where the large gulls nest, so do the Eiders, and within a three metre circle of a sitting Great Black-backed Gull, seven Eider nests were counted in both 1986 and 1987. Around the lighthouse there are no gulls, and just to endorse the argument, only five Eider nests were located in 1987. By far the greatest concentration of nests is found in the gravel pool area, a region also favoured by the increasing population of Great Black-backed Gulls, now totalling upwards of 70 pairs. Over 200 Eider nests were counted on the spit another section of the reserve where gulls dominate, and this region is also home to varying numbers of breeding Sandwich, Little, Arctic and Common Terns. Eight pairs of Roseate Terns bred here in 1961. Ringed Plovers do not thrive at South Walney and the population of no more than ten pairs, is found in areas where the gulls are not omnipotent.

***Ringed Plover***

Of the remaining breeding species only small numbers are found. Moorhens, Coots and Mallards may be found in the freshwater areas of the gate pool and central marsh, along with solitary pairs of Reed Bunting and Shoveler, and intermittently successful Sedge Warblers. The finger pools at the offices hold a pair of Little Grebe and occasionally Red-breasted Mergansers, but the surrounding scrub and derelict buildings are nest sites for Magpies, Dunnock, Blackbird, Pied Wagtail, Jackdaws and Stock Doves. The gull-less dunes are home to a couple of pairs of Skylarks and held Grey Partridge in the early 1980s, while Meadow Pipits seem to be lost as a breeding species, as do Lapwings, although both species tentatively set up territories in the early part of the year. In a similar vein, Black-headed Gulls frequent the central marsh and gate pool, but inevitably end up as guardians to the terns on the spit. Swallows and Starlings may find annual refuge in the residential parts of the reserve, while Linnets can now only be found at the lighthouse and at the gorse patch half a mile to the north of the reserve, a location that also plays host to Song Thrush, Blackbird and Dunnock. Little Owl has bred in the past, but the individual or individuals concerned, seem to be almost carefree in their mobility, and in the 1980s, the species has bred in any suitable site from the offices at South Walney to the farm buildings at Biggar.

***Stock Dove***

Past breeding species have included Mute Swan, Teal, Stonechat, Whitethroat and House Sparrow, and may have included Corncrake, Snipe, Redshank, Short-eared Owl and Cuckoo. Pairs of Pintail have shown interest in 1983 and 1985, and Tufted Ducks would seem a good bet for the future.

High tides at South Walney are probably the most profitable times to observe the gatherings of gulls, ducks and waders that use the area throughout the year. The tidal cycles mean that birds of these groups can no longer forage for the foods that are available at low tide; as such they are forced to sit out the high tide until the tide recedes and feeding opportunities once more appear. During autumn and winter, the safe shingle areas of the reserve hold large assemblies of Oystercatchers, Dunlin, Turnstones and Redshanks, with smaller flocks of Sanderlings, Ringed and Grey Plovers. However, passage periods may occasion larger collections of the last named species, most notably the Sanderlings in late May and early June. Winter may also see up to 100 Bar-tailed Godwits and late summer and early autumn can bring in up to a dozen Greenshanks and smaller groups of Black-tailed Godwits. Apart from the waders, which prefer the spit and the south shore of the reserve, gulls, Eiders and Cormorants are also seen in varying abundance, roosting on the former locality. The high tides push Great Crested Grebes into the Channel, most numerous between July and November, and storm-driven birds, such as auks, divers and scoters may be encountered.

Winter means that flocks of Wigeon, Teal, Mallards and Shelducks will be seen in the high tide waters of Lighthouse Bay and with the turn of the tide, the newly available exposures of mud will attract quickly, flocks of hungry waders that have been sitting out the often lengthy periods of full water. Full advantage for the bird-watcher can be obtained with patient watching from the superbly sited Pier hide.

A combination of westerly winds and high tides can often ensure profitable sea-watching. During winter, these conditions produce divers, Eiders, Common Scoters and a few auks, but early spring may be enlivened by Gannets, Fulmars and increasing numbers of divers, many on passage, with larger counts logged in late April and May. Even during the height of summer, the right conditions will force normally sea-bound species towards the Walney shore and Manx Shearwaters are often most numerous from June to August. Skuas, usually Arctic and less often Great, can be seen harrying the terns and gulls in late summer, but autumn gales generate enthusiasm amongst the devoted sea watchers hoping to see large movements of the pelagic seabirds and hopefully a sprinkling of such birds as Leach's Petrels.

The freshwater regions of gate pool and the central marsh guarantee Moorhens, Mallards and Coots throughout the year supplemented by Wigeon and Teal from autumn to spring. Additionally one would hope to see examples of Shoveler and Pintail, while on certain occasions, Garganey and Gadwall may be located. The margins of mud often provide feeding areas for Redshanks and Common Sandpipers. Greenshanks regularly overwinter and autumn passage waders may include Green and Wood Sandpipers, Ruffs, Black-tailed Godwits, Spotted Redshanks, Little Stints and Curlew Sandpipers. Careful watching may yield the odd autumn or winter Water Rail.

The dune areas along the western edge of the reserve are frequented by many species of passerines during spring and autumn. Wheatears, Meadow Pipits, Skylarks and wagtails, the last often found foraging amongst the high tide detritus, are especially abundant from late summer to early winter, and adverse weather conditions can result in Snow Buntings and Bramblings being forced to find food in a similar manner. Linnets and Greenfinches seek sustenance from the thistle and ragwort seeds, often in quite substantial flocks during autumn, and they are regularly preyed upon by Merlins, Kestrels and Sparrowhawks. The small amount of vegetation found at the offices, the central marsh, elderberry grove and the garden of the Coastguard's Cottage are the main haunts for anyone seeking migrating passerines such as warblers, chats and thrushes. Autumn can mean large falls of Willow Warblers and Goldcrests with lesser numbers of Whitethroats, Chiffchaffs, Redstarts and flycatchers. Towards late autumn and early winter, Blackbirds, Song Thrushes, Redwings and Fieldfares may be observed and with the fullness of winter, Robins, Dunnocks and Wrens take up their winter territories.

# North Walney National Nature Reserve

The long line of dunes that extend from Earnse Bay north encompassing saltmarsh on the east coast, dune heath in the centre and an assortment of pools was created a National Nature Reserve on 1st January 1985. The reserve is leased from the owners Vickers Shipbuilding and Engineering Limited, by the Nature Conservancy Council and is jointly managed by them and the Cumbria Wildlife Trust. Its 142 hectares exhibit a great variety of habitats including dunes, heath, saltmarsh, sandy beach, shingle and scrub. Nowadays it is principally known as a rich botanical site and the only island haunt for the Natterjack Toad. It is no longer the site for gull and tern colonies that were mentioned in the literature of the late 19th century. It seems apparent from reading the accounts of Harting (1864), Durnford (1883) and Kirkman (1905), that the ever-growing population of nearby Barrow-in-Furness, and their egg-collecting sorties pressurised the colonies to desert the north end for the safer sanctuary of the south end. However, the instincts of the terns and Black-headed gulls still occasion the appearance of individuals and pairs in spring contemplating the possibility of nesting in areas used by their ancestors. In fact, Arctic Terns nested at North Walney as late as 1969.

***Red-breasted Merganser***

Despite the loss of the terns and Black-headed Gulls, the reserve is still important in the island context for breeding birds. The dunes and rough grassland support a large population of Meadow Pipits and Skylarks, and the pools hold the island's only breeding Tufted Ducks in addition to 80% of Walney's Little Grebe population. This man-made habitat is host to a small flock of moulting Red-breasted Mergansers in late summer, and in recent years the species has bred here. Reed Buntings nest along the pool fringes and Sand Martins formerly occupied the bankings but have not been seen since the Second World War. The island's only breeding Mute Swans are hand fed by the devoted, but each year have to run the gauntlet of the mindless few. On the shingle beach,

Ringed Plovers and Oystercatchers invariably face a similar threat, and on hot mid-summer days, the disturbance to them seems incessant. The gorse scrub in the centre of the reserve provides the only constant Stonechat site on the island, and surrounding bushes can be alive with singing Whitethroats in early May, a few of which remain to breed. Migrant Willow Warblers can usually be noted in the same period, and in recent years, reeling Grasshopper Warblers have successfully bred. The harsh, chattering song of Sedge Warblers provides continual background music in the small 'phragmites' belts bordering the saltmarsh. A few pairs of Redshanks nest along the eastern side of the reserve and drumming Snipe can be watched in May.

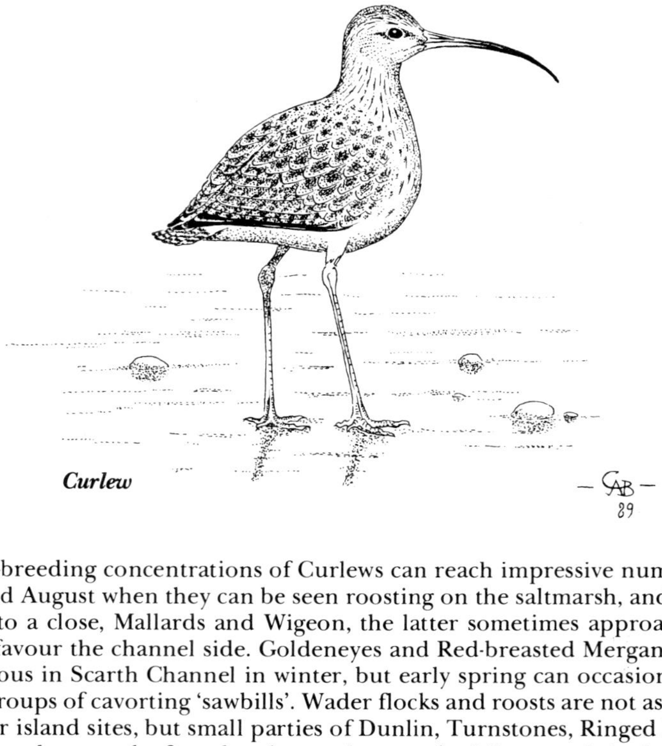


***Curlew***

Post-breeding concentrations of Curlews can reach impressive numbers in late July and August when they can be seen roosting on the saltmarsh, and as the year draws to a close, Mallards and Wigeon, the latter sometimes approaching 1,000 birds, favour the channel side. Goldeneyes and Red-breasted Mergansers may be numerous in Scarth Channel in winter, but early spring can occasion splendidly sized groups of cavorting 'sawbills'. Wader flocks and roosts are not as plentiful as at other island sites, but small parties of Dunlin, Turnstones, Ringed Plovers and Oystercatchers can be found at the northern end, while a good sized gathering of Sanderlings, normally over 70, skitter along the sand. Occasionally, Twite and Snow Buntings forage along the tideline or seek shelter on the leeward side of the dunes.

Coveys of Grey Partridge may be met with, but their numbers have dwindled over recent years as has the number of breeding pairs. Merlins regularly patrol the area during winter causing panic amongst the flocks of Skylarks, Meadow Pipits and Linnets. Small pools in the centre of the reserve can hold healthy collections of Snipe, often in partnership with Jacks.

During spring and autumn migration, the dunes witness itinerant Wheatears and Whinchats, while the pools can attract quite large numbers of Swifts and hirundines especially in July and August. The lack of extensive shrub vegetation precludes much in the way of passage birds such as warblers and thrushes, but careful scrutiny of the small areas of sallows and gorse could turn up trumps one day. Such diligence has been profitable amongst the gull roosts; in some years, Glaucous Gulls have been noted and the extremely large concentrations of young gulls after the breeding season, which assemble off the west shore, warrant a better look than they presently receive. Out at sea, feeding flocks of Gannets, approaching 200 birds, are regular in July and August, and observers have logged impressive numbers of Manx Shearwaters and Fulmars on the right days. Loose flocks of Red-throated Divers and tighter flocks of Common Scoters, sometimes with an odd Velvet, can be seen in autumn and winter off Scarth Channel.

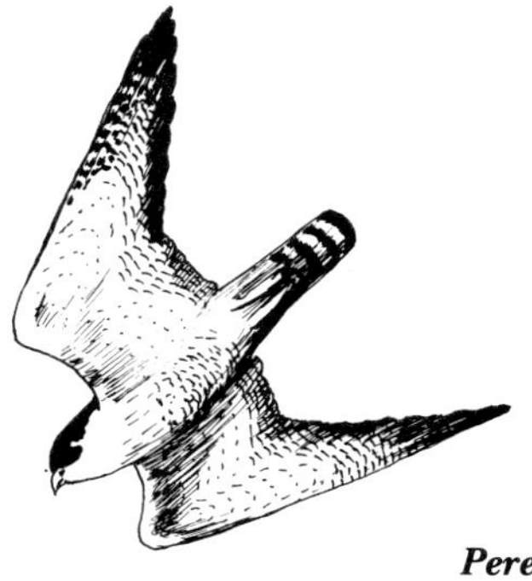

***Peregrine***

# Bird Protection and History of Recording

An Act of Parliament passed in 1533 prohibiting the destruction or taking of wild birds' eggs, appears to be the earliest ornithological reference to Walney. The first bird species mentioned is found in Dr. Leigh's "Natural History of Lancashire" (1700), who writes of "the Great Gull which breeds in vast quantities". F. S. Mitchell (Birds of Lancashire 1892) is of the opinion that this refers to the Great Black-backed Gull. Mid-Victorian visitors to the island included P. J. Mannex who, in his "History of Westmoreland with Furness and Cartmel" (1849), seems impressed by the myriads of sea-gulls and plants of the north end, including the Walney 'geranium', but describes the south end merely as an immense ridge of pebbles. Conversely, Harper Gaythorpe in his article on the Walney Gulleries (Vol.XII Barrow Naturalists' Field Club and Literary and Scientific Associations. Annual reports 1913) states that the "principal gullery and ternery on the island over 100 years ago was at the south end."

An island species list of sorts can be found in J. E. Harting's account of his shooting and collecting visit to Walney in May 1864. The day's excursion concentrated on the gulls and terns at the north end of the island including the killing of a Roseate, but is interesting for its reference to the abundance of Wheatears and the locating of a Rock Pipit's nest. W. A. Durnford's "List of birds found in the neighbourhood of Walney Island" (1883) is the first attempt at a comprehensive systematic list for the area and many of Durnford's observations are included in H. A. MacPherson's "A Vertebrate fauna of Lakeland" (1892) and F. S. Mitchell's "Birds of Lancashire" (1892).

Valuable information relating to the natural history of the island can be found in the Barrow Naturalists' Field Club reports of the late-Victorian and Edwardian years which catalogue the results of regular visits to all parts of Walney and the study of all orders.

Following F. B. Kirkman's "The Gulls and Terns on Walney" (1905), there is very little literary reference to the island until the publication of C. Oakes' "Birds of Lancashire" (1953), although C. H. Gowland's disturbing "Birdland" magazines, with their competitions and prizes of Peregrine eggs, are useful in providing breeding numbers for the south end. Oakes' definitive work records the sterling efforts of Robinson amongst the terns in the 1930s and includes photographs of the first Eider nest of 1949. Administratively part of Lancashire, MacPherson's Lakeland eyes had turned to Walney's flora and fauna at the end of the 19th century. With the unique Eider record, "Lakeland Ornithology" (1954) edited by E. Blezard, also includes a scoop photograph of the Eider and her nest. Indeed, Blezard's "Lakeland Birds" (1958) and R. Stokoe's "Birds of the Lake Counties" (1962), both give increasing space to Walney's observations and the Lancashire link seems to end with K. G. Spencer's "Status and distribution of birds in Lancashire" (1973) and county re-organisation in 1974, although Eric Hardy's "Birdwatching in Lancashire" (1979) refuses to relinquish. Lancashire's loss was certainly Cumbria's gain as evinced in both the annual Birds in Cumbria reports and the recent "Cumbrian Birds" by Malcolm Hutcheson (1986).

# Walney Bird Observatory

Regular observations and ringing commenced shortly after the establishment of South Walney Nature Reserve in July 1963, and Walney achieved full bird observatory status in 1965 under the guidance of Eric Pithers who fulfilled, until late 1966, the role of secretary to both the nature reserve and the observatory. In the first flushes of enthusiasm, heligoland traps were built in the garden of the Coastguards' Cottages and at the northern boundary wall while mist-netting was carried out in the few suitable areas and on the few days weather conditions permitted. During 1964, the first full year of operations, 722 birds were ringed, amongst which was Lancashire's very first Melodious Warbler, and over 1,000 birds were trapped in the following year including Great Britain's third White-throated Sparrow.

Until the early 1970s, a small but keen personnel continued to ring in the region of 600 to 700 birds per annum, the majority of which were migrating passerines in the spring and autumn months, caught in the existing heligoland traps. A further two traps were built in the central marsh and completed in 1967 and 1972 but despite this, ringing figures deteriorated and in 1974 and 1975 scarcely reached 350. Disillusioned observatory stalwarts linked the ringing decline with an increase in the gull colony and the supposed reticence of passerines to rest and feed while on migration in such a vital and pulsating colony. It is true that the spreading colony had taken over habitat where once Skylarks and Meadow Pipits nested but no credence can be given to the statement "very few migrants are seen (or trapped) in spring, or in early autumn until the gulls move away in mid-September" (Bird Observatories in Britain and Ireland 1976, p254.) A cursory look at the ringing totals will show that since 1976 annual totals have bettered the early years of the Observatory on three occasions and 1985, (still despite the presence of a large gull colony!), produced a record spring passage of Willow Warblers.

The reasons for the Observatory's nadir in the early 1970s are probably more due to an ebbing away of enthusiasm and the loss of a few young souls to further education, rather than to purely ornithological reasons and the gull colony seems to have become the unfortunate scapegoat. Many of the older Observatory hands could remember rather tranquil days with no more than a few hundred pairs of gulls in the early 1950s, and the ease with which spring migrant flight calls could be heard, but it is highly doubtful whether there was ever a time when "up to 90% of the passerines present could be caught with little difficulty" (Bird Observatories in Britain and Ireland 1976, p256).

Without the financial ability to employ a full-time warden, the Observatory relied on the efforts of a hard core of Barrow and Walney regulars but the greatest fillip to the Observatory's fortunes came with the appointment of Mike Thom by the Cumbria Naturalists' Trust as the full-time warden of South Walney Nature Reserve in 1975. Consequently, for the first time in its history, the area had complete daily coverage which boosted the collection and collation of daily observations and marked an upward trend in ringing totals. In the ensuing years, the Observatory has widened its sphere of operations not only in collecting data for the whole of the island, but also in the commencement of mist-netting in Willow Woods. In 1983 a fifth heligoland trap was built to complement the existing garden trap, and in 1986, No. 3 trap was totally rebuilt having been demolished in 1978.

Mention migration and one thinks of bird observatories. Mention bird observatories and one thinks of Fair Isle, Dungeness, Spurn, Gibraltar Point, Isle of May, Bardsey, Portland Bill, Calf of Man, Sandwich Bay, Cape Clear, Copeland or Skokholm. One does not automatically think of Walney. More often than not, Walney is mistaken for Welney. "Oh, where the ducks are" is the retort when introductions are made. Those who do know of Walney, think of it geographically as the bit that sticks off southwest Scotland. In the past, the island has been regarded as a bit of a backwater by the bird-watching fraternity — known for its large colony of gulls and its Eiders — and that's about all. It does not have the romantic attraction that the offshore bird observatory islands have; neither does it have the quantity and quality of birds that one associates with the south and east coast coastal observatories. Look at the ringing figures for other observatories — many of them can achieve 10,000 birds per annum and some of them do this despite being March to November observatories. If Walney rings 1,000 birds, it has had a good year! However, Walney could ring more birds than any other observatory; there are birds aplenty; thousands of pairs of gulls and their offspring, thousands of waders and Eiders, and hundreds of ducks. Finances, time and man power exclude all of the above except for the sterling work of the Morecambe Bay Wader Ringing Group and Ian Spence's Lesser Black-backed gull work in the 1980s. As such, the ringing is devoted almost exclusively to passerine migrants caught in the heligoland traps; consequently, a third of the ringing total is made up of warblers. The lack of cover and lack of windless days means that mist-netting operates all to infrequently. Additionally clap-netting opportunites usually occur when a clap-net is unavailable and tape-luring of such species as Meadow Pipits has yielded poor reward. The technique of 'dazzling' has been tried on many occasions, but the surrounding coastal lights and the lighthouse beam, mean that a great deal of effort is normally thwarted. It was calculated that almost 40 miles were walked for the catching of four birds in 1981. The many surrounding lights perhaps also account for the lack of lighthouse attractions — a syndrome well known at Bardsey. The lights are probably the reason for the lack of success in mist-netting for waders and duck at night — 14 nights consecutive mist-netting resulted in the catching of two Redshanks in 1986. The only notable 'dazzling' sorties have occurred during nights of strong winds and exceptionally heavy rain.

Many books refer to the mystery of migration. It can be a puzzle on Walney. It is virtually impossible to say what are the prime conditions for the appearance of migrants. In spring light southerly winds and dull conditions normally produce a small fall of passerines, while clear skies usually mean few birds. Calm and misty days are just as likely to occasion no birds as they are to provide many. There seems to be no hard and fast rule that one can apply to both spring and autumn as to the abundance or paucity of grounded migrants. Examples of the Walney enigma include September 11th 1982, a hot and clear morning with only one bird caught, a Paddyfield Warbler; and a calm and misty September 26th 1985, when only five passerines were in evidence — three Red-breasted Flycatchers, a Yellow-browed Warbler and a Pied Flycatcher. There are days when the weather maps indicate the perfect conditions and the island is birdless. However, over the years, certain rules have been learnt:

1) Almost undoubtedly, passerine migrants will not be seen or caught during storm force winds.

2) South Walney is a lazy person's observatory. There is absolutely no point in getting out of bed until half past seven. Birds only arrive at South Walney in the morning between 07.30 and 10.30. The skies are dead from the crack of dawn until the sound of Vicker's shipyard hooter.

3) Despite all the available water margins at South Walney, freshwater waders cannot be guaranteed. The low water of the central marsh seems an ideal spot for travelling waders, but other than the Common Sandpipers, there is normally a dearth of other species. Probably an over-flying wader has too much opportunity in the area — the whole of north Morecambe Bay area provides an abundance of suitable stop-over sites. Since 1980, only three exotic waders have frequented the marsh — a Pectoral Sandpiper in 1982, a Little Ringed Plover in 1983 and a White-rumped Sandpiper in 1984. What have the Weaver Bends in Cheshire got that Walney has not?

4) If you wish to see rare birds on South Walney, arrive in the late morning or early afternoon — because that is when the birds do.

A list of examples of trapped birds (all times are GMT):

| | |
|---|---|
| Bluethroat | — 25th May 1987 - 14.45 |
| Firecrest | — of nine birds caught, all have been after 09.00 |
| Red-breasted Flycatcher | — of six birds caught, four have been after 10.00 |
| Nightingale | — 14th June 1986 - 14.15 |
| Black Redstart | — of 14 birds caught, ten have been after 10.00 |
| Great Grey Shrike | — 7th November 1982 - 14.10 |
| Woodchat Shrike | — 20th May 1986 - 17.55 |
| White-throated Sparrow | — 18th June 1965 - 15.45 |
| Barred Warbler | — of four birds caught, one was at 09.45, another at 14.00 and a third at 19.40 |
| Icterine Warbler | — 23rd August 1977 - 12.30 19th August 1983 - 10.00 |
| Marsh Warbler | — 29th September 1986 - 16.00 |
| Melodious Warbler | — of ten birds caught, eight have been after 09.40, with five after 13.00 |
| Paddyfield Warbler | — 11th September 1982 - 10.30 |
| Reed Warbler | — 24th August 1979 - 14.00 and 25th August 1989 - 10.30 |
| Subalpine Warbler | — 6th June 1986 - 15.00 |
| Wood Warbler | — 16th May 1979 - 15.00; 20th July 1987 - 14.30 |
| Yellow-browed Warbler | — 5th October 1968 - 16.00 18th October 1985 - 17.15 |
| Lesser Whitethroat | — of seven birds caught, six have been after 09.45 |
| Wryneck | — 1st September 1966 - 15.30 and 9th September 1988 - 19.00 |

Sightings of other untrapped rare birds show a similar pattern:

| | | |
|---|---|---|
| Black Storks | (1985) | — 14.45 |
| Honey Buzzard | (1985) | — 15.15 |
| Crane | (1984) | — 16.30 |
| Little-Ringed Plover | (1983) | — 14.00 |
| Pectoral Sandpiper | (1982) | — 11.15 |
| Wilson's Phalarope | (1989) | — 11.00 |
| Bean Goose | (1983) | — 15.00 |
| Stone-curlew | (1985) | — 15.20 |
| Greater Sandplover | (1988) | — 14.20 |
| White-rumped Sand. | (1984) | — 12.30 |
| Buff-breasted Sand. | (1975) | — 13.30 |
| Ring-billed Gull | (1984) | — 13.00 |

| | | | | | |
|---|---|---|---|---|---|
| Richard's Pipit | (Nov 80) | — 16.30 | Tawny Pipit | (1980) | — 16.00 |
| | (Dec 80) | — 16.00 | | (9/8/82) | — 15.50 |
| | (1985) | — 14.10 | | (27/8/82) | — 17.30 |
| | (Sep 87) | — 14.15 | | (1984) | — 15.10 |
| Desert Wheatear | (1986) | — 12.30 | Icterine Warbler | (1984) | — 14.15 |
| Pallas's Warbler | (1982) | — 15.10 | Nutcracker | (1979) | — 11.00 |

***Tawny Pipit at the oyster farm***

# Walney Island Wildfowler's Association

Walney Island Wildfowler's Association began life in 1970 as a direct result of an increase in the number of irresponsible shooters using the land and foreshore on Walney. Subsequently, the group succeeded in leasing the farmland on the southern part of the island and the major part of the foreshore. In the early years, one third of the leased area was set aside as full sanctuary, and a great deal of work was undertaken to improve the wildfowl habitat. In recent years a wetland area at Hillock Whins has been created as a nursery for young ducks and in addition provides feeding and nesting opportunities for Teal, Moorhen, Shoveler, Mallard, Shelduck, Reed Bunting and Sedge Warbler. Sheep Island has benefitted from the planting of 1,000 small trees and the excavation of a scrape area. The wildfowlers' policy has resulted in the releasing of over 1,000 Mallards, including 400 alone in the period 1970 to 1976. Other less successful releasing schemes have included 25 Red-legged Partridge chicks at North Walney in 1973 (none of which were subsequently seen); up to 20 Pheasants in the Biggar village region since 1974 (with breeding in the following year); and the introduction of four Greylag Geese in 1982 at the north end.

Birds shot on Walney Island 1972-1977.

| | |
|---|---|
| Wigeon | 513 |
| Mallard | 266 |
| Teal | 230 |
| Curlew | 87 |
| Grey Partridge | 14 |
| Goldeneye | 9 |
| Pink-footed Goose | 6 |
| Scaup | 4 |
| Pintail | 3 |
| Pochard | 3 |
| Tufted Duck | 2 |
| Cormorant | 1 |
| Total | 1138 |

Reference:

Walney Island Wildfowler's Association, (R. Scarr, R. Warriner pers. comm.)

# The Ornithological Year

## 1st — 15th January

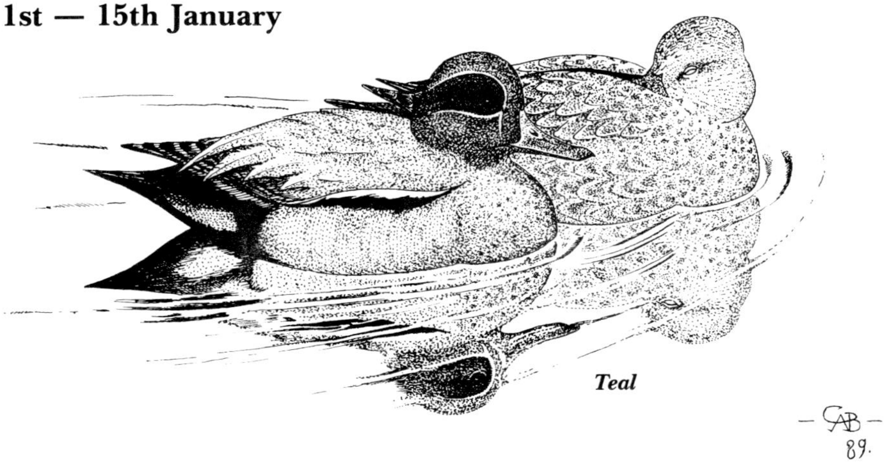

***Teal***

Wigeon and Shelducks dominate the saltmarshes throughout the island and Teal and Mallards are in plentiful supply, with the former especially in Lighthouse Bay. Small flocks of Pintail may appear at North Walney. Overwintering Greenshanks frequent the large gravel pools at South Walney along with Goldeneyes and Red-breasted Mergansers.

Sizeable flocks of Dunlin and Turnstones occur along the west shore of the island and North Walney can hold up to 150 Sanderlings, while Purple Sandpipers cling to the rocks at the Coastguard Station. Bar-tailed Godwits are regularly seen in small flocks in the Piel Channel area.

On calm windless days, Red-throated Divers can be seen in loose flocks in the Piel Bar area and a raft of up to 5,000 Eiders bob off the groyne. In mild Januarys, Gannets, Fulmars, Great and Pomarine Skuas have been recorded in Morecambe Bay. Hard weather may mean Tufted Ducks and Pochards using the largely unfrozen saline pools at South Walney and in turn, wintering duck numbers of all species will increase.

Passerines are normally at a premium — in mild winters gatherings of Linnets, Reed Buntings, Redwings and Fieldfares may frequent the Long Rein Point area, but severe weather may induce invasive flocks of Bramblings, Twite and Skylarks on to the saltmarshes.

## 16th — 31st January

If hard weather conditions prevail, Lapwings, Snipe and Golden Plovers will have deserted the island, and in such a period, Fieldfares and Redwings can be seen scouring the tidelines for sustenance. Snow Buntings and Bramblings may also occur, and in this particular period Walney witnessed its largest fall of the former species with up to 1000 birds. Pink-footed Geese are also seen in such conditions winging their way to more lenient pastures and Woodcock may be found sheltering in the dune marram or Willow Woods.

Apart from the wintering divers, Eiders and small flocks of Common Scoters, sea-watching usually provides very little, although solitary Red-necked Grebes may be seen in Walney Channel. Gull numbers are generally high — many Herring Gulls already staking their claims at South Walney and up to twenty Common Gulls foraging the high tide detritus near the spit. Great Black-backed Gull numbers peak at this time with large loafing groups near the refuse tip.

Passerines are not much in evidence although Long Rein Point can usually guarantee small assemblies of finches and tits may be found in Willow Woods.

## 1st — 15th February

Do not let February fool you. Skeins of grey geese can be seen moving north in the early part of the month. Watery sunshine can give a very false impression that winter is over and spring is almost upon us. Shelduck numbers begin to build up in all the island bays, Coots return to their territories on gate pool and the first Small Tortoiseshells of the year come out of hibernation. But all this is often a false spring and winter can be at its most bitter with chilling easterly winds sweeping across Morecambe Bay and keeping the agricultural waders in Ireland. In tandem with the conditions, Glaucous Gulls can often be located roosting on the spit at high tide. Northward bound Redwings may be grouded due to the inclemency of the weather and the grey geese of the early part of the month can be seen again returning south.

## 16th — 29th February

***Golden Plovers***

Hopefully the worst of the winter is over by mid month, but it is certainly not guaranteed. Mild overcast days can bring in a small trickle of Song Thrushes and Blackbirds, and the odd Stonechat may be seen perched on top of the gorse near the caravan site at South Walney. Chaffinches and Reed Buntings may be encountered at South Walney, the refuse tip or in the Biggar region.

Wigeon and Teal numbers begin to decline but the duck interest is maintained by the Eiders moving closer to the South Walney shores engaged in their tremendous courtship displays in Lighthouse Bay and near the pier. Similar springtime frolics can be seen in Piel Channel or Scarth Bight with maximum numbers of Red-breasted Mergansers. Waders at South Walney normally include large and impressive gatherings of Oystercatchers, Dunlin and Turnstones.

The sea will usually yield the first movements of northward bound divers and Lesser Black-backed Gulls begin to appear in ever-increasing numbers. Golden Plover and Lapwing flocks return after hard weather to the fields to the north of South Walney Nature Reserve and the latter are already giving territorial displays in the fields around Biggar.

## 1st — 15th March

There is often not a lot of difference between the end of February and the early days of March. Foul weather can often persist but this does not deter the ever-increasing activity on the gull colony with Herring Gulls taking up their territories and now looking immaculate after shaking off their winter dowdiness. The colony's numbers are swelled with each successive day as the Lesser Black-backed Gulls compete for the available nesting sites.

On the sea, spells spent in the sea-watching hides will usually provide a fair amount of activity with increased sightings of divers and the possibility of an early surge of Gannets and Fulmars with accompanying parties of Kittiwakes which are characteristically seen after strong westerly blows.

Small birds do not figure greatly in the day to day recording but Meadow Pipits in loose bands can be seen flitting low over the dunes at both ends of the island. Occasionally Black Redstarts and Stonechats may appear at South Walney and overcast days may presage heavier movements of Song Thrushes and Blackbirds. Invariably, eyes are turned southwards in the hope of an early Wheatear.

## 16th — 31st March

***Merlin and Meadow Pipit***

After the rigours of winter, there is eager anticipation during this period for the first glimpse of summer migrants. Generally it is provided by the screech of Sandwich Terns past the groyne, but occasionally, Wheatears at South Walney or Biggar Bank precede the terns. Chiffchaffs normally put in appearances two or three days later, often with accompanying Goldcrests and there is always the possibility of small groups of White Wagtails. More Blackbirds and Meadow Pipits move through the island, individuals of the latter species often being preyed upon by Merlins, in the last days of their winter residency on Walney.

From the groyne, large numbers of Black-headed Gulls can be observed heading towards Foulney Island, while divers are again in evidence as are parties of Gannets.

On the gull colony, the population is almost at its height with most of the Lesser Black-backed Gulls paired up and vocalising raucously. Many nests have been made and on calm evenings the whole colony seems to be engaged in copulatory activity.

Similar urgency is noted amongst the Eiders, many of which cavort ecstatically near the pier at high tide, and prospecting females can be seen with their partners on terra firma. Walney's winter dabblers have all but vanished but a few pairs of Teal can be found at South Walney or in the Rakes Lane area.

## 1st — 15th April

Meadow Pipit passage can reach into four figures during the early part of the month completely out-numbering any other small birds that may be present. Linnets can be seen at their breeding sites throughout the island, and on calm days during the first week returning Swallows and Willow Warblers should be seen. Small flocks of Skylarks, normally flying higher than the pipits, are a regular feature and the gorse areas hold parties of Goldcrests. Blackbirds and Song Thrushes are still moving through but the island population has already commenced nest-building.

Wader numbers are swollen by great flocks of Knot which swirl over the mudflats of Morecambe Bay and can be seen from far afield. Parties of Redshanks and Curlews feed in Haws Bed and along the Channel, briefly stopping over before continuing north. Great Northern Divers can be seen with the more numerous Red-thoateds off Hilpsford Point and along with increasing numbers of Sandwich Terns, the first Commons and Artics may be seen. Auks are never very abundant in spring but a few are usually seen in this period.

## 16th — 30th April

*Lesser Black-backed Gulls*

Despite annual differences in weather conditions during early spring, the first gull eggs are invariably found between the 16th and 18th April. Late springs, early springs, good springs and bad springs seem to have little effect upon the finding of the first egg. However, long warm days in this period probably induce a mass unburdening which has a direct effect upon whether the gull season and the raising of their young is a protracted affair. Eider nests become increasingly apparent, and Eider eggs appear alongside gull eggs incubated by unknowing adopters.

Migration activity can come in a rush. Willow Warblers on calm days may be numerous in the Walney hedgerows and the arrival of Redstarts although normally in low figures, brings a welcome splash of colour. Tree Pipits and Yellow Wagtails are usually recorded passing overhead in small numbers and it is probable that many go under-recorded, their calls having to compete with the slightly more raucous gulls. Common Sandpipers, never very common in spring, are seen at the gate pool or at the offices. Willow Woods generally holds the first Whitethroats, often before the first birds are seen elsewhere on the island. Grasshopper Warblers may be heard at Hillock Whins or at North Walney and Sedge Warblers, on occasions plentiful, in vegetation bordering the island's ditches.

A few late wintering birds may be seen; Fieldfare, Redwing and Brambling have all been recorded as individuals or small groups in recent years and there are instances of lingering Goldeneye and Scaup. The Walney fields have all but lost their roosts of Curlews, Golden Plovers, Lapwings and Redshanks, but in their place, small assemblies of Whimbrel sit out the high tides, notably in the Rakes Lane area.

## 1st — 15th May

Although the majority of passerine migrants have moved through in the last week of April, some species, notably Whinchats appear on the island fence posts during the first week of May. Early morning skies often hold increasing numbers of Swallows and the first House Martins, the latter species being fairly uncommon at South Walney in spring. Swifts are never abundant at this locality, but may be seen over Vickerstown or hawking at the North Walney pools. The first Cuckoo is most likely to be met with in the Rakes Lane area or amongst the sandhills of the north. Apart from Linnets, the only other finches at this period should include the occasional Redpoll, buzzing north over the south end, small parties of Goldfinch, and in later years, Siskin have been noted at Willow Woods. Small parties of Collared Doves seem to be an annual feature at South Walney, usually appearing at either end of the day.

Westerly winds can bring in large gatherings of Gannets and Fulmars, while the same conditions should still guarantee late divers and returning skuas, usually Arctic, less often Great. Tern activity is often heavy, already dominated by purposeful eel-seeking Sandwich Terns, many of which already have nests at Foulney Island, but increased numbers of Common Terns can also be seen. Early May has produced Black Terns, most often located flying into Walney Channel.

The large gathering of Knot have probably left the area by the end of the first week of May, but flocks of Ringed Plovers and Turnstones, often in large numbers, can be seen especially in the Rakes Lane and Biggar Bank region. At the former site, Whimbrel may reach up to fifty birds.

At South Walney, Eider chicks make an appearance towards the middle of the month, while Mallards and Moorhens may also be seen in the wetter parts of the island, chaperoning their offspring.

## 16th — 31st May

***Little Tern***

Gull chicks emerge at South Walney just as mid-month is passed. Data shows that Herring Gulls, Lesser Black-backed Gulls and Great Black-backed Gulls have all provided the first emergents. As the eggs near hatching, the parents' stubbornness to leave the nest site increases, and agitated gulls begin to vent their fury on human visitors and the grazing sheep and cattle. Eider mothers escort their ducklings to the water's edge where awaiting aunts take over the maternal duties. By the end of May, most Eiders are well into the incubation period, ensuring that their offspring hatch before the gull chicks make their huge demand on available food supplies. Territory holding terns have had their population swollen during the 1980s by an influx of late arrivers. This annual phenomenon may be linked to the activities of spring bank holiday recreationalists, who disturb potential breeding pairs at other tern sites within Cumbria.

Migration is virtually at an end except for the appearance of Spotted Flycatchers and at times a rush of Greenland Wheatears. However, the possibility of vagrant species keeps hopes high, and late May has yielded Hoopoe, Wryneck and Melodious Warbler at South Walney, and Red-backed Shrike and Golden Oriole in Willow Woods. The last-named site can often produce reeling Grasshopper Warblers, Lesser Whitethroat, Chiffchaffs and Willow Warblers, while in the skies above, Peregrines from across the channel, become more obvious.

An annual feature of late May is the arrival of substantially sized Sanderling flocks which can normally be found at high tide on the spit or at Hillock Whins.

They represent the last of the wader flocks until the breeding season in the Arctic is over.

## 1st — 15th June

*Eider duck and eiderlings*

Meadow Pipits and Skylarks are prominent in the rough grassland regions of the island. Linnets in the gorse areas are bringing food back to their clutches and Swallows can be seen at their traditional nest sites. Family parties of Song Thrushes and Blackbirds may be encountered in the urban parts of Walney. In the fields near Biggar, piping Redshanks warn off intruders and out of every large bush, Magpies fly off at the slightest approach. In the 1960s they were a rare bird on the island; by the mid-1980s they were seen everywhere.

Along the shingle shores, Oystercatchers and Ringed Plovers are either incubating or protecting their newly-hatched chicks and Shelducks can be seen with their youngsters.

Despite all this breeding frenzy, most birds being where they should be and doing what they should do, there is still the chance of meeting up with late migrants or wanderers. Spoonbills, Nightingale, Subalpine Warbler and Red-breasted Flycatcher have been seen at South Walney while North Walney has held Garganey and Woodchat Shrike.

Sea-watching can also be profitable with strong westerly winds and gloomy conditions yielding Manx Shearwaters, Gannets and Fulmars. At South Walney, the early hatched gull chicks are exercising their wings by mid-month, and cannibalistic parents may well find more food at their neighbour's nest to feed the ever-demanding offspring than at low-tide mussel beds. Already the majority of Eider drakes have left the area to form a large moult flock off Foulney Island and the Eider ducks can be seen with their charges off the west coast of Walney.

## 16th — 30th June

Displaced Lapwings, probably a result of grass cutting for silage, have assembled in loose flocks in some of the very same fields they have been forced to vacate. There is already a hint of post-breeding activity — almost a touch of autumn. Non-breeding or failed breeding birds begin to congregate, most noticeably Oystercatchers on the southwest shore at low tide and Cormorants on the spit. In a similar vein, small numbers of Curlews and Redshanks can be found in the salt marsh regions which they left barely six weeks earlier.

At North Walney, the Mute Swan cygnets can be found on the same pool as the young Tufted Ducks, Red-breasted Mergansers and Little Grebes. The local Peregrines will be patrolling the channel airstream, hopefully attended by their newly-fledged eyasses.

During the last week of the month, South Walney becomes almost deafening as six week old chicks take to the wing and are pursued relentlessly by territory holding gulls whose air space they have violated. Oystercatcher chicks are often at the same stage, that is, they can run better than they can fly.

Tern eggs begin to hatch, and the attentive parents are either journeying back and forth to the Duddon Estuary for sand eels or warding off any stray gulls, Magpies, Oystercatchers, Little Owls or Kestrels that have malevolent designs.

## 1st — 15th July

*Jackdaws at the offices*

The first day of autumn! And hints of it are provided by a trickle of passerines caught or seen at South Walney. Small numbers of Willow Warblers, Chiffchaffs and Whitethroats glean food from the vegetated heligoland trap areas and returning Whinchats, Wheatears, Pied and Yellow Wagtails are seen increasingly. Linnets and Reed Buntings occur, the former often still attending to the demands of young birds. Large gatherings of Starlings, many of them this year's birds forage the stubble fields and at night roost at the offices at South Walney. Jackdaws, in family troupes, roam over the gull colony, some of the younger members being set upon by parent gulls.

The wader flocks of Lapwings, Oystercatchers and Curlews, increase with each day of passing, and individuals of Greenshank and Grey Plover represent the precursors of the later passage flocks. At high tide in Lighthouse Bay, Great Crested Grebes, including a few candy-striped young, form small loose flocks, while at low tide, clubs of non-breeding gulls are supplemented by this season's newly-independents. However, large numbers are still on the colony and the smell of guano can be stifling. The whole area appears to be moving at times —

large flightless, brown youngsters 'legging it' to the safety of nettles and thistles. It is at this time that botulism-affected gulls are most numerous, some of them passing on their illness to their chicks, and providing a sad site to the otherwise vital and exuberant gull colony spectacle.

## 16th — 31st July

As the breeding season comes to a close, South Walney begins to receive its autumn visitors. The Shelducks disappear overnight, leaving their surviving fully grown chicks to fend for themselves. The first returning Teal, admittedly in only low numbers can be found in the central marsh and Eiders are noticeable by their absence.

Common Sandpipers frequent the pools at South Walney and other freshwater waders can include Green Sandpipers and Ruffs, while Haws Bed may hold individuals of Spotted Redshank and small parties of Black-tailed Godwits.

On calm days, hawking Black-headed Gulls are numerous over the mud flats and saltmarshes and ginger youngsters from high tide clubs on the sea-washed turf. It is with the same conditions that southward bound Swifts can occasionally be seen, flocks of one hundred plus, low over South Walney.

On the spit, newly-fledged tern chicks will still be attended to by their parents, but many of them will have deserted their natal site for a communal roost above the high tide. Flitting amongst them, Pied and Yellow Wagtails, foraging for sustenance on the tide line. A Cuckoo seen in this period probably represents the final sighting until the following April!

## 1st — 15th August

*Grey Heron*

The large gatherings of Walney bred terns and gulls form an undeniable attraction to any marauding Arctic or Great Skuas and in the early part of the month small parties of terns can be seen heading south out of Morecambe Bay. Return movements of other sea birds, notably Gannets, Fulmars, Manx Shearwaters and small numbers of auks can also be observed especially after 'good blows'.

Wader movement is also in evidence with Sanderlings, Dunlin, Turnstones and smaller flocks of Ringed Plovers, but apart from Ruffs, freshwater waders are generally in short supply.

Families of Swallows can often be seen assembling at the lighthouse before striking across the Bay, and similarly, wagtails join forces on the spit or at the groyne before undertaking the same flight.

The bushes at the offices will hold warblers, usually Willow, but Chiffchaffs and 'sylvia' warblers may also be met with. Linnets form fairly large flocks, feeding on the ragwort and thistles, while Meadow Pipits flit and feed, often being preyed upon by immature Kestrels and Merlins.

Moorhens and Teal become far more numerous in the freshwater regions at South Walney and Snipe once again utilise the margins of the gate pool and Wylock Marsh. Tummer Hill Marsh sees the arrival of Grey Herons and exceptionally large flocks of Curlews.

## 16th — 31st August

The breeding season is now virtually over and the island plays host to passage birds and the formation of the first over-wintering roosts. At both ends of the island, Wigeon begin to accumulate and the gate pool area of South Walney attracts peak numbers of Coot. Redshanks become very obvious and very numerous especially in the Lighthouse Bay area, while Whimbrels, alongside the huge Curlew flock, sit out high tide in the fields near Biggar. Oystercatchers are impressive in their numbers on the spit, and up to a dozen Greenshank may be found at the same site. More likely, the odd wader can also be located during this period — Green and Wood Sandpiper, Black-tailed Godwit, Ruff or Spotted Redshank.

On certain days the air can be alive with southbound passerines — usually rattling 'alba' wagtails, seeping 'flava' wagtails or chattering Swallows. In accompaniment may be Tree Pipits and Tree Sparrows. More obvious passerines include Wheatears and Whinchats, while the traps at South Walney yield the first autumn Robins, Redstarts and Spotted Flycatchers. Odd warblers have occurred in this period over past years, amongst which have been Melodious, Icterine and Barred. At the other end of the scale, flocking House Sparrows, can be found at South Walney, one of the few occasions when they can be almost guaranteed at this site. In very low numbers, the autumn wave of Goldcrests begins to appear on the island at Willow Woods, consorting with parties of Blue, and to a much lesser extent, Great Tits.

## 1st — 15th September

At South Walney, the gull colony has all but disappeared — only the sick and wounded are left. However, the area is not vacant. Meadow Pipits are very abundant, many arriving from the east and moving partially up the island before heading off towards the Isle of Man. Alongside them are smaller parties of Skylarks and admixed are Linnets and to a lesser degree Goldfinches, Greenfinches and Redpolls. Grey Wagtails begin to supersede the other wagtails in abundance and Robins and Dunnocks can be encountered in the unlikely sea-shore habitat.

The early part of the month usually witnesses tern movements, the majority being Sandwich, and the attending skuas are now just as likely to be Greats as Arctics. Sea-watching can bring its rewards with Manx Shearwaters and Fulmars, although Gannet numbers are normally less than in August. Auk passage continues steadily usually yielding Black Guillemots and Puffins, both in low figures.

The spit becomes increasingly important as a high tide refuge as the wader flocks accumulate and it is at this time that maximum Cormorant totals can be logged, with stormy conditions providing the occasional Shag.

It is not unknown for vagrants to occur during this period and in recent years, South Walney has recorded Honey Buzzard, Temminck's Stint, Marsh and Paddyfield Warbler. The heligoland traps begin to produce more Chiffchaffs than Willow Warblers, and it becomes evident that the returning summer migrants are appearing in lower numbers.

## 16th — 30th September

*Leach's Petrel*

At either end of the island, but more particularly the south, calm days are filled with the movements of diurnal migrants. Sea-watching is enlivened by the continual stream of Skylarks and Meadow Pipits journeying west or southwest. Smaller numbers of Grey Wagtails accompany them, while Swallows and martins can also be noted. After the September gales sweeping in from the Atlantic, the white rumps of House Martins can be replaced by the white rumps of Leach's Petrels. The storms may additionally yield a rarer shearwater, Pomarine Skua or Shag.

Ringing is chiefly confined to the autumn falls of Robins, Wrens and Dunnocks, although in good years, Goldcrests can arrive in large numbers. Attendant upon them are Sparrowhawks, while across the dunes, Merlin presence is almost daily.

North Walney often plays host to at least half a dozen Short-eared Owls, while similar numbers may be found hunting at Long Rein Point or South Walney.

At no time very numerous, Little Stints and Curlew Sandpipers can usually be located either in the central marsh, Haws Bed or near the refuse tip and Grey Phalarope has put in the odd appearance.

The first real winter arrivals, skeins of Pink-footed Geese, are seen winging south, and by the end of the month, cloudy nights are alive with migrating Redwings and Song Thrushes.

## 1st — 15th October

***Short-eared Owl***

Summer migrants have almost petered out by the begining of the month, their place taken by thrushes, pipits, Skylarks and finches. The last Willow Warbler, Whitethroat and Redstart will have usually passed through, though there will still be the odd Blackcap, Wheatear, Chiffchaff and Swallow. In certain years Blue Tits can be abundant, with fewer Great Tits and at times irruptive Coal Tits and Long-tailed Tits. Goldcrests should still be numerous and an occasional Treecreeper may put in an appearance either at South Walney or at Willow Woods. Linnets in large flocks are often located feeding on ragwort and small parties of Siskins in the early morning are heard flying over.

At no time regular, Barnacle geese in small groups have been seen in early October and the first returning Shelducks can be found in all the island salt marshes. The gate pool may yield a Water Rail patrolling the exposed mud and Moorhen numbers are often high. Merlins and Kestrels can be seen preying on both reserves and Peregrines are also noted while Short-eared Owls are a regular feature at a few favoured sites.

Less regular sightings in this period have included Crane, Hobby, White-rumped and Buff-breasted Sandpiper, Pallas's and Yellow-browed Warbler, Red-breasted Flycatcher and Ortolan Bunting. In addition, Rock Pipits are more obvious than at other times of the year and strong westerly winds can induce Leach's Petrels to appear close inshore.

## 16th — 31st October

Early mornings at South Walney can see large movements of finches moving south and appropriately, with the first of the winter's ground frosts, amongst the finches can be heard a few Bramblings and a few Twite. More often than not they simply fly over, but at times small groups of them can be found on the sea-washed turf or at the refuse tip. Chaffinches, Greenfinches and Goldfinches are abundant along with lesser numbers of Redpolls and Tree Sparrows. Consorting with them and sending them into frantic swirls are one or two Merlins, Sparrowhawks, Kestrels and Peregrines. Both ends of the island may witness an autumn Hen Harrier.

The period usually brings the first Goldeneye to the Walney pools and, while Wigeon, Teal and Shelduck numbers build up, the year's maximum Mallard count can be made. Similarly, Oystercatcher roosts reach a peak and the first autumn Jack Snipes can be located either at the gate pool, Wylock Marsh or in the damp areas of North Walney. Sheltering Woodcock can be flushed from the marram grass at South Walney or from the denser vegetation of Willow Woods. Wrens are fairly abundant at the south end and a few have already taken up their winter territories at the offices. The last House Martins are generally recorded during this period.

Occasionally large numbers of auks may be seen flying fast and low over the sea and westerly blows may yield good counts of Kittiwakes emerging from Morecambe Bay. A few divers, normally Red-throated may seek shelter off the groyne and there is still the chance of a menacing Great Skua.

An as yet unexplained phenomenon is the huge gatherings of corvids which appear late in the month moving south. The majority seem to be Jackdaws but mixed in with them are larger corvids; are they purely a local movement circulating around Morecambe Bay or are they bound for the milder Irish pasture? A single Chough has been seen amongst them, Jays on a couple of occasions and Magpies, with flocks of up to 20.

## 1st — 15th November

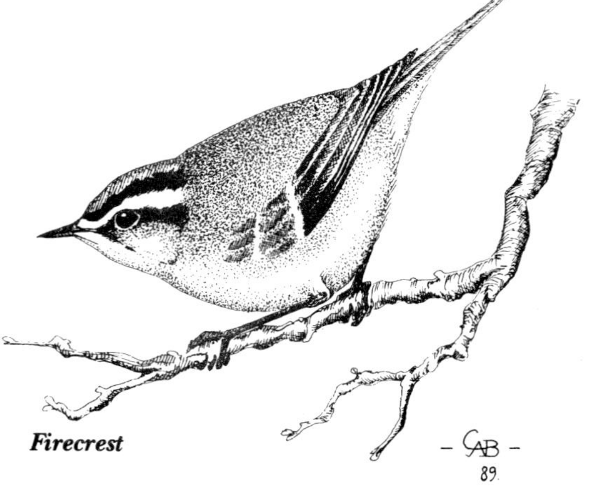

***Firecrest***

Walney seems to have a fairly good record for turning up oddities in the latter part of autumn. A well-remembered day, the 7th November 1982 produced Black Redstart, Firecrest, Great Grey Shrike, Long-eared Owl, Woodcock and Swallow. The next day provided a Yellow-browed Warbler of the 'humei' race and other odd birds in this period have included Richard's Pipit, Smew, Barbary Dove, House Martin, Leach's Petrel and of course the Desert Wheatear of 1986.

Calm misty mornings have occasioned large arrivals of thrushes among which have been late Ring Ousels on a couple of instances. However, the vast majority of passerines have passed through Walney by the middle of the month, although Goldcrests may still be abundant during the early days along with a few late tits which can normally be found in Willow Woods. North Walney can yield a few Stonechats and has yielded two very late Whinchats, while Reed Buntings and Rock Pipits may take up semi-residence at the north end. The last Blackcaps and Chiffchaffs can be found in the hedgerows and the wartime ruins may provide Black Redstart.

Wildfowl become increasingly numerous and along with the regulars of Wigeon, Teal, Mallard and Shelduck can be found Shovelers in Bass Pool, southbound Pink-footed Geese in large skeins and family groups of Whooper Swans, and to a lesser extent Bewick's Swans.

The corvid movements of late October are generally seen in early November and Little Owls are recorded daily. Their occurrence may indicate a small scale movement but as with other autumn birds of prey, there is a possibility that the same individuals are seen each day.

## 16th — 30th November

At South Walney passerines are generally at a premium. Apart from the territory-holding Robins, Wrens and Dunnocks at the offices, interest is provided by flocks of finches, pipits and a few Skylarks although there is always the possibility of Snow Bunting. The refuse tip can usually guarantee Linnets and maybe a small flock of Twite while Pied Wagtails also haunt the wetter areas. Willow Woods should yield Bullfinches and Reed Buntings and the fields around Biggar and Long Rein Point small gatherings of Linnets, Greenfinches, Reed Buntings and possibly Tree Sparrows. As long as the hawthorn bushes are full of berries, Redwings and Fieldfares may also spend the early part of winter in the area until the food supply is exhausted. Small parties of Rock Pipits forage the tideline at North Walney and Willow Woods may support the odd Long-tailed Tit amongst the more numerous Blue Tits.

All the island saltmarshes hold good numbers of Wigeon and particularly Tummer Hill Marsh holds congregations of Shelducks and high tide roosts of Curlews with the possibility of a late Whimbrel. White-fronted Geese do not appear regularly but late November has produced groups on a couple of occasions, and once a Bean Goose.

Sea-watching can be an arduous affair but small numbers of divers, auks and Kittiwakes may be supplemented by a late Gannet, Fulmar or skua and generally a small flock of Common Scoters may be in evidence. The winter flock of Eiders can be located off the groyne and the totals can be swelled by extra birds possibly of northern origin.'

The refuse tip holds peak numbers of Great Black-backed Gulls and already, zealous male Herring Gulls are taking up territories for the coming breeding season at South Walney.

## 1st — 15th December

***Snipe at the gate pool***

Wet Decembers hold large numbers of Lapwings and Golden Plovers in the agricultural fields especially those just to the north of South Walney Nature Reserve. High tide is normally the best time to see Golden Plovers although a search amongst the low tide boulders may also yield flocks. Groups of Snipe haunt the 'juncus' of gate pool, Wylock Marsh and North Walney and if hard weather conditions prevail, southward bound wisps can be seen high over the island. Grey Plovers are numerous at the high tide west coast wader roosts and in recent years numbers appear to be increasing. Stormy conditions may induce Long-tailed Duck, Black Guillemot or divers to seek the shelter of Haws Bed and possibly Scaup may also be seen.

As in November, the passerine interest is primarily confined to Willow Woods or the Biggar fields, but hard weather may cause the arrival of substantially sized lark, finch and thrush flocks which glean sustenance from the tide line. Mild conditions can occasion a Chiffchaff but in general one is hard pressed to find a 'small brown job'. A walk along the tide line is recommended during hard weather — South Walney produced a Nutcracker in 1979.

Large birds seem to dominate Walney during the winter. Scrutiny of gull roosts may yield a Glaucous Gull but generally they do not appear until the turn of the year and the more wintry conditions associated with late January and February. Wader flocks are normally composed of good numbers of Dunlin and Turnstone, although North Walney has a sizeable Sanderling flock and Purple Sandpipers can be found at Biggar Bank or the Coastguard Station.

## 16th — 31st December

Herring Gulls are already proclaiming their territories at South Walney in the early morning and high tide will see many pairs established and giving forth their long calls. Lesser Black-backed Gulls are not abundant and at South Walney rarely number more than 30. In normal winters, the pools should hold healthy collections of both Goldeneyes and Red-breasted Mergansers, and Cormorants, including white-headed birds, fish for eels.

Peregrines play havoc with the high tide roosting waders at South Walney and up to 100 Bar-tailed Godwits may be seen either at South Walney or at Earnse Bay. Oystercatchers form large roosts, their numbers supplemented by arrivals from the far north, and apart from the south end, gatherings can be seen at Biggar Bank, the refuse tip or Hillock Whins.

Tummer Hill Marsh holds its peak numbers of Shelducks and either there or at North Walney, small groups of Pintail may assemble. High tide may produce Snipe and Greenshank at Biggar marsh, but the latter species is virtually regular as an over-wintering bird in ones or twos on the pools at South Walney. Jack Snipe can also be located at their favoured island sites but only on rare occasions are they met with in any but low single figures.

Cold weather may cause the pools at North Walney to freeze up and following these conditions, Tufted Ducks and Pochards may appear at South Walney along with the odd Scaup. In addition, Little Grebes, having vacated North Walney after the breeding season, may be found in single figures on the large gravel pool at South Walney. Great Crested Grebes spend the winter in Walney Channel and Red-necked Grebe may also be recorded. Rare birds in this period are not easily met with, although a Gyrfalcon put in an impressive appearance in 1983.

***Shelducks***

# The Ornithological Year

## culled from Walney Bird Observatory Reports 1980 — 1986

### January 1984

***Snow Buntings***

For the first eleven days the weather was unseasonably mild and rain fell on six days. The lull was shattered on the 12th when severe westerly gales blasted the island until the 17th causing much domestic damage. Frost was recorded between the 18th and 21st, while warmer weather on the 22nd occasioned the first snow of the year. With the snow came a massive hard weather movement, most evident between the 24th and 27th, during which time Walney was swamped with northern birds. For the final few days, the weather remained calm and anticylonic. The total precipitation was 142.4 mm.

During the early part of January, passerines were almost exclusively confined to North Walney with four Long-tailed Tits and four Goldcrests in Willow Woods on the 1st and a Stonechat on the 5th. Divers were in evidence at South Walney with three Red-throated on the 1st and four on the 2nd, while both Black-throated and Great Northern were recorded between the 5th and the 8th. The most unseasonal visitor in that period was a Fulmar on the 2nd, on which date two Pintails, a Velvet Scoter, two Greenshanks and 61 Kittiwakes were also seen. Peregrine, Merlin and Kestrel were regulars at both ends of the island and the north produced a Green Woodpecker on the 10th, and a covey of Grey Partridge on the 12th. The subsequent severe gales brought a Red-necked Grebe to the south end on the 13th and a storm-driven Little Auk sought shelter under the Land Rover in the car-park on the same date. This bird was the second Little Auk in the month, the first was brought to South Walney having been found in the middle of the A590 near Dalton. Other birds storm-driven to the south end included two Snow Buntings on the 15th and six Red-throated Divers, a Great Northern and a Puffin on the 16th. On the 19th, the north end had a fine selection of species including a

Grey Heron, three Shovelers, a Pintail, 800 Curlews, a Jack Snipe, a Short-eared Owl, two Stonechats and three Bullfinches. Twite made their first winter appearance on the 20th with two birds at the south end, followed by three on the 21st, on which date a Water Rail was logged at the north end.

Obvious hard-weather movement was foreseen on the 22nd when a southerly movement of 490 Lapwings, 120 Snipe, 3100 Fieldfares and 310 Redwings left the south end of the island in a hectic three hour spell. The numbers did not let up on the following day with 4400 Fieldfares, 5100 Redwings, 130 Snipe, three Jack Snipe and 32 Bramblings beating a retreat. The hordes and variety which sought refuge on Walney on the 24th were impressive. South alone witnessed 1200 Pinkfeet, 1840 grey geese, 1200 Skylarks, a Shorelark, eight Mistle Thrushes, 55 Fieldfares, 20 Song Thrushes, 900 Redwings, 28 Blackbirds, 120 Meadow Pipits, 20 Chaffinches, 120 Bramblings, 250 Snow Buntings and a solitary, gull-mobbed Bittern. The North Walney picture was similar, highlighted by 139 Red-breasted Mergansers, a Woodcock, four Twite, 27 Bramblings and 81 Snow Buntings. Until the end of the month, numbers of northern birds were high. Each day brought more southward movement of Pinkfeet, but the flocks of Snow Buntings and Bramblings feeding on the saltmarsh will be a permanent memory for many people. On the 26th there were 308 Snow Buntings and 150 Bramblings at the south end, while the following day saw an increase to 350 for the buntings with an additional 180 of the same species on the north end with 130 Bramblings, six Woodcocks and a Hen Harrier. With a gradual let up in the severity of the weather, numbers naturally decreased and by the 29th only 60 Bramblings remained at the south end and two Snow Buntings at the north. A total of 99 species was seen on Walney Island, 87 occuring at the south end and 79 at the north.

## February 1981

*Black Redstart at the fort*

The weather in February was more in accord with typical winter conditions — producing gales on the 2nd, 6th and 7th and snow on the 21st, 22nd and 23rd. The last ten days were extremely bitter with steady southeasterly winds, but the most surprising feature was the rainfall total of 43.1 mm compared with 126.0 mm in February 1980.

The month began in fine style with five rare birds seen on the 1st. A drake and two duck Velvet Scoters rode the tide in Piel Channel, a single Snow Bunting was on the south shore, a Glaucous Gull was seen from the groyne, a Black Redstart remained throughout the month and the Richard's Pipit was seen for the last time. Prior to the gales of the 6th and 7th, duck numbers had diminished to 450 Teal and 500 Wigeon but the period from the 6th to the 9th was first class for sea-watching with an unprecedented number of divers. The 7th saw a single Red-throated Diver, 12 diver sp. and 20 auk sp.; the 8th brought two Red-throated Divers, four Great Northern Divers, four diver sp., 54 Common Scoters and four Razorbills with yet another Red-throated Diver on the 9th. Also regular between the 6th and the 9th were three Twite, two Snow Buntings and a Peregrine. The raft of Scaup provided consistent value reaching 11 birds on the 11th, but usually numbering nine, while on the same date a Mistle Thrush put in a rare appearance. Golden Plovers peaked at 300 on the 11th and 90 Grey Plovers roosted at high tide on the 16th. Less common were 100 Bar-tailed Godwits on the 16th and 30 Sanderlings on the 24th. The 20th and 21st added to the diver passage figures with four diver sp. on the 20th and four more on the 21st. Also on the 21st 30 Common Scoters were seen.

Towards the end of the month passerine movement was in evidence particularly during the snowy weather with 60 Skylarks and 13 Fieldfares on the 22nd; 18 Redwings, 30 Meadow Pipits and three Redpolls on the 23rd; 30 Goldfinches on the 26th and a single Siskin on the 28th. The fairly regular Peregrine was supplemented by a Sparrowhawk on the 17th and two wintering Greenshanks, after a 27 day absence, put in an appearance on the last day of the month. A total of 75 species was seen at South Walney.

## March 1982

*'Victor' the Velvet Scoter*

It was a pleasant task to record only 77.9 mm of rain during March 1982 compared with the abominable 219.7 mm of March 1981. The month was exceptionally sunny and the slight prevailing southwesterly winds in the latter part of the month aided the smooth arrival of migrants.

The early part of March was wet and windy and 12 Gannets made use of the southwest wind. A male Stonechat appeared to have taken up breeding territory in the garden from the 1st to the 4th but he absconded on the 5th. A Black-throated Diver rested off the west shore on the 8th while strong northwesterly winds on the 11th raised hopes in the sea-watching hide. These hopes were fulfilled with the sighting of three Manx Shearwaters including a bird of the Balearic race. The following day produced a further three Manx Shearwaters and 20 Kittiwakes. The winds did not abate and a thorough watch on the 13th yielded a wide range of species. Accompanying 30 Red-throated Divers, two Great Northern Divers and a single Black-throated Diver were a single Manx Shearwater, 15 Common Scoters, 40 Red-breasted Mergansers, seven Common Gulls, 35 Razorbills, five Guillemots and 30 auk sp., while on the shore were flocks of 150 Knot and 250 Turnstones. In addition a lone Peregrine disrupted the solemn group of 2000 Oystercatchers as they roosted on the spit. The activities of windsurfers are not normally beneficial to bird-watchers, but on the 13th, an enthusiastic 'boarder' caused the lifting of 31 Red-throated Divers from Piel Channel.

Clement migratory winds occurred on the 21st and the 22nd evidenced by the night movement of countless Redwings, while on the 22nd the first Sandwich Tern, Chiffchaff and Wheatear were seen. In addition to these regular species, a Black Redstart was trapped in the garden. The continuing kindly weather helped the northerly movement of passerines and two more Wheatears appeared on the 23rd followed by a single Goldcrest on the 24th. The next day, two Greylag Geese flew north while an early morning visitor on his own personal route north was a Snow Bunting. More summer migrants visited on the 26th with three Chiffchaffs and an incredibly early Garden Warbler. The 27th was a very well-watched day both on land and over the sea; Sandwich Terns totalled seven and with them were 30 Red-throated Divers, a single Great Northern Diver and a single Black-throated Diver, a Red-necked Grebe, a Glaucous Gull and two Brent Geese. Goldcrests poured through on the same day with over 20 seeking shelter in the scant vegetation of South Walney. Two Sand Martins flew north on the 28th and directly in front of Pier Hide, two Glaucous Gulls, one a near-adult, roosted at high tide. And still the Velvet Scoter remained. A total of 81 species was recorded at South Walney.

## April 1984

***Red-throated Diver***

— SAB —

Virtually the whole of the month was characterised by calm anticyclonic weather. Mist occurred on the 9th and 10th and the latter date produced the highest rainfall of the month 2.1 mm. Winds were almost negligible, but towards the end of April, gentle breezes emanated from the southeast sector. The advantageous conditions meant that there were few grounded passerines, although the 20th yielded a heavy fall of warblers over the whole of the island. The total rainfall for the month was 6.3 mm.

Little passerine migration was evident during the first week of April although Meadow Pipits moved daily northwards over South Walney, including 300 on the 1st. Divers were in evidence at south end with five Red-throateds and a Black-throated on the 1st when 20 Gannets were also recorded. The 2nd yielded the South Walney Velvet Scoter, a Greenshank and the long-staying Hooded Crow, while 10000 Knot visited the shore on the 3rd. The Hen Harrier was seen at the north end on the 1st and 6th when there were also 19 Teal, six Little Grebes, 13 Goldeneyes and two Wheatears. The 6th also produced the first Sand Martin of the year to south end. The 8th yielded a mixture of summer and winter visitors at both ends of the island. At the south, a Greenshank, two Fieldfares, a Black Redstart, six Robins, four Chiffchaffs and a Grey Wagtail were seen, while the north had three Fieldfares and a Brambling. Two Mute Swans began a two day residency at South Walney on the 9th. Eighteen Goldcrests flitted through the brambles on the same date, while a splendid summer-plumaged Black-tailed Godwit stayed in the central marsh throughout the 11th while 13th saw the return of the first Little Tern of the year, and North Walney logged a fair selection of raptors including two Sparrowhawks, a Peregrine and the regular Hen Harrier. Sea-watching at South Walney produced on the 14th, seven Red-throated Divers, one Great Northern, 20 Gannets, 18 Common Scoters, a Glaucous Gull and five Kittiwakes. In addition, the first Swallows of 1984 appeared on the 14th. Five hours of scrutiny of the gulls roosting on the spit on the 15th were rewarded with the first Cumbria record of a Ring-billed Gull, an adult, which was relocated on the 18th. Between these dates, a first-year Iceland Gull, the second Walney record, was found on the 17th. Also on the 17th, a maximum count of eight Bullfinches were in Willow Woods. The 19th brought the first Cuckoo and Common Sandpipers of the spring to South Walney while the sea provided ten Red-throated and four Great Northern Divers along with ten Little Terns.

At both ends of the island summer migrants were to the fore on the 20th with an estimated 400 Willow Warblers, 40 Goldcrests, four Redstarts, a Grasshopper Warbler and a Whinchat. In conjunction with these were 150 Golden Plovers, 11 Whimbrels, and ten Little Terns at the south end and seven Fieldfares and three Bramblings at the north. An equally mixed bag was seen at the south end on the 21st, with over 150 Sandwich Terns moving north, a Woodpigeon, a Short-eared Owl, four Sand Martins, a Redstart, 30 Willow Warblers and a Grasshopper Warbler, while the first Tree Pipits of the year were recorded on the 22nd followed by two Corn Buntings and a lone Twite on the next day. At the north end on the 23rd a Greenshank, four Whimbrels, two Whitethroats, two Redpolls, and a Merlin were seen, while a Great Tit at the south end on the 25th, constituted the first ever spring record. Only dribs of passerines were seen during the remaining five days of the month but noteworthy among them were a Ring Ousel and a Brambling at the north on the 29th. On the last day, an Osprey was seen over Walney Channel and a Corncrake with a broken wing was brought to the south end, having been caught at the foot of Hare Hill, half a mile to the north of the reserve.

Altogether, 116 species were seen during the month, 105 occuring at the south end and 80 at the north.

## May 1983

*Hoopoe*

May was characterised by almost three weeks of inclement weather and undoubtedly this contributed to the low numbers of passage migrants. Only four Whitethroats were recorded in the month compared with 21 in May 1982, and only three Common Sandpipers, compared with 14 in the previous May. Total rainfall for the month was 87.5 mm.

The month began in a very cold manner typified by two each of Red-throated and Black-throated Divers moving north and a Turtle Dove moving south. Also on the 1st, 400 Sandwich Terns and 70 Common Terns were logged during a three hour sea-watch. On the 3rd, 16 Wheatears and three Whinchats arrived, followed by four Tree Pipits, a Rock Pipit and eight flava wagtails on the 5th Whimbrel numbers were healthy, with up to 70 seen on the 8th. The only sighting of Grasshopper Warbler occurred on that date. A passage of over 300 Gannets was noted moving north on the 9th and of the same mind were 200 Dunlins. Summer and winter birds mixed on the 12th with two Garden Warblers, four Sedge Warblers and two Whinchats balanced by unusually late Wigeon and Merlin. A small movement of Collared Doves occurred on the 13th and 14th with six birds on the former and two on the latter. Also on the 14th, as well as 60 Gannets fishing off the west shore, two Arctic Skuas harried the returning sand-eel carrying terns. A Cuckoo and a House Martin were recorded on the 18th, while a further five Collared Doves passed through on the next day.

The surprise of the 19th, however, was a Hoopoe, which alighted on the car-maintenance pit at the side of the cottages and was later seen at the lighthouse. Possibly this bird had remained on the island for most of May because a Hoopoe, had been reported from near Biggar on two occasions during the 8th. Equally surprising was a Wryneck roosting in the last apology for an elder bush at South Walney on the 20th. It was obvious that the days immediately prior to these sightings had occasioned the wafting of southern species to these parts. In the days that followed, a Golden Oriole started a ten day residency at Willow Woods on the 20th and a Red-backed Shrike was also at that site on the 25th. The remainder of the month at South Walney yielded a few Spotted Flycatchers, a single Pied Flycatcher on the 26th and up to 80 Little Terns on the 29th.

With regard to breeding birds, it was very encouraging to note 25 pairs of Little Terns and two pairs of Common Terns on the spit. A count of Eider nests produced a total of 586, which probably means at least 700 nests in the Walney Island and Foulney Island area. A total of 87 species was recorded at South Walney in May.

## June 1986

***Common Tern***

The first two and half weeks of June continued to give the impression that summer was a long way off, with many days of westerly and northerly airflows. However, from the 18th until the end of the month, high pressure reigned over Europe, and Walney was presented with an almost continuous spell of hot, calm days which added little to the total rainfall of 72.6 mm for the whole month.

Previous Junes have thrown up a few surprises and in 1986 the tradition carried on in fine style with two long overdue firsts for the island. The first, a dapper male Subalpine Warbler came on the 6th; the second, a Nightingale, arrived on the 14th and provided an untypical show for the few fortunate witnesses. On the breeding front the tern colony, despite being down in Little Tern numbers, looked the healthiest since 1972, with not only Common and Little, but also Arctic and Sandwich. Additionally, a new breeding species was added to the island list with the discovery of a duck Shoveler accompanied by a half-grown youngster. The Eider colony was thoroughly counted, realising a staggering 946 nests — a far cry from the lone incubator of 1949.

The 1st saw a Sand Martin and seven House Martins at South Walney, while North Walney was host to two Grasshopper Warblers, 15 Sedge Warblers, ten Whitethroats and a Spotted Flycatcher. Sea-watching at the south end on the 2nd produced a Red-throated Diver and two Fulmars. Late migrants in the form of a Collared Dove, a Black Redstart and a Wheatear were at South Walney on the 4th and the May flock of 2000 Common Scoters were still in evidence on the 5th. In the late afternoon of the 6th, a male Subalpine Warbler was caught in No. 2 trap and after its release skulked sulkily for the benefit of the few. At North Walney, an unseasonal collection of 30 Grey Plovers on the 7th was followed by two more at the south on the 8th. The north held three Canada Geese on the 11th, a typical June record for the island. The only notable sea-watching occurred on the 12th with a single Great Crested Grebe, seven Fulmars, 41 Manx Shearwaters, 24 Gannets and five Kittiwakes. Two days later a small fall of passerines at South Walney included singles of Cuckoo, Whinchat, Redpoll, Nightingale, Willow

Warbler, Sand Martin and House Martin, accompanied by four Chiffchaffs.

By the start of the third week, waders were already returning with nine Sanderlings at South Walney on the 18th and 60 Lapwings, 120 Bar-tailed Godwits, 200 Knot, 50 Grey Plovers and 200 Turnstones on the 21st. Curlews began to assemble with 300 at the north on the 24th. A lull in activity was apparent in the final week of the month but a Common Sandpiper was at the south on the 29th as was an Arctic Skua on the 30th. A total of 87 species was logged on the island, with 79 at the south end and 46 at the north.

## July 1980

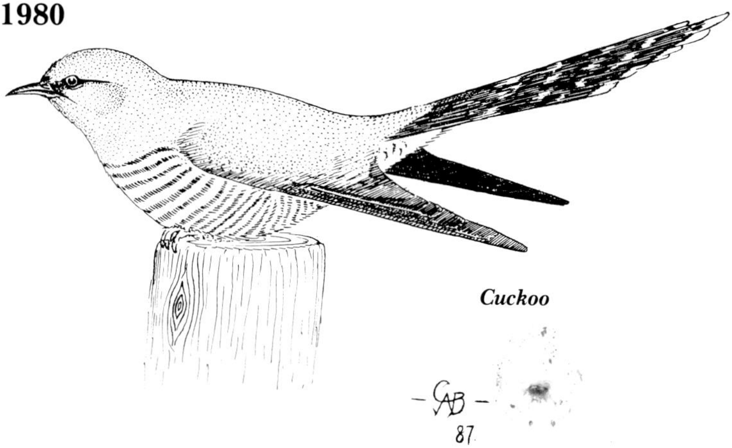

*Cuckoo*

In general, the month was typically July with many days of settled and humid weather. The only days of strong winds occurred on the 12th, from the southwest, and on the 17th, from the northwest. Total rainfall for the month was 50.2 mm.

July has the reputation of being a rather uneventful month, but the July of 1980, though not spectacular, was far from uneventful. Sea-watching and migration proved very fruitful. It has often been said that a sea-watching hide would be a marvellous asset on South Walney and in effect, the new hide overlooking Lighthouse Bay has helped in this sphere. Not only does it offer excellent views of the bay and channel, but also good sea-watching when the weather conditions are correct. On the 19th, a very wet and blustery day, a two hour watch at high tide produced five Gannets, three Manx Shearwaters, 200 Turnstones, two Spotted Redshanks, and 20 Little Terns plus the Walney regulars of breeding waders, gulls and Eiders. The three Manx Shearwaters flew up the channel as far as Piel Castle and did this on three occasions. The 22nd provided an Arctic Skua which spent ten minutes harrying terns, before disappearing towards the cranes of Vickers' shipyard. The month was good for wandering Grey Herons, with four on the 4th, and three on the 13th — both parties causing extreme concern among the gull colony.

Wader movement was interesting with 2500 Dunlin on the 26th, 150 Sanderlings on the 21st, five Greenshanks on the 18th and 30th, four Spotted Redshanks on the 18th, a Green Sandpiper on the 28th, up to 15 Common Sandpipers on the 14th and a Whimbrel on the 30th. The Common Sandpiper passage was very good — up to ten birds being seen on many days during the last three weeks. Further migrants included Cuckoos on the 15th and 23rd, 30 Swifts on the 28th, 40 Swallows on the 24th and 26th, five Wheatears on the 30th and 31st, four Whinchats on the 18th, a Garden Warbler on the 26th, seven Willow Warblers on the 21st. and up to 30 flava wagtails on the 20th, 24th and 28th. Another notable event was the first breeding of Whitethroat on the reserve. Additionally, a Kingfisher near the office pools on the 15th, was the first record since the late 19th century. A total of 77 species was recorded at South Walney.

## August 1983

***Little Ringed Plover***

Throughout August there was hardly a breath of wind and conditions were often near perfect for watching and catching birds. Total rainfall for the month was 60.9 mm.

Numbers of migrating passerines were well up on any previous year, of particular note were Tree Pipits of which 402 were logged compared with 152 and 67 in the Augusts of 1982 and 1981 respectively. The month was however slow to start, the only highlight of the first week being two Ruffs which arrived on the 6th and stayed till the 9th. A small fall of passerines on the 9th included Whinchats, Sedge Warblers, Garden Warblers, Pied Flycatchers and Spotted Flycatchers. An early lone Scaup was seen on the 11th, while the following day produced a profitable sea-watch with four Fulmars, 28 Gannets, a Great Skua and three Kittiwakes. A very early record was of eight Shelducks flying south on the 16th.

Ideal migration conditions were prevalent on the 17th, and the following few days were extremely hectic for all available watchers and ringers. The 17th brought 20 Wheatears, two Redstarts, 70 Willow Warblers, 30 Tree Pipits and two Grey Wagtails, while the 18th produced a further good fall of Willow Warblers and the tenth Melodious Warbler to be recorded on Walney. Coinciding with this for a few lucky Cumbrians was the second Icterine Warbler for the county, which was well received on the 19th. It was fortunate indeed to see two Hippolais Warblers in the hand on consecutive days. The first noteworthy day of Meadow Pipit passage was the 20th, when 60 birds flew south, while the following day during a three hour sea-watch, 600 Commic Terns per hour flew south, some harried by a lone Arctic Skua. Hirundine passage was also evident on the 21st with 300 Swallows, six House Martins and 12 Sand Martins; 30 Swifts, ten Robins, two Pied Flycatchers and 40 flava wagtails were also seen. Heavy southerly movement continued on the 22nd with four Redstarts, 70 Willow Warblers, five Whitethroats, three Spotted Flycatchers and 60 Tree Pipits followed by 300 Linnets on the 23rd.

Waders were scarce throughout most of the month, the Ruffs and six Greenshanks being the only delights, but on the 25th, a Spotted Redshank and a Green Sandpiper turned up in the central marsh. Passerines however continued to move through and it was pleasant to record the sixth Barred Warbler for Walney on the 26th, to be followed by the fourth Lesser Whitethroat for South Walney on the next day. Also on the 27th, sea-watching yielded 450 Gannets, ten Common Scoters, 16 Whimbrels, 40 Bar-tailed Godwits, a Great Skua and six Kittiwakes. The 29th brought the first new species for 1983, a Little Ringed Plover, which stayed for a further week in the central marsh. Finally, the last day of the month saw a single Black-tailed Godwit, eight Goldcrests, 40 flava wagtails, 25 Grey Wagtails and a Treecreeper, only the fifth ever recorded on Walney, which in lieu of trees, chose the World War Two searchlight emplacement on which to eke its livelihood. A total of 99 species was recorded at South Walney.

## September 1985

*Red-breasted Flycatcher*

September proved to be a much drier month than August with just 62.9 mm of rain and was an excellent month for both passerine and seabird movement. The month started in spectacular fashion when winds reached storm force on the 1st and seabirds poured past the west shore. Gannets and Fulmars totalled 250 each while other birds seen included three Curlew Sandpipers and a Black Tern. These sightings were, however, overshadowed by a Honey Buzzard which passed southward over the spit in the late afternoon.

The wind dropped dramatically on the 2nd when the only Lesser Whitethroat of the autumn was found. The calm conditions continued and migrants began to move through in quite large numbers. Wheatears increased to 45 on the 3rd, on which date 50 Grey Wagtails passed south and a splendid Richard's Pipit spent a short time strutting around the car park at South Walney. Wader passage was highlighted on the 4th by eight Commons and a single Green Sandpiper, a Ruff and six Greenshanks.

Westerly winds increased in force on the 7th and large numbers of Fulmars and Gannets were logged, totalling 200 of each species, accompanied by three Greats and a single Arctic Skua. Calm weather ensued for the following week bringing the only Melodious Warbler of the year to the south end on the 11th in the company of three Garden Warblers and seven Spotted Flycatchers. A touch of 'Jaws' came to South Walney on the 14th when a rather timid but awesome Basking Shark thrashed about in the shallow water of Lighthouse Bay. A Leach's Petrel was seen off the west shore on the 14th, followed by six Leach's Petrels, 50 Manx and a Cory's Shearwater on the 16th, and a further two Leach's on the 21st. From the 22nd onwards settled weather once more prevailed with light easterly winds and early morning mist on some days. On the 24th some varied passage occurred including 3500 Meadow Pipits, two Sand Martins, and a Siskin, while a Turtle Dove arrived and stayed for several days. The 25th brought similar passage to the previous day with the addition of a Pied Flycatcher. The 26th dawned dull and misty and, for a day, diurnal passage seemed to have come to an abrupt halt; however, sightings of three Red-breasted Flycatchers, a Yellow-browed Warbler, a Pied Flycatcher and a Snow Bunting supplied ample compensation. The first island record of a Stone-curlew came on the 28th, on which date two Short-eared Owls and a single Barn Owl were seen.

Throughout the month diurnal passage was very heavy with the skies seemingly full of southbound passerines on some mornings. Meadow Pipits were the predominant species amassing a total of almost 15000, with Skylarks the next most numerous with nearly 1350 during the month. A total of 133 species was seen during September, with 120 recorded at South Walney and 78 on North Walney.

## October 1984

*Crane mobbed by gulls*

The first week of the month was characterised by calm, clear anticyclonic weather which deteriorated rapidly when a series of depressions brought in muggy, drizzly conditions. Subsequently, gale force winds started on the 19th and continued until the 22nd but they were not strong enough to bring in pelagic seabirds. One depression after another filled the final abysmal week and 20.1 mm of rain fell on the 24th. The total rainfall for the month was 146.7 mm.

A total of 108 species was recorded on South Walney compared with 123 in October 1983. Despite this drop, two new birds were added to the island list. On the 5th a Crane was harried by gulls as it passed over South Walney and on the 21st a Red Grouse was located at North Walney. Passerine species had mixed fortunes with diurnal migrants in the form of Skylarks, alba wagtails and Grey Wagtails being well up on October 1983, but conversely there were only five Blackbirds compared with 68 twelve months previously, and only 178 Goldcrests compared with 670 in the October before.

On the 1st a Red-necked Grebe was spotted off the west shore, this venue also providing an Arctic Skua. A varied mix was seen on the 2nd including 155 Pinkfeet, the first of the autumn, and three Curlew Sandpipers, while a healthy 12 Stonechats were found at the north end. A lone Little Stint joined the Curlew Sandpipers on the 3rd and the next day, Walney recorded its second Hobby, an immature bird seen chasing Linnets over the central marsh. More Pinkfeet moved south on the 5th, on which date four Blackcaps, a Mistle Thrush, a Garden Warbler, 30 Magpies and a late Spotted Flycatcher were also seen. The star bird of the day, the Crane, appeared late in the afternoon as it flew north while being mobbed by gulls. Winter thrushes — 60 Redwings and nine Fieldfares — pushed south on the 6th after which passerine migration was at a standstill for seven days.

On the sea-watching front 21 Gannets, an Arctic Skua and a Sooty Shearwater were logged on the 8th; 35 Kittiwakes and an incredible eight Puffins on the 10th; a Sooty Shearwater on the 11th; 71 Guillemots on the 12th and a Great Northern Diver and a Manx Shearwater on the 13th. In addition, a Black Redstart was at the groyne on the 13th while further north a Reed Warbler was seen at Rakes Lane.

Large numbers of passerines moved over the south of the island on the 15th, 16th and 17th. Of particular note were 40 Robins, 1000 Linnets, 2500 Meadow Pipits, 60 Reed Buntings, 21 Tree Sparrows, two Yellowhammers and a Siskin. In complete contrast, North Walney attracted 12 Mute Swans to the main pool on the 17th. For the remainder of the month passerine movement was once more at a virtual standstill and consequently more emphasis was placed on sea-watching. Accordingly, a Little Gull and 40 Kittiwakes were recorded on South Walney on the 20th, while three Red-throated Divers, two Shags, 50 Kittiwakes and two Whooper Swans were seen on the 21st. The Red Grouse raised its head on North Walney on the 21st and five Sooty Shearwaters were seen off the south end on the 24th. By the last week of October typical winter birds had appeared. A Glaucous Gull and 54 Common Scoters were recorded on the 26th and a Great Northern Diver, ten Tree Sparrows and a Twite on the 27th. It was a great surprise to record the only Leach's Petrel of the year on the 29th, particularly since the westerly winds had not been abnormally strong. Also on the 29th, 76 Guillemots were close inshore at the south end, while a Water Rail was seen at the north end. A Black-throated Diver, two Blackcaps and two Little Owls on the 30th, were followed by a further two Blackcaps, a Woodcock and 400 Jackdaws on the last day of the month.

## November 1986

*Firecrest*

November was a mild month with only two nights of ground frost. In the main the month was rather unsettled with a dominating westerly airflow. A total of 103.4 mm of rain fell, less than during October 1986, but it seemed like more.

The island held 106 species in the month, 93 species at South Walney and 56 at the north end. There was less recording at North Walney due to the departure of the warden. The avian highlight for most people was the long-staying immature female Desert Wheatear which was found near the groyne on the 15th and remained until the 21st. An extremely obliging individual, delighting the many who saw it, and achieving immortality. A sensible Desert Wheatear would have migrated correctly and been safe in its winter quarters — but how mundane! Late autumn passage was still evident in the early part of the month with 17 Greylag Geese, 400 Jackdaws, 20 Carrion Crows and a Snow Bunting at the south end, while North Walney held two each of Jay and Siskin, all on the 1st. Thrush passage was heavyish on the 2nd with 30 Fieldfares and 50 Blackbirds; additionally, 42 Pink-footed Geese flew south as did eight Tree Sparrows and two Redpolls. The October White-fronted Geese were last seen on the 2nd, but the long-staying Barnacle Goose was still with the Curlews until the 9th. A Red Grouse was at the north end on the 3rd (and later seen on the 14th and 15th) while Willow Woods held the island's second Great Spotted Woodpecker. The first Bewick's Swans since 1982 were on the gravel pools at South Walney on the 4th and a late Great Skua was logged on the 5th. Sea-watching produced 25 Commons and one Velvet Scoter at South Walney on the 8th, on which date a Snow Bunting was at the refuse tip. Willow Woods provided a Blackcap and a second sighting of the Great Spotted Woodpecker on the 12th, while the south end played host to a Firecrest from the 13th until the 16th.

The influx of eyes on the 16th meant at least 300 times more coverage. As such, singles of Great Northern Diver, Gannet, Long-tailed Duck, Black Guillemot, Short-eared Owl, House Martin and Leach's Petrel plus two Black-throated Divers were located. Another House Martin was seen heading north on the 18th and, a few minutes later, five Snow Buntings were seen flying in the same direction. A warm, sunny 19th — so warm and sunny that the Desert Wheatear sang its Bedouin rhapsody — produced five Whooper Swans, 47 Pink-footed Geese, three Siskins and a Water Rail. A depression on the night of the 21st and 22nd shifted the Wheatear and though 60 Kittiwakes and three Little Gulls were off the west shore, it was little recompense for all those unfortunates who had travelled great distances to find that the bird had flown. After such fare, the remaining week lacked a little bit of lustre, yet a Great Skua was at the groyne on the 25th as was a Black Guillemot on the 27th and 30th, and an adult drake Long-tailed Duck flew over the cottages on the 28th. To end the month, a sprightly cock Black Redstart was at the north end refuse tip on the 29th.

## December 1983

***Short-eared Owl***

A total of 93 species was recorded at South Walney in December, a month during which there were only two days of frost but gallons of rain. The rainfall recorded, 206 mm, was amost three times as much as fell in December 1981. The mildness of the weather meant that hard weather passage was virtually non-existent and no doubt avian life benefitted after the harshness of the 1978 and 1981 winters.

Duck numbers remained relatively low, peak numbers of Wigeon occurred on the 1st with 260 birds, and of Teal on the 5th with 420 present. The first week was particularly interesting with a Great Northern Diver, Velvet Scoter, two Long-tailed Ducks and a lone Chiffchaff all logged on the 1st. A period of high pressure in the following three days brought an immaculate cock Black Redstart on the 2nd, while an immature male Lapland Bunting remained in residence at Snab Point from the 2nd till the 4th. While attempting to relocate the bunting on the 5th, a Water Pipit was found. The 5th also provided the peak count for Goldeneye — a very memorable six birds. A sea-watch on the 8th produced 43 Kittiwakes, all adults moving northwest, and in tow was an immature Sabine's Gull, which will provoke argument following publication of a letter in British Birds (Feb. 1983) questioning the validity of all British winter records. However, if there were going to be any winter stragglers in the northern hemisphere, surely 1983 was the year that they were going to occur, given the mildness of the winter and the extraordinary number of Sabine's Gulls recorded in the southwest of England in October.

A hard spell of weather commencing on the 10th, saw an influx of thrushes including 15 Songs, ten Redwings and 20 Blackbirds, while the 12th brought three Whooper Swans, two Woodcocks, two Short-eared Owls and 12 Fieldfares. Goose movement was evident during the cold period with skeins of 90 Pinkfeet flying south on the 15th and 16th, and 38 Greylags in the same direction on the 18th. Meanwhile on the 17th, a Gyrfalcon was located in the field next to South Walney Nature Reserve and it was subsequently seen at Rampside, across the channel, on the following day. Sea-watching was the most productive occupation in the last ten days of the month. Six Red-throated Divers were seen on the 21st and 22nd, with a bonus of Black-throated Diver, Black Guillemot and Little Gull also on the latter date. Red-throated Divers had increased to ten on the 23rd and an adult Glaucous Gull, the only one of December, was observed on the 24th. Boxing Day came up with two unlikely passerines, a Siskin at the offices, and a Chiffchaff in the central marsh. Finally to round off the old year came a Black-necked Grebe, a Fulmar, a Long-tailed Duck and the timely return of 'Victor', Walney's Velvet Scoter, which was last recorded on 14th April, but which prior to that date had been a resident 'turn' since late 1980.

*Lapwings*

# An Explanation of Available Statistics and Problems in Collating

John Dean

Except for the alphabetical index table on pages 69-77, the species are listed in the sequence proposed by Professor Voous; though one anomaly has been arbitrarily resolved. Most observatory lists include Snow Goose (*Anser caerulescens*) as a Category 'A' entry; but there must be a good measure of doubt regarding the ancestry and place of origin of these birds. It seems wrong to include one obvious escapee in the systematic list and exclude all other. All Walney's birds have been put into a single list, the text referring to those of a dubious nature, and sub-species are indicated by the presence of brackets around the generally accepted English name.

Each species is treated in the following order:

1. Generally accepted English name.
2. Latin equivalent.
3. Status:

| | | |
|---|---|---|
| i) | Vagrant | Up to 10 all-time records |
| ii) | Rare | 11-31 all-time records |
| iii) | Scarce | Averaging up to five birds per annum |
| iv) | Uncommon | Averaging 6-50 birds per annum |
| v) | Fairly common | Averaging 51-250 birds per annum |
| vi) | Common | Averaging 251-1000 birds per annum |
| vii) | Abundant | Averaging more than 1000 birds per annum |
| viii) | Exotica | Escape from captivity |
| ix) | Introduced | Usually with reference to wildfowl and game bird introduction |

4. Breeding (where applicable).
   Status and statistics of known, probable and possible breeding on Walney Island.
5. Selected information from previous literature.
6. The North Walney accounts and figures are gleaned and collated from the records of the Cumbria Wildlife Trust, the Nature Conservancy Council, Walney Bird Observatory and the notes of various enthusiasts. The latter have also been invaluable in providing information for the middle parts of the island.

   The majority of the summaries are, however, for South Walney only and are based on the daily records of Walney Bird Observatory for the 26 years 1964-1989. Because a full-time warden was first appointed in 1975, since which date cover has been much more complete, the period 1975 to 1989 is the basis usually used.
7. It is, of course, quite impossible to list all the available daily statistics and it becomes necessary to try to show patterns, both periodic and seasonal, by means of representative measures. None of the known measures are

completely satisfactory and, for reasons developed later in the chapter, the representative mainly used is the average (arithmetic mean) of the maximum daily count for the period covered. This average is simply a concise expression of the total and saves printing space. It enables a view to be expressed of the status of the species and its seasonal fluctuation. It does not give an indication of any change in status during the period nor of the regularity of presence of the species. These matters have to be dealt with in the text.

For some species, especially the less common ones, the form used is simply of "Days recorded 1975-1989". Under each month is a figure denoting the number of days that the species has been recorded in that month in the period 1975-1989, followed by the total number of days for that 15 year period. Any significant flocks or groups will be mentioned in the text.

A bird observatory has three basic functions — recognition, recording, reporting. It must not exist merely to observe since that information dies with the observer.

Recognition has two distinct aspects, expertise and ethic. There is a tendency to assume that wardens are all equally quick and expert in distinguishing species; but all of them are, in fact, at some stage of learning recognition and their education is never completed. There is no formal training as with ringers and the expertise is derived from on-the-job education.

Recognition is more important in some cases than in others; the degree of importance being, generally, inversely related to the abundance of the species. In the 19th century observers had the advantage, inappropriate now, of shooting a rarity and examining it at leisure. The only similar aid in modern times is the trapping of birds for ringing, but not all vagrants are prepared to cooperate. There are two types of vagrant or rarity with which an observatory has to contend and, curiously, the rarer the less the problem. British rarities are only acceptable if the British Birds Rarities Committee has vetted and approved; but local rarities (i.e. unusual for the observatory, locality or county) are often the sole responsibility of the warden and he has to make an ethical choice. This choice will depend, largely, on the number and known expertise of those who have seen the local rarity.

When, as in this book, a bird survey is attempted covering, not only the observatory and surrounding reserve but, also, the rest of an island that is 16 kilometres long, the judgement of what to count and what to omit is considerable; and the difficulties of also trying to include what has been seen during 150 years are obviously immense.

A summary of the available statistics is included earlier in this chapter, but a preliminary discussion of the records of an established observatory (or nature reserve, which, for South Walney is synonymus) is called for. It is the South Walney records which are the raw material for most of the statistics in the systematic list; those for the rest of the island being of comparatively recent or intermittent value, included as general interest and as a basis on which, hopefully, future statistics can be built.

The main record for South Walney is a daily log covering species which are not rarities to the area. Birds, not warranting a line in the daily log, are recorded as they occur, in the rarities log and provide a straightforward story. Different wardens have different problems, different opportunites, different ideas, and this is reflected in the manner in which the daily log is kept. It is apparent, looking at

Walney's daily log, that there have been days when it is partially or totally incomplete. Perhaps owing to other commitments, the warden devoted little time on a particular day to actual bird-watching; perhaps, as he was counting a flock, it was startled and took off; perhaps he was out shopping. Sometimes, having counted a species on one day, he merely put a tick on the following day. Sometimes there wasn't a warden. For one whole month foot and mouth disease made the reserve inaccessible.

Few other branches of nature study seem to be so obsessed with counting. It has become a way of life with observatories and bird books. Originally, "statistics" was used in the sense of "status" and this is still the important meaning for any ornithological study. It could well be that there is too much indiscriminate counting and too little purposeful counting. Far too little thought has been given to random sample days for birds such as Herring Gulls, Lesser Black-backed Gulls, Eiders and other abundant regulars.

Cover is a most important problem and is reflected in the role of the log's empty spaces. In "Hilbre, The Cheshire Island" (1982), the figures are based on observations for 2038 days in 11 years, i.e. one day in every two. It will not, of course, be alternate days and, although if there is a figure in for a particular day coverage is regarded as complete, there is no way of determining the daily quality, i.e. the number and experience of the observers, the hours observed and the visibility conditions etc. This is an inevitable difficulty and a calculation such as that for Hilbre is impossible for South Walney. All that can truthfully be said is that there has been more cover in the last fifteen years than in the previous fifteen.

One of the major snags of the daily log is the status of the empty spaces. A blank may indicate:

| | | |
|---|---|---|
| a) | Observer(s) present | Bird(s) not present |
| b) | Observer(s) present | Bird(s) present, but not seen/recorded |
| c) | Observer(s) not present | Bird(s) not present |
| d) | Observer(s) not present | Bird(s) present |

and the treatment of these is of considerable signigicance in any attempt to sum the records for consecutive days.

How then, given the imperfections of the raw material, are the logged figures to be summarised? Before answering this question, let us look at the motives that lie behind the production and publication of a book relating to the statistics of a bird observation point. The pioneer book of this nature for an observatory is, of course Dr. Sharrock's, "The Natural History of Cape Clear Island" (1974), in which he says:

"The primary purpose....is to summarise the results and achievements of ....work by Cape Clear Bird Observatory", and "This book is written for the general reader with an interest in natural history".

Reconciling these two ideas is not easy.

There are two types of tabulated statistics, those designed for expert reference and those for the general public. As the expert will "always" understand what is produced for the general public without the reverse being true, the tables must try to be both informative and simple. Both "Cape Clear" and this Walney book, being written by ornithologists from the viewpoint of bird observatories, must be heavily biassed towards birds. They are bird books with animal, vegetable and mineral attachments. For this book it is probable that there will be two main classes of reader, Cumbrian and Lancastrian naturalists who are interested in

Walney Island and ornithologists who may well skim or ignore the non-bird parts. If there is justification for a bird observatory, there must be justification for the dissemination of its observations to interested parties; and the intimate relationship between birds and geography, geology, flora and other fauna provokes a need for at least a picture of these latter. But the bird information must be in a form that the non-bird reader can enjoy.

Walney observatory has a massive collection of figures which are both invaluable and useless. Invaluable because they are the only "facts" that the obvservatory has; useless because they cannot be understood or appreciated as they stand. Somehow they must be turned into representations and it may well be that different species require different representations. The major questions are:

a) How regularly can this species be seen?
b) At what periods of the year can it be seen?
c) In what quantity can it be seen?
d) What is its status and has it changed or is it changing?

After considerable thought and soul-searching, the methods used by Dr. Sharrock for "Cape Clear" and followed, with some amendments, by Professor Craggs for "Hilbre", have been discarded. Both books use bird counts; unnecessary confusion is created by the use of the term "bird days" instead of "bird". Cape Clear adds the daily counts for 5-day periods over 11 years and divides by 55. Hilbre adds the daily counts for 15-day periods over 21 years. the second figure is, perhaps, easier to understand, but the two systems are similar. Bird counts are suitable where there is little chance of birds being counted twice, a condition which appears to confine their use to vagrants and other rarities and to birds which fly straight past. As a result it is not practicable to use such a method for birds that breed or birds that stop off for refreshment or birds that move to and fro. One of the consequences is that many common birds receive little numerical recognition in "Cape Clear" and "Hilbre"; another is that, to stretch the concept to as many species as possible, subjective adjustments take place, e.g. in "Hilbre"

Eider. One year excluded because a small flock did not conform.
Common Tern/Arctic Tern. Excluded because they move "to and fro".
Little Gull. "The same flock" included.

For a broad representation and an easy understanding for the general reader, calendar months appear to be sufficient. For a more detailed monograph on a single species or group of species, further delving in the daily log may be required. But too many figures are not helpful for a picture to be drawn.

Adding together daily counts leads to over-counting and inconsistent over-counting at that. If one takes the largest number seen on any one day in a calendar month, one has a number which is known to have been there. There could well be under-counting if there is a continual passage, but this factor can be taken into account in the text. The same birds may be counted in consecutive months but this does not matter provided they are not added together.

At South Walney, the first step was a condensation of the daily log by the production of grids showing monthly maxima over the whole period for each species. These give the warden a good general picture of the status of each species; but such grids are equally unprintable, with numbers sometimes varying between 1 and 30,000 for a single species. However, the arithmetic mean of the maxima for each month does produce, for most species, a useful indicator and many of the species in the systematic list are treated in this way.

There are two other variations from the "Cape Clear" technique. On page 37 of that book, "To give a clearer impression....certain pairs of groups of difficult species have been treated.... as if all birds were specifically identified, the unidentified birds being allocated according to the proportions of the identified ones in each period". This procedure would, of course, only be valid if the specifically identified were an adequate and random sample of the population, and it has not been followed. For instance, Common, Arctic and Common/Arctic Terns are treated as three species.

There are no histograms in the systematic bird list. In some books they may be thought to break up a text which might, otherwise, appear monotonous; but their prime purpose is to provide a visual aid to the understanding of figures. There are well-known snags. First, a histogram requires a translation from numerical to linear measurement and a scale drawing — operations always liable to error introduction. Secondly, in order to be understood other than merely as a pattern, they require translation back. For example, in "Cape Clear" (page 38), Great Northern Diver, the histogram shows for January 1-5 a height of approximately 2 cm. This means, presumably, that in 55 days (5 × 11 years) at this time of the year, 36 or 37 birds were recorded. The general reader is not going to do this very often, especially when he realises that he gets a quicker (and better ?) picture by reading the text. "Cape Clear" promises nothing more of the histograms than "a means of displaying the patterns of occurrences" (page 37). "Hilbre" attaches rather more than this to histograms (page 162) though it hardly helps the reader to have, not only half-a-dozen different scales to a page, but the calendar turned round from time to time.

Given the choice between:

Common Scoter — Average maxima 1975-1989

| J | F | M | A | M | J | J | A | S | O | N | D |
|---|---|---|---|---|---|---|---|---|---|---|---|
| 30 | 15 | 18 | 65 | 230 | 159 | 28 | 19 | 29 | 43 | 123 | 68 |

and:

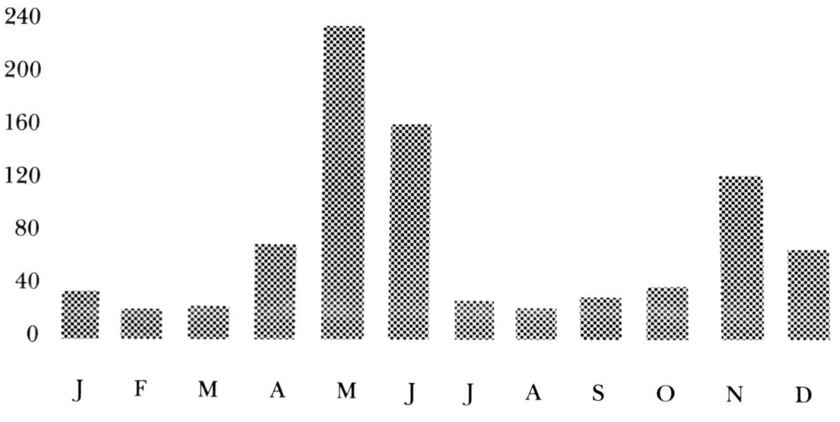


this book uses the former, for:

a) it has to be determined, anyway, before the histogram can be drawn,

b) being one step less, there is one potential error less,

c) it takes up less room,
d) its visual appreciation is not affected by changing vertical scales.

The average monthly maxima technique is used for most of the regularly recorded species. Other techniques are, however, used from time to time:

a) Bird counts for vagrant to uncommon species.
b) Days present where considered more appropriate, i.e. where the actual number of birds is in doubt.
c) Pairs or nests for breeding colonies.

For bird lists of any magnitude, or field guides, there is an obvious advantage in a recognised taxonomic approach and the order of Professor Voous is now widely accepted. It is used in the bird list for Walney. It has, however, tended to become something of a fetish (Voousdooism ?) and used where it is inappropriate and for short lists. The importance of the migration tables, for instance, lies in the dates and the calendar has been allowed to take precedence over taxonomy.

Despite the generally accepted Voous order by birders, it will not be appreciated by non-birders and they will be mystified as they look for information about various species. It is hoped that the table headed "**Index of Bird Records**" will make life easier for them and, also, be of interest to all readers. All the species recorded on Walney are in vernacular alphabetical order with a number reference to the systematic (Voous order) list. (Pp. 78-169). The figure below the month indicates the number of e.g. Januarys in the 15 year period 1975-1989 at South Walney. Thus '15' means the presence in that month every year at South Walney. The final number, the maximum number present on any one day and at any time at South Walney, is an indication of the top flock size. The advantages of this method of presentation are:

a) It is easy to understand.
b) All the figures are factual, not derived.
c) There is no error-inducing arithmetic and drawing.
d) Provided there is some coverage each month, the significance of gaps is much diminished.
e) It is easy to update.

***John Dean** spent his working life as a statistician and administrator with Stewarts and Lloyds and British Steel.*

# Index of Bird Records

(See Page 68)

| REF | | J | F | M | A | M | J | J | A | S | O | N | D | MAX |
|---|---|---|---|---|---|---|---|---|---|---|---|---|---|---|
| 159 | Auk, Little | 2 | 1 | 1 | — | — | — | — | — | — | 1 | 1 | 3 | 16 |
| 161 | Auk, sp. | 11 | 11 | 11 | 10 | 14 | 11 | 11 | 8 | 12 | 15 | 14 | 11 | 480 |
| 95 | Avocet | — | — | — | — | — | — | — | — | — | — | — | — | — |
| 25 | Bittern | 1 | — | — | — | — | — | — | — | — | — | — | — | 1 |
| 215 | Blackbird | 15 | 15 | 15 | 15 | 15 | 15 | 15 | 15 | 15 | 15 | 15 | 15 | 200 |
| 232 | Blackcap | 1 | — | — | 8 | 10 | 1 | 2 | 2 | 10 | 15 | 14 | 1 | 12 |
| 207 | Bluethroat | — | — | — | — | 1 | — | — | — | — | — | — | — | 1 |
| 268 | Brambling | 6 | 3 | 1 | 2 | — | — | — | — | — | 11 | 8 | 5 | 150 |
| 170 | Budgerigar | — | — | — | — | — | — | 1 | 2 | 1 | — | — | — | 1 |
| 276 | Bullfinch | — | — | — | — | — | — | — | — | 1 | — | — | — | 1 |
| 287 | Bunting, Corn | — | — | 2 | 3 | 1 | — | — | — | — | 2 | — | — | 2 |
| 280 | Bunting, Lapland | — | — | — | — | — | — | — | — | — | 2 | 3 | 2 | 2 |
| 284 | Bunting, Little | — | — | — | — | — | — | — | — | — | — | — | — | 1 |
| 283 | Bunting, Ortolan | — | — | — | — | — | — | — | — | — | — | — | — | 1 |
| 286 | Bunting, Red-headed | — | — | — | — | — | 1 | 1 | — | — | — | — | — | 1 |
| 285 | Bunting, Reed | 11 | 12 | 14 | 15 | 15 | 14 | 15 | 15 | 15 | 15 | 15 | 6 | 50 |
| 281 | Bunting, Snow | 8 | 5 | 1 | 1 | — | — | — | — | 2 | 2 | 10 | 6 | 356 |
| 74 | Buzzard | — | — | — | 1 | — | — | — | — | — | — | — | 1 | 1 |
| 68 | Buzzard, Honey | — | — | — | — | — | — | — | — | 1 | — | — | — | 1 |
| 267 | Chaffinch | 10 | 11 | 14 | 15 | 11 | 8 | 6 | 2 | 14 | 15 | 15 | 12 | 100 |
| 237 | Chiffchaff | 1 | — | 6 | 15 | 12 | 8 | 6 | 11 | 15 | 13 | 7 | 4 | 60 |
| 256 | Chough | — | — | — | — | — | — | — | — | — | 1 | — | — | 1 |
| 92 | Coot | 8 | 11 | 15 | 15 | 15 | 15 | 15 | 15 | 14 | 9 | 10 | 8 | 44 |
| 23 | Cormorant | 15 | 15 | 15 | 15 | 15 | 15 | 15 | 15 | 15 | 15 | 15 | 15 | 160 |
| 90 | Corncrake | — | — | — | 1 | — | — | — | — | — | — | — | — | 1 |
| 89 | Crake, Spotted | 1 | — | — | — | — | — | 1 | — | 1 | — | — | — | 1 |
| 93 | Crane | — | — | — | — | — | — | — | — | — | 1 | — | — | 1 |
| 275 | Crossbill | — | — | — | — | — | — | 1 | 1 | — | — | — | 1 | 1 |
| 259 | Crow, Carrion | 15 | 15 | 15 | 15 | 15 | 15 | 15 | 15 | 15 | 15 | 15 | 15 | 110 |
| 260 | Crow, Hooded | 1 | 3 | 5 | 7 | 9 | 3 | 3 | — | 2 | — | 3 | 1 | 5 |

| REF | | J | F | M | A | M | J | J | A | S | O | N | D | MAX |
|---|---|---|---|---|---|---|---|---|---|---|---|---|---|---|
| 171 | Cuckoo | — | — | — | 2 | 9 | 6 | 6 | 6 | — | — | — | — | 3 |
| 121 | Curlew | 15 | 15 | 15 | 15 | 12 | 13 | 14 | 15 | 15 | 15 | 15 | 15 | 1800 |
| 202 | Dipper | — | — | — | — | — | — | — | — | — | — | — | — | 1 |
| 2 | Diver, Black-throated | 7 | 5 | 7 | 5 | 4 | 1 | — | — | 5 | 3 | 1 | 4 | 5 |
| 3 | Diver, Great Northern | 7 | 6 | 8 | 11 | 4 | — | 1 | — | 7 | 12 | 8 | 9 | 4 |
| 1 | Diver, Red-throated | 11 | 12 | 10 | 12 | 11 | 5 | 1 | 7 | 12 | 13 | 12 | 10 | 50 |
| 4 | Diver, sp. | 13 | 10 | 9 | 14 | 8 | 1 | — | 2 | 10 | 13 | 9 | 11 | 30 |
| 100 | Dotterel | — | — | — | — | 1 | — | — | — | 1 | — | — | — | 1 |
| 167 | Dove, Barbary | — | — | — | — | — | — | — | — | — | 1 | 1 | — | 1 |
| 166 | Dove, Collared | 2 | — | 1 | 13 | 11 | 8 | 4 | 9 | 9 | 7 | 2 | 2 | 10 |
| 163 | Dove, Rock | ? | ? | ? | ? | ? | ? | ? | ? | ? | ? | ? | ? | ? |
| 164 | Dove, Stock | 11 | 12 | 12 | 15 | 12 | 13 | 12 | 15 | 13 | 10 | 10 | 14 | 20 |
| 168 | Dove, Turtle | — | — | — | — | 7 | 5 | 1 | 3 | 1 | 2 | — | — | 2 |
| 60 | Duck, Long-tailed | 3 | 5 | 2 | 4 | 1 | 1 | — | 2 | 1 | 6 | 7 | 6 | 8 |
| 55 | Duck, Ring-necked | — | — | — | — | — | — | — | — | — | — | — | — | 1 |
| 67 | Duck, Ruddy | — | — | — | — | — | — | — | — | — | — | 1 | — | 1 |
| 56 | Duck, Tufted | 11 | 11 | 8 | 7 | 5 | 2 | 2 | 3 | 8 | 9 | 5 | 6 | 20 |
| 112 | Dunlin | 15 | 15 | 15 | 15 | 15 | 11 | 14 | 15 | 15 | 15 | 15 | 15 | 15000 |
| 204 | Dunnock | 15 | 15 | 15 | 15 | 12 | 7 | 10 | 9 | 15 | 15 | 15 | 15 | 100 |
| 75 | Eagle, Spotted | — | — | — | — | — | — | — | — | — | — | — | — | 1 |
| 26 | Egret, Cattle | — | — | — | — | — | — | — | — | — | — | — | — | 1 |
| 58 | Eider | 15 | 15 | 15 | 15 | 15 | 15 | 15 | 15 | 15 | 15 | 15 | 15 | 5000 |
| 59 | Eider, King | — | — | — | 1 | 1 | 1 | — | — | — | — | — | — | 1 |
| 216 | Fieldfare | 11 | 9 | 12 | 11 | 3 | — | — | — | 1 | 14 | 15 | 12 | 5500 |
| 240 | Firecrest | — | — | — | 3 | 1 | 1 | — | — | 1 | 4 | 3 | — | 4 |
| 30 | Flamingo, Greater | — | — | — | — | — | — | — | — | — | — | — | — | 1 |
| 243 | Flycatcher, Pied | — | — | — | 1 | 4 | 1 | 1 | 12 | 6 | 6 | — | — | 4 |
| 242 | Flycatcher, R-b | — | — | — | — | — | 1 | — | — | 1 | 3 | — | — | 3 |
| 241 | Flycatcher, Spotted | — | — | — | 1 | 14 | 5 | 1 | 1 | 15 | 15 | — | — | 12 |
| 10 | Fulmar | 4 | 2 | 9 | 14 | 15 | 13 | 10 | 13 | 13 | 6 | — | 1 | 325 |
| 48 | Gadwall | 1 | — | — | 1 | 2 | — | — | — | 1 | 1 | — | — | 2 |

| REF | | J | F | M | A | M | J | J | A | S | O | N | D | MAX |
|---|---|---|---|---|---|---|---|---|---|---|---|---|---|---|
| 22 | Gannet | 2 | 2 | 9 | 12 | 15 | 13 | 14 | 14 | 15 | 14 | 7 | 1 | 700 |
| 52 | Garganey | — | — | — | — | 4 | 1 | — | 6 | — | 1 | — | — | 2 |
| 119 | Godwit, Bar-tailed | 15 | 14 | 14 | 12 | 6 | 5 | 6 | 14 | 15 | 15 | 11 | 13 | 350 |
| 118 | Godwit, Black-tailed | — | 1 | — | 4 | 4 | 5 | 6 | 11 | 9 | 4 | 5 | — | 200 |
| 239 | Goldcrest | — | — | 9 | 14 | 4 | 1 | — | 11 | 15 | 15 | 13 | 2 | 350 |
| 63 | Goldeneye | 15 | 14 | 13 | 7 | 2 | 2 | 2 | 2 | 4 | 14 | 15 | 15 | 100 |
| 270 | Goldfinch | 14 | 14 | 13 | 15 | 14 | 9 | — | 5 | 11 | 15 | 15 | 15 | 60 |
| 66 | Goosander | 1 | — | — | 1 | — | — | — | — | 1 | 1 | 1 | 2 | 7 |
| 42 | Goose, Barnacle | 3 | 1 | 1 | 1 | 1 | 1 | — | — | 2 | 4 | 2 | 1 | 105 |
| 35 | Goose, Bean | 1 | — | — | — | — | — | — | — | — | — | 1 | 1 | 1 |
| 43 | Goose, Brent | 4 | 5 | 5 | 7 | 4 | 2 | 1 | — | 2 | 6 | 3 | 5 | 21 |
| 41 | Goose, Canada | 1 | — | — | 4 | 2 | 6 | 2 | 1 | 3 | 2 | — | — | 30 |
| 39 | Goose, Grey | 12 | 4 | 3 | — | — | — | 1 | — | 4 | 6 | 10 | 8 | 1840 |
| 38 | Goose, Greylag | 5 | 1 | 4 | 3 | 3 | 3 | — | 3 | 4 | 5 | 4 | 5 | 94 |
| 36 | Goose, Pink-footed | 12 | 11 | 6 | 3 | 2 | 1 | 1 | 1 | 7 | 15 | 12 | 13 | 1360 |
| 40 | Goose, Snow | — | — | — | 1 | 3 | 1 | — | — | — | — | — | — | 2 |
| 37 | Goose, White-fronted | 1 | — | — | — | — | — | — | — | — | 2 | 2 | 2 | 14 |
| 9 | Grebe, Black-necked | — | — | — | — | — | — | — | 1 | — | 1 | — | 1 | 1 |
| 6 | Grebe, Great Crested | 14 | 12 | 14 | 12 | 13 | 11 | 12 | 13 | 14 | 15 | 15 | 14 | 25 |
| 5 | Grebe, Little | 13 | 12 | 11 | 12 | 9 | 8 | 8 | 9 | 12 | 13 | 15 | 14 | 8 |
| 7 | Grebe, Red-necked | 4 | 2 | 1 | — | — | — | — | — | 1 | 6 | 3 | 2 | 2 |
| 8 | Grebe, Slavonian | 1 | 1 | — | — | — | — | — | — | 1 | — | 3 | 1 | 1 |
| 269 | Greenfinch | 14 | 14 | 13 | 13 | 5 | 2 | 4 | 7 | 13 | 15 | 15 | 15 | 250 |
| 124 | Greenshank | 15 | 15 | 14 | 10 | 5 | 3 | 14 | 15 | 15 | 15 | 15 | 14 | 15 |
| 82 | Grouse, Red | — | — | — | — | — | — | — | — | — | — | — | — | 1 |
| 156 | Guillemot | 9 | 12 | 12 | 10 | 12 | 11 | 11 | 9 | 15 | 15 | 12 | 12 | 110 |
| 158 | Guillemot, Black | 2 | 2 | 2 | 2 | 2 | 4 | 2 | 7 | 11 | 8 | 9 | 4 | 3 |
| 140 | Gull, Black-headed | 15 | 15 | 15 | 15 | 15 | 15 | 15 | 15 | 15 | 15 | 15 | 15 | 510 |
| 142 | Gull, Common | 15 | 15 | 15 | 8 | 8 | 5 | 4 | 14 | 15 | 15 | 15 | 15 | 30 |
| 146 | Gull, Glaucous | 7 | 8 | 8 | 5 | 6 | — | — | 2 | 4 | 5 | 5 | 8 | 4 |
| 147 | Gull, Great Black-b. | 15 | 15 | 15 | 15 | 15 | 15 | 15 | 15 | 15 | 15 | 15 | 15 | 300 |
| 144 | Gull, Herring | 15 | 15 | 15 | 15 | 15 | 15 | 15 | 15 | 15 | 15 | 15 | 15 | 50000 |
| 145 | Gull, Iceland | — | 1 | — | 1 | — | — | — | — | — | — | — | — | 1 |
| 143 | Gull, Lesser Black-b. | 15 | 15 | 15 | 15 | 15 | 15 | 15 | 15 | 15 | 15 | 15 | 15 | 42000 |
| 138 | Gull, Little | — | 1 | 2 | 1 | 1 | 1 | — | 1 | 3 | 5 | 6 | 3 | 15 |

| REF | | J | F | M | A | M | J | J | A | S | O | N | D | MAX |
|---|---|---|---|---|---|---|---|---|---|---|---|---|---|---|
| 137 | Gull, Mediterranean | — | 1 | — | — | — | — | — | — | 1 | 1 | — | — | 1 |
| 141 | Gull, Ring-billed | 1 | — | — | 1 | — | — | — | — | — | — | — | — | 1 |
| 139 | Gull, Sabine's | — | — | — | — | — | — | — | — | — | — | 1 | 1 | 1 |
| 80 | Gyrfalcon | — | — | — | — | — | — | — | — | — | — | — | 1 | 1 |
| | | | | | | | | | | | | | | |
| 71 | Harrier, Hen | 2 | 2 | — | — | 2 | — | — | — | 2 | 4 | 1 | 2 | 2 |
| 70 | Harrier, Marsh | — | — | — | 2 | 6 | 4 | — | — | — | — | — | — | 3 |
| 72 | Harrier, Montagu's | — | — | — | 1 | — | — | — | — | — | — | — | — | 1 |
| 277 | Hawfinch | — | — | — | — | — | — | — | — | — | — | — | — | — |
| 27 | Heron, Grey | 7 | 2 | 1 | 3 | 4 | 11 | 12 | 13 | 15 | 10 | 12 | 8 | 5 |
| 79 | Hobby | — | — | — | — | 1 | — | — | — | — | 2 | — | — | 1 |
| 181 | Hoopoe | — | — | — | — | 1 | — | — | — | — | — | — | — | 1 |
| | | | | | | | | | | | | | | |
| 257 | Jackdaw | 15 | 15 | 15 | 15 | 15 | 15 | 15 | 15 | 15 | 15 | 15 | 15 | 1000 |
| 253 | Jay | — | — | — | — | — | — | — | — | — | 1 | — | — | 1 |
| | | | | | | | | | | | | | | |
| 77 | Kestrel | 13 | 14 | 12 | 12 | 10 | 9 | 10 | 15 | 15 | 15 | 15 | 15 | 9 |
| 179 | Kingfisher | — | — | — | — | — | — | 1 | — | — | — | — | — | 1 |
| 69 | Kite, Red | — | — | — | — | — | — | — | — | — | — | — | — | 1 |
| 148 | Kittiwake | 12 | 10 | 11 | 13 | 14 | 13 | 11 | 14 | 14 | 13 | 13 | 10 | 300 |
| 104 | Knot | 15 | 15 | 15 | 15 | 14 | 3 | 6 | 14 | 14 | 15 | 15 | 15 | 20000 |
| | | | | | | | | | | | | | | |
| 103 | Lapwing | 15 | 15 | 15 | 15 | 15 | 15 | 15 | 15 | 15 | 15 | 15 | 15 | 490 |
| 186 | Lark, Shore | 2 | 1 | — | — | — | — | — | — | — | — | — | 1 | 3 |
| 272 | Linnet | 15 | 15 | 15 | 15 | 15 | 15 | 15 | 15 | 15 | 15 | 15 | 15 | 825 |
| | | | | | | | | | | | | | | |
| 254 | Magpie | 13 | 13 | 13 | 13 | 13 | 12 | 11 | 14 | 13 | 15 | 14 | 14 | 30 |
| 50 | Mallard | 15 | 15 | 15 | 15 | 15 | 15 | 15 | 15 | 15 | 15 | 15 | 15 | 600 |
| 189 | Martin, House | — | — | — | 4 | 13 | 5 | 3 | 7 | 11 | 7 | 1 | — | 65 |
| 187 | Martin, Sand | — | — | 4 | 14 | 11 | 5 | 8 | 13 | 12 | 4 | 1 | — | 65 |
| 65 | Merganser, R-b | 15 | 15 | 15 | 15 | 15 | 14 | 13 | 15 | 15 | 15 | 15 | 15 | 120 |
| 78 | Merlin | 11 | 14 | 12 | 10 | 2 | — | — | 10 | 15 | 15 | 15 | 15 | 3 |
| 91 | Moorhen | 15 | 15 | 15 | 15 | 15 | 15 | 15 | 15 | 15 | 15 | 15 | 15 | 33 |
| | | | | | | | | | | | | | | |
| 206 | Nightingale | — | — | — | — | — | 1 | — | — | — | — | — | — | 1 |

| REF | | J | F | M | A | M | J | J | A | S | O | N | D | MAX |
|---|---|---|---|---|---|---|---|---|---|---|---|---|---|---|
| 177 | Nightjar | — | — | — | — | — | — | — | — | — | — | — | — | ? |
| 255 | Nutcracker | — | — | — | — | — | — | — | — | — | — | — | 1 | 1 |
| | | | | | | | | | | | | | | |
| 249 | Oriole, Golden | — | — | — | — | — | — | — | — | — | — | — | — | 1 |
| 76 | Osprey | — | — | — | 2 | 2 | 1 | — | 1 | — | — | — | — | 1 |
| 214 | Ousel, Ring | — | 1 | 1 | 5 | — | — | — | — | 1 | 5 | 2 | — | 1 |
| 172 | Owl, Barn | — | 1 | 1 | 1 | — | 1 | 3 | 1 | 8 | 5 | 4 | 2 | 2 |
| 173 | Owl, Little | 7 | 7 | 5 | 7 | 4 | 6 | 8 | 5 | 12 | 15 | 15 | 9 | 3 |
| 175 | Owl, Long-eared | — | — | — | — | — | — | — | — | 1 | 3 | 2 | 1 | 2 |
| 176 | Owl, Short-eared | 3 | 2 | 2 | 3 | 1 | — | — | 8 | 13 | 13 | 12 | 4 | 11 |
| 174 | Owl, Tawny | — | — | — | — | — | — | — | — | — | — | — | — | 1 |
| 94 | Oystercatcher | 15 | 15 | 15 | 15 | 15 | 15 | 15 | 15 | 15 | 15 | 15 | 15 | 20000 |
| | | | | | | | | | | | | | | |
| 169 | Parakeet, Ring-necked | — | — | — | — | — | — | — | — | — | — | — | — | 2 |
| 83 | Partridge, Red-legged | — | — | — | — | — | — | — | — | — | — | — | — | — |
| 84 | Partridge, Grey | 7 | 7 | 8 | 7 | 6 | 5 | 6 | 5 | 7 | 8 | 9 | 6 | 12 |
| 81 | Peregrine | 13 | 11 | 8 | 6 | 5 | 1 | 3 | 8 | 12 | 15 | 12 | 14 | 3 |
| 20 | Petrel, Leach's | — | — | — | — | — | — | — | — | 5 | 5 | 1 | — | 16 |
| 21 | Petrel, sp. | — | — | — | — | — | — | — | — | 1 | — | — | — | 1 |
| 19 | Petrel, Storm | — | — | — | — | — | 1 | 1 | — | 1 | 1 | — | — | 3 |
| 18 | Petrel, White-faced | — | — | — | — | — | — | — | — | — | — | — | — | 1 |
| 17 | Petrel, Wilson's | — | — | — | — | — | — | — | — | — | — | — | — | 1 |
| 131 | Phalarope, Grey | — | — | — | — | — | — | — | — | 2 | 3 | — | — | 1 |
| 130 | Phalarope, Red-necked | — | — | — | — | — | — | — | — | 1 | 1 | — | — | 1 |
| 129 | Phalarope, Wilson's | — | — | — | — | — | — | — | — | — | 1 | — | — | 1 |
| 85 | Pheasant | — | — | — | 1 | — | — | — | — | — | — | — | — | 1 |
| 51 | Pintail | 10 | 8 | 5 | — | 1 | 1 | — | 3 | 7 | 9 | 9 | 8 | 19 |
| 193 | Pipit, Meadow | 15 | 15 | 15 | 15 | 15 | 15 | 15 | 15 | 15 | 15 | 15 | 15 | 5000 |
| 190 | Pipit, Richard's | 1 | 1 | — | — | — | — | — | — | 3 | — | 2 | 1 | 1 |
| 194 | Pipit, Rock | 10 | 3 | 6 | 5 | 1 | 1 | — | — | 9 | 13 | 8 | 5 | 6 |
| 191 | Pipit, Tawny | — | — | — | — | — | — | — | 1 | 1 | 1 | — | — | 1 |
| 192 | Pipit, Tree | — | — | — | 10 | 9 | 1 | — | 15 | 14 | 4 | — | — | 100 |
| 195 | Pipit, Water | 1 | — | — | — | — | — | — | — | — | — | — | 2 | 1 |
| 101 | Plover, Golden | 15 | 14 | 13 | 13 | 6 | — | 2 | 13 | 15 | 15 | 15 | 15 | 850 |
| 102 | Plover, Grey | 14 | 15 | 15 | 14 | 10 | 3 | 6 | 15 | 15 | 15 | 15 | 15 | 208 |

| REF | | J | F | M | A | M | J | J | A | S | O | N | D | MAX |
|---|---|---|---|---|---|---|---|---|---|---|---|---|---|---|
| 97 | Plover, Little Ringed | — | — | — | — | 1 | — | — | 1 | 2 | — | — | — | 1 |
| 98 | Plover, Ringed | 15 | 15 | 15 | 15 | 15 | 15 | 15 | 15 | 15 | 15 | 15 | 15 | 800 |
| 54 | Pochard | 6 | 8 | 5 | 1 | — | 2 | — | 3 | 7 | 12 | 8 | 11 | 22 |
| 160 | Puffin | 3 | 4 | 2 | 1 | 3 | 3 | — | — | 5 | 6 | 3 | 3 | 8 |
| 86 | Quail | — | — | — | — | — | — | — | — | — | — | — | — | — |
| 87 | Quail, Blue-breasted | — | — | — | — | — | 1 | — | — | — | — | — | — | 1 |
| 88 | Rail, Water | 3 | 2 | 2 | — | — | — | — | — | 1 | 4 | 6 | 2 | 2 |
| 261 | Raven | — | 1 | — | — | — | 1 | — | — | — | — | — | — | 2 |
| 157 | Razorbill | 9 | 12 | 11 | 10 | 10 | 9 | 6 | 4 | 10 | 14 | 12 | 11 | 420 |
| 274 | Redpoll | 1 | 2 | 2 | 3 | 11 | 3 | 1 | 1 | 7 | 12 | 6 | 5 | 200 |
| 123 | Redshank | 15 | 15 | 15 | 15 | 14 | 13 | 15 | 15 | 15 | 15 | 15 | 15 | 2000 |
| 122 | Redshank, Spotted | 1 | — | — | — | — | — | 2 | 11 | 12 | 7 | 2 | — | 9 |
| 209 | Redstart | — | — | — | 13 | 12 | 1 | 4 | 13 | 14 | 6 | — | — | 9 |
| 208 | Redstart, Black | 2 | 1 | 3 | 5 | 3 | 1 | 1 | 1 | 3 | 6 | 9 | 3 | 4 |
| 218 | Redwing | 12 | 12 | 14 | 8 | — | — | — | — | 4 | 15 | 15 | 14 | 5100 |
| 205 | Robin | 15 | 15 | 15 | 15 | 9 | 2 | 1 | 15 | 15 | 15 | 15 | 15 | 75 |
| 180 | Roller | — | — | — | — | — | — | — | — | — | — | — | — | 1 |
| 258 | Rook | 6 | 5 | 10 | 10 | 10 | 7 | 5 | 4 | 8 | 14 | 10 | 8 | 121 |
| 114 | Ruff | — | — | — | 2 | 4 | 1 | 5 | 14 | 13 | 4 | — | — | 8 |
| 105 | Sanderling | 15 | 15 | 15 | 15 | 15 | 12 | 13 | 15 | 15 | 15 | 15 | 15 | 3000 |
| 162 | Sandgrouse, Pallas's | — | — | — | — | — | — | — | — | — | — | — | — | 21 |
| 113 | Sandpiper, B.-breasted | — | — | — | — | — | — | — | — | — | 1 | — | — | 1 |
| 127 | Sandpiper, Common | — | — | — | 12 | 11 | 7 | 14 | 15 | 14 | 7 | — | — | 15 |
| 110 | Sandpiper, Curlew | — | — | — | — | — | — | 1 | 2 | 11 | 4 | 1 | — | 10 |
| 125 | Sandpiper, Green | — | — | 1 | 1 | 1 | — | 2 | 11 | 7 | — | — | — | 6 |
| 109 | Sandpiper, Pectoral | — | — | — | — | — | — | 1 | 1 | — | — | — | — | 1 |
| 111 | Sandpiper, Purple | 9 | 8 | 7 | 7 | 4 | — | — | — | 3 | 9 | 12 | 11 | 10 |
| 108 | Sandpiper, W.-rumped | — | — | — | — | — | — | — | — | — | 1 | — | — | 1 |
| 126 | Sandpiper, Wood | — | — | — | — | — | — | 2 | 7 | 5 | 2 | — | — | 11 |
| 99 | Sandplover, Greater | — | — | — | — | — | — | 1 | 1 | — | — | — | — | 1 |
| 57 | Scaup | 6 | 6 | 5 | 4 | 1 | 1 | 1 | 3 | 3 | 5 | 6 | 6 | 18 |
| 61 | Scoter, Common | 13 | 12 | 14 | 14 | 14 | 13 | 10 | 14 | 15 | 15 | 13 | 11 | 2000 |

| REF | | J | F | M | A | M | J | J | A | S | O | N | D | MAX |
|---|---|---|---|---|---|---|---|---|---|---|---|---|---|---|
| 62 | Scoter, Velvet | 5 | 6 | 5 | 6 | 4 | 3 | 2 | 3 | 3 | 6 | 9 | 3 | 10 |
| 24 | Shag | 5 | 2 | 3 | 3 | 2 | 3 | — | 4 | 5 | 9 | 5 | 8 | 6 |
| 16 | Shearwater, Balearic | — | — | 1 | — | — | — | — | 1 | 1 | — | — | — | 1 |
| 11 | Shearwater, Cory's | — | — | — | — | — | 2 | — | 2 | 3 | — | — | — | 5 |
| 13 | Shearwater, Cory's/Gt. | — | — | — | — | — | — | — | 4 | — | — | — | — | 2 |
| 12 | Shearwater, Great | — | — | — | — | — | — | — | — | 2 | 1 | — | — | 1 |
| 15 | Shearwater, Manx | — | — | 4 | 4 | 9 | 13 | 11 | 8 | 11 | 5 | 1 | — | 440 |
| 14 | Shearwater, Sooty | — | 1 | 1 | — | 1 | — | — | 2 | 4 | 1 | — | — | 6 |
| 46 | Shelduck | 15 | 15 | 15 | 15 | 15 | 15 | 13 | 11 | 11 | 15 | 15 | 15 | 548 |
| 45 | Shelduck, Australian | — | — | — | — | — | — | — | — | — | — | 1 | 1 | 1 |
| 44 | Shelduck, Cape | — | — | — | — | — | — | — | — | 1 | 1 | — | — | 2 |
| 53 | Shoveler | 7 | 8 | 8 | 9 | 10 | 7 | 4 | 12 | 11 | 10 | 10 | 6 | 12 |
| 251 | Shrike, Great Grey | — | — | — | — | — | — | — | — | — | 2 | 1 | — | 1 |
| 250 | Shrike, Red-backed | — | — | — | — | — | — | — | — | — | — | — | — | — |
| 252 | Shrike, Woodchat | — | — | — | — | 1 | — | — | — | — | — | — | — | 1 |
| 271 | Siskin | 1 | — | 1 | — | — | — | 1 | — | 5 | 12 | 9 | 3 | 30 |
| 133 | Skua, Arctic | 1 | — | — | — | 5 | 10 | 11 | 10 | 10 | 8 | 2 | 1 | 9 |
| 135 | Skua, Great | 1 | — | 1 | 4 | 4 | 6 | 6 | 7 | 9 | 8 | 3 | 1 | 10 |
| 134 | Skua, Long-tailed | — | — | — | — | 1 | 1 | — | — | 1 | 1 | — | — | 2 |
| 132 | Skua, Pomarine | 1 | — | — | — | 1 | 3 | 3 | 2 | 5 | 4 | 1 | 1 | 2 |
| 136 | Skua, sp. | 1 | 2 | — | 2 | 2 | 4 | 3 | 4 | 6 | 3 | 2 | — | 8 |
| 185 | Skylark | 15 | 15 | 15 | 15 | 15 | 15 | 15 | 15 | 15 | 15 | 15 | 15 | 3000 |
| 64 | Smew | 1 | — | — | — | — | — | — | — | — | — | 1 | — | 2 |
| 116 | Snipe | 15 | 15 | 15 | 15 | 9 | 3 | 8 | 15 | 15 | 15 | 15 | 15 | 130 |
| 115 | Snipe, Jack | 7 | 6 | 1 | 2 | — | — | 1 | 2 | 4 | 7 | 5 | 9 | 4 |
| 266 | Sparrow, Golden | — | — | — | — | — | — | — | — | — | — | — | — | 1 |
| 264 | Sparrow, House | 7 | 6 | 5 | 11 | 13 | 11 | 13 | 15 | 14 | 13 | 12 | 5 | 70 |
| 265 | Sparrow, Tree | — | — | — | 4 | 5 | 1 | 1 | 6 | 7 | 9 | 5 | 2 | 34 |
| 279 | Sparrow, W.-throated | — | — | — | — | — | — | — | — | — | — | — | — | 1 |
| 73 | Sparrowhawk | 8 | 9 | 11 | 9 | 4 | 1 | 5 | 12 | 11 | 15 | 11 | 13 | 3 |
| 29 | Spoonbill | — | — | — | — | — | 1 | — | — | — | — | — | — | 3 |
| 263 | Starling | 15 | 15 | 15 | 15 | 15 | 15 | 15 | 15 | 15 | 15 | 15 | 15 | 8000 |
| 262 | Starling, Purp. Glossy | — | — | — | 1 | — | — | — | — | — | — | — | — | 1 |
| 106 | Stint, Little | 1 | — | — | 2 | 1 | — | 1 | 5 | 9 | 4 | — | — | 5 |
| 107 | Stint, Temminck's | — | — | — | — | — | — | — | — | 1 | — | — | — | 1 |

| REF | | J | F | M | A | M | J | J | A | S | O | N | D | MAX |
|---|---|---|---|---|---|---|---|---|---|---|---|---|---|---|
| 211 | Stonechat | 6 | 8 | 14 | 7 | 8 | 4 | 6 | 6 | 14 | 14 | 7 | 7 | 10 |
| 96 | Stone-curlew | — | — | — | — | — | — | — | — | 1 | — | — | — | 1 |
| 28 | Stork, Black | — | — | — | — | — | — | — | — | — | 1 | 1 | — | 2 |
| 188 | Swallow | — | — | 2 | 15 | 15 | 15 | 15 | 15 | 15 | 15 | 6 | — | 500 |
| 33 | Swan, Bewick's | — | 1 | 2 | — | — | — | — | — | — | 2 | 5 | 2 | 26 |
| 32 | Swan, Black | — | — | — | — | — | — | — | — | — | — | — | — | 1 |
| 31 | Swan, Mute | 4 | 8 | 7 | 6 | 7 | 9 | — | 2 | 8 | 9 | 7 | 7 | 14 |
| 34 | Swan, Whooper | 4 | 2 | 3 | 2 | — | — | — | — | — | 8 | 10 | 4 | 43 |
| 178 | Swift | — | — | — | — | 15 | 11 | 12 | 15 | 5 | 2 | 1 | — | 210 |
| | | | | | | | | | | | | | | |
| 49 | Teal | 15 | 15 | 15 | 15 | 12 | 8 | 11 | 15 | 15 | 15 | 15 | 15 | 2500 |
| 152 | Tern, Arctic | — | — | — | 3 | 15 | 15 | 15 | 15 | 7 | 1 | — | — | 36 |
| 155 | Tern, Black | — | — | — | — | 5 | 3 | 1 | 6 | 5 | 2 | — | — | 4 |
| 153 | Tern, Commic | — | — | — | 10 | 15 | 15 | 15 | 15 | 13 | 2 | — | — | 1800 |
| 151 | Tern, Common | — | — | — | 7 | 15 | 15 | 15 | 15 | 8 | 1 | — | — | 400 |
| 154 | Tern, Little | — | — | — | 7 | 15 | 15 | 15 | 11 | 4 | 2 | — | — | 120 |
| 150 | Tern, Roseate | — | — | — | — | 1 | 2 | 2 | 2 | 2 | — | — | — | 2 |
| 149 | Tern, Sandwich | — | — | 9 | 15 | 15 | 15 | 15 | 15 | 15 | 10 | — | — | 400 |
| 219 | Thrush, Mistle | 7 | 7 | 2 | 5 | 1 | 1 | 1 | 2 | 4 | 12 | 7 | 4 | 10 |
| 217 | Thrush, Song | 15 | 15 | 15 | 10 | 6 | 6 | 7 | 10 | 13 | 15 | 15 | 15 | 110 |
| 246 | Tit, Blue | 10 | 11 | 8 | 3 | 1 | 1 | 8 | 9 | 12 | 15 | 11 | 10 | 150 |
| 245 | Tit, Coal | — | — | — | 1 | — | — | — | — | 2 | 6 | — | — | 6 |
| 247 | Tit, Great | — | — | 1 | 1 | — | — | 1 | — | 9 | 12 | 2 | — | 6 |
| 244 | Tit, Long-tailed | — | — | — | — | — | — | — | — | — | 1 | 1 | — | 13 |
| 248 | Treecreeper | — | — | — | — | — | — | 2 | 2 | 1 | 3 | — | — | 1 |
| 128 | Turnstone | 15 | 15 | 15 | 15 | 15 | 12 | 14 | 15 | 15 | 15 | 15 | 15 | 2000 |
| 273 | Twite | 8 | 7 | 3 | 5 | — | — | — | — | 2 | 8 | 11 | 10 | 55 |
| | | | | | | | | | | | | | | |
| 197 | Wagtail, Blue-headed | — | — | — | — | — | — | — | — | 1 | — | — | — | 2 |
| 198 | Wagtail, Grey | — | 2 | 7 | 5 | 2 | 3 | 9 | 13 | 15 | 15 | 6 | 3 | 78 |
| 199 | Wagtail, Pied | 15 | 15 | 15 | 15 | 15 | 15 | 15 | 15 | 15 | 15 | 15 | 15 | 300 |
| 200 | Wagtail, White | 1 | 2 | 5 | 11 | 8 | — | — | 3 | 5 | 3 | 2 | — | 20 |
| 196 | Wagtail, Yellow | — | — | — | 12 | 13 | 5 | 15 | 15 | 15 | 5 | 1 | 1 | 120 |
| 228 | Warbler, Barred | — | — | — | — | — | — | — | 2 | 6 | 1 | — | — | 1 |
| 235 | Warbler, Bonelli's | — | — | — | — | — | — | — | — | — | — | — | — | — |

| REF | | J | F | M | A | M | J | J | A | S | O | N | D | MAX |
|---|---|---|---|---|---|---|---|---|---|---|---|---|---|---|
| 231 | Warbler, Garden | — | — | 1 | — | 9 | 1 | 5 | 15 | 14 | 12 | 3 | — | 7 |
| 220 | Warbler, Grasshopper | — | — | — | 3 | 8 | — | 1 | 1 | 6 | — | — | — | 2 |
| 225 | Warbler, Icterine | — | — | — | — | — | — | — | 3 | — | — | — | — | 1 |
| 223 | Warbler, Marsh | — | — | — | — | — | — | — | — | 1 | — | — | — | 1 |
| 226 | Warbler, Melodious | — | — | — | — | — | 1 | — | 4 | 3 | — | — | — | 2 |
| 222 | Warbler, Paddyfield | — | — | — | — | — | — | — | — | 1 | — | — | — | 1 |
| 233 | Warbler, Pallas's | — | — | — | — | — | — | — | — | — | 1 | — | — | 2 |
| 278 | Warbler, Palm | — | — | — | — | 1 | — | — | — | — | — | — | — | 1 |
| 224 | Warbler, Reed | — | — | — | — | 1 | — | — | 2 | — | — | — | — | 1 |
| 221 | Warbler, Sedge | — | — | — | 8 | 15 | 4 | 9 | 14 | 11 | — | — | — | 12 |
| 227 | Warbler, Subalpine | — | — | — | — | — | 1 | — | — | — | — | — | — | 1 |
| 238 | Warbler, Willow | — | — | 3 | 15 | 15 | 7 | 14 | 15 | 15 | 5 | 1 | — | 200 |
| 236 | Warbler, Wood | — | — | — | 1 | 2 | — | 1 | 1 | 1 | — | — | — | 1 |
| 234 | Warbler, Yl.-browed | — | — | — | — | — | — | — | — | 1 | 2 | 1 | — | 2 |
| 201 | Waxwing | — | — | — | — | — | — | — | — | — | — | 1 | — | 1 |
| 212 | Wheatear | — | 1 | 14 | 15 | 15 | 9 | 12 | 15 | 15 | 15 | 2 | — | 60 |
| 213 | Wheatear, Desert | — | — | — | — | — | — | — | — | — | — | 1 | — | 1 |
| 120 | Whimbrel | 1 | 1 | — | 11 | 12 | 7 | 14 | 15 | 15 | 9 | 2 | 1 | 64 |
| 210 | Whinchat | — | — | — | 8 | 15 | 3 | 11 | 15 | 15 | 9 | 1 | — | 14 |
| 230 | Whitethroat | — | — | — | 5 | 15 | 12 | 11 | 15 | 15 | 6 | — | — | 16 |
| 229 | Whitethroat, Lesser | — | — | — | — | 3 | 1 | 1 | 2 | 3 | 1 | — | — | 1 |
| 47 | Wigeon | 15 | 15 | 15 | 15 | 7 | 2 | 4 | 15 | 15 | 15 | 15 | 15 | 1000 |
| 117 | Woodcock | 4 | 3 | 2 | — | — | — | — | — | 1 | 1 | 7 | 3 | 14 |
| 184 | Woodpecker, Gt. Sptd. | — | — | — | — | — | — | — | — | — | — | — | — | 1 |
| 183 | Woodpecker, Green | — | — | — | 1 | — | — | — | 2 | — | — | — | — | 1 |
| 165 | Woodpigeon | 5 | 2 | 5 | 7 | 7 | 9 | 7 | 3 | 3 | 3 | 3 | 4 | 24 |
| 203 | Wren | 15 | 15 | 15 | 15 | 5 | — | 1 | 5 | 15 | 15 | 15 | 15 | 50 |
| 182 | Wryneck | — | — | — | — | 1 | — | — | — | 1 | 1 | — | — | 1 |
| 282 | Yellowhammer | 2 | 1 | 1 | 3 | — | 2 | — | 3 | 4 | 4 | 2 | — | 6 |

# Systematic List of Birds

## 1 RED-THROATED DIVER *Gavia stellata*

*Fairly common*

Durnford (1883), MacPherson (1892), and Oakes(1953) regard the species as a regular winter visitor and spring passage bird. Oakes suggests a northward movement during February and March, indicated by increased sightings in offshore waters along the Lancashire coast.

South Walney figures confirm this and include peaks of 30 on 28th March 1987 and 4th April 1981 and 50 on 14th March 1982. The regular October visits only involve small groups, the exception being 16 on 17th October 1976. Winter arrivals form loose flocks in the Piel Bar area, while passage is noted at Hilpsford Point and Biggar Bank.

Average maxima 1975-1989

| J | F | M | A | M | J | J | A | S | O | N | D |
|---|---|---|---|---|---|---|---|---|---|---|---|
| 5 | 7 | 10 | 12 | 3 | — | — | 1 | 3 | 3 | 2 | 4 |

Records from North Walney and Biggar Bank are sparse, but occurrence is probably as constant as at the south end. The maximum counts are 12 on 21st October 1985, and 25 on 15th February 1987.

## 2 BLACK-THROATED DIVER *Gavia arctica*

*Scarce*

The first sightings at South Walney relate to three birds on 2nd May 1972. Much of the increase since then is, doubtless, due to the provision of hides in the early 1980s and the species is, unquestionably, a regular visitor, especially in January and March with peaks of five on 21st February and 22nd April 1989. Birds are usually seen in the vicinity of Piel Bar or Hilpsford Point, although a heavily-oiled bird sought shelter in Haws Bed in October 1980.

Days recorded 1975-1989

| J | F | M | A | M | J | J | A | S | O | N | D | T |
|---|---|---|---|---|---|---|---|---|---|---|---|---|
| 9 | 14 | 15 | 8 | 5 | 1 | — | — | 9 | 4 | 1 | 6 | 72 |

At North Walney, a corpse was located on 31st December 1981.

## 3 GREAT NORTHERN DIVER *Gavia immer*

*Uncommon*

Durnford (1883) and MacPherson (1892) note its occurrence in Walney Channel almost every winter, and Durnford stated it became "at once the object of pursuit by all the gunners in the neighbourhood".

At South Walney it is a regular winter visitor and it passes in small numbers in spring and autumn. Wintering birds frequent the Piel Bar area, while on-flight sightings are at Hilpsford Point and Biggar Bank. The effect of hide building in the early 1980s is, once again, reflected in the figures: present on 16 days in the period 1975-1979 and on 83 days in the following five years. The maximum count is four on 8th February 1981, 11th January 1982 and 19th April 1984.

Days recorded 1975-1989

| J | F | M | A | M | J | J | A | S | O | N | D | T |
|---|---|---|---|---|---|---|---|---|---|---|---|---|
| 22 | 21 | 23 | 24 | 7 | — | 1 | — | 12 | 21 | 15 | 19 | 165 |

**4 DIVER SPECIES** *Gavia sp.*

*Fairly common*

The occurrence of unidentifiable divers has the same pattern as that of Red-throated Diver, with the majority appearing in late winter and early spring. South Walney peaks are 52 on 8th April 1966 and 30 on 13th March 1982. Small groups appear regularly in autumn and early winter.

**5 LITTLE GREBE** ***Tachybaptus ruficollis***

*Fairly common*

A pair bred, in 1983 and 1984, in man-made habitat at South Walney. Other records indicate possible nesting in 1968 and 1969, 1976 and 1978 and 1981-3. Wintering birds show an increase in the period 1975-1987, with a peak of eight on 23rd December 1986 and 13th December 1987.

Up to four pairs per annum have made use, since the mid-1950s, of excavated ponds at North Walney; but there is no evidence of over-wintering, the more open waters of Cavendish Dock (in Barrow) or South Walney, apparently, being required.

**6 GREAT CRESTED GREBE** ***Podiceps cristatus***

*Common*

Recorded at South Walney in all months, with peaks between July and November in the Haws Bed, Piel Island and Lighthouse Bay areas. The maximum count is 25 on 18th August 1989.

Average maxima 1975-1989

| J | F | M | A | M | J | J | A | S | O | N | D |
|---|---|---|---|---|---|---|---|---|---|---|---|
| 6 | 4 | 5 | 3 | 2 | 2 | 5 | 6 | 9 | 11 | 8 | 7 |

Small numbers are occasionally seen at North Walney from October to March including a maximum of five on 12th November 1985.

**7 RED-NECKED GREBE** ***Podiceps grisegena***

*Rare*

At South Walney an irregular visitor between September and March, most birds being seen in the Haws Bed and Piel Channel areas. Two birds have been recorded on five dates and one individual was seen on eleven days between 4th September and 16th October 1983. There is undoubtedly some duplication in the following statistics:

Days recorded 1975-1989

| J | F | M | A | M | J | J | A | S | O | N | D | T |
|---|---|---|---|---|---|---|---|---|---|---|---|---|
| 9 | 2 | 1 | — | — | — | — | — | 8 | 12 | 4 | 2 | 38 |

Two corpses were found on the tideline at North Walney in the winter of 1982, and one in April 1986.

### 8 SLAVONIAN GREBE — *Podiceps auritus*

*Rare*

There are six South Walney records from 1966-1974 and eight from 1975-1989. Except for birds seen on 8th May 1966 and 9th September 1984, all were recorded from October to February.

Individuals were seen off the north end on 22nd November 1964, and 22nd December 1968. An oiled summer plumaged bird was found on the shore near the Coastguard Station on 9th April 1988 and died the following day.

### 9 BLACK-NECKED GREBE — *Podiceps nigricollis*

*Vagrant*

There have been five birds off the southwest shore at South Walney, two on 22nd October 1981 and the others on 30th December 1983, 13th August 1985 and 20th August 1985.

### 10 FULMAR — *Fulmarus glacialis*

*Abundant*

Oakes (1953) describes the species as a rare vagrant to Lancashire and mentions a Walney-caught bird of 1929. Hilbre Island, after a single instance in 1957, records a gradual increase, and there have been annual examples, often tideline corpses, during the same period at Walney. The phenomenal upsurge in numbers and wider distribution of the species is illustrated by South Walney figures, but the extra coverage, in recent years, must be recognised. It appears regularly from April to late September, usually during or immediately after strong westerly winds, and large numbers can sometimes be seen off Hilpsford Point. Peak counts include 300 on 3rd May 1982 and 400 on 2nd September 1988. There are no records for November, but individuals have turned up, occasionally, in October, December, January and February.

Average maxima·1975-1989

| J | F | M | A | M | J | J | A | S | O | N | D |
|---|---|---|---|---|---|---|---|---|---|---|---|
| — | — | 3 | 6 | 26 | 18 | 9 | 47 | 57 | 2 | — | — |

Five-yearly totals of monthly maxima

| | | | |
|---|---|---|---|
| 1965—1969 | 102 | 1980—1984 | 701 |
| 1970—1974 | 34 | 1985—1989 | 1778 |
| 1975—1979 | 41 | | |

### 11 CORY'S SHEARWATER — *Calonectris diomedea*

*Rare*

Recorded on ten days at South Walney, all except one, after periods of southwest winds, in June to September from 1980 to 1985. Five birds were seen on 8th

August 1982 off Hilpsford Point and the same venue provided two on 15th and 16th June 1981, during a large movement of Manx Shearwaters, and two on 6th September 1983. None of these, nor other September sightings, have been submitted to the B.B.R.C., but one on 6th August 1972 has been accepted. North Walney has yielded individuals on 12th and 25th June 1985 and on 27th July 1986.

### 12 GREAT SHEARWATER *Puffinus gravis*

*Vagrant*

A bird which plunge-dived on three occasions into Morecambe Bay was seen on 20th September 1982 and one battled north off Hilpsford Point on 19th September 1983. A third individual appeared at North Walney on 2nd August 1985. All sightings followed strong westerly winds. The fourth record for the island occurred on 8th October 1988 when a specimen was seen flying out of Morecambe Bay.

### 13 CORY'S/GREAT SHEARWATER

*Rare*

Unidentified large Shearwaters have occurred as follows:

1 — 29th August 1965
1 — 5th September 1970
2 — 8th August 1973
2 — 10th September 1977
2 — 17th May 1980
2 — 8th August 1982
1 — 5th August 1985
1 — 20th August 1985
1 — 24th August 1985

### 14 SOOTY SHEARWATER *Puffinus griseus*

*Rare*

As with other Shearwaters, usually seen, from August to October following strong westerlies. Off Hilpsford Point four were seen on 4th September 1967, six on 18th September 1983 and five on 24th October 1984. Biggar Bank has provided three late-summer sightings between 1973 and 1979 while, uncharacteristically, South Walney has recorded birds on 26th February 1982 and 4th March 1983.

Average maxima 1975-1989

| J | F | M | A | M | J | J | A | S | O | N | D | T |
|---|---|---|---|---|---|---|---|---|---|---|---|---|
| — | 1 | 1 | — | 1 | — | — | 2 | 4 | 1 | — | — | 10 |

**15 MANX SHEARWATER** ***Puffinus puffinus***

*Fairly common*

Although suitable burrows are plentiful, Walney's proximity to mainland predators has probably prevented the species from nesting. Durnford (1883) describes the bird as being occasionally seen off the coast, but South Walney records show that it is regular, especially between April and September during and after westerly winds. Peak counts off Hilpsford Point include 48 on 30th April 1967, 204 on 2nd September 1970, 86 on 16th May 1976, 358 on 12th June 1984, 180 on 24th July 1988 and 400 on 12th August 1989. There have been four sightings in March and one in November.

Average maxima 1975-1989

| J | F | M | A | M | J | J | A | S | O | N | D |
|---|---|---|---|---|---|---|---|---|---|---|---|
| — | — | — | 1 | 11 | 53 | 31 | 58 | 6 | 2 | — | — |

**Ringing and recoveries**

The only indication of the origin of the species at South Walney relates to an individual ringed on Skokolm, Pembrokeshire (300 km south-southwest) in September 1953, and found dead on Walney in July 1956.

**16 (BALEARIC SHEARWATER)** ***Puffinus puffinus mauretanicus***

There have been three sightings all at South Walney of individuals on 11th March 1982, 2nd September 1988 and 30th August 1989.

**17 WILSON'S PETREL** ***Oceanites oceanicus***

*Vagrant*

A corpse of this pelagic species was reputedly found on the northwest shore of the island in November 1890. MacPherson obtained the skin from a Barrow blacksmith and sent it to O. Salvin at the British Museum. It was found to be "unaccountably small", but despite MacPherson's doubts, Oakes (1953) accepts the record and asserts that identification was confirmed. Spencer (1973) maintains that the record should be deleted and refers to Bourne (Ibis 109-1967) who, however, scarcely refers to its validity.

**18 WHITE-FACED PETREL** ***Pelagodroma marina***

*Vagrant*

The storm of November 1890 produced another petrel, the skin of which was also submitted to the British Museum. O. Salvin identified it as a "typical example of Pelagodroma marina" which "agreed closely with examples from the South Seas and Canary Islands now in the British Museum". There is none of the uncertainty so obvious in the Wilson's Petrel record. Nevertheless, Spencer (1973) dismisses the bird and again refers to Bourne (Ibis 109-1967), who, despite citing late in the year petrels, regards the Walney bird as "totally unacceptable", because "it is compromised by the company of a Wilson's Petrel at a time when nobody else noticed a wreck".

**19 STORM PETREL** ***Hydrobates pelagicus***

*Vagrant*

As with Manx Shearwater, nesting may have occurred on the island in the past, even if predation from the mainland is not difficult. MacPherson (1892), though not naming Walney, had seen specimens all around the Lake District coast, and Durnford (1883) describes the species as rare. At South Walney, there have only been ten records, eight of them since 1980. Two birds flew north off Hilpsford

Point on 13th September 1980, two were seen, untypically, in calm weather on 14th June 1983, while 1988 produced an individual on 26th July and three birds on 8th October. Another June bird was seen in 1960 and a lighthouse casualty was found dead on 4th October 1970. North Walney's only record is a tideline corpse of 23rd November 1981.

### 20 LEACH'S PETREL *Oceanodrama leucorhoa*

*Scarce*

MacPherson (1982) had experience of many "fresh" specimens from Morecambe Bay, but there are only 22 records at South Walney, all between 1979 and 1989. Single birds were seen on 20th September and 27th September 1979, seeking shelter in Haws Bed during severe westerly gales; 24 individuals were recorded off Hilpsford Point in similar conditions in September and October 1983. In 1986, an individual was caught and eaten by a Merlin on 21st October and a very late specimen was harried by gulls on 16th November. The island's largest ever count involved 16 birds moving out of Morecambe Bay on 8th October 1988. Biggar Bank yielded two flying north on 13th September 1980 and a corpse on 14th November 1977.

### 21 PETREL SPECIES

*Vagrant*

Two unidentifiable birds were off Hilpsford Point on 2nd September 1970 and a single on 14th September 1985.

### 22 GANNET *Sula bassana*

*Abundant*

Durnford (1883) notes that the species occurred at sea (the Irish) in considerable numbers. At South Walney large numbers are seen between April and October, often off Hilpsford Point or having been driven in by storms. Peak counts include:

| | | | |
|---|---|---|---|
| 120 | 1st April 1987 | 200 | 2nd July 1983 |
| 300 | 9th May 1983 | 700 | 12th August 1988 |
| 300 | 14th June 1983 | 260 | 21st September 1984 |

Adult birds predominate in June and July, mostly perhaps, from Scar Rocks in southwest Scotland; but given their vast ability to travel, birds from Grassholm or Ailsa Craig could be involved.

There is a single sighting for December, three for January, seven for February and 11 in November.

Average maxima 1975-1989

| J | F | M | A | M | J | J | A | S | O | N | D |
|---|---|---|---|---|---|---|---|---|---|---|---|
| — | — | 8 | 25 | 43 | 59 | 70 | 153 | 81 | 20 | — | — |

Fishing parties of more than 200 birds have been seen off North Walney in mid-summer.

**Ringing and recoveries**

Three birds, all ringed as nestlings, have been found on the island; two of them originating form Ailsa Craig in the Firth of Clyde, (180 km northwest), and the third from Great Saltee Island, Wexford, Eire (317 km southwest).

## 23 CORMORANT *Phalacrocorax carbo*

*Abundant*

MacPherson (1892) and Oakes (1953) describe the species as plentiful in spring and autumn. Lowest numbers at South Walney are in spring, when the spit is populated by non-breeding birds. An increase commences in July, with the arrival of failed breeders, and continues with an influx in early autumn. A drop is evident in winter when, probably, many seek the comparative shelter of Barrow's Cavendish Dock. The maximum count is 160 on 5th October 1987.

Average maxima 1975-1989

| | J | F | M | A | M | J | J | A | S | O | N | D |
|---|---|---|---|---|---|---|---|---|---|---|---|---|
| SW | 22 | 28 | 30 | 22 | 20 | 27 | 40 | 39 | 69 | 61 | 32 | 20 |
| NW | 6 | 11 | 9 | 7 | 5 | 6 | 9 | 13 | 10 | 10 | 9 | 6 |

**Ringing and recoveries**

A ten year old bird, ringed as a nestling at Mochrum, Wigtown (115 km northwest) was found dead on the tideline, and a twenty year old, again ringed as a nestling at Mochrum, was moribund at Cavendish Dock, Barrow-in-Furness.

**24 SHAG** ***Phalacrocorax aristotelis***

*Scarce*

Coastal dispersal produces autumn sightings of flying birds; records at South Walney, for the rest of the year, depend on usually solitary storm-driven birds, sheltering in the Piel Bar area. The maximum count is six on 5th September 1981.

Days recorded 1975-1989

| J | F | M | A | M | J | J | A | S | O | N | D | T |
|---|---|---|---|---|---|---|---|---|---|---|---|---|
| 7 | 4 | 6 | 7 | 2 | 3 | — | 8 | 22 | 21 | 22 | 14 | 116 |

North Walney produced individuals on 14th October 1979, and 7th October 1989, and a corpse in February 1984; while a specimen was at Jubilee Bridge on 1st September 1988.

**25 BITTERN** ***Botaurus stellaris***

*Vagrant*

Part of a huge hard weather movement on 24th January 1984, one flew south from South Walney, mobbed by gulls. Benson (pers. comm.) records a winter bird, c. 1936, at an ice-filled hollow near Willow Woods.

**26 CATTLE EGRET** ***Bubulcus ibis***

*Vagrant*

A single bird, accepted by the B.B.R.C., was with grazing cattle at South Walney on 26th July 1964; in the same period, a specimen was reported from Dumfries and Westmorland. Sharrock (1976) suggests that, although autumn records probably relate to escapes from captivity, early autumn vagrancy must also be considered.

**27 GREY HERON** ***Ardea cinerea***

*Fairly common*

For many years, occurrences were deemed appropriate to the rarities log; but in the period 1975-1984, the species was present on 232 days, compared with 81 days in the period 1965-1974. Most birds appear in the post-breeding months, autumn and early winter, with a maximum of four on 7th September 1975.

Days recorded 1975-1989

| J | F | M | A | M | J | J | A | S | O | N | D | T |
|---|---|---|---|---|---|---|---|---|---|---|---|---|
| 17 | 6 | 1 | 3 | 4 | 26 | 40 | 40 | 59 | 59 | 35 | 17 | 307 |

Tummer Hill Marsh is a regular haunt in late summer and autumn, with a siege of 11 on 21st October 1985 and ten on 31st August 1980.

At North Walney, the species is frequently seen, with a pattern similar to that of the south end.

**28 BLACK STORK** ***Ciconia nigra***

*Vagrant*

An adult and a juvenile flew off Wylock Marsh on 25th October 1985. Later that day, the adult was seen to fly east over Haws Bed while the juvenile remained in the area of the refuse tip and South End caravan site until 1st November.

It was later discovered that the ring-bearing juvenile was released from Hallbankgate near Carlisle on 24th October, after being in care since September. Despite this almost unbelievable sequence of events, both records have been accepted by B.B.R.C.

### 29 SPOONBILL *Platalea leucorodia*

*Vagrant*

At South Walney, there are three records, involving five birds. Single birds appeared on 29th October 1966 and 21st July 1970; but in 1982 three birds remained, contentedly, among the gulls in the central marsh from 8th June until they flew north on the evening of 11th June. Twenty-three days earlier, three adults put in a brief appearance at Railway Flash, Sandbach, Cheshire and, in the ensuing period, adults were present at Belvide and Blithfield reservoirs in Staffordshire.

### 30 GREATER FLAMINGO *Phoenicopterus ruber*

*Vagrant — probable escape*

One flew over South Walney towards Blackpool on 21st July 1973 and a corpse was found, on 13th January 1974, on the west shore at South Walney — possibly the same bird.

### 31 MUTE SWAN *Cygnus olor*

*Fairly common*

At South Walney, between 1962 and 1973, a pair bred with intermittent success, rearing 35 young. Since their departure, there has been a drastic decrease in records, with, for example, only two sightings in 1982. In the period 1975-1989, most birds have occurred between September and December, with peaks of seven on 27th December 1981 and 28th to 30th May 1985 and 14 on 16th November 1988.

A pair has nested, annually, since the mid-1950s in the excavated gravel pools on North Walney and in 1986 reared eleven cygnets.

**Ringing and recoveries**

Young birds and adults have been caught irregularly at South Walney, although some constant effort was directed towards nestlings during the late 1960s. Two individuals have been recovered or controlled at Cavendish Dock and a nestling of 1968 was at St. Helens, Lancashire (85 km south-southeast) in the winter of 1972. An individual, ringed as a cygnet at Marton Mere, Blackpool (30 km south-southeast) in August 1974, was at South Walney in October 1976.

### 32 BLACK SWAN *Cygnus atratus*

*Exotica*

South Walney's large gravel pool held a specimen on 28th April 1969.

### 33 BEWICK'S SWAN *Cygnus columbianus*

*Rare*

South Walney has 15 records in the period 1975-1989 and the only previous sighting was a single bird in mid-January 1969. A northward bound bird was seen on 18th February 1987, while March provided individuals on two dates in 1975 and a flock of 26, flying south, on the 13th in 1978; sixteen were off the west shore on 28th October 1978 and five flew over Coastguard Cottages on 28th October 1989; November occurrences consist of 19 birds on the 3rd off Sheep Island in 1976, two fleeting visitors in Wylock Marsh on the 5th in 1983, three using the gravel pools on the 4th in 1986 followed in 1988 by three on the 3rd and nine on the 4th and in 1989 by three on the 5th. Three individuals were present on 26th December 1975, two on 16th December 1986 at Snab Pools, while elsewhere, two were off Biggar Bank on 14th April 1978.

**34 WHOOPER SWAN** ***Cygnus cygnus***

*Uncommon*

In the period 1975-1989, birds have appeared annually at South Walney between October and April. Most sightings are of flying groups in November, many being family parties. Larger numbers have occurred in spring, including a herd of 43 off Sheep Island on 18th March 1976. Other sizeable flocks include 19 on 28th February 1984, 25 on 4th March 1984, and 24 on 4th April 1987.

Days recorded 1975-1989

| J | F | M | A | M | J | J | A | S | O | N | D | T |
|---|---|---|---|---|---|---|---|---|---|---|---|---|
| 5 | 3 | 3 | 2 | — | — | — | — | — | 21 | 19 | 4 | 57 |

There are only eight records pre-1975, but they include two early April instances.

North Walney sightings have been infrequent, the highest number being 17 which roosted on the salt marsh on 1st December 1983.

**35 BEAN GOOSE** ***Anser fabalis***

*Vagrant*

Coombes (in Oakes 1953) regards the bird as rare in Morecambe Bay and this is borne out by South Walney records. One was present on 25th October 1968, and a well-watched individual of the *fabalis* race landed among Shelduck in Haws Bed on the afternoon of 18th November 1983 and remained until after dusk. A solitary low-flying bird headed south on 14th January 1987 and in 1988 a bird of the *rossicus* race was with nine Pink-footed Geese on 9th December. A tideline corpse was found at the south end on 5th March 1970. North Walney held a single on 5th April 1985.

**36 PINK-FOOTED GOOSE** ***Anser brachyrhynchus***

*Abundant*

Skeins, occasionally exceeding 300 birds, are regular between late September and March, but with the majority of sightings in the October to February period. Most are moving purposefully, to or from their wintering grounds on the Fylde and only in foggy or icy weather do they settle on the island.

Average maxima 1975-1989

| J | F | M | A | M | J | J | A | S | O | N | D |
|---|---|---|---|---|---|---|---|---|---|---|---|
| 333 | 121 | 32 | 6 | — | — | — | — | 73 | 125 | 149 | 159 |

Hard-weather movements, usually associated with detrimental conditions to the north, force Scottish birds to supplement the Fylde population.

Examples of southerly movement during hard weather:

December 1981 — 2400 between 15th and 25th
January 1982 — 1314 between 6th and 10th
January 1984 — 1572 between 24th and 28th

Sightings of Pink-footed Goose and Grey Goose (q.v.) in the Friday to Monday period have occurred on 87 of the 126 days recorded during 1980-1984; this probably reflects disturbance due to wildfowling activities over weekend periods.

**37 WHITE-FRONTED GOOSE** ***Anser albifrons***

*Rare*

Oakes (1953) regards the species as a regular winter visitor, in small numbers, to Morecambe Bay while Wilson (1976) estimates a peak of 30 in February, usually of the Russian race.

At South Walney there are only five records, two of them involving long staying family groups of the *flavirostris* race. In 1970, two adults and three juveniles remained from 27th October until 20th November during which period one of the young birds died after losing a wing to the overhead power cables. An exceptionally mobile group of two adults and five juveniles was seen, between Biggar and Foulney Island, in the period 20th November 1984 to 9th January 1985. By contrast, 14 birds of the Russian race rested, north of Pho Hill, for less than half a day on 4th December 1982 and two birds of the Greenland race were in the same area from 31st October until 2nd November 1986, while in 1989 a further two winged south on 29th October.

### 38 GREYLAG GOOSE *Anser anser*

*Uncommon*

Has appeared at South Walney, since 1964, in every month except July, but mid-year sightings are probably feral birds, flocks of which have been introduced into the Lake District. Most occurrences are in the period September to January, with early autumn skeins probably representing true movement. Peak counts include 80 on 17th September 1982 and 210 on 1st October 1965. The paucity of February and March records suggests that northward movement by-passes Walney.

A pair nested unsuccessfully on North Walney in 1973, as did a pair at South Walney.

Walney Island Wildfowlers Association introduced four birds at the north end in 1982.

### 39 GREY GOOSE *Anser sp.*

*Common*

Silent skeins passing at great distances are a frequent feature of anticyclonic days from September to February. At South Walney, peak counts include 1840 on 24th January 1984 and 450 on 3rd and 4th October 1972. Other movements in company with Pink-footed Geese (q.v.), usually hard-weather induced, include:

December 1981 — 364 between 15th and 25th
January 1982 — 126 between 6th and 10th

Most are probably Pink-footed or Greylag, but there are other possibilities.

### 40 SNOW GOOSE *Anser caerulescens*

*Vagrant — probably feral*

White birds were recorded at South Walney on 31st May 1979 and 7th June 1979 and one was seen flying south over Walney Channel on 4th May 1984. Additionally an adult on 15th April 1988 was followed in May by two adults on 9th and 10th.

### 41 CANADA GOOSE *Branta canadensis*

*Uncommon*

Prior to 1980, South Walney had only five records, one of them a 1970 long-staying individual. In the eighties, appearances have been annual between April and October, usually of small flocks of up to ten birds; although 27 grazed near gate pool on 15th June 1982. Of 13 records since 1964, five have been in June.

During 1988 and 1989 the species became decidedly less scarce with sightings on 41 days including a flock of between 28 and 30 birds frequenting South Walney from late August until the end of September in the former year. Additionally a pair bred near Biggar village in 1989.

North Walney's records consist of two birds on 5th May 1985, three on 11th June 1986 and two on 1st April 1989.

## 42 BARNACLE GOOSE *Branta leucopsis*

*Scarce*

Mitchell (1892) declares that the species occurred in considerable numbers in Morecambe Bay and refers to Gerarde's "The Herball or General Historie of Plants" (1633), in which credence is given to the mythic emergence of Barnacle Geese from shells on Piel Island. Constancy and abundance are not evident at South Walney, with only 37 days of sightings since 1975, 15 of them in October. The maximum count is 105 which flew east over Morecambe Bay on 6th December 1983.

Days recorded 1975-1989

| J | F | M | A | M | J | J | A | S | O | N | D | T |
|---|---|---|---|---|---|---|---|---|---|---|---|---|
| 3 | 1 | 1 | 1 | 2 | 1 | — | — | 2 | 15 | 10 | 1 | 37 |

Biggar Bank witnessed 21 birds on 30th September 1978 and North Walney a solitary on 5th May 1985.

## 43 BRENT GOOSE *Branta bernicla*

*Uncommon*

MacPherson (1892) and Oakes (1953) cite Durnford (1883), who regarded the species as a regular winter visitor to Walney, although Oakes indicated increased scarcity. At South Walney there are records for all months except August, with most in the February to May period. A small flock frequents the Rampside and Foulney areas each winter and its excursions to South Walney can, normally, be related to disturbances (e.g. wind-surfing) across the channel. For the period between 1966 and 1982, the flock consisted of no more than five, but early December of the latter year saw the arrival of two adults and seven immatures; and by mid-April there were 11 more. Virtually all sightings are of dark-bellied birds, although 16 of the *hrota* race were in Haws Bed on 16th and 17th April 1965.

Days recorded 1975-1989

| J | F | M | A | M | J | J | A | S | O | N | D | T |
|---|---|---|---|---|---|---|---|---|---|---|---|---|
| 4 | 23 | 10 | 61 | 37 | 3 | 22 | — | 2 | 12 | 3 | 5 | 182 |

Seven birds were seen at North Walney on 15th January 1986.

**44 CAPE SHELDUCK** *Tadorna cana*

*Exotica*

South Walney was host to two drakes, which frequented Lighthouse Bay and the central marsh from 15th September to 3rd October 1984.

**45 AUSTRALIAN SHELDUCK** *Tadorna tadornoides*

*Exotica*

An immature female was with Shelduck in Haws Bed from 9th November 1989 until the end of the year.

**46 SHELDUCK** *Tadorna tadorna*

*Abundant*

All previous authors noted its abundance on Walney Island and Durnford (1883) describes a winter flock of 100 birds as, "only a small remnant of the thousands which, within the memory of man, used to frequent the warrens in this locality." There has, undoubtedly, been some decrease, especially within the last 100 years, but, even allowing for this and the fact that an average of 50 pairs per 10 km square has been recorded in North Kent (Sharrock 1976), Durnford's statement seems excessive. The Walney population makes extensive use of rabbit burrows, with approximately 25 pairs at North Walney Nature Reserve and 20 pairs at South Walney. At the north end, where the survival rate is far better than at the gull-dominated south end, there were in June 1968, 115 chicks. At South Walney, the species has been recorded in all months, but, between the end of June and late September, the sightings are usually of a few maturing young, left to fend for themselves when the adults depart to moult. By early October, returning birds set up feeding territories in all the Channel-side salt marshes; by mid-winter the Walney population reaches c.900, with a maximum of 600 at Tummer Hill Marsh in December 1977.

The peak count at South Walney is 548 in February 1989.

Average maxima 1975-1989

| | J | F | M | A | M | J | J | A | S | O | N | D |
|---|---|---|---|---|---|---|---|---|---|---|---|---|
| SW | 169 | 164 | 127 | 97 | 86 | 65 | 20 | 7 | 7 | 48 | 147 | 170 |
| NW | 238 | 249 | 224 | 230 | 215 | 143 | 48 | 16 | 5 | 59 | 220 | 224 |

**Ringing and recoveries**

The only Shelduck ringed by the observatory was found six months later in September 1978, freshly dead at Grusser Knechtsand, Stade, West Germany (800 km east). The only other recovery is of a bird ringed at Ainsdale, Formby, Lancashire (50 km south) in June 1920 and located at South Walney in January 1930.

**47 WIGEON** *Anas penelope*

*Abundant*

At South Walney the species has appeared in all months and is, invariably, present from August to April. Scarce in mid-summer, there is a build-up towards the end of August, when birds frequent the central marsh, Lighthouse Bay and Walney Channel. By November the total Walney population can exceed 1,500, with maxima of 2,010 at North Walney in November 1982, 1,000 at South Walney in January 1980 and 1981, and 965 at Tummer Hill Marsh in January 1970. During February and March the exodus becomes evident and by mid-April only a few stragglers remain.

Average maxima 1975-1989

| | J | F | M | A | M | J | J | A | S | O | N | D |
|---|---|---|---|---|---|---|---|---|---|---|---|---|
| SW | 534 | 447 | 184 | 21 | 1 | — | — | 12 | 160 | 389 | 456 | 479 |
| NW | 417 | 165 | 14 | — | — | — | — | — | 59 | 567 | 846 | 635 |

## 48 GADWALL *Anas strepera*

*Rare*

Sightings at South Walney have been very sporadic with 17 short-staying birds between 1971 and 1989. Pairs have occurred in May 1971 and 1987, June 1980 and January 1985 and singles between April and October.

A flock of 14 was at the north end in October 1978 and an individual on 25th September 1989.

## 49 TEAL *Anas crecca*

*Abundant*

Never more than a very occasional breeder, a duckling was noted at South Walney Nature Reserve in June 1957 and a pair have nested near the Coastguard Station in Central Walney c. 1957. Pairs are seen, well into May, chiefly around the Rakes Lane area, and breeding may have occurred. As with Wigeon, the species is virtually ever-present from August to April at South Walney. Numbers increase from the middle of August, when birds are seen in the central marsh, Lighthouse Bay and Walney Channel areas. Peak numbers are reached between November and January and are often created by a hard-weather influx. During February, numbers decline and by mid-April most birds have gone. The highest count is 2500 in January 1980.

Elsewhere on Walney, the species is rather irregular, though moderate flocks are sometimes located on North Walney and Sandy Nook.

Average maxima 1975-1989

| | J | F | M | A | M | J | J | A | S | O | N | D |
|---|---|---|---|---|---|---|---|---|---|---|---|---|
| SW | 779 | 396 | 143 | 39 | 2 | 2 | 3 | 92 | 247 | 439 | 514 | 707 |
| NW | 75 | 13 | 10 | 3 | — | — | — | 1 | 7 | 36 | 93 | 108 |

## 50 MALLARD *Anas platyrhynchos*

*Abundant*

The rural areas of Central Walney probably hold 40-50 nesting pairs. At South Walney Nature Reserve, up to 15 pairs nest annually, with limited success due to predation; while a similar number breed at North Walney. The species is resident throughout the year with peak numbers at South Walney in October, and at

North Walney in November and December. Maximum counts of 600 have occurred in October 1977 (South Walney) and November 1972 (North Walney). Small wintering flocks are regular in Tummer Hill and Wylock Marshes.

Average maxima 1975-1989

| | J | F | M | A | M | J | J | A | S | O | N | D |
|---|---|---|---|---|---|---|---|---|---|---|---|---|
| SW | 147 | 112 | 59 | 26 | 25 | 30 | 32 | 92 | 149 | 192 | 147 | 153 |
| NW | 138 | 95 | 33 | 18 | 20 | 10 | 9 | 40 | 69 | 128 | 157 | 165 |

**Ringing and recoveries**

Irregularly caught at South Walney and none have been ringed since 1979. There have been five recoveries, the furthest dead near Roose (6 km north). Walney Island Wildfowlers Association have released over 700 birds between 1970 and 1978 and have had at least 25 recoveries, most of which have been local, the most distant being a bird shot at Leighton Moss (25 km northeast).

## 51 PINTAIL *Anas acuta*

*Uncommon*

Appearing chiefly in small groups during autumn and winter, the species rarely stays for any length of time, although one prospecting pair visited South Walney in 1983 and another in 1985. A flock of 1500 winters in the Kent Estuary and considerable, though smaller, numbers are in the Duddon and Levens Estuaries; birds in flight at South Walney possibly relate to movements between these gatherings. Peak counts at South Walney include 16 on 3rd December 1978, 15 on 23rd October 1981 and 19 on 10th March 1985.

Days recorded 1975-1989

| J | F | M | A | M | J | J | A | S | O | N | D | T |
|---|---|---|---|---|---|---|---|---|---|---|---|---|
| 22 | 12 | 12 | — | 1 | 1 | — | 8 | 27 | 28 | 19 | 22 | 152 |

Equally sporadic are the North Walney sightings of which there were 48 between September and April in the period 1975-1989; an influx of 125 in December 1977 were, probably, tourists from the Duddon flock.

## 52 GARGANEY *Anas querquedula*

*Rare*

South Walney has 14 records, 12 of them since 1974. Five relate to spring birds with pairs on 19th May 1987 and 20th and 21st May 1989 and solitary drakes in 1960, 1976 and 1986; the second bird frequenting the gate pool from 9th to 20th May. Most of the other sightings were short staying individuals in August.

North Walney's sole record is of a drake on 1st June 1985. A superb drake was at Long Rein Point on 13th May 1988. This locality also held an autumn drake on six days between 19th August and 5th September after first being located at South Walney on 17th August.

## 53 SHOVELER *Anas clypeata*

*Uncommon*

After prospecting pairs, in the Rakes Lane area, had aroused suspicions in the previous three years, breeding was confirmed at South Walney in 1986.

The species appears most frequently in spring and autumn, with small groups of up to 12 birds making use of the central marsh, gate pool, Lighthouse Bay and, occasionally, Bass Pool and Haws Bed. Long staying individuals and parties are not uncommon and the peak count is a remarkable 30 on 14th April 1962.

Days recorded 1975-1989

| J | F | M | A | M | J | J | A | S | O | N | D | T |
|---|---|---|---|---|---|---|---|---|---|---|---|---|
| 37 | 41 | 30 | 58 | 66 | 20 | 17 | 58 | 44 | 58 | 57 | 42 | 528 |

Sightings at North Walney consist of four birds in April 1960, three in January 1984, and two on 15th March and 2nd May 1986 while in 1988 eight were seen on 15th May.

### 54 POCHARD *Aythya ferina*

*Uncommon*

Most sightings are in the period October to February, with individuals or small groups on the gravel pools, especially when hard weather conditions prevail. A flock of 22 was present in January 1979, and one of 40 on 25th October 1969.

Days recorded 1975-1989

| J | F | M | A | M | J | J | A | S | O | N | D | T |
|---|---|---|---|---|---|---|---|---|---|---|---|---|
| 46 | 44 | 10 | 1 | — | 3 | — | 10 | 13 | 48 | 56 | 52 | 283 |

At North Walney, the pattern is similar, with small numbers consorting with the resident Tufted Ducks between September and March; the maximum count an unprecedented 21 on 20th March 1984.

### 55 RING-NECKED DUCK *Aythya collaris*

At North Walney a drake was seen on 9th June 1989 possibly the same individual that had frequented Coniston Water and Cavendish Dock since February 1989.

### 56 TUFTED DUCK *Aythya fuligula*

*Fairly common*

A population of up to five pairs has existed in the excavated pools of North Walney since the mid-1950s and 20 ducklings were at the site in July 1984. Its frequency on the island, prior to utilising the north end, is possibly reflected by Durnford (1883), whose sole record is of one shot in 1876. Birds are now present at North Walney, throughout the year, with an average of 20 outside the breeding season. A flock of 50 at this locality on 21st February 1988 is unparalleled.

The only records at South Walney, prior to 1976, relate to small numbers from September to December, with a maximum of 18 in October 1968. Since 1976, however, appearances have been more frequent. Individuals and small groups use the deep gravel pools and are usually seen during hard weather with 12 in December 1981. Unprecedented numbers appeared in 1985 with up to 20 birds between January and May. Created habitat at South Walney Nature Reserve may encourage nesting in the future.

Days recorded 1975-1989

| J | F | M | A | M | J | J | A | S | O | N | D | T |
|---|---|---|---|---|---|---|---|---|---|---|---|---|
| 65 | 92 | 73 | 54 | 10 | 6 | 5 | 4 | 10 | 52 | 61 | 48 | 480 |

### 57 SCAUP *Aythya marila*

*Uncommon*

Described by Wilson (1976) as "surprisingly scarce", the species is irregular, being absent in 1970, 1978 and 1984. Sightings are, normally, of small groups or individuals, but a maximum of 11 birds wintered between January and March 1981 and a flock, peaking at 18 in January 1982 were around from late October 1981 until early April 1982.

Days recorded 1975-1989

| J | F | M | A | M | J | J | A | S | O | N | D | T |
|---|---|---|---|---|---|---|---|---|---|---|---|---|
| 49 | 73 | 77 | 12 | 1 | 3 | 1 | 3 | 13 | 23 | 55 | 53 | 363 |

North Walney records are scarce, with 17 between 1975 and 1987, including a peak of seven on 1st November 1980, and four long staying birds in the spring of 1986.

**58 EIDER** ***Somateria mollissima***

*Abundant*

The literature declares the species to have been a very rare vagrant and, according to MacPherson (1892), "was quite unknown to the Morecambe Bay fishermen". However, in 1949, a nest was discovered on the spit at South Walney, described by Oakes (1953) as "a surprising event", since there had only been three previous Lancashire sight records (one at Barrow in 1860 and two in the Crosby area in 1938 and 1939). In the ensuing 35 years, the increase in breeding birds has been meteoric and Walney now has over 1000 nests. The nearest breeding population is in southwest Scotland and the Walney-Foulney site provides an isolated but flourishing colony, the only one on the west coast of England.

The vast amount of crustacea in the locality probably encouraged the small flock of wintering birds which, according to Benson (pers. comm.), was first noted at the end of the 1930s. The success of the colony, however, must be seen in relation to the success of the co-existing gull colony and the protective umbrella that the gulls provide.

Dr. W. H. Drury maintains that, on the Maine coast of the U.S.A., "the comeback of the Eiders coincided with the gull's population climb" (Audubon, Nov. 1972). In 1950, at South Walney, there were 520 pairs of Lesser Black-backed Gull, 180 pairs of Herring Gull and one, solitary, Eider nest; in 1987 there were approximately 25,000 pairs of gulls and 1000 Eider nests which had increased to 1200 nests in 1988. Despite the apparent threat from predatory gulls, the Eiders are robust enough, not only to look after their creches of young, but also to commandeer gull nests and, even, eggs. (Perry, British Birds Aug. 1982).

**Number of Eider nests at South Walney:**

| | |
|---|---|
| 1949 — 1 | 1971 — 264 |
| 1952 — 1 | 1976 — 375 |
| 1962 — 20 | 1981 — 577 |
| 1966 — 125 | 1986 — 1000 |

In the late 1970s, Eiders began nesting at the north end of the island and 15 nests were located in 1984. Elsewhere on Walney, successful breeding has occurred at various sites along the Channel. Dova Haw held four pairs in 1980, whilst Sheep Island had 29 nests in 1977 and 36 in 1984. Both sites have, unfortunately, experienced disturbance from collectors. Nests have not yet been found on Piel Island, which is surprising, since Foulney Island supports a growing colony.

**Number of Eider nests on Foulney Island:**

| | |
|---|---|
| 1962 — 1 | 1977 — 21 |
| 1965 — 3 | 1980 — 35 |
| 1968 — 8 | 1983 — 55 |
| 1971 — 10 | 1986 — 70 |
| 1974 — 18 | |

During the winter months, a flock of up to 5,000 birds has been counted off South Walney and, as the breeding season approaches, birds begin to move towards their nesting areas. By April, congregations of up to 4,000 are performing courtship displays in Haws Bed and Lighthouse Bay. After breeding has taken place, the ducks escort their young to the southwest shores of the island, while the drakes assemble in a large moult flock off Foulney Island. The species seems extremely sedentary and local to the Walney-Foulney region, although the winter population is, probably, supplemented by northern birds. Elsewhere in Cumbria, records are scarce and relate to individuals and small parties; but on the Lancashire side of Morecambe Bay, sightings are increasing, with 21 off Rossall in May 1984 and 30 at Heysham, after gales, on 18th January 1983.

**59 KING EIDER** ***Somateria spectabilis***

*Vagrant*

The two South Walney records relate, perhaps, to the same bird, seen, also, off Southwest Scotland in the same years. In 1979, a drake, the fourth English record since 1915, was present on seven days from 10th to 23rd June, and in 1980, on six days from 12th April to 2nd May. Both occurrences were accepted by B.B.R.C.

**60 LONG-TAILED DUCK** ***Clangula hyemalis***

*Scarce*

Described by both MacPherson (1892) and Oakes (1953) as a rare winter visitor, the species was absent in 1972, 1975, 1978 and 1984.

Sea watching has increased the number of sightings, including a peak of eight, flying north off Hilpsford Point on 10th October 1981; but many birds are longish-staying, making use of the more sheltered waters of Haws Bed and the gravel pools. Between 10th October 1988 and 25th April 1989 one to three birds were present almost daily except for five on 4th November 1988 and four on 5th and 8th.

Days recorded 1975-1989

| J | F | M | A | M | J | J | A | S | O | N | D | T |
|---|---|---|---|---|---|---|---|---|---|---|---|---|
| 29 | 22 | 25 | 21 | 1 | 3 | — | 8 | 26 | 19 | 32 | 30 | 216 |

North Walney records are sparse and consist of four birds in late March and early April in 1960, 1961 and 1962, up to two long-staying individuals in late 1985, and a single almost daily until 15th February 1986.

## 61 COMMON SCOTER *Melanitta nigra*

*Fairly common*

MacPherson (1892) and Mitchell (1892) portray the species as very abundant in Morecambe Bay. MacPherson writes of the fondness of Barrow gunners for having, "a few shots at the Black Duck"; while Mitchell describes the taking of Common Scoter in douker nets as common practice on the Furness shores, and illustrated this with a scene of nets near Piel Island. It is implicit, in both accounts, that the species was quite plentiful and more numerous than in recent times. Large wintering congregations are, occasionally, seen off South Walney, with peaks of 2,000 in October 1964 and 5,000 in April 1965. Such figures have not been approached in the period 1975-1989, when maximum counts have been 600 in November 1980 and 500 in November 1982. However, in 1986, a summering flock of at least 2,000 birds was off South Walney between late April and early July. There are sightings for all months, but most occur between August and May.

Average maxima 1975-1989

| J | F | M | A | M | J | J | A | S | O | N | D |
|---|---|---|---|---|---|---|---|---|---|---|---|
| 30 | 15 | 18 | 65 | 230 | 159 | 28 | 19 | 29 | 43 | 123 | 68 |

Records from North Walney are few, although small numbers have been seen in most months. Peak counts include 50 on 19th April 1987 and 95 on 26th November 1985.

## 62 VELVET SCOTER *Melanitta fusca*

*Scarce*

Although recorded at South Walney in all months, the figures have had to be adjusted because of the adoption of South Walney by a drake, dubbed 'Victor', who from early 1981 until spring 1984 moved, with each tide, in and out of Piel Channel. In the period 1975-1980, there were only four records. Victor, however, induced others of the species to keep him company and, during his stay, four were seen on 3rd July 1981, three were seen on 3rd July 1981, three were present on five days in the same year, and there were three on 31st December 1982. Additionally amongst the large gathering of Common Scoters in May 1986, at least ten Velvets were observed on 13th.

Days recorded 1975-1989 (excluding 'Victor')

| J | F | M | A | M | J | J | A | S | O | N | D | T |
|---|---|---|---|---|---|---|---|---|---|---|---|---|
| 6 | 9 | 7 | 7 | 9 | 1 | 2 | 3 | 4 | 9 | 9 | 5 | 71 |

At North Walney, the only birds sighted were two on 4th December 1983, and 16th January 1987.

## 63 GOLDENEYE *Bucephala clangula*

*Common*

At South Walney, the species can be consistently seen between October and March, becoming less regular and numerous in April. Records for May to September are chiefly created by oversummering individuals in 1976 and 1986. Birds arrive at the south end in mid-October and form loose flocks in the gravel pools and Piel Channel. Peak numbers occur in December and January, hard weather inland being responsible for the maximum of 100 in December 1981.

Average maxima 1975-1989

| J | F | M | A | M | J | J | A | S | O | N | D |
|---|---|---|---|---|---|---|---|---|---|---|---|
| 16 | 14 | 6 | 1 | — | — | — | — | — | 6 | 13 | 23 |

At North Walney, flocks of up to 30 are regular, and frequent Scarth Channel

*North Walney National Nature Reserve — looking east over Scarth Channel and Scarth Bight with the tip of Sandscale Haws Nature Reserve, Lowsy Point, in the top left.*
*(Frank Quayle)*

*South Walney Nature Reserve — looking north-northeast over Lighthouse Bay, the Spit, Piel Island and Roa Island with Barrow-in-Furness in the background.*
*(Frank Quayle)*

*Walney Island — looking north-northwest from the northern tip of South Walney Nature Reserve over Coastguard Cottages, Gate Pool and from bottom to top, the island's bays, Haws Bed, Wylock Marsh and Tummer Hill Marsh.*
*(Frank Quayle)*

***Walney Channel and Jubilee Bridge — looking north-northwest with Vickerstown on the left, Vickers' shipyard on the right and Black Combe in the distance.***
*(Frank Quayle)*

***Vickerstown and Tummer Hill Marsh — looking west-northwest towards the Irish Sea.***
*(Frank Quayle)*

***Biggar Village — looking northeast over Walney Channel to Ramsden and Cavendish Docks. Rakes Lane can be seen in the bottom right of the picture.***
*(Frank Quayle)*

*The gull colony at South Walney Nature Reserve at the height of the breeding season.*
(George Higginbotham)

*Lesser Black-backed Gulls and chicks at South Walney Nature Reserve in June. The male, larger and thicker-set than the female, is standing on the left.*
(George Higginbotham)

*Herring Gull at the nest with chicks in June, South Walney Nature Reserve. This male is shielding his offspring with partially-opened wings.*
(George Higginbotham)

*Great Black-backed Gull on eggs at South Walney Nature Reserve in May. This female will share her incubation duties with her partner.*
*(George Higginbotham)*

*Shelducks in winter at South Walney Nature Reserve congregating at the food source provided by the outflow of the Gate Pool.*
*(Jack Sheldon)*

*Eider on eggs at South Walney Nature Reserve in May. Stray wisps of eiderdown, used to line the nest and help keep the eggs warm, can be seen under her breast.*
*(George Higginbotham)*

*Oystercatcher on eggs at South Walney Nature Reserve in May. The bill is open and the wings are slightly spread in an attempt to keep cool.*
(George Higginbotham)

*Ringed Plover on eggs at South Walney Nature Reserve in May. This is a female indicated by the dark brown ear-coverts.*
(George Higginbotham)

*Lapwing on eggs near Rakes Lane in May. Still an abundant breeding bird on the island, with many fields holding two or three pairs.*
(George Higginbotham)

*Common Terns and chick at South Walney Nature Reserve in June. The discarded eggshell, similar in colouring to the chick, can be seen under the left foot of the right-hand bird.*
(George Higginbotham)

*Stonechat at South Walney Nature Reserve in June. This male, perched on top of gorse, is carrying food to feed its offspring.*
(Frank Quayle)

*Reed Bunting at the nest near Rakes Lane in May. This male is carrying food to feed its offspring.*
(George Higginbotham)

*Eiders at South Walney Nature Reserve in April. The Gate Pool area is one of the best sites to witness the courtship display of this species.*
*(Tim Dean)*

*Oystercatcher flock at Scar End Point in November. High-tide assemblies can be seen at many island locations.*
*(Jack Sheldon)*

*White-throated Sparrow at South Walney Nature Reserve on 17th June 1965. This North American resident became the third record for Great Britain.*
*(Jack Sheldon)*

*King Eider at South Walney Nature Reserve on 12th April 1980. A bird of the high Arctic, this drake was the second record for the island.*
(Nat Dawson)

*Paddyfield Warbler at South Walney Nature Reserve on 11th September 1982. Breeding in Central Asia and wintering further south, this individual became the eighth record for Great Britain and the easiest of all previous records to twitch.*
(Dave Satterthwaite)

*Pallas's Warbler at South Walney Nature Reserve on 13th October 1982. This bird, one of two at South Walney on that date, should really have been winging its way from Siberia to South East Asia.*
(Tim Dean)

between October and March with peaks of 32 in November 1983 and February 1984.

### 64 SMEW *Mergus albellus*

*Vagrant*

Two drakes were in Scarth Channel on 3rd January 1962 and a drake was off the southwest shore of the island on 25th January 1977. Two redheads were in Wylock Marsh on 14th November 1985 and one at the pier on 19th November 1985.

### 65 RED-BREASTED MERGANSER *Mergus serrator*

*Common*

In line with the expansion of the species in northwest England, nesting has probably occurred since the early 1960s. The Walney population, up to five pairs, seems confined to the ends of the island. A pair may have nested at South Walney in 1965 but, although young birds had been seen at sea in many subsequent years, breeding was not confirmed until 1984 and 1985. At the north end, there has been at least one pair since 1980, and regular sightings of young indicate the presence of other successful breeders. The species is present throughout the year with maximum counts of 120 on 11th February 1979 at South Walney, and 172 on 5th March 1986 at North Walney.

Average maxima 1975-1989

| | J | F | M | A | M | J | J | A | S | O | N | D |
|---|---|---|---|---|---|---|---|---|---|---|---|---|
| SW | 28 | 46 | 35 | 27 | 9 | 5 | 4 | 3 | 7 | 15 | 28 | 41 |
| NW | 23 | 24 | 32 | 22 | 16 | 7 | 7 | 6 | 25 | 22 | 22 | 24 |

### 66 GOOSANDER *Mergus merganser*

*Rare*

At South Walney there are nine records since 1962. Five birds were off the west shore on 29th December 1976, four in Haws Bed on 13th April 1983 and three in the large gravel pool on 16th December 1981. The large gravel pool also attracted individuals in September 1962, August 1974, January 1977, November 1982 and October 1987. In 1989 a flock of seven female-types were seen at sea on 26th September.

### 67 RUDDY DUCK *Oxyura jamaicensis*

A drake in winter plumage was on the gate pool at South Walney on 30th November 1989.

### 68 HONEY BUZZARD *Pernis apivorus*

*Vagrant*

One flew south over the spit at South Walney on 1st September 1985.

### 69 RED KITE *Milvus milvus*

*Vagrant*

One flew south over Walney Channel on 6th April 1969.

### 70 MARSH HARRIER *Circus aeruginosus*

*Rare*

Since 1975, all appearances at South Walney have been between 14th April and 18th June usually of singles, except for three birds on 14th May 1980 and two on

22nd May 1989. (Hilbre Island recorded four birds in the period 1st to 11th May 1980). Prior to 1975, there are May sightings for 1966 and 1972, and a lone August appearance by a female on 20th and 21st in 1966.

Days recorded 1975-1989

| J | F | M | A | M | J | J | A | S | O | N | D | T |
|---|---|---|---|---|---|---|---|---|---|---|---|---|
| — | — | — | 2 | 7 | 4 | — | — | — | — | — | — | 13 |

Rakes Lane yielded a single on 14th April 1978, and wandering individuals have been at North Walney on 16th May 1982, 31st May 1985 and 23rd June 1986.

### 71 HEN HARRIER *Circus cyaneus*

*Scarce*

At South Walney since 1975, all sightings have been between 8th September and 11th February, except for early May records in 1978 and 1986. Single birds are the norm although two were over Lighthouse Bay on 25th October 1979. Prior to 1975, there were three October appearances and one for September in a dozen years.

Days recorded 1975-1989

| J | F | M | A | M | J | J | A | S | O | N | D | T |
|---|---|---|---|---|---|---|---|---|---|---|---|---|
| 5 | 4 | — | — | 2 | — | — | — | 2 | 9 | 1 | 2 | 25 |

At North Walney, in some years, there have been regular sightings of over-wintering birds staying until mid-April. Though there are no confirmed records, nesting may well have occurred in the past.

### 72 MONTAGU'S HARRIER *Circus pygargus*

*Vagrant*

Durnford (1883) writes of a specimen killed on Walney in 1872, dated, subsequently, as 1874 by MacPherson (1892), Mitchell (1892), and Oakes (1953). A male was seen in Lighthouse Bay, Wylock Marsh, and Sandy Nook on 20th April 1981, and a similar individual frequented the Wirral a few days earlier.

### 73 SPARROWHAWK *Accipiter nisus*

*Fairly common*

A pair nested at the north end in the 1930s (Benson, pers. comm.), but wartime activity destroyed their habitat. Since the mid 1970s a pair has bred annually near North Scale. Prior to 1975, South Walney had only 16 records in a dozen years, but, since 1975, less victimisation nationwide and increased coverage has produced sightings in all months.

Days recorded 1975-1989

| J | F | M | A | M | J | J | A | S | O | N | D | T |
|---|---|---|---|---|---|---|---|---|---|---|---|---|
| 22 | 26 | 32 | 17 | 5 | 1 | 11 | 62 | 96 | 95 | 38 | 40 | 445 |

**Ringing and recoveries**

Only three were caught prior to 1981, since then, perhaps reflecting the increase indicated above, 15 more have been ringed, three of them at Willow Woods. Controls have been of Walney birds and maybe indicate a degree of sedentariness.

### 74 BUZZARD *Buteo buteo*

*Vagrant*

Between 1962 and 1980 there are eight South Walney records. Four were seen in April and May, and the remainder between August and December, with two of them in September. Given its sedentary habits, Buzzard is one of Walney's unlikeliest raptors. No spring records have been forthcoming since April 1978, although spring appearances of Marsh Harrier have increased since 1980. Sightings of the species at Hilbre Island in April and May are non-existent. A tideline corpse was found on Walney's southwest shore in August 1966.

### 75 SPOTTED EAGLE *Aquila clanga/naevia*

*Vagrant*

A tideline corpse, found by fishermen in 1875 on the west shore of the island, was examined by Durnford who stated it to be *Aquila naevia.* Mitchell (1892) refers to it as the less improbable *Aquila clanga* and, though MacPherson (1892) accepts Mitchell's identification he maintains that there must be doubt as to its actual specification. Spencer (1973) thinks that it is best ignored!

### 76 OSPREY *Pandion haliaetus*

*Rare*

Durnford (1883) and MacPherson (1892) refer to the species as an occasional, rare visitor. There are 11 records involving, probably, eight birds, with six of the records between April and early June in the period 1965 to 1989. Most are short staying, but one remained at South Walney from 4th September to 6th September 1965 and another fished in Piel Channel on 2nd and 3rd June 1981. The late April sighting in 1984 was flying over Osprey Drive, before heading north above Walney Channel!

### 77 KESTREL *Falco tinnunculus*

*Fairly common*

Durnford (1883) describes the species as resident although the current Walney population is no more than three pairs. Suitable nesting sites are few, but a pair used the Coastguard Station from 1968 until 1982 and pairs have bred successfully on a navigation light in Tummer Hill Marsh. A pair has, also, nested in Piel Castle and has been seen regularly, harrying the Little Terns at Foulney and South Walney.

A small passage occurs in late summer and early autumn, with peaks of nine on 30th August 1975 and 4th September 1981.

Days recorded 1975-1989

| J | F | M | A | M | J | J | A | S | O | N | D | T |
|---|---|---|---|---|---|---|---|---|---|---|---|---|
| 105 | 94 | 64 | 59 | 27 | 27 | 39 | 132 | 256 | 277 | 152 | 130 | 1362 |

At North Walney, few days pass without a sighting, with up to three on many days and a peak of seven on 6th September 1985.

**Ringing and recoveries**

Irregularly caught at South Walney although 1981 produced three individuals. A Walney nestling was found dying in October 1962 at Ormskirk, Lancashire (65 km south-southeast) four months after being ringed, and a juvenile of September 1971 was found dead in the following February at Garforth, Yorkshire (127 km east-southeast).

### 78 MERLIN *Falco columbarius*

*Fairly common*

Durnford (1883) refers to over-wintering and most South Walney records between 1975 and 1984 are for the period August to March. Summer sightings are scarce, but May produced individuals in 1980 and 1983 and in July 1964, while North Walney had two on 5th June 1983. There is a small passage in late summer and early autumn with a maximum of three on 9th October 1984, 21st October 1986, 19th October 1987 and 5th September 1989.

Days recorded 1975-1989

| J | F | M | A | M | J | J | A | S | O | N | D | T |
|---|---|---|---|---|---|---|---|---|---|---|---|---|
| 54 | 54 | 48 | 34 | 2 | — | — | 37 | 117 | 210 | 126 | 79 | 761 |

At North Walney, up to two birds are seen fairly regularly between October and March.

### 79 HOBBY *Falco subbuteo*

*Vagrant*

Durnford (1883) records the species as being "rarely met with", and MacPherson (1892) asserts it had not been seen in Furness. Sightings are increasing at South Walney where a male flew over Walney Channel on 4th May 1981, an immature pursued Meadow Pipits on 4th October 1984 and a bird of similar age was logged on five days between 12th and 27th October 1985.

North Walney was host to a single on 6th October 1984.

### 80 GYRFALCON *Falco rusticolus*

*Vagrant*

The only record, accepted by the B.B.R.C., is of a juvenile, at South Walney on 17th December 1983 and, across Walney Channel, at Rampside on the following day. Reports suggest that the bird remained in the South Furness area until the middle of January 1984.

### 81 PEREGRINE *Falco peregrinus*

*Fairly common*

Durnford (1883) records the species as occasionally met with on the coast. At South Walney, there have been sightings in all months in the period 1975 to 1989 with most occurring from September to March. Appearances have been more numerous in recent years, reflecting the success of the Lake District population.

An individual showing the characteristics of the race *calidus* was seen on 11th October 1980.

Days recorded 1975-1989

| J | F | M | A | M | J | J | A | S | O | N | D | T |
|---|---|---|---|---|---|---|---|---|---|---|---|---|
| 57 | 41 | 20 | 6 | 5 | 1 | 5 | 17 | 45 | 84 | 66 | 69 | 416 |

At North Walney, locally breeding birds have been recorded almost daily since 1982.

## 82 RED GROUSE *Lagopus lagopus*

*Vagrant*

There have been occasional reports of birds at North Walney, but the only accepted records are of singles on 21st October 1984 and on five days in October and November 1986.

## 83 RED-LEGGED PARTRIDGE *Alectoris rufa*

*Introduced*

Walney Island Wildfowlers Association released 25 chicks at North Walney in 1973 but there have been no subsequent sightings.

## 84 GREY PARTRIDGE *Perdix perdix*

*Uncommon*

Appearances at South Walney over the last 25 years have varied considerably. There is only one record from 1965 to 1968, and only two from 1972 to 1975. An increase was evident from 1976, with coveys of up to 12 birds in 1979 and early 1980, but since 1981, sightings have dwindled dramatically. Nesting was last noted in 1983.

Days recorded 1965-1989

| | | | | |
|---|---|---|---|---|
| 1965 — 1 | 1970 — 4 | 1975 — 0 | 1980 — 47 | 1985 — 2 |
| 66 — 0 | 71 — 12 | 76 — 15 | 81 — 76 | 86 — 0 |
| 67 — 0 | 72 — 2 | 77 — 20 | 82 — 53 | 87 — 7 |
| 68 — 0 | 73 — 0 | 78 — 8 | 83 — 26 | 88 — 0 |
| 69 — 10 | 74 — 0 | 79 — 21 | 84 — 9 | 89 — 4 |

North Walney shows a similar pattern. A diminishing breeding population, now less than five pairs, and fewer sightings of smaller coveys. In the early 1980s, moderate assemblies were met with almost daily between October and February, with a maximum of 53 in late November 1983.

### 85 PHEASANT *Phasianus colchius*

*Introduced*

Since 1974, Walney Island Wildfowlers Association has released up to 20 birds, chiefly in the Biggar village area. Breeding has taken place in the year following, but not subsequently. A female was at South Walney between 7th and 10th April 1977, and two birds were caught in Shearwater Crescent and Black Butts Lane, Vickerstown on 26th June and 16th July 1984 respectively. North Walney held a single on 8th February 1986, and two birds in 1987 on 8th March and 13th April.

### 86 QUAIL *Coturnix coturnix*

*Vagrant*

The only records are of singing males at Walney airfield on 20th June 1985 and 5th July 1987.

### 87 BLUE-BREASTED QUAIL *Coturnix chinensis*

*Exotica*

A moribund example was found at Biggar Bank on 30th June and died on 2nd July 1988.

### 88 WATER RAIL *Rallus aquaticus*

*Uncommon*

Although ample habitat is available, especially at the north end, nesting has yet to be confirmed. Since 1975 the species has been seen at South Walney on 37 days, 33 of them since March 1985. Most sightings involve single birds at the offices, central marsh and gate pool, but include two birds on 10th October 1986.

Days recorded 1975-1989

| J | F | M | A | M | J | J | A | S | O | N | D | T |
|---|---|---|---|---|---|---|---|---|---|---|---|---|
| 6 | 3 | 3 | — | — | — | — | — | 3 | 9 | 7 | 6 | 37 |

Icy conditions at North Walney can occasion fairly regular appearances and since 1980, individuals have been seen on 32 days. Biggar marsh occasionally yields solitary birds.

### 89 SPOTTED CRAKE *Porzana porzana*

*Vagrant*

Birds have appeared at the gate pool on 26th September 1983 and 21st July 1985, and a winter sighting was in the central marsh from 7th to 11th January 1986. The first island record was at North Walney on 5th October 1981.

### 90 CORNCRAKE *Crex crex*

*Rare*

In 1864, according to Harting "landrails were frequently met with," and the island probably supported a healthy population. Immediately prior to the Second World War, there were up to six pairs at both North and South Walney. There has been no evidence of breeding since 1939, although birds were heard in the spring of 1945, 1960 and 1964. A bird with a broken wing was found on 30th April 1984, beneath the cliffs of Hare Hill, but despite veterinary attention, it died in captivity nine days later.

### 91 MOORHEN *Gallinula chloropus*

*Common*

Breeding takes place annually, with up to seven pairs at South Walney, up to three pairs at North Walney and up to five pairs around Biggar village. At South Walney, numbers peak between July and December, with a maximum of 33 on 4th September 1989.

Average maxima 1975-1989

| J | F | M | A | M | J | J | A | S | O | N | D |
|---|---|---|---|---|---|---|---|---|---|---|---|
| 4 | 5 | 5 | 6 | 6 | 4 | 6 | 10 | 16 | 14 | 8 | 7 |

**Ringing and recoveries**

At South Walney a concerted effort was made to catch the species using drop traps resulting in seven birds during September and October of 1986. Previous years have produced occasional birds but no more than the six of 1982. A juvenile of late October 1980 was found dead at Great Urswick, Ulverston (13km east) in the following year.

### 92 COOT *Fulica atra*

*Fairly common*

The island population of no more than seven pairs is almost exclusive to South Walney Nature Reserve, although nesting has occurred irregularly at North Walney. Peak numbers occur at South Walney between April and October, with a maximum of 44 on 24th August 1987.

Average maxima 1975-1989

| J | F | M | A | M | J | J | A | S | O | N | D |
|---|---|---|---|---|---|---|---|---|---|---|---|
| 1 | 4 | 5 | 8 | 9 | 9 | 10 | 15 | 9 | 4 | 2 | 1 |

### 93 CRANE *Grus grus*

*Vagrant*

At South Walney, a B.B.R.C. accepted adult flew in from Morecambe Bay on 5th October 1984 and continued north pursued by gulls.

### 94 OYSTERCATCHER *Haematopus ostralegus*

*Abundant*

All previous authors refer to the species' abundance on the island as a breeding bird. The present population of about 120 pairs nests on shingle, saltmarsh and pasture, with between 70 and 80 pairs at South Walney Nature Reserve and up to 20 pairs at the north end. Post-breeding and wintering birds congregate on the spit at South Walney, the refuse tip, Biggar Bank and North Walney, with peak numbers between August and March. At South Walney, maximum counts of 30,000 have been in October 1964, August 1965 and January 1967, while more recently, 20,000 were counted in August 1976. At North Walney the largest assembly was 12,000 in September 1975.

Average maxima (thousands) 1975-1989

| | J | F | M | A | M | J | J | A | S | O | N | D |
|---|---|---|---|---|---|---|---|---|---|---|---|---|
| SW | 5.2 | 5.6 | 5.3 | 2.1 | 1.0 | 0.6 | 1.4 | 6.2 | 6.6 | 8.0 | 6.7 | 5.6 |
| NW | 2.3 | 2.1 | 1.7 | 0.7 | 0.5 | 0.3 | 0.6 | 1.7 | 3.3 | 2.7 | 3.1 | 3.3 |

**Ringing and recoveries**

Morecambe Bay Wader Ringing Group have received over 150 reports of their birds, most from northern latitudes, indicating the importance of the area to winter visitors. There are 40 recoveries from East Scotland; 26 from Norway; 15 from the Faeroes; 13 from West Scotland; 12 from the Shetlands; 11 from the Orkneys; nine from West England; five from Iceland; four from Wales; three from Denmark; two from East England; and singles from Spitzbergen, St. Kilda, Northern Ireland and France.

### 95 AVOCET — ***Recurvirostra avosetta***

*Vagrant*

Specimens have occasionally appeared in Morecambe Bay, but the only Walney report is of two birds at Sandy Nook on 8th May 1983.

### 96 STONE-CURLEW — ***Burhinus oedicnemus***

*Vagrant*

One flew over the central marsh at South Walney on 28th September 1985.

### 97 LITTLE RINGED PLOVER — ***Charadrius dubius***

*Vagrant*

There are three records all at South Walney commencing in 1983 with a juvenile that remained in the central marsh from 29th August until 7th September. In 1988 an individual was in Haws Bed on 6th September and an adult in 1989 was present at the refuse tip on 25th May. If the species continues to colonise England as it has done in the last 20 years, sooner or later both ends of the island could hold breeding pairs.

### 98 RINGED PLOVER — ***Charadrius hiaticula***

*Abundant*

Oakes (1953) considered Walney to be the main Lancashire nesting haunt and, in the 1980s, breeding, by up to 40 pairs, occurs along the west coast, with, occasionally, nests on the east shore. Up to 30 pairs nested in the late 1960s and early 1970s at South Walney Nature Reserve, but the same site in the eighties has yielded, annually, a mere seven nests. The north end currently supports 20 pairs.

During May, peak passage numbers occur at both ends of the island and at Biggar Bank, and large returning flocks are recorded in August. Maxima are 800 at South Walney in May 1981 and 1045 at North Walney in August 1978, while 3,000 were at Biggar Bank in May 1980.

Average maxima 1975-1989

| | J | F | M | A | M | J | J | A | S | O | N | D |
|---|---|---|---|---|---|---|---|---|---|---|---|---|
| SW | 29 | 24 | 20 | 20 | 95 | 17 | 27 | 91 | 70 | 67 | 40 | 28 |
| NW | 37 | 37 | 21 | 32 | 98 | 12 | 24 | 135 | 51 | 50 | 44 | 38 |

**Ringing and recoveries**

Birds ringed by the Morecambe Bay Wader Ringing Group have been recovered in Norway, West France, Hampshire, Gloucestershire, Gwent, Gwynedd and Fife; the best documented being an individual caught at Biggar Bank on 26th May 1978, controlled at Giske, Norway (1,000 km northeast) on 20th August 1979 and found dead on 27th August 1980 at the Seine Estuary, France (600 km southeast). In addition, there have been controls on Walney of birds ringed in Norway, Netherlands, Fife and Cornwall.

**99 GREATER SAND PLOVER**

An individual, the ninth record for Great Britain, was located at Low Bank near the refuse tip on 19th July and remained in the vicinity until 5th August 1988.

**100 DOTTEREL** ***Charadrius morinellus***

*Vagrant*

There are only three records, all at South Walney. One was present, almost daily, from 23rd September to 27th October 1969; another was off the west shore on 4th May 1982; and a third was seen in the dunes on 19th September 1984. The 1982 bird was part of a well-recorded passage in West Cumbria, with a maximum of 15 at Silecroft golf course (22 km north-northwest) between 29th April and 6th May.

**101 GOLDEN PLOVER** ***Pluvialis apricaria***

*Common*

At South Walney peak numbers occur in mid-winter. In the period 1975 to 1989 the maximum count was 850 in February 1975, although 1200 had been logged in the same month of 1972. The arable land to the north of South Walney Nature Reserve is the main roosting and feeding ground at high tide, while at low water the flocks move, either to fields in the Rampside area, or to the boulder zones on Walney's west shore.

Average maxima 1975-1989

| J | F | M | A | M | J | J | A | S | O | N | D |
|---|---|---|---|---|---|---|---|---|---|---|---|
| 203 | 233 | 114 | 176 | 25 | — | — | 52 | 142 | 257 | 194 | 188 |

North Walney records are scanty, but include 200 on 8th November 1985. Prior to this, the maximum at the north end was 15 on 8th January 1980.

**102 GREY PLOVER** ***Pluvialis squatarola***

*Common*

MacPherson (1892), citing Bolton, regards the bird as scarce in the Walney area;

but there is definite evidence of an increase in passage and wintering numbers during the period 1965 to 1989. The average annual maxima was 28 from 1965 to 1989 and 103 from 1975 to 1984, but fluctuations from year to year are considerable.

Average maxima 1975-1989

| | J | F | M | A | M | J | J | A | S | O | N | D |
|---|---|---|---|---|---|---|---|---|---|---|---|---|
| SW | 50 | 57 | 39 | 26 | 6 | 4 | 2 | 26 | 46 | 63 | 85 | 62 |
| NW | 64 | 94 | 73 | 11 | 1 | 5 | 1 | 9 | 14 | 61 | 67 | 85 |

Elsewhere on Walney, 200 were at the Coastguard Station on 21st March 1981 and 120 at Rakes lane on 14th April 1978; while smaller flocks are regularly on Biggar Bank and, occasionally at Tummer Hill Marsh. North Walney held 270 birds on 21st February 1988, which represents the highest ever island count.

### 103 LAPWING *Vanellus vanellus*

*Abundant*

The species breeds in the low-lying fields between Ocean Road and South Walney Nature Reserve, with a total of 70 to 80 pairs. Up to 10 pairs bred at South Walney Nature Reserve in the 1960s, but suitable sites have now been relinquished to the gull colony. North Walney holds a population of about 20 pairs, breeding either in the arable fields or on the saltmarsh. Peak numbers, probably consisting of Cumbrian bred birds, begin to build up in late July and early August, and these are supplemented, in late autumn and early winter, by migrants from further north. The record count at South Walney is 1000 in February 1973, with a similar number at North Walney in both August 1978 and December 1984. At times of severe weather, birds desert the island completely and fly west, probably to more congenial pastures in Ireland.

Average maxima 1975-1989

| | J | F | M | A | M | J | J | A | S | O | N | D |
|---|---|---|---|---|---|---|---|---|---|---|---|---|
| SW | 179 | 102 | 77 | 21 | 13 | 36 | 48 | 84 | 133 | 239 | 238 | 231 |
| NW | 122 | 132 | 115 | 33 | 34 | 38 | 58 | 227 | 195 | 185 | 162 | 213 |

Elsewhere on the island, Tummer Hill Marsh holds a roost which reached 800 on 21st December 1972.

**Ringing and recoveries**

Of 63 pulli ringed on Walney since 1964, the only recovery was found four and a half years later in December 1972 on the island. However, "pre-observatory" birds include an August 1955 specimen located near Oporto, Portugal (1,500 km south-southwest) in January 1956, and a May 1961 individual found in early 1962 at Lussant, Charente-Maritime, France (1,000 km south).

### 104 KNOT *Calidris canutus*

*Abundant*

Previous authors refer to its abundance, and Oakes (1953) regards the bird's spring passage as "impressive." At South Walney the species is virtually ever present. Peak numbers occur from December until May, with record counts of 30,000 in January 1965 and 40,000 in April 1966. North Walney roosts are much smaller, although 3000 appeared in December 1974 and January 1975.

Average maxima 1975-1989

| | J | F | M | A | M | J | J | A | S | O | N | D |
|---|---|---|---|---|---|---|---|---|---|---|---|---|
| SW | 881 | 2859 | 3992 | 3928 | 1719 | 414 | 60 | 28 | 197 | 404 | 429 | 1568 |
| NW | 714 | 623 | 342 | 19 | 15 | — | — | — | 18 | 99 | 320 | 251 |

Elsewhere on the island, 2000 were recorded at the Coastguard Station in May 1973, and smaller flocks visit Biggar Bank and Tummer Hill Marsh.

**Ringing and recoveries**

Birds caught in winter by the Morecambe Bay Wader Ringing Group have been recovered in subsequent breeding seasons in the high Arctic. From Iceland there are ten recoveries; six from Greenland; seven from East England; three from West Germany; two each from Netherlands and West England; and singles from Denmark, France and Portugal. A typical and well documented example concerns a specimen caught on 21st February 1970, controlled at Eyri, Iceland (1,300 km northwest) on 23rd May and controlled again on 17th February 1973 on Foulney Island.

### 105 SANDERLING *Calidris alba*

*Abundant*

A small wintering flock, mostly at North Walney, is supplemented by much larger numbers in May and June, with peaks of 3000 at South Walney in May 1987 and 1950 at the north end in May 1977. A return passage, although smaller than in springtime, is evident in late July and in August, especially at South Walney.

Average maxima 1975-1989

| | J | F | M | A | M | J | J | A | S | O | N | D |
|---|---|---|---|---|---|---|---|---|---|---|---|---|
| SW | 15 | 18 | 16 | 16 | 473 | 160 | 84 | 119 | 64 | 29 | 16 | 20 |
| NW | 66 | 87 | 104 | 84 | 664 | 42 | 4 | 42 | 33 | 106 | 28 | 59 |

Flocks of up to 300 have been seen elsewhere on the island, notably at the Coastguard Station, Rakes Lane and Biggar Bank.

**Ringing and recoveries**

Birds ringed in spring on Walney have been recovered in subsequent winters in France and Morocco. In addition, six further recoveries all relate to the west coast between Southwest Scotland and mid-Lancashire during spring and autumn passage.

## 106 LITTLE STINT *Calidris minuta*

*Scarce*

At South Walney the species has been seen on 60 days in the period 1975 to 1989, with the majority occurring from late July to early October and with a maximum of five on 23rd September 1984. There is a single instance for January in 1977 and the only spring sightings refer to two birds at the refuse tip on 30th April 1982 and individuals in the central marsh on 30th April and 2nd May 1989.

Days recorded 1975-1989

| J | F | M | A | M | J | J | A | S | O | N | D | T |
|---|---|---|---|---|---|---|---|---|---|---|---|---|
| 1 | — | — | 2 | 1 | — | 7 | 5 | 33 | 11 | — | — | 60 |

## 107 TEMMINCK'S STINT *Calidris temminckii*

*Vagrant*

The only record is of a single bird in the lighthouse pool at South Walney on 6th September 1983.

## 108 WHITE-RUMPED SANDPIPER *Calidris fusciollis*

*Vagrant*

Walney's only record appeared in the central marsh at South Walney on 13th October 1984. The B.B.R.C. accepted both this and a sighting at Hodbarrow, 18 km to the north, on 1st and 2nd August 1984.

## 109 PECTORAL SANDPIPER *Calidris melanotos*

*Vagrant*

An adult was in South Walney's central marsh from 31st July until 3rd August 1982.

### 110 CURLEW SANDPIPER *Calidris ferruginea*

*Scarce*

Between 1975 and 1989 the species has appeared at South Walney on 45 days. September and October are the favoured months and birds have been seen in the central marsh and Haws Bed, the latter locality providing six birds on 12th September 1970 and four on 4th October 1983. South Walney witnessed unprecedented numbers during autumn 1988 with records on 13 days including ten birds on 4th September 1988 and eight on 5th.

Average maxima 1975-1989

| J | F | M | A | M | J | J | A | S | O | N | D | T |
|---|---|---|---|---|---|---|---|---|---|---|---|---|
| — | — | — | — | — | — | 1 | 4 | 28 | 11 | 1 | — | 45 |

The only sighting at North Walney involves two birds on 13th September 1987 while at Long Rein Point, 1988 yielded two birds on 28th August and 5th September.

### 111 PURPLE SANDPIPER *Calidris maritima*

*Fairly common*

Oakes (1953) refers to small or moderate numbers being regular winter visitors to the western shores of the island. The major roosts are at Biggar Bank and the Coastguard Station, where the species has occured in all months, except June and July, with peak numbers between November and April. Maxima are 98 at Biggar Bank on 25th January 1970 and 78 at the Coastguard Station on 25th March 1978. At South Walney in the period 1975 to 1989, the species has been recorded between September and May with a maximum of ten in May 1977.

Average combined maxima for South Walney, Biggar Bank and the Coastguard Station 1962-1989.

| J | F | M | A | M | J | J | A | S | O | N | D |
|---|---|---|---|---|---|---|---|---|---|---|---|
| 50 | 29 | 61 | 32 | 4 | — | — | — | 12 | 6 | 29 | 34 |

### 112 DUNLIN *Calidris alpina*

*Abundant*

Previous authors note the abundance of the species, especially during the winter months. Peak counts at all Walney sites occur during winter and early spring with maxima of 15,000 at South Walney in February 1976, 4,600 at North Walney in December 1977, and 8,000 at Rakes Lane in April 1978.

Average maxima 1975-1989

| | J | F | M | A | M | J | J | A | S | O | N | D |
|---|---|---|---|---|---|---|---|---|---|---|---|---|
| SW | 1996 | 3073 | 1702 | 1913 | 1590 | 20 | 510 | 874 | 337 | 850 | 1363 | 1480 |
| NW | 581 | 598 | 256 | 280 | 215 | 2 | 10 | 30 | 49 | 217 | 309 | 646 |

**Ringing and recoveries**

The Morecambe Bay Wader Ringing Group has a wealth of impressive information accumulating from their cannon-netting catches. Sweden has yielded nine recoveries; West Germany and Finland six each; Denmark five; France four; Morocco three; two each from Poland and Mauretania; and singles from East Germany, Iceland and the Netherlands. Specimens ringed elsewhere and recovered on Walney include 13 birds from Norway; five from Sweden; three each from Finland and East Germany; two each from Netherlands and Poland; and singles from France, Greenland, Mauretania, U.S.S.R. and West Germany.

**113 BUFF-BREASTED SANDPIPER** ***Tryngites subruficollis***

*Vagrant*

This visitor from North America, accepted by B.B.R.C., was located on 5th October 1974 in the company of roosting Dunlin at Scar End Point.

**114 RUFF** ***Philomachus pugnax***

*Uncommon*

Between 1975 and 1989 the species has appeared on 177 days at South Walney, but, of the individuals involved, not one has been prepared to sample a Walney winter. There are rare spring arrivals but sightings occur in August and September when individuals or small groups frequent the central marsh or the gravel pool areas. The maximum count is eight on 16th August 1981. Unprecedented numbers visited South Walney in autumn 1988 with records on 26 days including six birds on 30th August and seven on 8th September.

Days recorded 1975-1989

| J | F | M | A | M | J | J | A | S | O | N | D | T |
|---|---|---|---|---|---|---|---|---|---|---|---|---|
| — | — | — | 4 | 7 | 1 | 13 | 88 | 53 | 11 | — | — | 177 |

**115 JACK SNIPE** ***Lymnocryptes minimus***

*Uncommon*

From 1975 to 1989 the species has appeared on 98 days at South Walney, with most sightings during the last three months of the year. The peak count is four in December 1966 and in November 1975, with the gate pool area being the favourite haunt. For the first year since 1979, there were no records at South Walney during 1988.

Days recorded 1975-1989

| J | F | M | A | M | J | J | A | S | O | N | D | T |
|---|---|---|---|---|---|---|---|---|---|---|---|---|
| 9 | 11 | 1 | 3 | — | — | 1 | 2 | 7 | 18 | 24 | 22 | 98 |

Wylock Marsh, Biggar marsh and North Walney are other localities where individuals are sometimes seen, including five at the last site on 20th October 1986. One was seen at Biggar on 8th May 1983.

**Ringing and recoveries**

Mist nets in the gate pool area caught three birds in 1966. One of the two October specimens was killed in January 1968 at Lugo, Spain (1300 km south-southwest).

**116 SNIPE** ***Gallinago gallinago***

*Common*

The fields to the south of Ocean Road hold no more than a pair as does the north end where, prior to the Second World War, there were up to six pairs. Displaying birds were at South Walney Nature Reserve in 1966 and 1971 but breeding was not attempted. At South Walney, peak numbers occur between October and March, with the gate pool area being the most favoured haunt. Hard weather movements were particularly noticeable in December 1981 with 115 birds on the 5th, and in January 1984 with a flock of 130 flying south on the 23rd.

Average maxima 1975-1989

| J | F | M | A | M | J | J | A | S | O | N | D |
|---|---|---|---|---|---|---|---|---|---|---|---|
| 33 | 20 | 20 | 8 | 1 | — | 1 | 17 | 19 | 34 | 38 | 37 |

Small numbers frequent the wetland areas of North Walney with a maximum of 35 on 12th November 1985; elsewhere on the island, birds are regularly noted in Wylock, Biggar and Tummer Hill Marshes.

**Ringing and recoveries**

Enthusiastic mist netting in the late 1960s accounted for 39 birds. Since then, examples have been occasionally caught in heligolands during severe weather. An adult of October 1966 was killed near Gravelines, Calais, France (500 km southeast) in August 1970, and a juvenile of September 1969 was controlled near Malvern, Worcestershire (230 km south-southeast) in January 1972.

### 117 WOODCOCK *Scolopax rusticola*

*Scarce*

Durnford (1883) implies that the species was regular on Walney, noting that it usually arrived with the Short-eared Owls. The island wildfowlers confirm its regularity in small numbers, especially at North Walney, where six were seen on 27th December 1983. South Walney records do not, however, reflect these opinions, as, since 1958, there have only been 45 sightings. Birds have appeared from September to May, with a maximum of 14 on 17th December 1981 coinciding with hard weather inland.

Days recorded 1975-1989

| J | F | M | A | M | J | J | A | S | O | N | D | T |
|---|---|---|---|---|---|---|---|---|---|---|---|---|
| 9 | 3 | 2 | — | — | — | — | — | 2 | 1 | 10 | 17 | 44 |

### 118 BLACK-TAILED GODWIT *Limosa limosa*

*Uncommon*

MacPherson (1892) finds no evidence of the species in Morecambe Bay, but singles or small groups have been recorded at South Walney on 133 days between 1975 and 1989. Most sightings have been from August to November with an unprecedented 200 on 4th November 1979. Before 1972 there are occasional records of overwintering individuals.

Days recorded 1975-1989

| J | F | M | A | M | J | J | A | S | O | N | D | T |
|---|---|---|---|---|---|---|---|---|---|---|---|---|
| — | 1 | — | 5 | 11 | 5 | 16 | 36 | 45 | 9 | 5 | — | 133 |

Elsewhere on the island 25 were at Earnse Bay on 23rd July 1985 while in 1988, 37 birds were at Long Rein Point on 9th September.

## 119 BAR-TAILED GODWIT *Limosa lapponica*

*Common*

MacPherson (1892) states that small parties frequented Walney. Peak numbers are seen at South Walney from October to March with a maximum of 800 in January 1969. Smaller flocks are seen at Tummer Hill Marsh and North Walney, with 600 at the latter locality on 15th February 1985.

Average maxima 1975-1989

| | J | F | M | A | M | J | J | A | S | O | N | D |
|---|---|---|---|---|---|---|---|---|---|---|---|---|
| SW | 86 | 55 | 35 | 14 | 12 | 10 | 7 | 11 | 12 | 38 | 35 | 49 |
| NW | 23 | 49 | 22 | 2 | — | — | — | — | — | 3 | 5 | 6 |

## 120 WHIMBREL *Numenius phaeopus*

*Fairly common*

In spring, flocks gather in the fields to the south of Ocean Road, with a maximum of 50 on 8th May 1983 in the Rakes Lane area; autumn birds, more dispersed, are recorded in the Walney Channel vicinity. At South Walney, peaks occur in early May and August with a maximum of 100 on 7th August 1967. Since 1966, wintering individuals have been logged on seven days in November, three in December, eight in January and one in February. Included in these figures is a bird that was seen on 13 days between 8th November 1984 and 24th January 1985.

Average maxima 1975-1989

| J | F | M | A | M | J | J | A | S | O | N | D |
|---|---|---|---|---|---|---|---|---|---|---|---|
| — | — | — | 4 | 16 | 1 | 4 | 8 | 4 | 1 | — | — |

Elsewhere on the island, small numbers are regularly seen at Tummer Hill Marsh, Biggar Bank, Water Garth Nook and North Walney, including 50 at the last named on 8th August 1986.

## 121 CURLEW *Numenius arquata*

*Abundant*

In 1968, at South Walney Nature Reserve, a Curlew was observed behaving as if nesting, but further information is not documented. Large roosts begin to assemble in late July at North Walney, Tummer Hill Marsh, and in the fields to the south of the refuse tip. The peak count is 3500 at Tummer Hill Marsh in August 1971, while flocks of 2000 have been recorded at South Walney in October 1965 and August and October 1972, and at North Walney, also, in October 1965.

Average maxima 1975-1989

| | J | F | M | A | M | J | J | A | S | O | N | D |
|---|---|---|---|---|---|---|---|---|---|---|---|---|
| SW | 291 | 405 | 246 | 113 | 9 | 34 | 200 | 182 | 412 | 448 | 348 | 267 |
| NW | 422 | 472 | 387 | 129 | 44 | 130 | 290 | 418 | 633 | 496 | 471 | 420 |

**Ringing recoveries**

Birds ringed by the Morecambe Bay Wader Ringing Group indicate a very definite Finnish connection. A catch in August 1971 at Biggar has produced six recoveries, three of them from Finland in subsequent springs. The link is further enforced by another two Finnish recoveries, one of which was found dead in May 1984 at Vassa (1,800 km northeast) almost eight years after being caught.

## 122 SPOTTED REDSHANK *Tringa erythropus*

*Uncommon*

Since 1975 the species has been seen at South Walney on 124 days with most

appearances being single birds from August to October. Nine were present on 15th August 1977 and five on 4th October 1982. Records outside this period of the year are declining; only three in 1975-1989 compared with 28 in 1964-1974.
Days recorded 1975-1989

| J | F | M | A | M | J | J | A | S | O | N | D | T |
|---|---|---|---|---|---|---|---|---|---|---|---|---|
| 1 | — | — | — | — | — | 4 | 29 | 66 | 22 | 2 | — | 124 |

The only other island sightings are of individuals at North Walney on 14th January 1982, 28th August 1985 and 20th and 21st September 1987 while Long Rein Point held an immaculate individual on 16th May 1988, the first spring record on the island since 1972.

### 123 REDSHANK *Tringa totanus*

*Abundant*

MacPherson (1892) records a single pair in the late 19th century, but, in line with the expansion of the species in the north and west of Britain since the mid-19th century, Walney's breeding population stands at between 12 and 15 pairs. The fields around Biggar village hold up to ten pairs and the remainder nest at the north end. By early autumn, large flocks have assembled at both ends of the island and at Tummer Hill Marsh, with a maximum of 5,000 at South Walney in October 1967 and 2,000 at North Walney in October 1972.
Average maxima 1975-1989

| | J | F | M | A | M | J | J | A | S | O | N | D |
|---|---|---|---|---|---|---|---|---|---|---|---|---|
| SW | 467 | 393 | 373 | 319 | 26 | 23 | 257 | 590 | 720 | 910 | 559 | 378 |
| NW | 265 | 303 | 223 | 137 | 27 | 24 | 44 | 325 | 319 | 284 | 326 | 242 |

**Ringing recoveries**

Morecambe Bay Wader Ringing Group have received two Icelandic recoveries. Furthermore, two Iceland-ringed individuals have been controlled in late autumn on Walney.

### 124 GREENSHANK *Tringa nebularia*

*Fairly common*

At South Walney, there are records throughout the year, although, since 1964, there are only five in June. Small groups arrive in mid-July, followed by increasing numbers during autumn; a few birds overwinter peaking at seven in the Decembers of 1964, 1967 and 1989. Lighthouse Bay, the gravel pools and the central marsh are regularly used, and a maximum of 25 was recorded on 5th September 1965.
Average maxima 1975-1989

| J | F | M | A | M | J | J | A | S | O | N | D |
|---|---|---|---|---|---|---|---|---|---|---|---|
| 2.7 | 2.0 | 1.7 | 0.8 | 0.5 | 0.3 | 3.3 | 6.3 | 9.7 | 6.9 | 4.3 | 2.4 |

Sightings in other parts of the island are regular; North Walney held five on 22nd August 1982 and three on 22nd September 1972 while up to 20 birds frequented Long Rein Point in August 1988.

### 125 GREEN SANDPIPER *Tringa ochropus*

*Scarce*

Since 1975 South Walney has records on 78 days. Sightings have normally been found from July to September including four in the central marsh on 20th August 1977. Spring records are rare and involve singles on 7th April 1974 and 11th March 1978. Surpassing all other years however was 1988 with records on 26 days between mid-August and mid-September and including six birds on three dates with most sightings at South Walney or the refuse tip.

Days recorded 1975-1989

| J | F | M | A | M | J | J | A | S | O | N | D | T |
|---|---|---|---|---|---|---|---|---|---|---|---|---|
| — | — | 1 | 3 | 1 | — | 3 | 43 | 27 | — | — | — | 78 |

## 126 WOOD SANDPIPER *Tringa glareola*

*Scarce*

At South Walney the species has been present on 86 days. One stayed from 25th August until 13th October 1980. Apart from an individual on 31st July 1982, all sightings have been in August and September. An unprecedented influx in August 1980 peaked at 11 on 14th and remained in the central marsh for six days.

Days recorded 1975-1989

| J | F | M | A | M | J | J | A | S | O | N | D | T |
|---|---|---|---|---|---|---|---|---|---|---|---|---|
| — | — | — | — | — | — | 2 | 31 | 39 | 14 | — | — | 86 |

## 127 COMMON SANDPIPER *Actitis hypoleucos*

*Common*

From mid-July to mid-September, the species can be seen, almost daily at South Walney; with a maximum of 29 on 4th August 1966. Spring passage, though regular, involves fewer birds; but eight were present on 1st May 1969.

Average maxima 1975-1989

| J | F | M | A | M | J | J | A | S | O | N | D |
|---|---|---|---|---|---|---|---|---|---|---|---|
| — | — | — | 1.5 | 1.6 | 0.5 | 4.7 | 6.1 | 2.5 | 0.8 | — | — |

Occasional sightings, usually of single birds, have been recorded at North Walney.

## 128 TURNSTONE *Arenaria interpres*

*Abundant*

Previous authors refer to the all-the-year-round abundance of the species on Walney. June provides fewest records and peak numbers occur during the spring and autumn passages; South Walney had a maximum of 2,000 in August 1980, Rakes Lane 500 in May 1978 and North Walney 510 in September 1988.

Average maxima 1975-1989

| | J | F | M | A | M | J | J | A | S | O | N | D |
|---|---|---|---|---|---|---|---|---|---|---|---|---|
| SW | 169 | 181 | 219 | 193 | 258 | 41 | 143 | 515 | 355 | 256 | 185 | 181 |
| NW | 44 | 54 | 44 | 25 | 40 | 2 | 1 | 43 | 108 | 70 | 63 | 70 |

**Ringing recoveries**

Individuals ringed on Walney have been recovered in Poland, France, Denmark and Morocco. In addition, there have been a further nine recoveries of birds, usually wintering, along the west coast of England and Wales. The long-distance prize goes to a specimen ringed on 6th June 1974 at Ellesmere Island, Hudson Bay, Canada (4,480 km west) and controlled on Walney on 29th October 1977.

## 129 WILSON'S PHALAROPE *Phalaropus tricolor*

*Vagrant*

A first-winter bird, accepted by B.B.R.C., was at South Walney on 1st October 1989.

**130 RED-NECKED PHALAROPE** ***Phalaropus lobatus***

*Vagrant*

One visited the refuse tip on 19th and 20th September 1975 and, on 5th October 1980, a storm-driven individual was close to the groyne at South Walney.

**131 GREY PHALAROPE** ***Phalaropus fulicarius***

*Vagrant*

MacPherson (1892) mentions a bird shot in autumn 1891, but records are sparse — only nine from 1959 to 1989, all at South Walney and all between early September and mid-November. One long-staying individual was in the central marsh from 4th to 22nd September 1974 and an equally obliging specimen was on the gate pool from 29th September until 7th October 1982.

**132 POMARINE SKUA** ***Stercorarius pomarinus***

*Scarce*

There are two records prior to 1981; one quoted in MacPherson (1892), shot in the autumn of 1879 and the other, an adult at South Walney on 24th May 1964. Since 1981 there have been 42 records at the south end, only five of them being adults. This increase in sightings in the 1980s is probably because of better identifying from the luxury of the new hides, rather than a genuine flood in numbers. One bird stayed in the South Walney-Morecambe Bay area from 14th November 1982 until 16th January 1983.

Days recorded 1975-1989

| J | F | M | A | M | J | J | A | S | O | N | D | T |
|---|---|---|---|---|---|---|---|---|---|---|---|---|
| 2 | — | — | — | 1 | 3 | 4 | 5 | 8 | 11 | 4 | 2 | 40 |

At North Walney two birds on 3rd and 4th August 1985 were followed by an individual on 6th.

**133 ARCTIC SKUA** ***Stercorarius parasiticus***

*Uncommon*

Although recorded as rare by 19th century authors, the species is a regular spring and autumn migrant in small numbers. Between 1975 and 1989, there were sightings on 176 days, with most during the August to October period. What are probably non-breeding birds arrive in late June and in July to prey on the Walney and Foulney gull and tern colonies. The maximum count was an exceptional 11 on 14th July 1970.

Days recorded 1975-1989

| J | F | M | A | M | J | J | A | S | O | N | D | T |
|---|---|---|---|---|---|---|---|---|---|---|---|---|
| 1 | — | — | 9 | 20 | 25 | 13 | 42 | 41 | 22 | 2 | 1 | 176 |

### 134 LONG-TAILED SKUA *Stercorarius longicaudus*

*Vagrant*

MacPherson (1892) reports the shooting of about a dozen specimens on Walney in 1891, three of which he was able to examine. At least 12 others appeared in Cumbria around the same time. In more modern times the only records are of single birds at South Walney on 26th May and 13th June 1985. followed in 1988 by two adults on 8th October 1988 and a juvenile, white-headed light-phase wire casualty, which died under anaesthetic on 12th September 1989.

### 135 GREAT SKUA *Stercorarius skua*

*Uncommon*

Spencer's (1973) assertion that this species is less numerous than Arctic Skua off the Lancashire coast is borne out by South Walney records, which total 117 days between 1975 and 1989, with August, September and October providing over half of them. There are only seven records prior to 1981, and the recent increase may be due partly to better coverage (although better coverage has had no significant effect on Arctic Skua sightings), and partly to the recent rapid advance in Britain of Great Skua as a breeding bird.

Days recorded 1975-1989

| J | F | M | A | M | J | J | A | S | O | N | D | T |
|---|---|---|---|---|---|---|---|---|---|---|---|---|
| 2 | — | 1 | 5 | 4 | 11 | 11 | 36 | 24 | 16 | 6 | 1 | 117 |

Ten birds off South Walney on 12th August 1988 represents the largest ever island count.

### 136 SKUA SPECIES *Stercorarius sp.*

Since 1981 there have been 30 records at South Walney of unspecified skuas. Most have occurred in September and October, with a maximum of eight on 8th September 1983; but, intriguingly, six turned up on 26th February 1982.

### 137 MEDITERRANEAN GULL *Larus melanocephalus*

*Vagrant*

Six adults have appeared, singly, at South Walney; on 13th and 25th February 1982, 1st, 13th and 20th September 1984 and 18th October 1986.

### 138 LITTLE GULL *Larus minutus*

*Scarce*

Between 1975 and 1989, the species has been recorded on 31 days at South Walney. Most occurrences have been of single birds, except for two on 28th November 1976, nine, in Walney Channel on 18th October 1982 and 15 adults on both 17th December 1985 and 8th March 1986.

Days recorded 1975-1989

| J | F | M | A | M | J | J | A | S | O | N | D | T |
|---|---|---|---|---|---|---|---|---|---|---|---|---|
| — | 1 | 4 | 2 | 1 | 2 | — | 1 | 4 | 7 | 6 | 3 | 31 |

As a rule, Walney misses out on the moderate assemblies (peaking at 70-90 on 14th January 1984) which, appearing after WSW winds in winter, are a regular feature in Heysham Harbour. B. Minshull (pers. comm.), travelling on the Heysham-Douglas ferry, recorded ten adults on 13th November 1982 and 17 adults plus three immatures on 18th December 1982. All were approximately 10 km southwest of Walney.

## 139 SABINE'S GULL *Larus sabini*

*Vagrant*

There are two records, both of immature birds at South Walney. One was in Lighthouse Bay on 28th November 1980 and the other off the groyne on 8th December 1983.

## 140 BLACK-HEADED GULL *Larus ridibundus*

*Abundant*

The Walney colony, which, according to Mitchell (1892) can be traced back to the 18th century, has fluctuated, in both fortune and numbers, during the last 100 years. Durnford (1883) notes large numbers nesting at the north end, where the species received protection from local farmers, and a much smaller population at the south end. MacPherson (1892) reports a move from north to south induced, probably, by egg collecting — the culprits, an increasing Barrow population. Oakes (1953) asserts that South Walney's peak was in the years immediately prior to the First World War and even in 1938 there were more than 1,500 nesting pairs. Since 1945, the colony has declined significantly, due perhaps, to wartime depredations and to an increase in the number of large gulls. Barnes notes approximately 100 pairs in 1947 and, from then to the present day, no more than 45 pairs have nested in any year, and in some, there has been no breeding whatsoever. At North Walney, up to six pairs make nesting attempts in the arable fields or on the saltmarsh. The descendants of Walney's large 19th century colony are probably now resident on Foulney Island, which supports up to 1,000 pairs.

The following charts the fluctuations of the species on Walney and Foulney Islands. The earlier opinions are from contemporary authorities and can only be taken at face value. All figures are quoted as pairs.

**Black-headed Gulls breeding on Walney and Foulney**

| | SOUTH WALNEY | NORTH WALNEY | FOULNEY |
|---|---|---|---|
| 1865 | Smaller numbers than at North Walney | Very large numbers | |
| 1891 | Move from N. Walney | Move to S. Walney | |
| 1911–1914 | "Peak" numbers | | |
| 1938 | 1500 | | |
| 1947 | 100 | | |
| 1949 | 15 | | |
| 1957 | 10 | | |
| 1961 | 12 | | |
| 1962 | 18 | | |
| 1963 | 1 | | |
| 1964 | 3 | | |
| 1965 | 0 | | |
| 1966 | 20 | | |
| 1967 | 0 | | |
| 1968 | Small colony | | |
| 1971 | 20 | | |
| 1973 | 0 | | Numbers increasing to |
| 1981 | 0 | | 814 |
| 1982 | 10 | | 1000 |
| 1983 | 10 | | 1100 |
| 1984 | 4 | | 750 |
| 1985 | 40 | | 750 |
| 1986 | 45 | | 650 |
| 1987 | 30 | | 700 |
| 1988 | 0 | | 1000 |
| 1989 | 1 | | 750 |

Considering the large numbers that now breed on adjacent Foulney Island, sightings at South Walney although occurring regularly, are of relatively small numbers. Peak numbers are 510 returning birds to Foulney on 13th March 1989 and 300 post-breeding birds in Haws Bed on 16th August 1984. The island's main roosts are at Tummer Hill Marsh, Wylock Marsh and the north end, at which a maximum 2,050 were logged in September 1978.

Average maxima 1975-1989

| | J | F | M | A | M | J | J | A | S | O | N | D |
|---|---|---|---|---|---|---|---|---|---|---|---|---|
| SW | 28 | 34 | 72 | 51 | 26 | 28 | 48 | 70 | 55 | 33 | 21 | 32 |
| NW | 141 | 118 | 120 | 46 | 35 | 45 | 109 | 243 | 379 | 142 | 123 | 165 |

**Ringing and recoveries**

There are three examples all involving birds ringed as nestlings. An individual caught in mid-June 1959 at Noorden, Zuid Holland, Netherlands (600 km east-southeast) was found dead on Walney in late February 1969; a bird from Limfjorden, Jylland, Denmark (900 km east), was a Walney tide-line corpse in October 1975; and a Barrow-found specimen of October 1984 had been ringed in mid-May 1978 at Milicz, Wroclaw, Poland (1,500 km east).

### 141 RING-BILLED GULL *Larus delawarensis*

*Vagrant*

There are two records both accepted by B.B.R.C., and both involving adults on the spit; the first on 15th and 18th April 1984 and the second on January 31st 1986.

### 142 COMMON GULL *Larus canus*

*Fairly common*

Between August and March, the species is recorded regularly at South Walney with small numbers at the groyne or roosting on the spit. The maximum count is 40 in October 1969 and March 1970.

Average maxima 1975-1989

| J | F | M | A | M | J | J | A | S | O | N | D |
|---|---|---|---|---|---|---|---|---|---|---|---|
| 11 | 10 | 6 | 3 | 2 | — | 1 | 2 | 3 | 12 | 8 | 6 |

The species is not as frequent elsewhere on the island, with a peak of 18 on 21st February 1986 at the north end.

**Ringing and recoveries**

Few details are available for a bird ringed at Stavanger, Norway (800 km north-east) and recovered on Walney in 1958. However, another Norwegian bird, ringed on Neroga Island, Stangvik in July 1955, was found on Walney in December 1957.

### 143 LESSER BLACK-BACKED GULL *Larus fuscus*

*Abundant*

Durnford (1983) describes the species as resident, but nesting at South Walney was not recorded until 1926; and that was unsuccessful. By 1934, however, more than 200 pairs were nesting there, an increase attributed by Oakes (1953) to the destruction of two small colonies in North Lancashire and to a superabundance of egg-collecting at Foulshaw Moss (Westmorland). Band (quoted in Oakes 1953) considers that, in 1947, "not fewer than 500 pairs were breeding at South Walney" and, in the ensuing years, the colony increased rapidly. Brown's meticulous count of 1965 realised 9,500 pairs; 17,500 pairs were obtained by MacRoberts and MacRoberts (1972) for 1969; and Verbeek (1977) reckoned on 21,000 pairs for 1974. The population has subsequently remained fairly constant with Hosey and Goodridge (1980) producing 19,000 pairs for 1978, and later estimates showing some 15,000 pairs in 1988.

Many previously available nesting sites have been lost to sand and gravel extraction and avian botulism may also have aided the small decline.

Post breeding numbers drop sharply at the end of August and birds return in force during late February and early March. Mid-winter figures are generally low with an average monthly maximum of about twenty.

**Ringing and recoveries**

No other species has been subjected to as much study on South Walney. Between 1961 and 1966, over 14,700 pulli were ringed and Ian Spence conducted a slightly less energetic study between 1981 and 1987, with the ringing of 6,043 pulli. The 1960s study indicated that most first-year birds followed the western seaboard through Britain, France, Portugal and Spain to North Africa. The recoveries also showed that a few birds travelled across Britain in a southeasterly direction over the Midlands and southeast England. There were three instances of birds summering in Belgium and Holland. The 1980s study showed a similar pattern, but strangely from 196 recoveries, there have been none from France. A breakdown of the combined studies yields 11 recoveries from France between Morbihan and Landes (all from the 1960s study); seven in north Spain between Santander and La Coruna; eight in south Spain between Sevilla and Malaga; a solitary east Spain recovery from Valencia; 51 in Portugal, with most between Porto and Lisboa; 26 from Morocco between Tangier and El Aaiun (the latter being the most southerly recovery of a South Walney Lesser Black-backed Gull), two in Belgium, and singles in Denmark, Holland and the Canary Islands. Virtually all of these recoveries relate to first and second -year birds. Both Wilson (1966) and Spence (1987) conclude that most first and second -year birds are back in Britain nine months after leaving. However, both also confirm that some birds linger in Iberia and Morocco, although Spence's recoveries indicate that no third-summer or older birds have been recovered from this wintering area.

As with the Herring Gull, there is evidence of inter-colonial recruitment indicated by the following:

ringed as a pullus on 31st July 1968 at Eilean Balnagowan, Loch Linnhe, Strathclyde was found dead at South Walney (318 km south -southeast) on 23rd August 1980; and another pullus ringed on 26th June 1986 on the Calf of Man, Isle of Man, was found at South Walney (103 km east) on 12th July 1987.

The oldest Walney individual was ringed as a pullus on 7th July 1962, and found dead at South Walney on 13th November 1988, aged 26 years and 130 days.

An odd return was of a pullus ringed at South Walney on 2nd July 1964 whose ring was subsequently found on a Mallard shot over the River Soar in Leicestershire.

## 144 HERRING GULL *Larus argentatus*

*Abundant*

Harting (1864), Durnford (1883), MacPherson (1892) and Mitchell (1892) note the abundance of the species, but all categorically state that breeding did not occur. According to Oakes (1953), sporadic nesting at the south end began in 1904, but it was not until 1928 that, in company with Lesser Black-backed Gulls, the species was securely established. By 1934 the population had increased to 35 pairs while in 1947, Band (quoted in Oakes 1953) counted 120 pairs. Brown's survey in 1965 produced 9,500 pairs and subsequent counts until the late 1970s indicated an astonishing increase. MacRoberts and MacRoberts (1972) recorded 17,500 pairs for 1969 and Verbeek (1977) calculated 25,000 pairs. Since Hosey and Goodridge's study of 1978, when a figure of 22,000 pairs was obtained, the species has suffered an equally remarkable decline to 12,000 pairs in 1984 and 8,000 pairs in 1988. Sand and gravel extraction has reduced the available nesting sites and it is possible that avian botulism may also have contributed in no small way.

Territories are vacated by the end of August, but large numbers remain in Morecambe Bay throughout the autumn and early winter and some pairs are back on site by the third week in October. In mid-winter, there are huge congregations on the spit at South Walney and at the refuse tip.

**Ringing and recoveries**

During the early 1960s a large number of Herring Gull pulli were ringed at South Walney by a variety of ringers. The majority of recoveries for these birds indicate that they rarely move out of the coastal area of Northwest England and are chiefly found between Walney Island and Southport (c. 55 km south). There are relatively few exceptions but do include the following pulli; ringed on 9th July

1961 and found dead at Dunkineely, Co. Donegal, Eire (390 km west-northwest) on 18th March 1962; ringed on 4th July 1963 and found dead in Jutland, Denmark (800 km east) on 5th June 1972; ringed on 24th August 1968 and found dying at Leyburn, North Yorkshire (100 km east-northeast) on 15th April 1970; ringed on 23rd April 1966 and found dead at Silloth, Cumbria (88 km north) on 22nd October 1974; ringed 3rd July 1982 and found dead in West Kennet, Marlborough, Wiltshire (307 km south-southeast) on 2nd February 1986; ringed 3rd July 1983 and found at Ramsey, Isle of Man (82 km west) on 21st March 1984. Inter-colonial recruitment is indicated by a 1963 South Walney pullus being culled at the Tarnbrook Fell colony, Lancaster (39 km east) on 15th May 1978. Additionally, further inter-colonial connections are indicated by the following pulli recoveries:

ringed at Newborough Warren, Anglesey and found dead on the nest at South Walney (125 km northeast) on 3rd May 1976; ringed at Puffin Island, Anglesey on 17th June 1967 and found at South Walney (100 km northeast) on 2nd September 1976; ringed on the Calf of Man, Isle of Man on 1st July 1976 and found at South Walney (105 km east) on 23rd August 1980; ringed at Little Ross Island, Dumfries on 10th July 1979 and found at South Walney (98 km southeast) on 15th July 1987. As yet the oldest bird is an individual of just over 21 years, ringed as a pullus on 6th July 1965 at South Walney and recovered dead on 1st July 1986.

There have been a handful of rather odd recoveries; one flew into a bulldozer in Barrow-in-Furness in 1966 two years after ringing; another collided with a glider (or possibly vice-versa) over North Walney in 1980 four years after ringing; and another ringing return thought-provokingly stated "ring found in hotel bedroom, Ulpha, Cumbria".

## 145 ICELAND GULL *Larus glaucoides*

*Vagrant*

South Walney's only sightings involve an adult on 21st December 1963, a first-winter bird on 17th April 1984 and a third-winter bird on 26th February 1989; although a second-winter bird was on playing fields in Central Walney on 14th April 1985. As Durnford (1883) states, the species is certainly a 'rare visitor', and it is surprising that the more comprehensive observation of the last ten years has not increased, as it has with Glaucous Gull, the number of sightings.

## 146 GLAUCOUS GULL *Larus hyperboreus*

*Scarce*

At South Walney, between 1962 and 1974, there are ten records involving, probably, six individuals. From then until the end of 1989, the species has been recorded on 162 days. The increase, in all likelihood, is due to greater scrutiny of gull roosts. The majority of sightings are between late February and early May including a peak of four, two adults and two first winter birds, on 20th February 1984.

Days recorded 1975-1989

| J | F | M | A | M | J | J | A | S | O | N | D | T |
|---|---|---|---|---|---|---|---|---|---|---|---|---|
| 14 | 42 | 38 | 17 | 17 | — | — | 2 | 7 | 7 | 9 | 9 | 162 |

At North Walney, an adult was visible, almost daily, from January to April and from September to December 1982; other individuals have been occasionally seen in late winter.

## 147 GREAT BLACK-BACKED GULL *Larus marinus*

*Common*

During the 17th century, according to Leigh (quoted in Mitchell 1892), vast numbers of the species bred at South Walney. Barnes (pers. comm.) notes a single pair in 1946, but Spencer (1973) describes the colony as long disused with resettlement starting in 1955. Almost annually since that year, there have been small increases and in 1985 there were 44 nests, 54 in 1987 and 70 in 1989. Most pairs make use of the more isolated shingle outcrops and islets left behind by the sand and gravel extractions.

**Number of nests 1955-1985**

| '55 | '60 | '65 | '70 | '75 | '80 | '85 | '90 |
|---|---|---|---|---|---|---|---|
| 1 | 5 | 8 | 10 | 18 | 24 | 44 | '75 |

Winter roosts gather on the Spit at South Walney, on Sheep Island, Wylock Marsh and Tummer Hill Marsh, and at North Walney; the island's mid-winter population contains up to 300 birds.

**Ringing and recoveries**

Of 421 pulli ringed, 362 have been caught since 1982. A colour ringing scheme commenced in 1985 and hopefully will determine whether the increase of Great Black-backed Gulls at South Walney is due to Walney born birds returning to set up territory. The fruits should be seen in spring 1989 and 1990. Meanwhile the ringing programme has shown certain trends amongst the dispersal of young birds with most first and second-year recoveries from the coastal strip between the Esk Estuary, Cumbria and the Dee Estuary, Cheshire. There are four exceptions all involving birds ringed as pulli at South Walney:

ringed on 29th June 1985 and recovered at Kendal (48 km northeast) on the 13th April 1986; ringed on 3rd July 1983 and found at Ramsey, Isle of Man (82 km west) on 17th January 1984; ringed on 24th June 1987 and found at Carlingford Lough, Co. Louth, Eire (195 km west) on 7th November 1987; ringed on 1st July 1987 and found at Ballyteigue Burrow, Co. Wexford, Eire (313 km southwest) on 24th January 1988. Older birds are supposed to be much more sedentary but South Walney's only adult recovery ringed on 18th June 1977 was found dead on 5th May 1982 at Rockcliffe, Carlisle, Cumbria (102 km north-northeast) possibly on territory. In addition a slightly younger bird ringed on 27th June 1981 was found dead at Langness, Isle of Man (103 km west) on 31st October 1983 and a precocious individual, perhaps keen on establishing territory, was culled at

Tarnbrook Fell, Lancaster (39 km east) on 20th May 1987, having been ringed at South Walney on 19th June 1984.

## 148 KITTIWAKE *Rissa tridactyla*

*Common*

Durnford (1883) describes the species as more plentiful in winter, but this is not reflected in South Walney records. These indicate its appearance in all months, with most in spring and autumn and fewest in July and December. Westerly winds and squally conditions often bring birds into Morecambe Bay and, even, into Walney Channel; but most sightings are off Hilpsford Point with peaks of 345 on 9th September 1965 and 300 on 8th September 1984.

Average maxima 1975-1989

| J | F | M | A | M | J | J | A | S | O | N | D |
|---|---|---|---|---|---|---|---|---|---|---|---|
| 22 | 16 | 25 | 19 | 12 | 9 | 6 | 28 | 39 | 51 | 28 | 10 |

Off North Walney 144 were seen on 24th May 1988.

**Ringing and recoveries**

A nestling ringed at Goulien, Finisterre, France (677 km south), was a tideline corpse on 26th December 1983 at South Walney.

## 149 SANDWICH TERN *Sterna sandvicensis*

*Abundant*

According to Oakes (1953), the species had nested at the north end since 1843, but had declined to 40 pairs by 1880. The site was abandoned in 1889 and the birds appear to have moved to South Walney, where nesting had been recorded since 1879. Numbers continued to decrease and there was no breeding in 1901. By 1909, recolonisation had begun with four pairs, rising to 30 pairs in 1912. Another decline took place during the First World War, but, afterwards, there was steady expansion, peaking in 1930 when Robinson (mentioned in Oakes 1953) ringed 535 young birds. The colony was virtually destroyed in 1932 by predatory Herring and Lesser Black-backed Gulls (Oakes). Most of the Sandwich Terns appear to have moved to Ravenglass (50 km to the north of South Walney), where 12 pairs in 1930 had become 360 pairs in 1932 (British Birds Vol.26). A second site at South Walney fared rather better, however, and in 1938 over 300 young were ringed. Defensive activities during wartime, which included billeting of up to 200 troops at the south end, reduced the colony, but, by 1947, 40 pairs were nesting and this had advanced to 350 pairs by 1949. Between 1951 and 1968, the number of nesting pairs was never more than 21 and from 1958 to 1964, there was no breeding whatsoever. A brief recolonisation took place in 1969 when 250 pairs nested, but from 1972 breeding birds were totally absent, until 1986 when 45 pairs bred, followed by 180 pairs in 1987. The table on page 124 attempts to list the data available.

Returning birds arrive at South Walney in small numbers towards the end of March, and large flocks are occasionally seen from mid-April to early May with records of 400 on 20th April 1966 and 1st May 1983. From May onwards, the species is regularly sighted around the Walney coast, usually journeying to and from their major feeding area, the Duddon Estuary. By the end of the breeding season, small movements south are noticeable offshore with 250 on 25th August 1968 and 100 on 5th September 1983.

Average maxima 1975-1989

| J | F | M | A | M | J | J | A | S | O | N | D |
|---|---|---|---|---|---|---|---|---|---|---|---|
| — | — | 5 | 68 | 79 | 99 | 91 | 49 | 47 | 3 | — | — |

**Sandwich Terns breeding** (p-pairs; n-nests; y-young; p.a.-per annum)

| | SOUTH WALNEY | NORTH WALNEY | FOULNEY ISLAND |
|---|---|---|---|
| 1843 | | some breeding | |
| 1864 | | 17(p) | |
| 1879 | 3(p) | | |
| 1880 | | 40(p) | |
| 1890 | 6(p) | | |
| 1909-13 | 18(p)p.a. | | |
| 1921-24 | 30-92(y) | | |
| 1925 | 117(y) | | |
| 1926-29 | 63-399(y) | | |
| 1930 | 535(y) | | |
| 1932 | wiped out | | |
| 1933 | 50(p) | 25(p) | |
| 1940 | 300(y) | | |
| 1946 | | 1(p) | |
| 1947 | 40(p) | | |
| 1949 | 350(p) | | |
| 1950 | 45(p) | | |
| 1954-57 | 11-21(p) | | |
| 1958-61 | | | 2-3(p) |
| 1962 | 2(p) | | 230(p) |
| 1963 | | | 400(p) |
| 1964 | | | 500(p) |
| 1965 | | | 1(p) |
| 1966 | | | |
| 1967 | | | 20(p) |
| 1968 | 'successful' | | |
| 1969 | 250(p) | | |
| 1970 | 200(p) | | |
| 1971 | 200(p) | | |
| 1974 | | | 184(n) |
| 1975 | | | 30(p) |
| 1976 | | | 150(p) |
| 1977 | | | 350(n) |
| 1978 | | | 350(n) |
| 1979 | | | 700(p) |
| 1980 | | | 600(n) |
| 1981 | | | 500(n) |
| 1982 | | | 1400(p) |
| 1983 | | | 275(n) |
| 1984 | | | 1600(p) |
| 1985 | | | 1000(n) |
| 1986 | 45(n) | | 400(n) |
| 1987 | 180(n) | | 550(n) |
| 1988 | | | 700(p) |
| 1989 | | | 770(p) |

## 150 ROSEATE TERN *Sterna dougallii*

*Scarce*

Despite shooting three birds in 1864, Hartings's account of his visit to Walney is full of identification uncertainties; although Durnford, 20 years later, states that the species formerly nested. Oakes (1953) regards the species as breeding at long and irregular intervals and asserts that single pairs were nesting in 1865 and 1876. Although no site is specified, North Walney is the likely source of 19th century records; whereas the next confirmed records of one pair in 1926 and six pairs in 1927 were probably at South Walney. This site held three pairs in 1945 and breeding was successful in 1949. The longest period of colonisation was from 1958 to 1961 culminating in eight nests in the final year. Roseate Terns were first recorded as nesting on Foulney Island by Hancock (Mitchell 1892) in 1840, while single nests were found at North Walney in 1864, 1865 and 1876.

**Roseate Terns breeding** (nests, except where stated)

| | SOUTH WALNEY | NORTH WALNEY |
|---|---|---|
| 1926 | 1 pair | |
| 1927 | 6 pairs | |
| 1945 | 3 pairs | |
| 1949 | successful | |
| 1958 | 3 | 2 pairs |
| 1959 | 6 | 6 |
| 1960 | 5 | 6 |
| 1960 | 8 | 5 |
| 1962 | | 5 |
| 1963 | | 12 |
| 1964 | | 7 |
| 1967 | | 2 |

No records in other years to 1989.

Between 1963 and 1989 the species has been recorded on only 31 days at South Walney; more significantly, perhaps only one record is within the period 1972 to 1981 and the species is now scarce. The maximum count is five on 31st August 1967.

Days recorded 1975-1989

| J | F | M | A | M | J | J | A | S | O | N | D | T |
|---|---|---|---|---|---|---|---|---|---|---|---|---|
| — | — | — | — | 1 | 3 | 2 | 2 | 2 | — | — | — | 10 |

Elsewhere on the island, two birds were seen at Biggar Bank on 14th August 1963 and two at North Walney on 30th May and 7th June 1983.

## 151 COMMON TERN *Sterna hirundo*

*Abundant*

In the late 19th century, the species bred at the north end , and, in 1864, Harting counted "about a score of nests". As with the Sandwich Tern, disturbance by the ever-growing Barrow population caused a shift to South Walney and a decline in breeding, with only 12 nests in 1905. South Walney was abandoned either pre-First World War or during it; but the species returned in 1919 and increased to such an extent that 460 young were ringed in 1929, 610 in 1930 and 911 in 1935. Wartime defence activities hampered the success of the colony, but 1947 produced an improvement with 250 nests. From 1954 there was a decline (compare Sandwich Tern) with one nest in 1960 and 1961 and none from 1962 to

1969. Brief recolonisation took place during 1970 to 1972 with up to 300 pairs, but, since then, nesting has only been annual in the 1980s with, encouragingly 40 pairs in 1985 and 1986, followed by 70 pairs in 1987.

**Common Terns breeding** (p-pairs; n-nests; y-young; p.a.-per annum)

| | SOUTH WALNEY | NORTH WALNEY | FOULNEY ISLAND |
|---|---|---|---|
| 1864 | | 20(n) | |
| 1905 | 12(n) | | |
| 1913 | 100(n) | | |
| 1929 | 460(y) | | |
| 1930 | 610(y) | | |
| 1934 | 879(y) | | |
| 1935 | 911(y) | | |
| 1938 | 700(y) | 12(p) | |
| 1947 | 250(n) | | |
| 1954 | 65(n) | | |
| 1955 | 47(n) | | |
| 1956 | 56(n) | | |
| 1957 | | | 102(n) |
| 1959 | 5(p) | | 450(n) |
| 1960 | 1(p) | | 450(n) |
| 1961 | 1(p) | | 450(n) |
| 1962 | 2(p) | | 550(n) |
| 1963-67 | | | 600(n)-96(n) |
| 1968 | 'successful' | | |
| 1969 | 'successful' | | 10(p) |
| 1970 | 300(p) | | |
| 1971 | 200(n) | | |
| 1972 | 35(p) | | |
| 1973-80 | | | 120(n)p.a. on average |
| 1981 | 1(n) | | 62(n) |
| 1982 | 10(p) | | 120(n) |
| 1983 | 20(p) | | 67(n) |
| 1984 | 20(p) | | 116(n) |
| 1985 | 40(p) | | 48(n) |
| 1986 | 45(p) | | 20(n) |
| 1987 | 70(p) | | 5(n) |
| 1988 | 4(p) | | 60(p) |
| 1989 | | | 40(p) |

At South Walney, returning birds are seen at the end of April and larger flocks are recorded in May with a peak of 120 on 9th May 1986. Throughout the breeding season, birds are seen around the Walney coast, flying to and from the Duddon Estuary; and towards the end of July, movements south are seen offshore, with occasional heavy passage, such as 600 on 14th July 1970 and 400 on 30th August 1989.

Average maxima 1975-1989

| J | F | M | A | M | J | J | A | S | O | N | D |
|---|---|---|---|---|---|---|---|---|---|---|---|
| — | — | — | 4 | 36 | 26 | 37 | 62 | 17 | — | — | — |

**Ringing and recoveries**

Two birds, both ringed as nestlings have been found on Walney. A June 1982 specimen from Shotton, Clwyd, North Wales (105 km south) was found dead in the following September and a July 1983 individual from the Ribble Estuary, Lancashire (45 km south) was located on the tide-line in the subsequent September.

## 152 ARCTIC TERN *Sterna paradisaea*

*Common*

Harting found four nests at the north end in 1864 and, as with the other breeding terns, there was a shift to the south end towards the end of the century. According to Kirkman, 50 pairs were at this locality in 1905, while Rogers (Oakes 1953) counted 100 nests in 1913. This is probably the maximum attained by the species and there is no further evidence of breeding at the south end until 1930. No figures are available, but Robinson (Oakes 1953) notes a small but steady increase between 1932 and 1935. Gowland found 15 pairs in 1949 and Sheldon 75 pairs in 1955; but the colony was then abandoned until 1970 when a brief recolonisation peaked at 150 nests in 1971. Since that year, despite Common Tern and Little Tern success at South Walney, Arctics have only appeared in 1986 when eleven nests were located, 1987 with 18 nests, and 1988 with four.

**Arctic Terns breeding** (n-nests; p-pairs; p.a.-per annum)

| | SOUTH WALNEY | NORTH WALNEY | FOULNEY ISLAND |
|---|---|---|---|
| 1864 | | 4(n) | |
| 1905 | 50(p) | | |
| 1913 | 100(p) | | |
| 1932-35 | small increase | | |
| 1949 | 15(p) | | |
| 1955 | 75(n) | | 38(n) |
| 1956-64 | | | Average 148(n) p.a. |
| 1965 | | 4(p) | 100(n) |
| 1966 | | 10(p) | 40(n) |
| 1967 | | | 60(n) |
| 1968 | 'successful' | | 25(n) |
| 1969 | 'successful' | 1(n) | 10(p) |
| 1970 | 50(p) | | |
| 1971 | 150(p) | | |
| 1972 | 2(n) | | |
| 1973-85 | | | Average 90(n) p.a. |
| 1986 | 11(n) | | 36(n) |
| 1987 | 18(n) | | 25(n) |
| 1988 | 4(n) | | 44(p) |
| 1989 | | | 35(p) |

N.B. Predation by a Little Owl on Foulney Island in 1964; and by one at South Walney in 1986 which produced nine corpses.

Identification problems have probably led to past under-recording of this species, but, even with greater diligence in the 1980s, it is still not a daily performer during its season. Peak counts include 36 on 5th July 1987 and 30 on 25th April 1981.

Average maxima 1975-1989

| J | F | M | A | M | J | J | A | S | O | N | D |
|---|---|---|---|---|---|---|---|---|---|---|---|
| — | — | — | 2 | 6 | 8 | 7 | 4 | 1 | — | — | — |

**Ringing and recoveries**
Two Scottish birds, both ringed as nestlings, have been found on Walney. An individual from Tentsmuir, Fife (250 km northeast) was recovered in July 1961 and a specimen from Brora, Highland Region (420 km north) was a Little Owl victim of July 1986. In addition, a Foulney Island ringed pullus of 1964 was another unfortunate of July 1986.

**153 COMMIC TERN** ***Sterna sp.***
*Abundant*
Migrating Common or Arctic Terns are seen regularly off Walney's southwest coast in August and September with peaks at South Walney of 2,000 on 28th August and 5,000 on 1st September 1966. More recently, the maximum has been 1,800 in three hours on 21st August 1983.

**154 LITTLE TERN** ***Sterna albifrons***
*Common*
Harting found three nests at the north end of the island in 1864 and Durnford (1883) regarded the species as more plentiful than the Sandwich Tern. MacPherson found 18 nests in 1891 and, although the precise site is not stated, it can be assumed that, at the end of the 19th century, the species, like the other breeding terns, moved to the south end. There, Kirkman counted six pairs in 1905 and Rogers eight nests in 1907 and 14 pairs in 1913. According to Oakes (1953), this figure was the peak until 1932, when Robinson reported an increase. No records are available for the period of the Second World War, but it is likely that defence activities resulted in reduced breeding. Figures for 1946 show 12 pairs at the north end and two pairs at the south, while Bowden, in 1949, noted about 40 pairs on the island. Since 1950, nesting has been sporadic at South Walney. No more than six pairs had nested in any year until 1969, when a flurry of activity resulted in ten pairs, followed by 14 pairs in 1971. Absent for the next nine years, the early 1980s have seen increased breeding success, from one pair in 1981 to 24 pairs in 1984 and 30 pairs in 1985. The apparent loyalty of the species to traditional sites induces prospecting pairs, each year, to North Walney and in 1979, six pairs attempted breeding. The newly formed South Walney colony probably consists of birds displaced from North Walney, Sandscale, Millom and, to a lesser extent, Foulney Island.

**Little Terns breeding** (p-pairs; n-nests)

| | SOUTH WALNEY | NORTH WALNEY | FOULNEY ISLAND |
|---|---|---|---|
| 1864 | | 3(n) | |
| 1891 | 18(n) | | |
| 1905 | 6(p) | | |
| 1907 | 8(n) | | |
| 1910 | 12(n) | | |
| 1913 | 14(p) | | |
| 1932 | 'small increase' | | |
| 1946 | 2(p) | 12(p) | |
| 1947 | 3(p) | | |
| 1955 | | | 6(n) |
| 1956 | | | 5(n) |
| 1957 | 6(n) | | 13(n) |
| 1958 | 2(n) | 29(n) | |
| 1959 | | | 36(n) |
| 1960 | | | 29(n) |
| 1961 | 3(n) | | 39(n) |
| 1962-66 | | 'present' | 29(n) decreasing to |
| 1967 | | | 5(p) |
| 1968 | 'successful' | | 4(n) |
| 1969 | 10(p) | 'nested' | 7(p) |
| 1970 | 10(p) | | |
| 1971 | 14(n) | | 4(n) |
| 1979 | | | 15(p) |
| 1980 | | | 7(n) |
| 1981 | 1(n) | | 25(n) |
| 1982 | 14(n) | | 9(n) |
| 1983 | 25(n) | | 40(n) |
| 1984 | 25(n) | | 50(p) |
| 1985 | 30(n) | | 18(n) |
| 1986 | 8(n) | | 21(n) |
| 1987 | 18(n) | | 2(n) |
| 1988 | 7(p) | | 17(p) |
| 1989 | | | 8(p) |

Small numbers are seen at South Walney towards the end of April and, throughout the breeding season, birds are commonly seen around the Walney coast journeying to and from the Duddon Estuary. Small groups of birds moving south are regularly seen in early autumn with a maximum of 30 on 6th September 1967.

Average maxima 1975-1989

| J | F | M | A | M | J | J | A | S | O | N | D |
|---|---|---|---|---|---|---|---|---|---|---|---|
| — | — | — | 2 | 14 | 23 | 28 | 11 | 1 | — | — | — |

**Ringing and recoveries**

There are three examples all recovered on Walney in the late 1950s. Birds from Angus, Scotland (280 km north-northeast) and Suffolk (350 km southeast) were found in June 1959, and an individual from Aberlady, Lothian, Scotland (175 km north-northeast) was located in July 1957, two years after being ringed.

## 155 BLACK TERN *Chlidonias niger*

*Rare*

At South Walney, the species has been recorded on 24 days in the period 1975-1989. Most records relate to autumn sightings, but peak numbers have occurred in late spring with four on 4th June 1971 and 4th May 1980.

Days recorded 1975-1989

| J | F | M | A | M | J | J | A | S | O | N | D | T |
|---|---|---|---|---|---|---|---|---|---|---|---|---|
| — | — | — | — | 5 | 3 | 1 | 6 | 6 | 3 | — | — | 24 |

A single was seen at North Walney on 9th October 1982.

## 156 GUILLEMOT *Uria aalge*

*Fairly common*

Durnford (1883) and MacPherson (1892) both refer to the frequency with which corpses were found on Walney's tideline. South Walney figures indicate a southerly passage in autumn which was recognised by Spencer (1973), but which scarcely add up to the spring flocks mentioned by Oakes (1953). January provides fewest sightings and August yields the lowest numbers. The peak count is 110 birds on 10th October 1989.

Average maxima 1975-1989

| J | F | M | A | M | J | J | A | S | O | N | D |
|---|---|---|---|---|---|---|---|---|---|---|---|
| 5 | 5 | 2 | 2 | 5 | 7 | 1 | 1 | 4 | 22 | 6 | 4 |

**Ringing and recoveries**

A bird ringed on Bardsey Island, North Wales (180 km southwest) in June 1954 was found dead on Walney in the following December. Additionally, a nestling from the Isle of Canna, Inner Hebrides, Highland Region, Scotland (300 km northwest) ringed in July 1983 was recovered dead in January 1984.

## 157 RAZORBILL *Alca torda*

*Fairly common*

Durnford (1883) and Oakes (1953) state that the species occurred in considerable numbers off the coast during autumn and winter. Records at South Walney are, however, decidedly scant before 1980 compared with figures since, and at one time sightings were confined to the rarities log. The bird has appeared in all months, but with an occasional spring passage including peaks of 30 on 13th February and 13th March 1982 and a more obvious autumn passage with 110 on 23rd October 1981 and 420 on 10th October 1989.

Average maxima 1975-1989

| J | F | M | A | M | J | J | A | S | O | N | D |
|---|---|---|---|---|---|---|---|---|---|---|---|
| 4 | 5 | 5 | 2 | 3 | 3 | 1 | — | 2 | 50 | 4 | 3 |

**Ringing and recoveries**

The only indication of the species' origin is indicated by a single recovery of an adult ringed on Berneray, Western Isles, Scotland (375 km northeast) in June 1979 and found dead on Piel Island in December 1983.

### 158 BLACK GUILLEMOT *Cepphus grylle*

*Scarce*

At South Walney, the species has been recorded on 115 days in the period 1975 to 1989. Most are seen between August and November with a maximum of three on 25th August 1980 and 27th September 1981. Storm-driven birds occasionally take up short term residence, usually in Walney Channel.

Days recorded 1975-1989

| J | F | M | A | M | J | J | A | S | O | N | D | T |
|---|---|---|---|---|---|---|---|---|---|---|---|---|
| 4 | 2 | 2 | 2 | 2 | 5 | 3 | 11 | 30 | 32 | 16 | 6 | 115 |

One was seen off Biggar Bank on 31st July 1984.

### 159 LITTLE AUK *Alle alle*

*Rare*

Durnford (1883) states that the species had been washed up on the shores of the island and MacPherson (1892) cites an example of a corpse retrieved in November 1890. At South Walney, all records have occurred during or after periods of strong northwesterlies. Two birds were seen on 24th April 1966, singles on 17th May 1970 and 10th October 1976 and, on 8th March 1981, 16 flew west out of Morecambe Bay. Two storm-driven birds were off the west shore on 29th November 1982 and on 13th January 1984, one sheltered under a Land Rover at Coastguard Cottages. Also in 1984, one remained in the large gravel pool from 15th to 20th December.

Individuals were seen on 9th January and 9th December 1985, 10th February 1986 and two birds flying into Morecambe Bay on 4th December 1987. A single was on North Walney on 9th February 1984 and a corpse was picked up there on 26th January 1982.

### 160 PUFFIN *Fratercula arctica*

*Scarce*

Durnford (1883), MacPherson (1892) and Oakes (1953) refer to tideline specimens and, prior to 1973, South Walney's only two records were of dead birds. 1973 produced a single on 6th May and in the period 1975 to 1989, the species has been recorded on 44 days. Most have been seen in the autumn, with peaks of eight on 10th October 1984 and six on 30th October 1978.

Days recorded 1975-1989

| J | F | M | A | M | J | J | A | S | O | N | D | T |
|---|---|---|---|---|---|---|---|---|---|---|---|---|
| 3 | 5 | 3 | 2 | 4 | 4 | — | — | 6 | 10 | 4 | 3 | 44 |

### 161 AUK SPECIES

*Common*

Sightings of unidentified auks have occurred at South Walney in all months with, in some years, a marked passage during October and November. The peak count is 480 on 24th October 1981.

Average maxima 1975-1989

| J | F | M | A | M | J | J | A | S | O | N | D |
|---|---|---|---|---|---|---|---|---|---|---|---|
| 4 | 6 | 4 | 3 | 7 | 6 | 2 | 2 | 4 | 89 | 15 | 5 |

### 162 PALLAS'S SANDGROUSE *Syrrhaptes paradoxus*

*Vagrant*

Major irruptions into Europe occurred in 1863, 1888, 1908 and birds were seen on the island in the first two of these. MacPherson (1892) maintains that the earliest public announcement of the species in England appeared in 'The Times' of 26th May 1863, which reported a covey of 14 on Walney Island, two of which had been shot. The irruption of 1888 reached Walney on 19th May and included 21 birds on 4th June, 57 at North Walney on 11th June and eight at South Walney on 17th June. During this period, seven were shot and sent for preservation, while another two were killed, one in late summer and one on 20th December. The suggestion of nesting on the island is pure conjecture, but it happened in Yorkshire in that year and young were seen in Elgin in 1889.

### 163 ROCK DOVE/FERAL PIGEON *Columbia livia*

*Common*

The single Rock Dove record on 14th December 1969 at South Walney is best ignored, considering the frequency with which homing pigeons use the island on their travels.

### 164 STOCK DOVE *Columbia oenas*

*Fairly common*

Though Durnford (1883) asserts that the species nested in considerable numbers on Walney Island, Kirkman could find only one pair in 1905. Oakes (1953) records the bird as regularly nesting but diminishing during the 1940s, while Benson (pers. comm.) states that it has not nested on North Walney since the Second World War. At South Walney, nesting by one to three pairs has probably occurred annually for many years, but the only reports of confirmed breeding are for 1974, 1982 and from 1985 to 1988. Single-figure numbers are fairly constant during the year, but passages are occasionally recorded with 14 on 6th April 1980. Autumn and winter gatherings, with a maximum of 20 on 5th November 1983 and 23rd February 1986, probably involve the Piel Island population of four or five pairs.

Average maxima 1975-1989

| J | F | M | A | M | J | J | A | S | O | N | D |
|---|---|---|---|---|---|---|---|---|---|---|---|
| 4.8 | 4.7 | 3.8 | 4.5 | 3.0 | 3.5 | 4.1 | 4.5 | 2.8 | 2.1 | 4.5 | 4.6 |

Elsewhere on Walney, appearances are spasmodic, although the species is probably under-recorded; the maximum of three was at North Walney on 1st April 1984.

### 165 WOODPIGEON *Columba palumbus*

*Uncommon*

There are few nesting records, but Benson (pers. comm.) states that the species did not nest on North Walney prior to the Second World War. Since then and the subsequent growth of Willow Woods, two to three pairs nest there each year, one or two pairs in North Scale village and two or three in the Biggar and Long Rein Point area. Despite this proximity to breeding birds, sightings at South Walney are scarce. In the period 1975 to 1989 birds were only seen on 100 days, mostly in June and November; but occasionally, hard weather movement is noted with 24 birds on 3rd December 1981 and six on 26th January 1984.

Days recorded 1975-1989

| J | F | M | A | M | J | J | A | S | O | N | D | T |
|---|---|---|---|---|---|---|---|---|---|---|---|---|
| 5 | 3 | 7 | 7 | 9 | 17 | 8 | 7 | 4 | 3 | 21 | 9 | 100 |

At North Walney, large flocks occasionally have been seen feeding in the fields of stubble, with 96 on 24th November 1983 and 70 on 1st December 1983.

### 166 COLLARED DOVE *Streptopelia decaocto*

*Fairly common*

Since the mid-70s, a small breeding population has established itself in the gardens of North Scale and Vickerstown amounting, probably, to between 10 and 12 pairs. At South Walney, the first sighting was of a single bird on 27th April 1963, but records increased only slowly well into the 1970s; since then birds have appeared more frequently and in greater numbers.

Days recorded

| | J | F | M | A | M | J | J | A | S | O | N | D | T |
|---|---|---|---|---|---|---|---|---|---|---|---|---|---|
| 1963-67 | — | — | — | 3 | 1 | 1 | 2 | 1 | 3 | 1 | — | — | 12 |
| 1968-72 | — | — | 1 | 4 | 3 | 1 | — | — | 5 | 4 | — | — | 18 |
| 1973-77 | — | — | — | 5 | 13 | 2 | — | 1 | 2 | — | — | — | 23 |
| 1978-82 | 1 | — | — | 20 | 19 | 3 | 2 | 4 | 6 | 7 | — | — | 62 |
| 1983-87 | 1 | — | — | 19 | 16 | 9 | 2 | 6 | 10 | 3 | 2 | 3 | 71 |

A marked spring passage has been observed in recent years with peaks of nine on 6th May 1976 and ten on 23rd May 1979. Autumn passage is also regular, but involving smaller numbers.

### 167 (BARBARY DOVE) *Streptopelia 'risoria'*

Examples of this domesticated variety turned up at South Walney on 7th November 1983 and 31st October 1988.

### 168 TURTLE DOVE *Streptopelia turtur*

*Rare*

Benson (pers. comm.) states that a pair nested near the airfield immediately prior to the Second World War. At South Walney in the period 1975 to 1989, the species has been seen on 39 days, mostly in May with two birds on 10th May 1978. An extremely early individual was present on 26th March 1964.

Days recorded 1975-1989

| J | F | M | A | M | J | J | A | S | O | N | D | T |
|---|---|---|---|---|---|---|---|---|---|---|---|---|
| — | — | — | — | 21 | 6 | 1 | 3 | 4 | 4 | — | — | 39 |

Biggar Bank provided two birds on 8th May 1983, while North Walney's solitary example appeared on 3rd June 1985.

### 169 RING-NECKED PARAKEET *Psittacula krameri*

*Vagrant — probable escape*

Two were at the South Walney offices on 2nd September 1972.

### 170 BUDGERIGAR *Melopsittacus undulatus*

*Exotica*

Four single birds have been recorded at South Walney, on 26th August 1967, 30th August 1981, 24th July 1982 and 4th September 1987. The 1981 individual roosted briefly with a flock of 200 Dunlin.

## 171 CUCKOO *Cuculus canorus*

*Uncommon*

Although Harting (1864) was 'surprised to hear a cuckoo in the sandhills', the island has undoubtedly held a few pairs. Breeding is annual at North Walney, a pair frequents the Rakes Lane area and breeding was confirmed at South Walney in 1976. At South Walney, the species has been recorded on 45 days in the period 1975 to 1989, mostly in late spring and early August. Though appearing annually, only a few individuals are normally involved with peaks of five on 5th May 1968 and three on 2nd June 1982.

Days recorded 1975-1989

| J | F | M | A | M | J | J | A | S | O | N | D | T |
|---|---|---|---|---|---|---|---|---|---|---|---|---|
| — | — | — | 2 | 15 | 11 | 7 | 10 | — | — | — | — | 45 |

At North Walney, sightings are often daily in May and June, usually of no more than two birds.

## 172 BARN OWL *Tyto alba*

*Uncommon*

Suitable nesting sites are no longer numerous, although Benson (pers. comm.) reckons that, prior to the Second World War, four pairs nested at North Walney. Since then, but irregularly, one or two pairs have bred in the vicinity of North Scale village. At South Walney the species has been recorded on 50 days in the period 1975 to 1989 with the majority in the autumn. There were no sightings for the period 1966 to 1970.

Days recorded 1975-1989

| J | F | M | A | M | J | J | A | S | O | N | D | T |
|---|---|---|---|---|---|---|---|---|---|---|---|---|
| — | 1 | 1 | 6 | — | 1 | 3 | 1 | 13 | 13 | 8 | 3 | 50 |

### 173 LITTLE OWL *Athene noctua*

*Uncommon*

One or two pairs have probably nested at the south end at least since 1969. The diet of the 1982 pair included adult Little Terns, and a 1986 individual killed one Common Tern and nine each of Arctic and Little Terns. Benson (pers. comm.) reports that a pair has nested infrequently at North Walney during the period 1975 to 1984.

Single birds can be seen almost daily at South Walney from September to December.

Days recorded 1975-1989

| J | F | M | A | M | J | J | A | S | O | N | D | T |
|---|---|---|---|---|---|---|---|---|---|---|---|---|
| 16 | 16 | 15 | 18 | 9 | 21 | 20 | 8 | 46 | 103 | 69 | 25 | 366 |

### 174 TAWNY OWL *Strix aluco*

*Rare*

Prior to 1983 there were only two island records; an individual in the Wylock Marsh area on 17th May 1971 and at South Walney on 24th September being mobbed by a Kestrel. Regular watching in Willow Woods has produced sightings on 11 occasions between 1983 and 1989 with specimens on three days each in April and May, two each in September and November and one in October.

### 175 LONG-EARED OWL *Asio otus*

*Rare*

Durnford (1883) notes that the species was "unusually plentiful" in the winter of 1875. At South Walney there are nine records in the period 1975 to 1989, all occurring between September and December, but involving only three years, 1976, 1981 and 1982. The only record prior to 1975 is of an individual on 10th April 1965.

Days recorded 1975-1989

| J | F | M | A | M | J | J | A | S | O | N | D | T |
|---|---|---|---|---|---|---|---|---|---|---|---|---|
| — | — | — | — | — | — | — | — | 1 | 5 | 2 | 1 | 9 |

Willow Woods held up to three birds in March and April of 1986, an individual on five days in autumn 1988 and up to three birds between January and April in 1989.

**Ringing and recoveries**

Of three birds ringed by the observatory, two were caught on the 5th December 1976 and the third on 16th October 1981. One of the December individuals was shot in the following August near Ronga, Mariskaya, U.S.S.R. (3,200 km east).

### 176 SHORT-EARED OWL *Asio flammeus*

*Uncommon*

MacPherson (1892) records the species breeding in 1885 and, according to Oakes (1953), it was well established on the island in the 19th century. Four pairs nested in 1906, but despite the regular presence at the north end of birds in spring, no breeding success has since been confirmed. At South Walney, the species has been recorded in all months except June and July with the majority of sightings from September to November and a maximum of eleven on 22nd October 1981. Unusually, six were seen almost daily during February and March 1965.

Days recorded 1975-1989

| J | F | M | A | M | J | J | A | S | O | N | D | T |
|---|---|---|---|---|---|---|---|---|---|---|---|---|
| 5 | 2 | 2 | 4 | 3 | — | — | 10 | 135 | 118 | 51 | 10 | 340 |

On North Walney, appearances are usually more regular than at the south end. The maximum count at North Walney was six on 16th October 1988.

**Ringing and recoveries**

Of the two birds ringed at South Walney, the specimen of September 1972 was shot two months later near Benavente, Zamora, Spain (1,400 km south).

### 177 NIGHTJAR *Caprimulgus europaeus*

*Vagrant*

MacPherson (1892) records "drowsy" birds on the sandhills of the coast and Oakes (1953) describes Walney Island as a local haunt of the species. Walney's habitat is not typically suitable for the species and there is the strong possibility that churring birds may have been mistaken for the calls of the abundant Natterjack Toad. There have been no sightings since Oakes.

### 178 SWIFT *Apus apus*

*Fairly common*

Up to ten pairs breed in some of Vickerstown's older residencies, but a decline has been noted in recent years. Irregular sightings occur at South Walney during the summer with a maximum of 210 on 27th July 1982. There is an April record in 1968 and occasional appearances, since 1964, in September and October, with peaks of 27 on 5th September 1965 and two on 5th October 1976. An extremely late individual was seen on 9th November 1988.

Average maxima 1975-1989

| J | F | M | A | M | J | J | A | S | O | N | D |
|---|---|---|---|---|---|---|---|---|---|---|---|
| — | — | — | — | 6 | 6 | 21 | 36 | — | — | — | — |

Summer on North Walney sees birds feeding daily over the ponds with a maximum of 80 on 12th August 1986. On 6th November 1982 a misguided individual was seen winging north.

### 179 KINGFISHER *Alcedo atthis*

*Vagrant*

Durnford (1883) records a lighthouse casualty of the early 1870s; the only other example was over the gravel pools at South Walney on 16th July 1980.

### 180 ROLLER *Coracias garrulus*

*Vagrant*

MacPherson (1892) reports one killed in June 1860.

### 181 HOOPOE *Upupa epops*

*Vagrant*

Another MacPherson (1892) report of killing on the island; this one in the spring of 1884. There are three subsequent sightings: a long-staying bird at South Walney from 20th to 30th May 1974, another in the Rakes Lane area on 8th May 1983, and the third (perhaps the same bird) at South Walney on 19th May 1983. Two days earlier, one was at Heysham Harbour.

### 182 WRYNECK *Jynx torquilla*

*Vagrant*

Records at South Walney show single birds on 10th September 1963, 5th September 1965, 20th May 1983 and 20th October 1982, while one stayed from

1st to 6th September 1966. A less fortunate individual ventured into Vickerstown on 10th September 1976 and was killed by a cat. A juvenile, the seventh island record, was caught at South Walney on 9th September 1988.

### 183 GREEN WOODPECKER *Picus viridis*

*Vagrant*

All the records have appeared in the 1980s perhaps reflecting further expansion of the species in northern Britain. There are four single records at South Walney. A male alighted on a chimney pot at the cottages on 5th April 1981 and stayed briefly, chortling; an adult was at the offices on 24th August 1982; an immature was at the same locality on 27th August 1982; and a young female was ringed on 8th August 1984. The species breeds at Sandscale, five km north of the island, but despite this, North Walney has only three records, on 10th January 1984, 18th September 1984 and 10th August 1987.

### 184 GREAT SPOTTED WOODPECKER *Dendrocopos major*

*Vagrant*

One flew along the Channel side tideline at South Walney on 20th August 1970. Willow Woods has held individuals on 4th and 12th November 1986, 15th September 1988 and in 1989 on 27th January, 19th November and 9th December.

### 185 SKYLARK *Alauda arvensis*

*Abundant*

Described by Kirkman (1905) as abundant, it is, as a breeding species, declining on Walney Island. On South Walney Nature Reserve, 35 pairs bred in 1967, but appropriate nesting sites have been forfeited to the expanded gull colony. By 1984 only three pairs were nesting, all in the region by the lighthouse that is avoided by gulls. The undisturbed rough grazing lands of the island still hold successful breeders, but building developments and recreational interests are affecting the species in the Biggar Bank area. North Walney, where about 50 pairs bred in 1984, will hopefully remain a stronghold. The total island population may reach 100 pairs.

At South Walney, regular heavy passage occurs throughout September and October with a maximum of 3,000 on 29th September 1984. Hard weather movements can also take place and, in 1979, a flock of 2,000 stayed for five days in late January.

Average maxima 1975-1989

| J | F | M | A | M | J | J | A | S | O | N | D |
|---|---|---|---|---|---|---|---|---|---|---|---|
| 269 | 104 | 21 | 15 | 10 | 8 | 13 | 11 | 517 | 311 | 26 | 50 |

### 186 SHORE LARK *Eremophila alpestris*

*Vagrant*

MacPherson (1892) mentions three birds shot on Walney on 29th October 1890. At South Walney, birds were seen on 9th and 10th February 1963, on 11th December 1966 and on 24th January 1984, while one stayed throughout January and February of 1967. In 1977, three birds were on the spit from 8th January until 19th February and three were on the west shore on 15th December 1981.

**187 SAND MARTIN** ***Riparia riparia***

*Fairly common*

Durnford (1883) records the species as nesting, especially "in gravel pits where land slips have occurred", and Oakes (1953) notes a site on the Channel side of the island. Benson (pers. comm.) states that a small colony was at the north end immediately prior to the Second World War. Since then, breeding has been sporadic with three pairs at the south end in 1962, "undisturbed pairs" (Walney Bird Observatory Annual Reports) in 1964 and 1967, and most lately, three pairs at Hare Hill in 1979. There are suitable sites for breeding on the island but, at present, the species is in decline due to its wintering problems.

At South Walney, 1981, 1982, 1987 and 1989 produced March sightings, but the majority are logged in April, August and September with peaks of 190 on 17th July 1965 and 46 on 26th August 1980.

Average maxima 1975-1989

| J | F | M | A | M | J | J | A | S | O | N | D |
|---|---|---|---|---|---|---|---|---|---|---|---|
| — | — | 0.6 | 3.0 | 6.4 | 0.6 | 2.8 | 7.3 | 4.4 | 1.3 | 0.2 | — |

Average maxima a. 1980-1983 b. 1984-1987

| | J | F | M | A | M | J | J | A | S | O | N | D |
|---|---|---|---|---|---|---|---|---|---|---|---|---|
| a. | — | — | 1.0 | 6.2 | 5.0 | 1.5 | 7.0 | 18.2 | 7.0 | 1.5 | — | — |
| b. | — | — | 0.2 | 2.5 | 0.5 | 0.5 | 1.5 | 0.5 | 4.2 | 1.2 | 1.0 | — |

The highest count since April 1982 involved 65 birds on 4th May 1989. A hopeful sign compared with recent years.

**188 SWALLOW** ***Hirundo rustica***

*Abundant*

There are probably 15 to 20 breeding pairs on the island, making use of derelict Second World War explacements, covered railway wagons converted into pony stables, and old farm outbuildings. At South Walney, a steady stream of migrants is evident by mid-April, but heaviest passage comes towards the middle of May with a maximum of 120 on 5th May 1989. Return movement commences in late July and continues to mid-October, with peaks of 110 on 29th July 1982, 500 on

28th August 1982, 1,000 on 3rd September 1964 and 1,100 on 6th October 1966.
Average maxima 1975-1989

| J | F | M | A | M | J | J | A | S | O | N | D |
|---|---|---|---|---|---|---|---|---|---|---|---|
| — | — | — | 9 | 40 | 9 | 26 | 176 | 166 | 69 | 1 | — |

Records from North Walney usually involve small numbers feeding daily over the pools but include a roost of 2,000 on 15th September 1984.

**Ringing and recoveries**

Of 342 birds ringed, 260 have been nestlings. The recoveries all relate to pulli; two of them controlled at Thwaite Flat, Dalton-in Furness (11 km north) and the third at Fairburn Ings, Castleford, Yorkshire (125 km east) on 9th September 1963, six weeks after being ringed.

### 189 HOUSE MARTIN *Delichon urbica*

*Uncommon*

Up to five pairs breed in the Vickerstown area of the island. The species appears irregularly at South Walney with unusually, 50 on 30th September 1986 and 65 on 16th September 1987. Ones and twos are the normal sighting.

Average maxima 1975-1989

| J | F | M | A | M | J | J | A | S | O | N | D |
|---|---|---|---|---|---|---|---|---|---|---|---|
| — | — | — | 0.6 | 2.5 | 1.2 | 0.2 | 2.1 | 15.2 | 0.06 | 0.07 | — |

### 190 RICHARD'S PIPIT *Anthus novaseelandiae*

*Vagrant*

There are six South Walney records. In 1980 one remained from 8th to 10th November near Pho Hill, while a second stayed near the cottages, feeding among the cattle, from 20th December until 1st February 1981. Both these were accepted by the B.B.R.C. Subsequent sightings relate to short staying individuals on 3rd September 1985, 25th September 1987 and 11th November 1987, while in 1989 an elusive bird was present from 17th to 19th September.

### 191 TAWNY PIPIT *Anthus campestris*

*Vagrant*

Three records at South Walney have been accepted by the B.B.R.C.; one at the oyster farm on 18th October 1980, one at the cottages on 9th August 1982 and one at the lighthouse on 27th August 1982. Additionally, the extreme southern tip of the island held an individual on 1st September 1984.

### 192 TREE PIPIT *Anthus trivialis*

*Fairly common*

Spring passage is noticeable at South Walney during late April and early May, but with no more than four birds appearing on any day. A much larger return movement begins in mid-August and continues until mid-September, with peaks of 100 on 31st August 1986 and 120 on 16th September 1987.

Average maxima 1975-1989

| J | F | M | A | M | J | J | A | S | O | N | D |
|---|---|---|---|---|---|---|---|---|---|---|---|
| — | — | — | 1.1 | 1.4 | — | — | 24.8 | 22.7 | 0.6 | — | — |

## 193 MEADOW PIPIT *Anthus pratensis*

*Abundant*

Harting (1864) describes the bird as common and, though still breeding on Walney, it has declined because of 20th century urbanisation in the central area. At South Walney Nature Reserve a more recent decrease, as with other ground nesting species, is due to forfeiture of suitable sites to the gulls. Twenty pairs bred in 1967; none in 1984. North Walney has up to 50 pairs and the whole island may support 100 pairs. At South Walney, moderate diurnal passage is logged in late March and in April, with peaks of 400 on 28th March 1984 and 5,000 on 10th April 1966. Movement in autumn is considerably heavier with many days yielding 1,000 plus birds, and peaks of 5,000 on 26th September 1989 and 5,000 on 8th October 1966.

Average maxima 1975-1989

| J | F | M | A | M | J | J | A | S | O | N | D |
|---|---|---|---|---|---|---|---|---|---|---|---|
| 61 | 16 | 121 | 307 | 11 | 7 | 34 | 79 | 2264 | 1237 | 57 | 14 |

Visible passage totals at South Walney

| | 20 Mar — 15 Apr | 1 Sep — 31 Oct |
|---|---|---|
| 1980 | 1490 | 14040 |
| 1981 | 505 | 8897 |
| 1982 | 186 | 10377 |
| 1983 | 1585 | 20308 |
| 1984 | 3866 | 23569 |
| 1985 | 2266 | 24177 |
| 1986 | 382 | 26560 |
| 1987 | 1640 | 31385 |
| 1988 | 2571 | 33610 |
| 1989 | 438 | 30915 |

### Ringing and recoveries

The observatory has ringed 433 birds, chiefly pulli in May and southward moving birds in autumn. There have been four recoveries all from the western seaboard of southern Europe. Spain provides three examples; an adult 'taken' near Cadiz (2,000 km south) on 4th May 1966 having been ringed in the previous September; an adult, on Walney on 2nd September 1970, and shot near Orio, Guipuzcoa (1,200 km south) on 29th October; and a juvenile 'found' near Liano, Santander (1,200 km south) on 26th December 1971 less than three months after being ringed. The fourth recovery refers to a juvenile of autumn 1969 that took a day less than two months to reach St. Nazaire, France (800 km south).

## 194 ROCK PIPIT *Anthus petrosus*

*Uncommon*

All previous authors refer to Harting's finding of a nest in 1864 and this remains the sole record. Oakes (1953) doubts if nesting was ever regular on Walney and Robinson (quoted in Oakes 1953) asserts that breeding did not occur from 1910 to 1933, although birds were on the island in June of the last year. At South Walney, the species has been seen in all months except July and August, but records are decidedly sporadic. Passage birds appear in October and small groups or single birds are recorded almost every winter. Late October peaks of 12 birds occurred in 1964, 1966 and 1969.

Days recorded 1975-1989

| J | F | M | A | M | J | J | A | S | O | N | D | T |
|---|---|---|---|---|---|---|---|---|---|---|---|---|
| 18 | 9 | 7 | 6 | 1 | 1 | — | — | 14 | 54 | 17 | 7 | 134 |

At North Walney small groups are regularly noted in late autumn and overwintering. Peak counts include eight on 15th October 1989 and 15 on 22nd November 1987 and 12th November 1988.

## 195 WATER PIPIT *Anthus spinoletta*

*Vagrant*

There are three records, all at South Walney, with single birds on 5th January 1981, 18th December 1981 and 5th December 1983.

## 196 YELLOW WAGTAIL *Motacilla flava flavissima*

*Common*

At South Walney, small numbers move north during late April and early May. Heavier reverse movements occur from mid-July to mid-September with peaks of 100 on 1st September 1972 and 120 on 27th August 1982. An extremely late individual was in the central marsh area from 25th November until 9th December 1978.

Average maxima 1975-1989

| J | F | M | A | M | J | J | A | S | O | N | D |
|---|---|---|---|---|---|---|---|---|---|---|---|
| — | — | — | 2 | 5 | — | 11 | 36 | 16 | 1 | — | — |

## 197 (BLUE-HEADED WAGTAIL) *Motacilla flava flava*

*Vagrant*

The only record concerns two birds at the South Walney offices on 7th September 1975.

## 198 GREY WAGTAIL *Motacilla cinerea*

*Common*

Benson (pers. comm.) states that a pair nested at North End Farm immediately prior to the Second World War. At South Walney, the species has been recorded in all months except January, although sightings are sporadic but for the period late August until mid-October. Peak counts include 30 on 26th August, 78 on 29th September and 25 on 6th October 1984.

Average maxima 1975-1989

| J | F | M | A | M | J | J | A | S | O | N | D |
|---|---|---|---|---|---|---|---|---|---|---|---|
| — | 0.1 | 0.6 | 0.4 | 0.1 | 0.2 | 1.1 | 9.8 | 33.3 | 10.5 | 0.4 | 0.2 |

Visible passage totals at South Walney

| | 1980 | 1981 | 1982 | 1983 | 1984 | 1985 | 1986 | 1987 | 1988 | 1989 |
|---|---|---|---|---|---|---|---|---|---|---|
| August | 63 | 10 | 5 | 51 | 80 | 28 | 35 | 4 | 16 | 22 |
| September | 450 | 150 | 178 | 206 | 385 | 306 | 261 | 282 | 295 | 401 |
| October | 24 | 20 | 3 | 39 | 103 | 53 | 97 | 55 | 47 | 4 |

## 199 PIED WAGTAIL *Motacilla alba yarelli*

*Abundant*

As a nesting species it is scarce, with no more than three pairs on the island in recent years. Small numbers move north through South Walney during March and April, but the return passage from late July until mid-October is much heavier with peaks of 110 on 31st August 1987, 300 on 25th September 1986, 30th September 1988, 1st October 1986 and 1st October 1989.

Average maxima 1975-1989

| J | F | M | A | M | J | J | A | S | O | N | D |
|---|---|---|---|---|---|---|---|---|---|---|---|
| 4 | 3 | 7 | 8 | 4 | 3 | 19 | 40 | 110 | 130 | 10 | 5 |

Visible passage totals at South Walney

| | 1980 | 1981 | 1982 | 1983 | 1984 | 1985 | 1986 | 1987 | 1988 | 1989 |
|---|---|---|---|---|---|---|---|---|---|---|
| August | 412 | 279 | 246 | 204 | 144 | 211 | 274 | 379 | 285 | 687 |
| September | 616 | 660 | 377 | 522 | 767 | 437 | 1427 | 724 | 1740 | 512 |
| October | 338 | 460 | 86 | 440 | 535 | 832 | 912 | 645 | 450 | 559 |

**Ringing and recoveries**

Of 128 birds ringed by the observatory, 20 relate to nestlings, and 48 have been caught in August. There are two recoveries; one from Barrow in May 1967, two years after being ringed; and a juvenile caught in August 1967, died after hitting a window at Sytchampton, Stourport, Worcestershire (220 km south-southeast) on 31st October 1971.

**200 (WHITE WAGTAIL)** ***Motacilla alba alba***

*Uncommon*

At South Walney the species is generally uncommon except for a small passage in spring with peaks of 20 on 24th April 1975 and 11 on 16th April 1983.

Average maxima 1975-1989

| J | F | M | A | M | J | J | A | S | O | N | D |
|---|---|---|---|---|---|---|---|---|---|---|---|
| 0.1 | 0.1 | 0.8 | 4.0 | 1.7 | — | — | 0.3 | 0.3 | 0.4 | 0.3 | — |

**201 WAXWING** ***Bombycilla garrulus***

*Vagrant*

The first record is of a bird that stayed briefly in the cottage garden at South Walney on 26th November 1982. The second island record was a specimen at Willow Woods on 2nd and 3rd November.

**202 DIPPER** ***Cinclus cinclus***

The only record is of an individual on the beck to the south of Willow Woods on 28th October 1988.

**203 WREN** ***Troglodytes troglodytes***

*Common*

There are ample nest sites in the urban areas of the island, in Willow Woods and in the hedgerows, but precise breeding figures are non-existent. More certain is that breeding at either end of the island has only rarely been detected.

The species is virtually absent at South Walney from May to August, but there is noticeable passage from September until November, with a few birds holding territories into March. Durnford (1883) recorded it on the shores of Walney "at the migratory season", and, in more recent years, there have been maxima of 50 on 30th September 1964, 50 on 10th October 1988 and 40 on 13th November 1989.

Average maxima 1975-1989

| J | F | M | A | M | J | J | A | S | O | N | D |
|---|---|---|---|---|---|---|---|---|---|---|---|
| 7 | 5 | 5 | 3 | — | — | — | — | 12 | 24 | 17 | 10 |

**Ringing and recoveries**

The observatory has ringed 837 birds, over half of them in October, and virtually all autumn examples classified as juveniles. From this vast amount of information there is but one recovery; an adult found dead at Biggar in early May 1969 after being ringed at South Walney in the previous October.

**204 DUNNOCK** ***Prunella modularis***

*Common*

As with other garden birds, the urban areas of Walney Island provide ample opportunity for nesting; but exact numbers are hard to gauge. Successful breeding has been recorded at the offices and in the cottage garden at South Walney Nature Reserve. Here, also, a moderate passage occurs between September and November with 30 on 30th September 1988, 100 on 10th October 1988 and 35 on 9th November 1983. Up to ten birds regularly hold winter territories at South Walney.

Average maxima 1975-1989

| J | F | M | A | M | J | J | A | S | O | N | D |
|---|---|---|---|---|---|---|---|---|---|---|---|
| 6 | 5 | 4 | 3 | 2 | 1 | 1 | 2 | 11 | 27 | 15 | 10 |

**Ringing and recoveries**

Of 509 birds ringed, over half have been caught in October. There are only three recoveries, two very local. However, an adult caught on the Calf of Man (110 km west) on 21st July 1967 was controlled at Walney on 27th October 1968.

**205 ROBIN** ***Erithacus rubecula***

*Common*

As with Wren and Dunnock, nesting sites are chiefly in the gardens and hedgerows of Biggar, Vickerstown and North Scale; with few breeding records at the extreme ends of the island where cover is less. At South Walney, there are a few scattered sightings between May and August, but by the end of the latter month, there is a steady trickle southwards which continues into early November. Peak counts include 40 on 28th October 1983, and, in 1984, 20 on 26th August, 75 on 16th September and 30 on 2nd November. During winter, up to ten birds hold territories at South Walney.

Average maxima 1975-1989

| J | F | M | A | M | J | J | A | S | O | N | D |
|---|---|---|---|---|---|---|---|---|---|---|---|
| 5 | 4 | 4 | 2 | 1 | — | — | 9 | 28 | 25 | 15 | 8 |

**Ringing and recoveries**

Over 50% of the 1,231 birds ringed since 1964 have been caught in September. An east-west movement is indicated by three recoveries from the Isle of Man of autumn ringed birds in winter. Additionally, there are three recoveries of individuals found in subsequent breeding seasons to the east of Walney, namely Durham, Northumberland and Inverness. A southward movement of 61 km was achieved by a bird ringed on Walney on 25th September 1986 and controlled at Homer Green, Merseyside on 27th September.

**206 NIGHTINGALE** ***Luscinia megarhynchos***

*Vagrant*

The only record is a single at South Walney on 14th June 1986.

**207 BLUETHROAT** ***Luscinia svecica***

*Vagrant*

A young male of the red-spotted race was caught at South Walney on 25th May 1987.

**208 BLACK REDSTART** ***Phoenicurus ochruros***

*Scarce*

At South Walney in the period 1975 to 1989, the species has been seen on 137 days. Most of the winter sightings can be attributed to an overwintering pair of 1980/81. Autumn birds tend to stay longer than the spring arrivals, and can be *in situ* for up to a week. The peak count at South Walney is four on 14th March 1983, with, perhaps, up to seven different birds between the 11th and 14th of that month. A yellow-gaped bird caught on 14th July 1985, obviously only recently out of the nest, stimulated a great deal of speculation as to its possible origin.

Days recorded 1975-1989

| J | F | M | A | M | J | J | A | S | O | N | D | T |
|---|---|---|---|---|---|---|---|---|---|---|---|---|
| 28 | 14 | 20 | 5 | 3 | 1 | 1 | 1 | 3 | 11 | 31 | 19 | 137 |

Birds have also been seen at Biggar Bank on three occasions in the period 1976 to 1983; and North Walney has held singles almost annually in the 1980s between

October and December except for a males on 31st March 1989 and 3rd April 1985.

**Ringing and recoveries**

Of 11 birds ringed by the observatory, an adult male on 4th June 1986 was found dying on an oil rig 320 km north of Aberdeen, Scotland (618 km north) on 5th July 1986.

**209 REDSTART** ***Phoenicurus phoenicurus***

*Uncommon*

Small numbers can usually be seen on the island during late April and early May. A maximum four appeared on the 26th April 1984 and on 3rd May 1985. Autumn passage is generally slightly heavier and occurs from late August to the end of September with peaks of nine on 7th September 1988 and seven on 7th September 1981.

Days recorded 1975-1989

| J | F | M | A | M | J | J | A | S | O | N | D | T |
|---|---|---|---|---|---|---|---|---|---|---|---|---|
| — | — | — | 28 | 44 | 3 | 4 | 38 | 57 | 13 | — | — | 187 |

There are occasional records from Willow Woods with a maximum of five on 8th September 1989.

**Ringing and recoveries**

Predominantly caught in May and September, the observatory has ringed a total of 120 birds producing one recovery; an adult female, trapped on 31st August 1982 was found dead in Madrid, Spain (1,515 km south) on 23rd September. Additionally, a young male ringed on 7th September 1976 at Gibraltar Point, Lincolnshire (250 km east-southeast) was controlled at Walney ten days later.

**210 WHINCHAT** ***Saxicola rubetra***

*Fairly common*

There are a few April records at South Walney, with an unprecedented eight on 30th April 1983; the main wave, with small daily numbers, coming in the first half of May. The peak passage takes place from towards the end of July until the last days of September, with a maximum 14 on 31st August 1982.

Days recorded 1975-1989

| J | F | M | A | M | J | J | A | S | O | N | D | T |
|---|---|---|---|---|---|---|---|---|---|---|---|---|
| — | — | — | 18 | 104 | 5 | 45 | 107 | 127 | 18 | 2 | — | 426 |

**Ringing and recoveries**

August and September have produced well over 60% of the 187 birds caught by the observatory. The only recovery is of a juvenile ringed on 25th August 1980 and 'taken' at Berrechid, Morocco (2,300 km south-southwest) on 10th April 1983.

**211 STONECHAT** ***Saxicola torquata***

*Uncommon*

Durnford (1883) and MacPherson (1892) record the species as being fairly numerous on the island; while Oakes (1953) states that a series of harsh winters (1939, 1940 and 1941) affected the numbers breeding. During the 1960s, up to eight pairs nested on Walney with at least two pairs at South Walney Nature Reserve. The last confirmed nesting at the latter was in 1976, and all subsequent breeding has been confined to the north end of the island. This comprised no more than four pairs per annum in the 1970s and, following severe winters in the late 70s and early 80s, plus a loss of habitat, the population has decreased further. In 1984, only two pairs bred.

South Walney records reflect the decline in breeding numbers. Until 1978, birds were regularly seen in all months with peaks of ten on 13th July 1969, 19th August 1969 and 27th August 1977. In 1979 there were only five sightings and the only promising signs subsequently were six birds on 12th March 1983 and seven on 13th October 1988.

Days recorded at South Walney

| | J | F | M | A | M | J | J | A | S | O | N | D |
|---|---|---|---|---|---|---|---|---|---|---|---|---|
| 1963-67 | 6 | 8 | 17 | 10 | 13 | 9 | 14 | 31 | 28 | 31 | 12 | 2 |
| 1968-72 | — | 6 | 14 | 25 | 42 | 28 | 46 | 85 | 68 | 52 | 9 | 10 |
| 1973-77 | 27 | 14 | 13 | 14 | 17 | 18 | 8 | 46 | 50 | 68 | 32 | 19 |
| 1978-82 | 8 | 9 | 19 | 6 | 5 | — | — | 4 | 17 | 22 | 8 | 15 |
| 1983-87 | — | 2 | 16 | 3 | 2 | 4 | 2 | — | 8 | 16 | 6 | 7 |

The picture at North Walney is slightly more promising with nine on 20th October 1983 and 12 on 2nd November 1984.

**Ringing and recoveries**

Of 206 birds ringed by the observatory, 131 have been caught in the period August to October. There are three recoveries, two of which are from Walney (one shot(!) in March 1972), and a juvenile ringed on 7th August 1970 and killed by a car at Eskmeals (35 km north-northwest) on 25th September 1971.

**212 WHEATEAR** ***Oenanthe oenanthe***

*Common*

All previous authors refer to the abundance of the species on the island, but only MacPherson (1892) and Oakes (1953) specifically mention breeding; the latter remarking on a decrease. Benson (pers. comm.) states that a pair nested at North End Farm in the 1930s. Suitable sites are available in the many turf and boulder walls, but the only indications in recent years have been a newly-fledged bird in 1980 and adults carrying food in 1985. Both events were in the Rakes Lane region. The first arrivals at South Walney are during the last week of March and moderate numbers appear daily until the end of May, with a peak of 58 on 6th April 1987 and with 20 on many May days. Greenland birds are often numerous towards the end of May and these are probably what Harting refers to when, after his visit of 30th May 1864, he states that never had he "observed anywhere Wheatears so large or so finely coloured". Autumn birds return to South Walney at the end of July and trickle through daily until mid-October, with peaks of 60 on 31st August 1980 and 45 on 3rd September 1985.

Average maxima 1975-1989

| J | F | M | A | M | J | J | A | S | O | N | D |
|---|---|---|---|---|---|---|---|---|---|---|---|
| — | — | 3 | 18 | 14 | 1 | 2 | 25 | 22 | 4 | — | — |

**213 DESERT WHEATEAR** ***Oenanthe deserti***

*Vagrant*

A young female was located at South Walney on 15th November 1986. The sandy shore and a plentiful supply of mealworms ensured its residence until the evening of the 21st, by which time over 700 people had witnessed it, some of whom heard it sing on the 19th. Accepted by B.B.R.C. as the 24th record for Great Britain.

**214 RING OUSEL** ***Turdus torquatus***

*Scarce*

At South Walney the species has been recorded on 16 days in the period 1975 to 1989. The majority of sightings are in April and October, with a maximum of six birds on 20th October 1969. Single birds appeared, unusually, on 19th and 20th February 1984 and on 4th and 5th November 1983.

Days recorded 1975-1989

| J | F | M | A | M | J | J | A | S | O | N | D | T |
|---|---|---|---|---|---|---|---|---|---|---|---|---|
| — | 2 | 1 | 5 | — | — | — | — | 1 | 5 | 2 | — | 16 |

North Walney was visited by single birds on 24th April 1983, 20th April 1984, 6th April 1987, 2nd November 1988 and 9th April 1989, while at Rakes Lane a female was evident on 20th April 1988.

## 215 BLACKBIRD *Turdus merula*

*Common*

As with other typical garden birds, most breeding takes place in the urban areas of the island. Nesting is recorded in most years at South Walney Nature Reserve, but the two pairs of 1971 and 1982 are the maximum. At the south end of the island, spring movement is occasionally heavy, with peaks of 90 on 15th March 1965 and 21 on 11th April 1976. Summer sightings usually relate to locally nesting birds, but by the middle of October regular passage is often daily with 60 on 18th October 1981 and an exceptional 200 on 4th November 1983.

Average maxima 1975-1989

| J | F | M | A | M | J | J | A | S | O | N | D |
|---|---|---|---|---|---|---|---|---|---|---|---|
| 9 | 5 | 10 | 5 | 3 | 3 | 3 | 3 | 4 | 15 | 30 | 8 |

**Ringing and recoveries**

Over 66% of 1,238 birds ringed since 1964 have been caught in March, October and November. There have been 17 recoveries involving seven countries and indicating a definite east-west movement. There are three instances of overwintering in Ireland and three of birds during breeding months in Scandinavia. An adult male ringed on Walney on 1st December 1973 was shot at Sippola, Finland (1,300 km northeast) on 11th April 1975. A swift short-distance east-west movement concerns a young female ringed at Spurn Point, Yorkshire (220 km east) and controlled on Walney on 27th October 1973, nine days later.

## 216 FIELDFARE *Turdus pilaris*

*Fairly common*

The first wave of autumn birds is recorded at South Walney by the second week of October and passage is normally of short duration; usually ending by the middle of November, with peaks of 150 on 6th October 1976 and 250 on 13th November 1977. Hard weather sometimes provides spectacular movements; during late January and early February 1984 a total of 16,770 birds were counted over a ten day period. Returning birds occur from late March to mid-April with peaks of 70 on 10th March 1968 and 110 on 9th April 1987, with occasional individuals lingering into early May.

Average maxima 1975-1989

| J | F | M | A | M | J | J | A | S | O | N | D |
|---|---|---|---|---|---|---|---|---|---|---|---|
| 25 | 26 | 8 | 10 | — | — | — | — | — | 31 | 35 | 7 |

(The 1984 spectacular has been omitted from the table)

Elsewhere on the island small flocks can often be seen in the Biggar village area peaking at 37 on 28th December 1989, while at North Walney regular autumn passage has witnessed a maximum 60 on 26th October 1985 and during the hard weather of January 1984 a flock of 245 foraged along the tideline.

## 217 SONG THRUSH *Turdus philomelos*

*Common*

An uncounted population breeds in the residential areas, but very few at the ends of the island; South Walney usually having one or two pairs. At South Walney, patterns of movement are similar to those of Blackbird, but numbers are fewer. February and March occasionally produce passage on a moderate scale and the peaks of 50 on 28th February 1965 and 70 on 2nd March 1965 are quite exceptional. Locally breeding birds are seen regularly during the summer and the daily passage south starts at the beginning of October and continues until the middle of November. Peaks of 100 occurred on 8th October 1966 and 4th November 1983 and numbers are supplemented by hard weather arrivals with 110 on 14th December 1981.

Average maxima 1975-1989

| J | F | M | A | M | J | J | A | S | O | N | D |
|---|---|---|---|---|---|---|---|---|---|---|---|
| 7 | 4 | 4 | 1 | 1 | 1 | 1 | 1 | 2 | 17 | 15 | 13 |

**Ringing and recoveries**

Of 592 birds ringed, just over 34% have been caught in October. There are eight recoveries including spring controls from the Isle of May, Scotland (240 km northeast) and an oil-rig in the North Sea (471 km north-northeast) which may indicate birds returning to breed in Scandinavia after wintering in the west.

## 218 REDWING *Turdus iliacus*

*Fairly common*

The first autumn birds appear at South Walney during late September, preceding Fieldfare by up to one week. Passage can be recorded almost daily until the end of November with peaks of 400 on 14th October 1985 and 150 on 4th November 1983. Redwing joined with Fieldfare in the 1984 winter spectacular, with 8,040 being counted in a ten day period, from late January, of hard weather. Returning birds move north during February and March with peaks of 250 on 11th March 1981 and 300 on 3rd February 1984. Small parties are occasionally seen in April with a maximum of 12 on 8th April 1984.

Average maxima 1975-1989

| J | F | M | A | M | J | J | A | S | O | N | D |
|---|---|---|---|---|---|---|---|---|---|---|---|
| 32 | 30 | 27 | 3 | — | — | — | — | 1 | 52 | 29 | 14 |

(The 1984 spectacular has been omitted from the table)

At North Walney, small parties are fairly regular on passage or in mid-winter, with 250 on 20th October 1985 an untypical maximum.

**Ringing and recoveries**

Of 239 birds ringed by the observatory, 55 of them were caught in 1977. Of the two recoveries, one is from Barrow and the other, a dead individual found near Severodvinsk, Arkhangelsk, U.S.S.R. (2,689 km northeast) on 28th June 1979, nearly four months after being ringed.

## 219 MISTLE THRUSH *Turdus viscivorous*

*Uncommon*

Up to five pairs breed in the Central Walney region but, despite this, sightings at South Walney are comparatively scarce. In the years 1975 to 1989 there are records on 127 days mostly from October to February. Spring and autumn sightings are probably of genuine passage birds, while winter records are made up of hard weather arrivals with eight on 24th December 1981 and ten on 5th January 1982.

Days recorded 1975-1989

| J | F | M | A | M | J | J | A | S | O | N | D | T |
|---|---|---|---|---|---|---|---|---|---|---|---|---|
| 21 | 12 | 5 | 6 | 1 | 1 | 1 | 2 | 4 | 44 | 14 | 16 | 127 |

North Walney has records on 11 days in the period 1983 to 1989, with eight birds on 14th October 1985.

## 220 GRASSHOPPER WARBLER *Locustella naevia*

*Uncommon*

Nesting may have taken place on the island for many years, but only since 1983 has it been confirmed, with two, possibly three pairs at the north end. At South Walney the species has been recorded on 37 days in the period 1975 to 1989. The first arrivals appear at the south end in late April and birds can be seen into the middle of May, with six on 24th April 1966 and four on 8th May 1964. Autumn sightings are generally far less numerous and the 12 records of August 1966 are remarkable.

Days recorded 1975-1989

| J | F | M | A | M | J | J | A | S | O | N | D | T |
|---|---|---|---|---|---|---|---|---|---|---|---|---|
| — | — | — | 6 | 19 | — | 1 | 3 | 8 | — | — | — | 37 |

At North Walney and Willow Woods sightings or hearings of up to three birds can be daily in May and June.

## 221 SEDGE WARBLER *Acrocephalus schoenobaenus*

*Fairly common*

Up to 12 pairs nest on the island with five or six at the north end and the remainder in the Biggar and Rakes Lane area. April sightings at South Walney are unusual with only ten days since 1975. The bulk of the spring passage is confined to the first three weeks of May with peaks of 12 on 9th May 1984 and 4th May 1989. The reverse process begins in late July with the arrival of birds, probably locally bred, and continues to late September with peaks of ten on 27th August 1965 and five on 8th September 1967. There are two October records, single birds on 9th October 1971 and 7th October 1972.

Days recorded 1975-1989

| J | F | M | A | M | J | J | A | S | O | N | D | T |
|---|---|---|---|---|---|---|---|---|---|---|---|---|
| — | — | — | 10 | 92 | 37 | 26 | 81 | 24 | — | — | — | 270 |

(June days are mostly made up of a breeding pair at South Walney in 1981)

**Ringing and recoveries**

May and August have provided 84% of the 202 birds ringed by the observatory. A juvenile, caught on 19th July 1982 was controlled at Marton Mere, Blackpool, Lancashire (29 km south-southeast) on 14th May 1984. In addition, Walney controlled on 27th July 1975, an individual ringed on the Ile du Migron, Loire Atlantique, France (800 km south) on 13th September 1974.

## 222 PADDYFIELD WARBLER *Acrocephalus agricola*

*Vagrant*

A first-year bird was caught at South Walney on 11th September 1982 and released in the central marsh, where it remained until the evening of 13th September. This constituted the eighth record for Great Britain, attracted 500 visitors and was accepted by B.B.R.C.

## 223 MARSH WARBLER *Acrocephalus palustris*

*Vagrant*

A young bird was trapped and ringed at South Walney on 29th September 1986.

## 224 REED WARBLER *Acrocephalus scirpaceus*

*Rare*

As a Cumbrian breeding bird, the species is at the northern limit of its British range and the paucity of Walney records reflects this; there are only 11 sightings for the whole island. At South Walney the only records are of individuals on 13th May and 24th August 1979 (the former date the first island record) and 25th

August 1989. Spring sightings have occurred at Biggar village on 9th May 1983, North Walney on 27th May and 30th June 1985, 7th June 1987 and 15th May 1988 and at Willow Woods on 29th April 1988. The last-named site held autumn birds on 18th September and 6th October 1984.

**225 ICTERINE WARBLER** ***Hippolais icterina***

*Vagrant*

There are three records, all of South Walney singles, on 23rd August 1977, 19th August 1983 and 23rd August 1984.

**226 MELODIOUS WARBLER** ***Hippolais polyglotta***

*Rare*

All but one of the Walney sightings have been at the south end; the exception being an individual at the Coastguard Station on 3rd September 1981. Ten of the South Walney birds have been logged in the 1980s, including two on 27th August 1982.

Records at South Walney 1964-1989

| | | | | | |
|---|---|---|---|---|---|
| 1964 | 12th September | 1970 | 18th August | 1983 | 18th August |
| 1965 | 30th August | 1980 | 10th August | | 23rd/24th September |
| 1967 | 30th May | 1981 | 25th August | 1984 | 17th June |
| 1969 | 20th September | 1982 | 27th August | 1985 | 11th September |

**227 SUBALPINE WARBLER** ***Sylvia cantillans***

*Vagrant*

A male, accepted by B.B.R.C., was trapped and ringed at South Walney on 6th June 1986.

**228 BARRED WARBLER** ***Sylvia nisoria***

*Rare*

Eleven birds have been recorded, ten of them at South Walney, the other in Willow Woods on 3rd September 1989. Nine of the South Walney birds have been seen in the 1980s including two in August 1980 and October 1988.

Records at South Walney 1964-1989

| | | | |
|---|---|---|---|
| 1977 | 7th September | 1983 | 26th August |
| 1980 | 17th August | 1986 | 6th September |
| | 31st August till | 1988 | 9th/10th October |
| | 3rd September | | 23rd/24th October |
| 1981 | 11th September | 1989 | 21st September |
| 1982 | 16th September | | |

**229 LESSER WHITETHROAT** ***Sylvia curruca***

*Rare*

A pair bred — a fairly uncommon Cumbrian event — in Willow Woods in 1984. Prior to that year there were only nine island records, seven of them at South Walney and including two birds on 5th September 1965. Since 1984, alongside the possible species' expansion in the north, Willow Woods has produced up to three birds on 19 days. In addition, at South Walney sightings have become annual although never producing more than one bird.

Days recorded 1975-1989

| J | F | M | A | M | J | J | A | S | O | N | D | T |
|---|---|---|---|---|---|---|---|---|---|---|---|---|
| — | — | — | — | 3 | 2 | 2 | 2 | 4 | 1 | — | — | 14 |

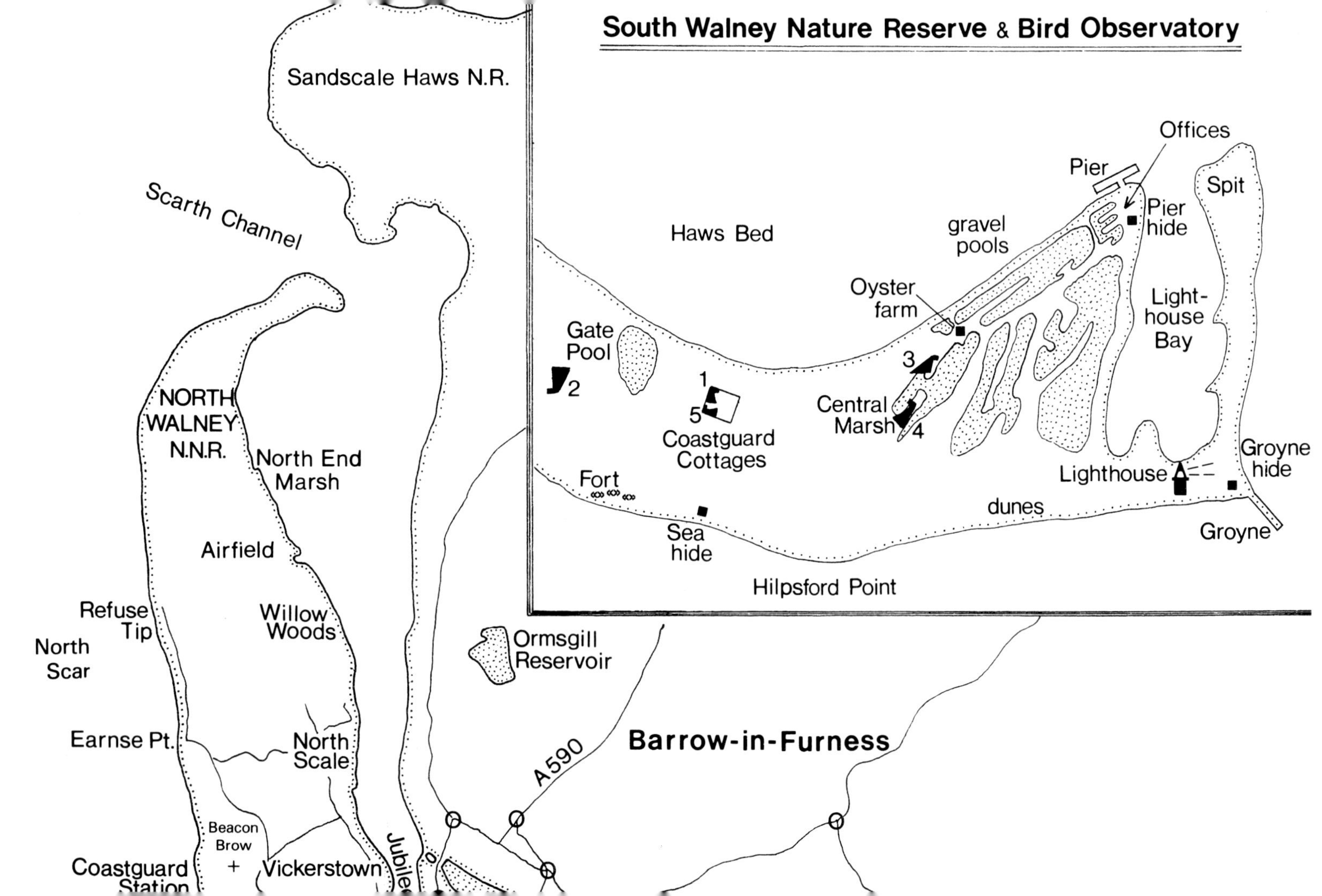
South Walney Nature Reserve & Bird Observatory
Sandscale Haws N.R.
Scarth Channel
Haws Bed
Offices
Pier
Pier hide
Spit
gravel pools
Oyster farm
Light-house Bay
Gate Pool
2
1
5
3
Central Marsh
4
Coastguard Cottages
Fort
Lighthouse
Groyne hide
dunes
Groyne
Sea hide
Hilpsford Point
NORTH WALNEY N.N.R.
North End Marsh
Airfield
Refuse Tip
North Scar
Willow Woods
Ormsgill Reservoir
Earnse Pt.
North Scale
Barrow-in-Furness
A590
Beacon Brow
Coastguard Station
Vickerstown
Jubilee

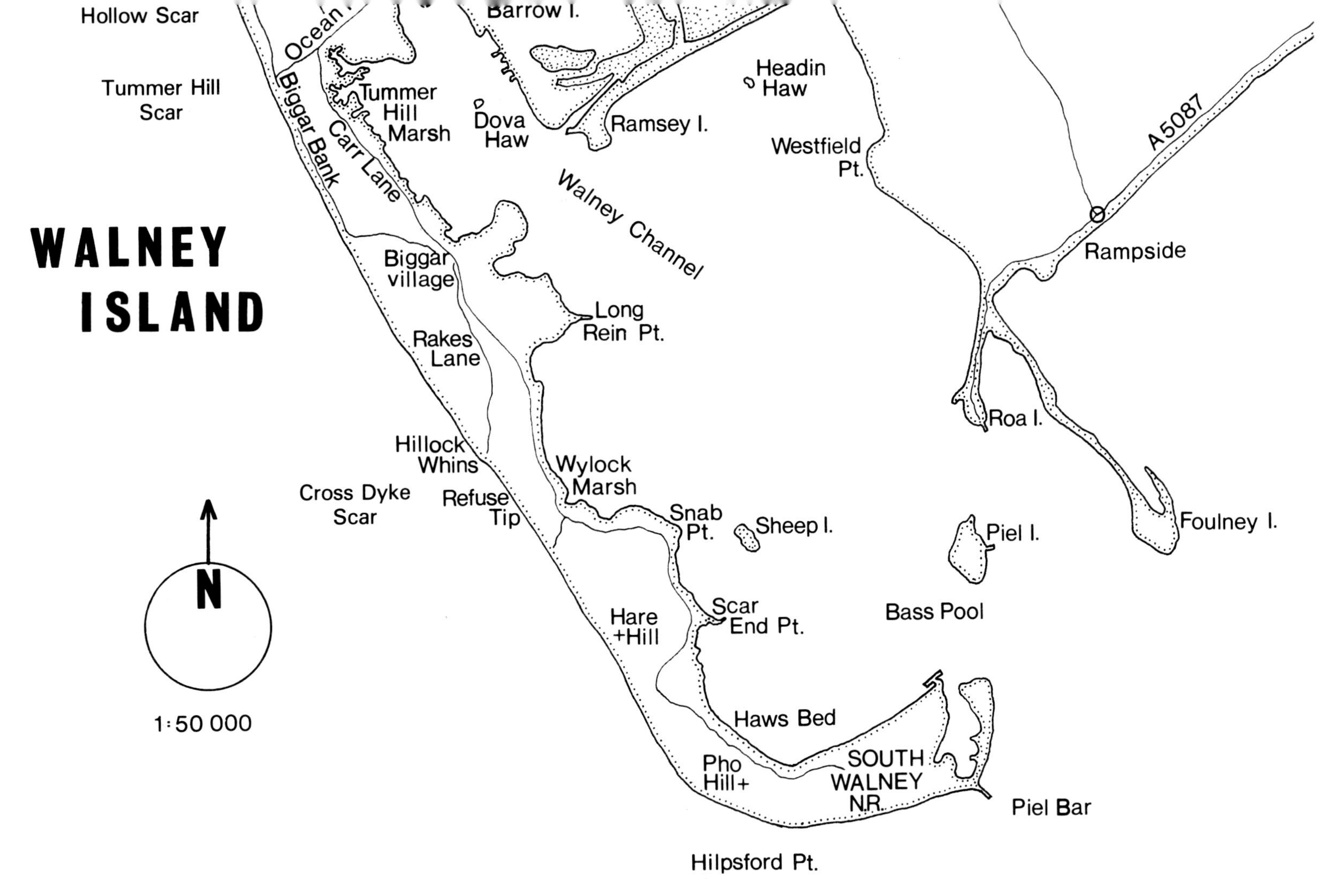
WALNEY ISLAND
Hollow Scar
Tummer Hill Scar
Ocean
Barrow I.
Biggar Bank
Carr Lane
Tummer Hill Marsh
Dova Haw
Headin Haw
Ramsey I.
Westfield Pt.
A5087
Rampside
Walney Channel
Biggar village
Long Rein Pt.
Rakes Lane
Roa I.
Hillock Whins
Wylock Marsh
Cross Dyke Scar
Refuse Tip
Snab Pt.
Sheep I.
Piel I.
Foulney I.
Hare +Hill
Scar End Pt.
Bass Pool
Haws Bed
Pho Hill+
SOUTH WALNEY N.R.
Piel Bar
Hilpsford Pt.
N
1:50 000

## 230 WHITETHROAT *Sylvia communis*

*Fairly common*

Up to 20 pairs nest on the island with, roughly, half at the north end and half in the Rakes Lane area. Birds are often on territory at the north end by the last week of April, sometimes a week prior to the first sightings at South Walney. At the latter site, daily passage is witnessed until the end of May with an exceptional 24 on 6th May 1965. Returning birds appear at the end of July and continue until the last week of September with peaks of 30 on 27th August 1967 and 20 on 12th September 1968. In 1969 there were no spring sightings and South Walney figures reflect the disastrous effect on the Whitethroat poulation of the Sahel drought of 1968/69 and 1973/74.

Average maxima 1975-1989

| | J | F | M | A | M | J | J | A | S | O | N | D |
|---|---|---|---|---|---|---|---|---|---|---|---|---|
| 1963-67 | — | — | — | 3 | 14 | 1 | 2 | 16 | 9 | — | — | — |
| 1968-72 | — | — | — | 1 | 2 | 1 | 1 | 5 | 7 | — | — | — |
| 1973-77 | — | — | — | — | 1 | — | 1 | 4 | 2 | — | — | — |
| 1978-82 | — | — | — | — | 6 | 1 | 1 | 3 | 3 | — | — | — |
| 1983-87 | — | — | — | 1 | 3 | 1 | 1 | 3 | 3 | 1 | — | — |

**Ringing and recoveries**

The observatory has ringed 841 birds, 70% caught in May and August. There are three Iberian recoveries; a juvenile ringed on 2nd September 1964 was 'wounded' near Setubal, Estremadura, Portugal (1,800 km south-southwest) on 5th October; a juvenile ringed on 2nd September 1965 was 'taken' near Renteria, Guipuzcoa, Spain (1,000 km south) on 15th September 1968; and an adult female, caught on 9th September 1967 was found ten days later near Irun, Guipuzcoa, Spain (1,000 km south).

## 231 GARDEN WARBLER *Sylvia borin*

*Uncommon*

Recorded at South Walney on 164 days in the period 1975 to 1989, 134 of them from early August to late October. There have been 13 May sightings, all of them since 1979, with a maximum four birds on 19th May 1984. Autumn passage is spread broadly from early August until late October with a peak of four on three dates in the 1980s and seven birds on 9th September 1988.

Days recorded 1975-1989

| J | F | M | A | M | J | J | A | S | O | N | D | T |
|---|---|---|---|---|---|---|---|---|---|---|---|---|
| — | — | 1 | — | 18 | 1 | 7 | 46 | 60 | 28 | 3 | — | 164 |

Records from Willow Woods are occasional, the most notable being three on 6th May 1985.

## 232 BLACKCAP *Sylvia atricapilla*

*Uncommon*

Sighted at South Walney between 1975 and 1989 on 203 days, with 128 of them in October or November. Passage birds occur over a long period embracing the whole of April and May and from September until the end of November, with a maximum 12 on 4th October 1976. Surprisingly, between 1964 and 1967 no autumn birds were recorded.

Days recorded 1975-1989

| J | F | M | A | M | J | J | A | S | O | N | D | T |
|---|---|---|---|---|---|---|---|---|---|---|---|---|
| 1 | — | — | 16 | 31 | 2 | 2 | 2 | 19 | 92 | 36 | 2 | 203 |

Willow Woods has occasionally held birds between April and November including a maximum three on 13th October 1986 and 21st April 1988.

### 233 PALLAS'S WARBLER *Phylloscopus proregulus*

*Vagrant*

During October and November 1982, 127 birds of this species were recorded in Great Britain. Of these, the only west coast sightings were at Wooltack Point, Dyfed on 30th October and two at South Walney, accepted by B.B.R.C., on 13th October.

### 234 YELLOW-BROWED WARBLER *Phylloscopus inornatus*

*Vagrant*

Birds have been recorded on six dates, all at South Walney. An individual on 8th and 9th November 1982 was thought to be of the race *humei*; one on September 1985 appeared with three Red-breasted Flycatchers (on this day, three more Yellow-browed Warblers were across the bay at Heysham); two arrived on 18th October 1985; and single birds were seen on 5th October 1968 and 5th October 1981.

### 235 BONELLI'S WARBLER *Phylloscopus bonelli*

*Vagrant*

A singing bird, accepted by B.B.R.C., was in sycamore trees above Chairman's Walk, Central Walney, on 7th May 1984.

**236 WOOD WARBLER** *Phylloscopus sibilatrix*

*Rare*

Prior to 1979 the only record was an individual at South Walney on 27th August 1965. Since 1979 when a specimen was at South Walney on 16th and 17th May, singles have been present on 11th April 1985, 4th May 1989, 20th July 1987 and 5th September 1982.

Spring birds are possibly annual at Willow Woods; 1985 produced singles on three days in May and two on 17th May; 1988 yielded two on 15th May while in 1989 an individual was singing on 7th May.

**237 CHIFFCHAFF** *Phylloscopus collybita*

*Fairly common*

A few pairs, probably no more than three, nest in Willow Woods or Chairman's Walk.

At South Walney, spring birds are usually evident by the end of March and small numbers arrive throughout April and May, with an unprecedented 50 on 3rd April 1988. September and early October provide heavier passage with peaks of 30 on 12th September 1968 and 60 on 20th September 1980. Occasionally there are birds in November and December and there is a single January instance.

Average maxima 1975-1989

| J | F | M | A | M | J | J | A | S | O | N | D |
|---|---|---|---|---|---|---|---|---|---|---|---|
| 0.1 | — | 2.1 | 7.3 | 1.7 | 0.7 | 0.6 | 1.1 | 8.7 | 2.5 | 0.5 | 0.3 |

**Ringing and recoveries**

Just under 50% of the 497 birds ringed by the observatory have been caught in September. There is a single recovery; an adult ringed on 16th September 1965 was killed by wires at Enniskillen, Fermanagh (280 km west) on 10 May 1966.

**238 WILLOW WARBLER** *Phylloscopus trochilus*

*Abundant*

Up to six pairs nest on the island, with two or three pairs in Willow Woods and the others around Biggar. Spring arrivals at South Walney usually start during early April and continue until mid-May, with 200 on 20th April 1984 as the maximum. Autumn return passage begins in late July, with heaviest numbers during August and early September and peaks of 100 on 9th August 1986, 22nd August 1987 and 40 on 10th September 1983.

Average maxima 1975-1989

| J | F | M | A | M | J | J | A | S | O | N | D |
|---|---|---|---|---|---|---|---|---|---|---|---|
| — | — | 0.4 | 37 | 22 | 0.7 | 6 | 48 | 11 | 0.3 | 0.1 | — |

**Ringing and recoveries**

Over 65% of the 4,745 birds ringed by the observatory have been caught in August. There are eight recoveries and six controls, many indicating swift movements. In this category comes an individual ringed on 1st September 1972 and caught near Minho, Portugal (1,500 km southwest) on 19th September and a specimen ringed on 20th April 1984 near Watchet, Somerset (330 km south) was controlled at Willow Woods on the following day.

**239 GOLDCREST** *Regulus regulus*

*Abundant*

Never recorded at South Walney in January, February, or July and only twice in December. The spring passage begins in mid-March and continues until the end of April; the March maximum is 80 on 27th March 1989 and the April peak 200 on 6th April 1983. A few birds are seen at the end of August, but the main autumn passage occurs in September and October with peaks of 250 on 10th September 1983 and 350 on 7th October 1983. No birds were seen in the spring of 1980, probably due to a combination of a poor 1979 breeding season and a subsequent harsh winter.

Average maxima 1975-1989

| J | F | M | A | M | J | J | A | S | O | N | D |
|---|---|---|---|---|---|---|---|---|---|---|---|
| — | — | 12 | 35 | 1 | — | — | 4 | 52 | 46 | 3 | — |

Willow Woods occasionally records birds overwintering with for example four on 10th January 1984.

**Ringing and recoveries**

Of 1,131 birds caught by the observatory, 77% have been ringed in September and October, 260 in 1983 alone. There are four recoveries; an adult of 19th March 1966 was dead at Bolton-le-Sands, Lancashire (27 km east) nine days later; a young female, ringed on 4th October 1981, was killed by a cat on 6th January 1982 near Northallerton, Yorkshire (119 km east); a young female, another feline victim, on 1st November 1983 near Le Porge, Gironde, France (1,032 km south), 30 days after being ringed; a young female controlled at Dungeness, Kent (449 km southeast) on 30th October 1983, 20 days after being ringed.

## 240 FIRECREST *Regulus ignicapillus*

*Rare*

Birds have been recorded on 27 days at South Walney in the period 1975 to 1989, with a peak of four among an influx of 200 Goldcrest on 6th April 1983. The only sighting prior to 1975 is of an individual on 6th October 1971.

Days recorded 1975-1989

| J | F | M | A | M | J | J | A | S | O | N | D | T |
|---|---|---|---|---|---|---|---|---|---|---|---|---|
| — | — | — | 7 | 1 | 1 | — | — | 1 | 8 | 9 | — | 27 |

Other singles were seen at Long Rein Point on 11th November 1980 and in Willow Woods on 20th April 1983, 23rd October and 24th October 1983.

## 241 SPOTTED FLYCATCHER *Muscicapa striata*

*Uncommon*

Although suitable habitat exists in Central Walney, breeding has never been confirmed.

Spring sightings at South Walney are almost confined to May and early June, with a maximum of eight on 23rd May 1989, although two were seen on 29th April 1972, one in Vickerstown on 30th April 1983 and one at South Walney on the same date in 1986. August and September provide the majority of autumn sightings with 12 on 26th August 1989 and seven on 26th August 1984. Of the 138 days recorded at South Walney in the period 1975 to 1987, 41 were in 1983-1984.

Days recorded 1975-1989

| J | F | M | A | M | J | J | A | S | O | N | D | T |
|---|---|---|---|---|---|---|---|---|---|---|---|---|
| — | — | — | 1 | 53 | 9 | 1 | 54 | 65 | 4 | — | — | 187 |

Willow Woods has yielded occasional records, with an unprecedented maximum of ten on 22nd August 1987.

**Ringing and recoveries**

The observatory has ringed 147 birds mostly in May, August and September. There is a solitary recovery; a juvenile ringed on 13th August 1966 was 'caught alive and being held' near Enugu, Nigeria (5,200 km southeast) on 4th October 1966.

## 242 RED-BREASTED FLYCATCHER *Ficedula parva*

*Vagrant*

Birds have been recorded on seven days all at South Walney with singles on 1st October 1972, 14th October 1974, 14th October 1977, 8th June 1984, 16th October 1986 and 21st October 1988. On 26th September, three birds, two of which were trapped and ringed, appeared in the cottage garden.

## 243 PIED FLYCATCHER *Ficedula hypoleuca*

*Uncommon*

In the period 1975 to 1989, the species has been recorded on 59 days at South Walney. Spring passasge is negligible but there is a small passage in August and September with a maximum four on 18th August 1975. Two birds appeared on the extreme date of 21st November 1970.

Days recorded 1975-1989

| J | F | M | A | M | J | J | A | S | O | N | D | T |
|---|---|---|---|---|---|---|---|---|---|---|---|---|
| — | — | — | 1 | 4 | 2 | 1 | 25 | 18 | 8 | — | — | 59 |

The only records for the rest of the island are individuals in Willow Woods on 25th April 1983 and 3rd May 1985, another sighting in James Dunn Park on the following day and a specimen in a garden in Central Walney on 26th April 1987.

## 244 LONG-TAILED TIT *Aegithalos caudatus*

*Rare.*

In only two years has the species been seen at South Walney. Eleven birds were present on 26th October 1973 and some of them remained, in the vicinity of the offices, until 2nd December. In 1983, a party of five flew south on 28th October and 13 stayed briefly on 16th November.

Individuals or small parties can appear annually in Willow Woods during late autumn and winter, with peaks of 12 on 20th November 1983, 11 on 5th October 1984, and nine on 9th December 1985 and eight on 2nd November 1988.

## 245 COAL TIT *Parus ater*

*Scarce*

Birds have been seen on 19 days at South Walney between 1965 and 1989 involving, perhaps, a score of individuals. All sightings have been in October except for solitary specimens on 17th April 1983, 29th September 1985 and 18th September 1988. October 12th has produced three birds on four occasions, in 1977, 1978, 1980 and 1988 and six were in the central marsh region on 7th October 1983.

Willow Woods occasionally holds a few birds in autumn or winter, with an unusual 11 on 20th October 1985.

**Ringing and recoveries**

With only nine birds ringed, it is remarkable that there is a recovery. One of the October 1983 birds, ringed on 7th was controlled at Lancaster (26 km east) on 16th March 1984.

## 246 BLUE TIT *Parus caerulus*

*Fairly common*

Willow Woods has up to five pairs in most years and urban Walney has a breeding population of indeterminate size.

A few instances of overwintering occur at South Walney, but most birds are seen in September and October with 100 on 30th September 1988 and 150 on 5th October 1988.

Average maxima 1975-1989

| J | F | M | A | M | J | J | A | S | O | N | D |
|---|---|---|---|---|---|---|---|---|---|---|---|
| 2 | 2 | 2 | — | — | — | 2 | 1 | 12 | 27 | 4 | 3 |

**Ringing and recoveries**

Of 331 birds ringed by the observatory, 73% have been caught in September and October. The seven recoveries are all fairly local, ranging from Ulverston, Rampside, Piel Island and Haverthwaite. The individual with the longest pedigree was ringed at Walney on 3rd October 1981, controlled at Bispham, Blackpool (25 km south-southeast) on 26th October and again controlled, this time at Lakeside, Windermere (30 km east) on 24th March 1984.

## 247 GREAT TIT *Parus major*

*Uncommon*

As a nesting species it is certainly scarce, with no more than ten pairs in the North Scale village, Willow Woods and Biggar areas.

It has been seen on 60 days at South Walney in the period 1975 to 1989 with two spring records; 25th April 1984 and 27th March 1989. Most have appeared in September and October with peaks of five on 28th September 1980 and 28th October 1983, followed in 1988 by six on 30th September and 10th October.

Days recorded 1975-1989

| J | F | M | A | M | J | J | A | S | O | N | D | T |
|---|---|---|---|---|---|---|---|---|---|---|---|---|
| — | — | 1 | 1 | — | — | 1 | 14 | 39 | — | 4 | — | 60 |

## 248 TREECREEPER *Certhia familiaris*

*Rare*

From 1964 to 1989 there are 12 records of single birds at South Walney; all appeared in the period 18th July to 28th October, with 1983 and 1985 producing two sightings each and 1989 yielding singles on 18th July, 9th and 12th September and 2nd October. There are occasional examples at Chairman's Walk and Willow Woods, the latter holding individuals on 4th November 1983, 20th and 24th October 1985 and 1st and 3rd January 1986.

## 249 GOLDEN ORIOLE *Oriolus oriolus*

*Vagrant*

A singing immature male was in Willow Woods between 20th May and 30th May 1983.

**250 RED-BACKED SHRIKE** ***Lanis collurio***

*Vagrant*

The scrubland near Willow Woods has recorded individuals on 25th May 1983 and 16th May 1985.

**251 GREAT GREY SHRIKE** ***Lanius excubitor***

*Vagrant*

All six records of this species were at South Walney, on 27th October 1968, 11th October 1975, 27th October 1975, 13th October 1976, 7th and 8th November 1982.

**252 WOODCHAT SHRIKE** ***Lanius senator.***

*Vagrant*

One was near the airfield from 2nd to 7th June 1984; and at South Walney another male remained from 20th to 30th May 1986. Both records have been accepted by B.B.R.C.

**253 JAY** ***Garrulus glandarius***

*Vagrant*

There are eight records of single birds. The Willow Woods area has seen individuals on 24th October and 14th November 1983, 11th May 1984, 1st November 1986 and 26th April 1988. The remaining occurrences involve specimens at South Walney on 27th October 1972 and 26th October 1986, while a garden in Vickerstown was visited on 24th October 1983.

**254 MAGPIE** ***Pica pica***

*Common*

Durnford (1883) describes the species as "seldom" and Benson (pers. comm.) says that it was "unheard of" on the island in the 1930s. Since the early 1970s, as in many other areas, there has been a considerable increase in the number of pairs breeding; at present (1990), the island's population is about 20 pairs, with five of them at South Walney.

Up to 1974 the species was present on only 37 days, 23 of them in September and October and seven of these in October 1972. Since 1974 the situation has changed considerably, with birds present throughout the year, and a distinct movement south in October and November with a peak of 30 on 5th October 1984.

Average maxima 1964-1989

| | J | F | M | A | M | J | J | A | S | O | N | D |
|---|---|---|---|---|---|---|---|---|---|---|---|---|
| 1964-76 | — | — | 0.2 | 0.07 | 0.3 | — | — | 0.07 | 0.3 | 1.1 | 0.6 | 0.3 |
| 1977-89 | 9.2 | 6.9 | 7.3 | 5.4 | 5.8 | 5.8 | 5.5 | 5.6 | 8.3 | 14.6 | 8.6 | 7.0 |

Small numbers are regular at the north end with a maximum of 22 on 9th January 1985, while in the Biggar village area, a roost of 42 were counted on 19th February 1987.

**Ringing and recoveries**

A total of 38 birds have been ringed, chiefly pulli in June. There are three recoveries, two of them very local, and the third, a nestling of May 1982, dead at Little Bispham, Blackpool (23 km south-southeast) at the end of July 1983.

### 255 NUTCRACKER *Nucifraga caryocatactes*

*Vagrant*

An individual, accepted by B.B.R.C., was disturbed from the tideline in Lighthouse Bay on 1st December 1979.

### 256 CHOUGH *Pyrrhocorax pyrrhocorax*

*Vagrant*

One flew south from South Walney on 21st October 1981 and one was seen in the dunes of North Walney on 16th January 1986.

### 257 JACKDAW *Corvus monedula*

*Common*

Nesting is only known at South Walney Nature Reserve where, in the ruins of the buildings that housed sand and gravel operations, up to four pairs have bred annually for at least the years 1963 to 1989. These pairs are probably overspill from Piel Island, whose castle holds both a breeding population and a winter roost. At South Walney, winter flocks and post-breeding numbers remain fairly constant, although large movements south have been noted in late October and early November with 1,000 on 13th October 1985, 850 on 30th October 1987 and 600 on 1st November 1987 as peaks.

Average maxima 1975-1989

| J | F | M | A | M | J | J | A | S | O | N | D |
|---|---|---|---|---|---|---|---|---|---|---|---|
| 46 | 63 | 63 | 46 | 30 | 37 | 50 | 46 | 30 | 381 | 153 | 60 |

**Ringing and recoveries**

Of 49 birds ringed, 12 of them pulli, there are four recoveries, three from Walney. The fourth relates to a nestling of May 1976 shot dead on 16th April 1986 at Pilling, Lancashire (24 km south-southeast).

### 258 ROOK *Corvus frugilegus*

*Fairly common*

A rookery of about 12 nests existed in Central Walney until the mid-1960s. At South Walney appearances are quite irregular, although small movements are seen each year in October and November, with peak counts of 25 on 21st October

1975 and 30 on 3rd November 1980. Hard weather sometimes induces arrivals with a maximum of 121 on 18th December 1981 and 70 on 15th January 1982.
Average maxima 1975-1989

| J | F | M | A | M | J | J | A | S | O | N | D |
|---|---|---|---|---|---|---|---|---|---|---|---|
| 7 | 2 | 3 | 3 | 3 | 2 | 2 | 2 | 2 | 9 | 7 | 13 |

Many of the records in the above table are of birds seen at the refuse tip, a daily excursion for many of the species.

At North Walney, birds have been recorded in all months, with a maximum of 34 on 30th June 1985.

## 259 CARRION CROW *Corvus corone corone*

*Common*

Between 10 and 15 pairs breed on the island, the majority in the vicinity of Willow Woods, North Scale and the airfield. The rest of Walney lacks suitable habitat, although a pair has nested at South Walney Nature Reserve on two occasions; using the pier in 1967 and the large elderberry in 1982.

Small numbers are seen at South Walney regularly throughout the year and there are southerly movements in October and November, with peaks of 40 on 15th October 1979 and 23rd October 1987 and 20 on 1st November 1986. Hard weather produced temporary influxes of 110 on 5th January 1979 and 60 on 19th December 1981.

Average maxima 1975-1989

| J | F | M | A | M | J | J | A | S | O | N | D |
|---|---|---|---|---|---|---|---|---|---|---|---|
| 11 | 3 | 5 | 5 | 3 | 2 | 1 | 2 | 5 | 15 | 7 | 8 |

The species can be seen almost daily during the year at the north end with 126 recorded on 13th November 1983.

## 260 (HOODED CROW) *Corvus corone cornix*

*Scarce*

Recorded at South Walney on 66 days in the period 1975 to 1989. Most sightings have been in spring and winter with a maximum of five during severe weather on 19th December 1981.

Days recorded 1975-1989

| J | F | M | A | M | J | J | A | S | O | N | D | T |
|---|---|---|---|---|---|---|---|---|---|---|---|---|
| 3 | 13 | 8 | 8 | 17 | 4 | 4 | — | 2 | — | 5 | 2 | 66 |

## 261 RAVEN *Corvus corax*

*Vagrant*

Benson (pers. comm.) reports that a single frequented the north end during the winters of 1945 to 1952. There are only three recent sightings with 1985 producing an individual over Water Garth Nook on 20th March and three flying south at the Coastguard Station on 5th August 1985, followed in 1989 by two birds which flew in from the Irish Sea on 14th February at South Walney. That site also yielded a tideline corpse on 17th June 1987.

## 262 PURPLE GLOSSY STARLING *Lamprotornis purpureus*

*Exotica*

This exotic was caught at South Walney on 17th April 1982; two weeks later, rather ingloriously, it was found dead in the Ladies toilet on Piel Island.

## 263 STARLING *Sturnus vulgaris*

*Abundant*

The residential areas of the island hold a plentiful supply of nesting pairs. Breeding is much scarcer at the ends of Walney, although during the extracting operations of the 1950s and 1960s South Walney had up to ten pairs nesting in the assorted buildings. With the subsequent removal of these sites, numbers declined until only two pairs bred in 1984.

Foraging flocks occur throughout the year at South Walney, the biggest between July and October and including 2,000 on 9th October 1976, 8,000 on 30th August 1979, 2,500 on 26th July 1980 and 2nd September 1980. Hard weather movements have been logged occasionally, with 2,000 on 15th January 1967 and 26th January 1969.

Average maxima 1975-1989

| J | F | M | A | M | J | J | A | S | O | N | D |
|---|---|---|---|---|---|---|---|---|---|---|---|
| 415 | 489 | 427 | 350 | 85 | 506 | 763 | 1686 | 880 | 729 | 574 | 355 |

Elsewhere on the island, large flocks are likely to be encountered in the fields around Biggar village, Tummer Hill Marsh and North Walney.

**Ringing and recoveries**

There are 21 recoveries from the 1,373 birds ringed by the observatory since 1964. Thirteen of them are very local but others include Bradford, Yorkshire (98 km east-southeast) in the following spring; Alvechurch, Worcestershire (206 km south-southeast), four winters later in 1984; and Ednaston, Derbyshire (159 km southeast) on 29th August 1985, 377 days after being ringed on Walney.

The furthest recovery was of an individual caught on Walney on 16th January 1979 and found dead near Lubeck, Schleswig-Holstein, West Germany (907 km east).

## 264 HOUSE SPARROW *Passer domesticus*

*Abundant*

Walney's urban areas hold considerable numbers of breeding birds, but elsewhere the species is rather scarce. There is no evidence of breeding on either of the two nature reserves, but a small isolated colony exists (1980s) at Old South End Farm.

At South Walney, the species appears intermittently, but there is often southerly dispersal noted between August and October with peaks of 75 on 10th August 1966, 50 on 9th September and 40 on 15th October 1981. Small groups occasionally overwinter with 40 on 4th January 1976.

Average maxima 1975-1989

| J | F | M | A | M | J | J | A | S | O | N | D |
|---|---|---|---|---|---|---|---|---|---|---|---|
| 7 | 4 | 2 | 5 | 6 | 5 | 8 | 21 | 14 | 11 | 4 | 2 |

## 265 TREE SPARROW *Passer montanus*

*Uncommon*

Recorded at South Walney on 110 days in the period 1975 to 1989. There is little pattern about these records, with 59 of these days in just four years 1976, 1978, 1983 and 1984, and presence on 30 days in the last year alone. Few sightings occur outside August to November; small flocks include peaks of 34 on 15th August 1976, 30 on 20th October 1983, 22 on 15th September 1984 and 21 on 6th November 1984.

Days recorded 1975-1989

| J | F | M | A | M | J | J | A | S | O | N | D | T |
|---|---|---|---|---|---|---|---|---|---|---|---|---|
| — | — | — | 4 | 9 | 2 | 1 | 29 | 21 | 24 | 18 | 2 | 110 |

**266 GOLDEN SPARROW** ***Passer luteus***

*Exotica*

A male was at North Scale on 14th May 1989.

**267 CHAFFINCH** ***Fringilla coelebs***

*Common*

Nesting, by up to 20 pairs, is chiefly confined to Willow Woods, the hedgerows of Biggar and North Scale villages and the allotments and less disturbed areas of urban Walney.

At South Walney, late February produces small flocks with a maximum of 21 on 29th February 1980. From then until mid-autumn appearances are irregular. Southerly movement becomes noticeable between September to November with peaks of 100 on 26th October 1975, 40 on 2nd and 5th November 1983 and 51 on 29th September 1984. Overwintering flocks sometimes appear after hard weather, with 20 on 5th January 1979 and 24th January 1984.

Average maxima 1975-1989

| J | F | M | A | M | J | J | A | S | O | N | D |
|---|---|---|---|---|---|---|---|---|---|---|---|
| 4 | 5 | 3 | 3 | 1 | 1 | — | — | 14 | 29 | 16 | 4 |

**Ringing and recoveries**

Over 33% of the 203 birds ringed by the obervatory since 1964 have been caught in October. Of five recoveries, two are very local, and the others are of autumn ringed birds located at Maybole, Ayrshire (160 km north); Alston, Cumbria (99 km northeast); and Dalston, Cumbria (82 km north).

**268 BRAMBLING** ***Fringilla montifringilla***

*Uncommon*

Southerly passage normally takes place in October and November with 11 on 18th October 1968 and 16 on 2nd November 1983. Severe weather occasionally produces fairly spectacular influxes when flocks are seen foraging along the tideline. In January 1979 up to 120 stayed for most of the month and 70 appeared in mid-December 1981. During an exceptionally cold spell in late January 1984, 150 remained into early February.

Days recorded 1975-1989

| J | F | M | A | M | J | J | A | S | O | N | D | T |
|---|---|---|---|---|---|---|---|---|---|---|---|---|
| 34 | 7 | 1 | 2 | — | — | — | — | — | 27 | 22 | 11 | 104 |

During the cold weather of January — February 1984, 130 took refuge at the north end, while Willow Woods recorded three birds on 30th March 1984 and two on 20th April 1984.

**269 GREENFINCH** ***Carduelis chloris***

*Common*

The island nesting population, utilising Willow Woods and the village hedgerows and allotments of Central Walney, is of the order of 20 to 30 pairs.

Spring passage at South Walney is sparse, with 15 on 20th April 1966 the maximum recorded; but southerly movement, often of fairly large flocks, takes place from late September until early November, with 250 on 18th October 1976 and 5th November 1983. Overwintering flocks appear regularly with 300 on 22nd February 1977, 120 on 6th December 1979 and 7th January 1980.

Average maxima 1975-1989

| J | F | M | A | M | J | J | A | S | O | N | D |
|---|---|---|---|---|---|---|---|---|---|---|---|
| 32 | 37 | 6 | 3 | 1 | — | — | 3 | 8 | 57 | 77 | 47 |

**Ringing and recoveries**

Over 80% of the 853 birds ringed by the observatory have been caught in September and October. There are 15 recoveries; seven are very local; two from Lancaster (27 km east); three from the Fylde (26 km southeast); and two from the Wirral (72 km south). Outside this north-south movement is an individual killed by a cat in Durham (135 km northeast) on 30th April 1974, five months after being ringed on Walney, and a control from Dalston, Cumbria (90 km north) on 22nd December 1984, two years and two months after being caught on Walney.

## 270 GOLDFINCH *Carduelis carduelis*

*Common*

Central Walney is the only known nesting area, but not more than three pairs actually breed. Peak numbers at South Walney occur in October and November, with 60 on 23rd October 1987 and 35 on 2nd November 1984. Overwintering foraging flocks appear regularly, with 50 on 8th January 1987 and 50 on 24th February 1987.

Average maxima 1975-1989

| J | F | M | A | M | J | J | A | S | O | N | D |
|---|---|---|---|---|---|---|---|---|---|---|---|
| 17 | 16 | 15 | 8 | 5 | 2 | — | — | 9 | 29 | 18 | 13 |

## 271 SISKIN *Carduelis spinus*

*Uncommon*

Recorded at South Walney on 124 days between 1975 and 1989, 57 of them between September 1985 and November 1987. The peak counts are 20 on 23rd September 1986, 18th and 19th September 1986, and 30th September 1989, followed by 30 on 5th October 1988. The paucity of records is surprising considering the proximity of the Lake District population.

Days recorded 1975-1989

| J | F | M | A | M | J | J | A | S | O | N | D | T |
|---|---|---|---|---|---|---|---|---|---|---|---|---|
| 1 | — | 1 | — | — | — | 1 | — | 28 | 69 | 21 | 3 | 124 |

In recent years, small numbers have been noted in spring and autumn at Willow Woods.

## 272 LINNET *Carduelis cannabina*

*Abundant*

The gorse patches and hedgerows of the island currently (1990) hold up to 70 pairs, but this is decreasing as the habitat is gradually lost. At South Walney Nature Reserve, at least 10 pairs bred in the 1960s, but by 1984, due to the loss of the gorse areas there were only two pairs.

At South Walney, heavy passage is occasionally witnessed in April and May with a peak of 200 on 21st April 1966. Larger numbers are seen between August and October with a flock of 300 on 23rd August 1983 and day totals of 825 on 26th September 1984 and 700 on 4th October 1984. Overwintering flocks, like the 350 of January 1987, are fairly unusual.

Average maxima 1975-1989

| J | F | M | A | M | J | J | A | S | O | N | D |
|---|---|---|---|---|---|---|---|---|---|---|---|
| 73 | 22 | 14 | 43 | 32 | 27 | 41 | 93 | 292 | 304 | 34 | 15 |

The species is seen regularly at North Walney with a maximum count of 294 during harsh weather on 24th January 1984.

**Ringing and recoveries**

Almost 60% of 1,226 birds have been ringed in June and August. In past years, mist-netting has been conducted successfully on Sheep Island, culminating in the 130 birds ringed in 1970. There are six recoveries, the most distant being a juvenile ringed in June 1966 and killed in October of that year at St. Medard-en-Jalles, Gironde, France (1,300 km south). An April adult female was taken by a cat in Tamworth, Staffordshire (187 km southeast) in August 1971. The remaining four recoveries were all found dead locally.

## 273 TWITE *Carduelis flavirostris*

*Uncommon*

Recorded at South Walney on 282 days in the period 1975 to 1989. Southbound birds are seen almost annually in October and November peaking at 22 on 23rd October 1971 and 32 on 6th November 1987. An overwintering flock, possibly the same birds, has been a regular feature of the late 1980s. In November 1987 a flock of 22 appeared on 26th increased to 26 by January 1988 and remained until 2nd April. In the following November the 35 of the 8th, increasing to 42 by January 1989 finally left on 7th April. The pattern was continued in November of 1989 when a flock of 35, first located on the 12th and peaking at 50 by the end of December, remained until well into 1990. Severe weather sometimes brings small parties, 55 staying from 16th to 22nd December 1981. Spring sightings are intermittent but include 17 on 15th March 1972.

Days recoıded 1975-1989

| J | F | M | A | M | J | J | A | S | O | N | D | T |
|---|---|---|---|---|---|---|---|---|---|---|---|---|
| 46 | 31 | 64 | 20 | — | — | — | — | 3 | 10 | 39 | 69 | 282 |

Elsewhere on the island, occasional sightings include six at Biggar Bank on 26th October 1983 and 11 at the north end refuse tip on 3rd December 1982.

## 274 REDPOLL *Carduelis flammea*

*Uncommon*

The species breeds in considerable numbers at Angerton Marsh, 16 km to the north, but despite suitable haitat on Walney Island and, during the 1980s, singing birds in Willow Woods, there is no evidence of breeding.

Sightings at South Walney before April are rare but there is a distinct northward passage in May with a peak of five on 1st May 1966. A flock of 200 on 28th September 1980 is untypical, but there is obvious movement from late September to mid November with peaks of 24 on 21st September 1966, 20 on 25th November 1968 and 18 on 23rd October 1981.

Days recorded 1975-1989

| J | F | M | A | M | J | J | A | S | O | N | D | T |
|---|---|---|---|---|---|---|---|---|---|---|---|---|
| 1 | 2 | 2 | 5 | 22 | 3 | 1 | 2 | 10 | 49 | 12 | 12 | 121 |

Apart from the singing birds of Willow Woods, there are few records for the north end, but exceptions are eight on 6th November 1983 and five on 13th May 1984 and 16th May 1986.

## 275 CROSSBILL *Loxia curvivostra*

*Vagrant*

The only records are from South Walney where individuals have been seen on 8th December 1987 and 17th July 1989 followed by two southbound birds on 22nd August.

**276 BULLFINCH** *Pyrrhula pyrrhula*

*Uncommon*

Walney's only site, Willow Woods, has held up to three pairs for at least the period 1974 to 1989. The species is very sedentary and South Walney's only record is of a single male on 8th September 1967. A male at Biggar on 26th November 1988, represents only the second ever sighting in the southern half of the island.

**277 HAWFINCH** *Coccothraustes coccothraustes*

*Vagrant*

Benson (pers. comm.) states that a pair nested near the airfield gates immediately prior to the Second World War. The only other records are of single birds in Willow Woods on 20th April 1983 and James Dunn Park on 19th September 1984.

**278 PALM WARBLER** *Dendroica palmarum*

*Vagrant — possibly ship-assisted*

A male corpse of this North American species was found on the west shore of the island on 18th May 1976. This was a first record for Great Britain and was allocated to Category D by the B.O.U. Records Committee.

**279 WHITE-THROATED SPARROW** *Zonotrichia albicollis*

*Vagrant*

The third record for Great Britain, accepted by B.B.R.C., was a male trapped in the cottage garden at South Walney on 17th June 1965. The bird was released in Barrow cemetery on the following day.

**280 LAPLAND BUNTING** *Calcarius lapponicus*

*Rare*

MacPherson (1892) "fell in with a solitary Lapland Bunting on 17th October 1890". Short staying birds were at South Walney on 26th April and 5th October

1968, 27th September and 1st November 1970, 5th November 1984 and in 1987 on 23rd October and 5th November interspersed by two birds on 2nd November. Longer staying birds, all singles, were on the south shore from 30th November to 1st December 1982, at Snab Point from 2nd to 4th December 1983 and an immature male at the refuse tip from 18th to 21st October 1989.

### 281 SNOW BUNTING *Plectrophenax nivalis*

*Uncommon*

Most sightings refer to individuals or small groups but hard weather has brought in sizeable numbers notably 30 on 27th December 1957 and 13 on 10th January 1960. However, the flocks which arrived at South Walney in late January 1984 were quite unprecedented with 350 on 24th, 308 on 26th, and 356 on 27th.

Days recorded 1975-1989

| J | F | M | A | M | J | J | A | S | O | N | D | T |
|---|---|---|---|---|---|---|---|---|---|---|---|---|
| 33 | 14 | 1 | 1 | — | — | — | — | 3 | 2 | 24 | 26 | 104 |

North Walney's contribution to the totals in late January 1984 included 81 birds on 24th and 180 on 27th. Records prior to these chiefly involve singles between October and February although ten were present on 26th December 1957 and five on 30th December 1982. A flock of 15 were present on 30th December 1987.

### 282 YELLOWHAMMER *Emberiza citrinella*

*Scarce*

There are no breeding records for the 1980s although Benson (pers. comm.) reports that, up to the mid 1970s, pairs nested at the Coastguard Station and near Willow Woods.

The species appears sporadically at South Walney but was absent from 1968 to 1974. Peak counts include 12 on 27th December 1963, eight on 19th September 1965 and three on 22nd April 1983.

Days recorded 1975-1989

| J | F | M | A | M | J | J | A | S | O | N | D | T |
|---|---|---|---|---|---|---|---|---|---|---|---|---|
| 2 | 1 | 2 | 7 | — | 2 | — | 3 | 5 | 8 | 2 | — | 32 |

North Walney records two birds on 20th November 1983 and one on each of 15th December 1983 and 4th June 1985.

**283 ORTOLAN BUNTING** *Emberiza hortulata*

*Vagrant*

The first island record was a single at the lighthouse on 7th October 1963. A male at Willow Woods on 1st May 1988 constituted the second island and Cumbrian record.

**284 LITTLE BUNTING** *Emberiza pusilla*

*Vagrant*

Accepted by B.B.R.C., a single bird was feeding with Meadow Pipits on the tideline at South Walney on 22nd September 1965.

**285 REED BUNTING** *Emberiza schoeniclus*

*Common*

The island supports a population of up to 20 pairs, the majority being at the north end and in the Biggar village area. The loss of suitable habitat at South Walney has led to a decline from ten pairs in 1964 to just one pair by the early 1980s. The species is, however, seen throughout the year at South Walney with overwintering flocks peaking at 26 on 15th February 1984. Spring movement is normally insignificant and 50 on 30th March 1965 most unusual. From the end of August until mid-November, small parties move south with 50 on 22nd September 1988, 16th October 1967 and 11th October 1980, and 20 on 15th November 1983.

Average maxima 1975-1989

| J | F | M | A | M | J | J | A | S | O | N | D |
|---|---|---|---|---|---|---|---|---|---|---|---|
| 3 | 5 | 4 | 4 | 4 | 3 | 3 | 6 | 12 | 21 | 5 | 4 |

The species can also be seen during the year at the north end with regular winter flocks of up to 40 birds. Similar sized parties are occasionally seen during winter around Biggar.

**Ringing and recoveries**

Almost one third of the observatory's 439 birds have been caught in August. Two of the four recoveries relate to birds controlled on the Wirral between November and January, and a third is of a young male ringed in July 1978 and controlled at Shotton, Clwyd (93 km south) in October 1979.

**286 RED-HEADED BUNTING** *Emberiza bruniceps*

*Vagrant — possible escape*

Individuals have been seen at the refuse tip on 27th June 1979 and 19th July 1986.

**287 CORN BUNTING** *Miliaria calandra*

*Rare*

MacPherson (1892) records the species nesting on the island but there have been no other examples, although up to six pairs breed across Walney Channel, at Rampside. South Walney was host to a potential breeder when a singing male was present from 19th to 25th June 1971.

Recorded on only nine days in the period 1975 to 1989 with March and April providing six of these including two birds on 17th March 1984 and 23rd April 1984. A maximum three birds were seen on 31st March 1969.

# Breeding Birds

**Birds breeding on Walney Island** (based on years 1980-1989)

**Abundant,** more than 200 pairs per year

Eider
Gull, Herring
Gull, Lesser Black-backed

**Common,** 101 to 200 pairs per year

Lapwing
Oystercatcher
Pipit, Meadow
Skylark
Starling

**Fairly common,** 21 to 100 pairs per year

Blackbird
Chaffinch
Dunnock
Greenfinch
Gull, Black-headed
Gull, Great Black-backed
Linnet
Magpie
Mallard
Plover, Ringed
Robin
Shelduck
Sparrow, House
Thrush, Song
Tit, Blue
Wren

**Uncommon,** 11 to 20 pairs per year

Bunting, Reed
Dove, Collared
Moorhen
Redshank
Swallow
Tern, Common
Tern, Little
Warbler, Sedge
Whitethroat

**Scarce,** 5 to 10 pairs per year

Coot
Crow, Carrion
Duck, Tufted
Grebe, Little
Partridge,Grey
Swift
Tit, Great
Warbler, Willow
Woodpigeon

**Rare,** less than 5 pairs or not breeding annually

| | |
|---|---|
| Bullfinch | Owl, Little |
| Chiffchaff | Shoveler |
| Cuckoo | Snipe |
| Dove, Stock | Sparrowhawk |
| Duck, Tufted | Stonechat |
| Goldfinch | Swan, Mute |
| Goose, Canada | Tern, Arctic |
| Goose, Greylag | Tern, Sandwich |
| Jackdaw | Thrush, Mistle |
| Kestrel | Wagtail, Pied |
| Martin, House | Warbler, Grasshopper |
| Merganser, Red-breasted | Wheatear |
| Owl, Barn | Whitethroat Lesser |

**Last records of birds no longer breeding on Walney Island**

| | | |
|---|---|---|
| 1979 | Sand Martin | 3 nests Hare Hill |
| 1975 | Pheasant (introduced) | Nest near Biggar |
| c.1975 | Yellowhammer | Nest near Coastguard Station |
| c.1965 | Rook | 12 nests Central Walney |
| 1961 | Roseate Tern | 8 nests South Walney |
| 1957 | Teal | One duckling South Walney |
| Inter-war | Corncrake | 12 nests |
| 1918-1939 | Turtle Dove | Nest near airfield |
| 1918-1939 | Grey Wagtail | Nest at North End Farm |
| 1918-1939 | Hawfinch | Nest near airfield |
| 1906 | Short-eared Owl | 4 nests North Walney |
| 1890 | Corn Bunting | ? |
| 1864 | Rock Pipit | One nest |

# Summer Migrants at South Walney 1964-1989

| | Arrival dates | | Departure dates | |
|---|---|---|---|---|
| | Median | Earliest | Median | Latest |
| Goldcrest | 24 March | 6.3.83 | 5 Nov. | 6.12.83 |
| Wheatear | 25 March | 24.2.84 | 20 Oct. | 11.11.84 |
| Chiffchaff | 2 April | 12.3.78 | 27 Oct. | 18.12.71 |
| Sandwich Tern | 24 March | 14.3.68 | 30 Sep. | 26.10.86 |
| Firecrest (a) | 18 April | 4.4.76 | 30 Oct. | 16.11.86 |
| Ring Ousel | 6 April | 19.2.84 | 25 Oct. | 5.11.83 |
| | | | | |
| Black Redstart (a) | 6 April | 9.3.83 | 8 Nov. | 9.12.84 |
| Swallow | 14 April | 27.3.66 (c) | 24 Oct. | 10.11.76 (c) |
| Willow Warbler | 12 April | 27.3.89 | 27 Sep. | 8.11.82 |
| Sand Martin | 17 April | 25.3.81 | 24 Sep. | 1.11.87 |
| Redstart | 23 April | 9.4.89 | 27 Sep. | 25.10.88 |
| | | | | |
| Yellow Wagtail | 20 April | 6.4.80 | 27 Sep. | 26.11.78 |
| Whimbrel (a) | 21 April | 7.4.69 | 4 Oct. | 24.10.65 |
| Tree Pipit | 22 April | 4.4.64 | 25 Sep. | 22.10.81 |
| Common Sandpiper | 26 April | 16.4.83 | 20 Sep. | 30.10.80 |
| 'Commic' Tern | 24 April | 12.4.70 | 23 Sep. | 23.10.69 |
| | | | | |
| Great Skua (a) | 29 April | 24.3.84 | 12 Oct. | 20.10.83 |
| Common Tern (d) | 1 May | 10.4.87 | 7 Sep. | 8.10.88 |
| Little Tern | 2 May | 13.4.84 | 26 Aug. | 8.10.88 |
| Grasshopper Warbler | 2 May | 14.4.71 | 9 Sep. | 28. 9 .89 |
| Blackcap (a) | 28 April | 5.4.85 | 9 Nov. | 21.11.75 (c) |
| | | | | |
| Whinchat | 1 May | 19.4.88 | 4 Oct. | 6.11.89 |
| Sedge Warbler | 30 April | 19.4.88 | 13 Sep. | 9.10.71 |
| Whitethroat | 2 May | 7.4.65 | 26 Sep. | 26.11.64 |
| Arctic Tern (d) | 6 May | 17.4.81 (c) | 9 Sep. | 8.10.88 (c) |
| Garden Warbler | 10 May | 26.3.82 | 8 Oct. | 5.11.89 |
| | | | | |
| Cuckoo | 14 May | 19.4.84 | 7 Aug. | 16. 9 .65 |
| Swift | 10 May | 28.4.68 | 26 Aug. | 4.11.88 |
| Arctic Skua | 7 May | 5.4.79 | 10 Oct. | 2.12.79 |
| Reed Warbler (b) | — | 13.5.79 | — | 24. 8 .79 |
| Turtle Dove | 28 May | 26.3.64 | 26 Aug. | 6.10.86 |
| | | | | |
| House Martin | 5 May | 21.4.68 (c) | 8 Oct. | 19.11.86 |
| Black Tern | 27 May | 4.5.80 (c) | 1 Sep. | 12.10.83 |
| Spotted Flycatcher | 15 May | 29.4.72 | 16 Sep. | 24.10.88 |
| Pied Flycatcher | 15 May | 26.4.87 | 16 Sep. | 21.11.70 |
| Wood Warbler (b) | 16 May | 11.4.85 | — | 20. 7 .87 |
| Wryneck (b) | — | 20.5.83 | — | 20.10.83 |
| Lesser Whitethroat (b) | 24 May | 4.6.84 | — | 12.10.87 |

# Winter Migrants at South Walney 1964-1989

| | Arrival dates | | Departure dates | |
|---|---|---|---|---|
| | Median | Earliest | Median | Latest |
| Greenshank | 17 Jul. | 1. 7 .71 (c) | 11 Apr. | 30.5.76 |
| Golden Plover | 9 Aug. | 11. 7 .82 | 26 Apr. | 31.5.71 (c) |
| Grey Plover | 11 Aug. | 8. 7 .82 | 4 May | 29.5.69 |
| Wigeon | 23 Aug. | 6. 7 .83 | 22 Apr. | 31.5.76 |
| Merlin | 24 Aug. | 5. 7 .64 | 10 Apr. | 31.5.76 |
| Pink-footed Goose | 3 Oct. | 15. 9 .88 | 16 Feb. | 1.3.83 |
| Redwing | 6 Oct. | 9. 9 .76 | 4 Apr. | 23.4.67 |
| Jack Snipe | 8 Oct. | 30. 7 .84 | 12 Mar. | 17.4.66 |
| Fieldfare | 15 Oct. | 28. 9 .84 | 20 Apr. | 7.5.76 |
| Brambling | 23 Oct. | 7.10.83 | 1 Mar. | 24.4.85 |
| Goldeneye (a) | 18 Oct. | 6. 9 .87 | 12 Apr. | 6.5.71 |
| Whooper Swan | 28 Oct. | 8.10.88 | 26 Mar. | 6.4.86 |

Notes:

(a) Overwintering or oversummering birds excluded wherever possible.

(b) Insufficient records for median calculation.

(c) Date equalled in subsequent year(s).

(d) See, also, 'Commic' Tern.

# Tables of Ringing

## Birds ringed by Walney Bird Observatory 1964-1989

| | J | F | M | A | M | J | J | A | S | O | N | D | T |
|---|---|---|---|---|---|---|---|---|---|---|---|---|---|
| Auk, Little | — | 1 | — | — | — | — | — | — | — | — | — | — | 1 |
| Blackbird | 51 | 63 | 226 | 80 | 5 | 15 | 29 | 74 | 21 | 366 | 360 | 74 | 1364 |
| | | | | | 9p | 4p | | | | | | | 13p |
| Blackcap | — | — | — | 18 | 27 | 1 | 2 | 5 | 18 | 93 | 15 | — | 179 |
| Brambling | 2 | — | — | 1 | — | — | — | — | — | — | — | — | 3 |
| Bullfinch | — | — | — | 5 | 2 | — | — | 10 | — | 1 | — | — | 16 |
| Bunting, Reed | 4 | 5 | 30 | 49 | 11 | 15 | 67 | 145 | 45 | 68 | 3 | 3 | 445 |
| | | | | | 2p | 16p | 4p | | | | | | 22p |
| Bunting, Snow | 2 | — | — | — | — | — | — | — | — | — | — | — | 2 |
| Chaffinch | 1 | 2 | 21 | 18 | 11 | 5 | 1 | 18 | 28 | 97 | 18 | 3 | 223 |
| | | | | | 4p | | | | | | | | 4p |
| Chiffchaff | — | — | 12 | 110 | 65 | 21 | 9 | 40 | 310 | 58 | 5 | 3 | 633 |
| Coot | 2 | — | — | — | — | — | — | — | — | — | 1 | — | 3 |
| Crow, Carrion | — | — | — | — | 1 | — | — | — | — | — | — | — | 1 |
| | | | | | | 3p | | | | | | | 3p |
| Cuckoo | — | — | — | — | 2 | 3 | 2 | 5 | — | — | — | — | 12 |
| Curlew | — | — | 2 | — | — | — | — | — | — | — | — | 1 | 3 |
| Dove, Collared | — | — | — | 2 | 1 | — | 1 | — | — | — | — | — | 4 |
| Dove, Stock | — | — | — | — | — | — | — | 1 | — | — | — | — | 1 |
| | | | | | 1p | 1p | | | | | | | 2p |
| Dove, Turtle | — | — | — | — | — | 1 | — | — | — | — | — | — | 1 |
| Dunlin | — | 1 | — | — | 1 | — | — | 14 | — | 1 | 1 | — | 18 |
| Dunnock | 12 | 4 | 11 | 13 | — | 1 | 8 | 57 | 198 | 311 | 40 | 6 | 661 |
| | | | | | 3p | | | | | | | | 3p |
| Eider | — | 1 | — | 2 | 41 | 14 | — | — | — | — | — | — | 58 |
| Fieldfare | 4 | — | 1 | 6 | 1 | — | — | — | — | 5 | 2 | — | 19 |
| Firecrest | — | — | — | 2 | 1 | — | — | — | 1 | 3 | 2 | — | 9 |
| Flycatcher, Pied | — | — | — | 1 | 2 | — | — | 36 | 10 | 5 | — | — | 53 |
| Flycatcher, R-b. | — | — | — | — | — | 1 | — | — | 2 | 3 | — | — | 6 |
| Flycatcher, Spot. | — | — | — | — | 51 | 17 | — | 66 | 42 | 1 | — | — | 177 |

| | J | F | M | A | M | J | J | A | S | O | N | D | T |
|---|---|---|---|---|---|---|---|---|---|---|---|---|---|
| Godwit, Blk.-tailed | — | — | — | — | — | — | — | — | 1 | — | — | — | 1 |
| Goldcrest | — | — | 70 | 232 | 5 | — | — | 30 | 871 | 578 | 21 | — | 1807 |
| Goldfinch | 3 | 11 | 3 | 15 | 5 | — | — | — | 2 | 19 | 17 | — | 75 |
| Grebe, Gt. Crested | — | 1 | — | — | — | — | — | — | — | — | — | — | 1 |
| Greenfinch | 52 | 9 | 5 | 5 | — | — | 1 | 9 | 13 | 384 | 387 | 87 | 952 |
| Guillemot | — | — | — | — | — | — | — | — | — | — | — | 1 | 1 |
| Gull, Black-hd. | | | | | | | 3p | | | | | | 3p |
| Gull, Great B-b. | — | — | — | — | — | — | — | — | 1 | — | — | — | 1 |
| | | | | | | 481p | 204p | | | | | | 685p |
| Gull, Herring | 3 | 5 | 51 | 83 | 1 | 47 | 4 | 95 | 4 | — | — | — | 293 |
| | | | | | | 132p | 50p | | | | | | 182p |
| Gull, Lsr. B-b. | — | 1 | 25 | 89 | 1 | 32 | 12 | 31 | 2 | — | — | — | 193 |
| | | | | | | 192p | 76p | | | | | | 268p |
| Jackdaw | — | — | 1 | 1 | — | 11 | 20 | 2 | — | 1 | — | 1 | 37 |
| | | | | | 3p | 8p | 1p | | | | | | 12p |
| Kestrel | — | — | — | 2 | — | — | — | 1 | 6 | 1 | 1 | 2 | 12 |
| Lapwing | | | | | 48p | 15p | | | | | | | 63p |
| Linnet | 7 | 12 | 31 | 81 | 49 | 240 | 88 | 469 | 151 | 35 | — | 2 | 1165 |
| | | | | | 29p | 37p | 31p | | | | | | 97p |
| Magpie | — | — | — | — | 1 | 7 | 9 | 6 | 2 | 2 | 1 | — | 28 |
| | | | | | 15p | | | | | | | | 15p |
| Mallard | 8 | — | — | 3 | 1 | 1 | 1 | 4 | — | — | — | — | 18 |
| Martin, House | — | — | — | — | — | — | — | — | — | 1 | — | — | 1 |
| Martin, Sand | — | — | — | — | — | — | — | 2 | — | — | — | — | 2 |
| Merlin | — | — | — | — | — | — | — | — | — | 2 | — | — | 2 |
| Moorhen | 4 | 1 | 5 | 5 | 5 | 1 | 1 | 5 | 13 | 9 | 5 | — | 54 |
| Nightingale | — | — | — | — | — | 1 | — | — | — | — | — | — | 1 |
| Ousel, Ring | — | — | — | 2 | — | — | — | — | — | 1 | — | — | 3 |
| Owl, Barn | — | — | — | — | — | — | — | — | 1 | — | — | — | 1 |
| Owl, Little | — | — | — | — | — | — | — | — | — | 8 | 1 | 1 | 10 |
| Owl, Long-e. | — | — | — | — | — | — | — | — | — | 1 | — | 2 | 3 |
| Owl, Short-e. | — | — | — | — | — | — | — | — | 1 | 1 | — | — | 2 |
| Oystercatcher | 46 | 4 | 3 | 1 | 2 | — | — | 13 | — | 1 | — | — | 70 |
| | | | | | 2p | 45p | 77p | 7p | | | | | 131p |

| | J | F | M | A | M | J | J | A | S | O | N | D | T |
|---|---|---|---|---|---|---|---|---|---|---|---|---|---|
| Partridge, Grey | — | — | 1 | 10 | — | — | — | — | — | — | 1 | — | 12 |
| Phalarope, Grey | — | — | — | — | — | — | — | — | 1 | — | — | — | 1 |
| Pipit, Meadow | 5 | 2 | 23 | 53 | 10 | 8 | 19 | 92 | 175 | 64 | 10 | 3 | 464 |
| | | | | | 74p | 14p | 4p | | | | | | 92p |
| Pipit, Rock | 1 | — | — | — | — | — | — | — | — | — | — | — | 1 |
| Pipit, Tree | — | — | — | 1 | 4 | — | — | 28 | 11 | — | — | — | 44 |
| Plover, Grey | — | — | — | — | — | — | — | — | — | — | 1 | — | 1 |
| Plover, Ringed | — | — | — | — | — | — | — | 3 | 11 | — | — | 1 | 15 |
| | | | | | 24p | 4p | 18p | 5p | | | | | 51p |
| Rail, Water | — | — | — | — | — | — | — | — | — | — | 1 | — | 1 |
| Redpoll | — | — | — | 1 | 1 | — | — | — | 2 | 3 | 2 | — | 9 |
| Redshank | 3 | — | — | — | — | — | — | 1 | 5 | 5 | 1 | — | 15 |
| Redstart | — | — | — | 29 | 62 | 8 | 6 | 50 | 81 | 8 | — | — | 244 |
| Redstart, Black | — | — | 2 | 3 | 1 | 1 | 1 | 1 | — | 1 | 3 | 1 | 14 |
| Redwing | 39 | 44 | 40 | 17 | — | — | — | — | 1 | 56 | 20 | 32 | 249 |
| Robin | 7 | 5 | 40 | 39 | 12 | 1 | 3 | 344 | 899 | 208 | 21 | 4 | 1583 |
| Rook | — | — | — | 1 | — | — | — | — | — | — | — | — | 1 |
| Ruff | — | — | — | — | — | — | — | 3 | 1 | — | — | — | 4 |
| Sanderling | — | — | — | — | 3 | — | — | — | 1 | — | — | — | 4 |
| Sandpiper, Com. | — | — | — | — | — | — | — | 13 | 1 | — | — | — | 14 |
| Sandpiper, Wood | — | — | — | — | — | — | — | 1 | — | — | — | — | 1 |
| Shelduck | — | 1 | — | — | — | — | — | — | — | — | — | — | 1 |
| Shrike, Gt. Grey | — | — | — | — | — | — | — | — | — | — | 1 | — | 1 |
| Shrike, Wd/chat | — | — | — | — | 1 | — | — | — | — | — | — | — | 1 |
| Siskin | — | — | — | — | — | — | — | — | — | — | 3 | — | 3 |
| Skylark | 6 | 19 | 13 | 6 | 4 | 5 | 1 | 2 | 1 | 1 | — | — | 58 |
| | | | | | 53p | 31p | 8p | | | | | | 92p |
| Snipe | 5 | 10 | 2 | — | — | — | — | 12 | 9 | 20 | 1 | 7 | 66 |
| Snipe, Jack | — | — | — | — | — | — | — | — | — | 2 | — | — | 3 |
| Sparrow, House | — | 1 | 5 | 6 | 2 | 3 | 26 | 89 | 24 | 21 | — | — | 177 |
| | | | | | | 4p | | | | | | | 4p |
| Sparrow, Tree | — | — | — | 3 | 1 | — | — | 8 | 11 | — | 1 | — | 24 |
| Sparrow, W/thd | — | — | — | — | — | 1 | — | — | — | — | — | — | 1 |
| Sparrowhawk | — | 4 | — | — | 2 | — | — | 4 | 7 | 7 | 1 | 1 | 26 |

| | J | F | M | A | M | J | J | A | S | O | N | D | T |
|---|---|---|---|---|---|---|---|---|---|---|---|---|---|
| Starling | 126 | 35 | 2 | 13 | 36 | 207 | 193 | 275 | 200 | 144 | 40 | 63 | 1334 |
| | | | | | 137p | 25p | 12p | | | | | | 174p |
| Stint, Little | — | — | — | — | — | — | — | — | 1 | — | — | — | 1 |
| Stonechat | — | 2 | 7 | 3 | 7 | 5 | 24 | 40 | 51 | 44 | 9 | 1 | 193 |
| | | | | | 13p | | | | | | | | 13p |
| Swallow | — | — | — | — | 2 | 4 | 7 | 37 | 33 | 1 | — | — | 84 |
| | | | | | | 72p | 87p | 76p | 23p | 2p | | | 260p |
| Swan, Mute | — | — | 1 | — | — | — | 1 | — | — | 7 | — | — | 9 |
| | | | | | | | | 8p | | | | 8p | |
| Teal | — | 2 | — | 1 | — | — | — | — | — | 4 | 2 | 1 | 10 |
| Tern, Arctic | | | | | | 8p | 5p | | | | | | 13p |
| Tern, Common | — | — | — | — | — | — | — | 4 | — | — | — | — | 4 |
| | | | | | | 3p | 42p | 21p | | | | | 66p |
| Tern, Little | | | | | | | 34p | | | | | | 34p |
| Tern, Sandwich | | | | | | | 4p | | | | | | 4p |
| Thrush, Mistle | — | — | — | 1 | — | — | — | — | — | 1 | — | 2 | 4 |
| Thrush, Song | 29 | 69 | 40 | 14 | 2 | 3 | 5 | 17 | 38 | 235 | 123 | 79 | 654 |
| | | | | | 22p | | | | | | | | 22p |
| Tit, Blue | 1 | 1 | — | 5 | 1 | — | 28 | 48 | 136 | 238 | 16 | 2 | 476 |
| Tit, Coal | — | — | — | 1 | — | — | — | — | 3 | 7 | — | — | 11 |
| Tit, Great | — | — | — | — | — | — | 1 | 20 | 17 | 27 | — | — | 65 |
| Tit, Long-t. | — | — | — | — | — | — | — | — | — | 11 | 15 | — | 26 |
| Treecreeper | — | — | — | — | — | — | 3 | — | 1 | 1 | — | — | 5 |
| Twite | — | — | 1 | — | — | — | — | — | — | — | — | — | 1 |
| Wagtail, Grey | — | — | — | — | — | — | 1 | 1 | 15 | 5 | — | — | 22 |
| Wagtail, Pied | — | 1 | — | 2 | 5 | 2 | 20 | 54 | 31 | 4 | 1 | 1 | 121 |
| | | | | | 11p | 6p | 3p | | | | | | 20p |
| Wagtail, Yellow | — | — | — | — | — | — | 6 | 17 | 8 | — | — | — | 31 |
| Warbler, Barred | — | — | — | — | — | — | — | 2 | 1 | 1 | — | — | 4 |
| Warbler, Garden | — | — | — | — | 16 | 3 | 7 | 59 | 41 | 21 | 2 | — | 149 |
| Warbler, Grassh. | — | — | — | 17 | 23 | — | — | 2 | 3 | — | — | — | 45 |
| Warbler, Ict/ne. | — | — | — | — | — | — | — | 2 | — | — | — | — | 2 |
| Warbler, Marsh | — | — | — | — | — | — | — | — | 1 | — | — | — | 1 |
| Warbler, Melod. | — | — | — | — | 1 | 1 | — | 6 | 2 | — | — | — | 10 |

| | J | F | M | A | M | J | J | A | S | O | N | D | T |
|---|---|---|---|---|---|---|---|---|---|---|---|---|---|
| Warbler, Paddyf. | — | — | — | — | — | — | — | — | 1 | — | — | — | 1 |
| Warbler, Reed | — | — | — | — | — | — | — | 1 | — | — | — | — | 1 |
| Warbler, Sedge | — | — | — | 4 | 99 | — | 18 | 95 | 12 | 1 | — | — | 229 |
| | | | | | | | 4p | | | | | | 4p |
| Warbler, Subalp. | — | — | — | — | — | 1 | — | — | — | — | — | — | 1 |
| Warbler, Willow | — | — | 2 | 603 | 826 | 27 | 234 | 3383 | 269 | 3 | — | — | 5347 |
| Warbler, Wood | — | — | — | — | 1 | — | 1 | — | — | — | — | — | 2 |
| Warbler, Yl-brd. | — | — | — | — | — | — | — | — | — | 2 | — | — | 2 |
| Wheatear | — | — | 2 | 28 | 15 | — | 1 | 31 | 10 | 1 | — | — | 89 |
| Whinchat | — | — | — | 2 | 47 | 1 | 22 | 60 | 65 | 7 | 1 | — | 205 |
| Whitethroat | — | — | — | 11 | 241 | 29 | 32 | 386 | 184 | 3 | — | — | 886 |
| Whitethroat, Lsr. | — | — | — | — | — | 2 | 1 | 8 | 2 | 1 | — | — | 14 |
| Wigeon | 1 | — | — | — | — | — | — | — | — | — | — | — | 1 |
| Woodcock | — | 2 | — | — | — | — | — | — | — | — | 1 | 2 | 5 |
| Woodpecker, Grn. | — | — | — | — | — | — | — | 1 | — | — | — | — | 1 |
| Woodpigeon | — | — | — | — | — | — | — | 1 | — | — | — | — | 1 |
| Wren | 9 | 2 | 16 | 79 | 5 | — | 3 | 23 | 287 | 598 | 97 | 26 | 1145 |
| Wryneck | — | — | — | — | — | — | — | — | 2 | — | — | — | 2 |
| Yellowhammer | 1 | — | 1 | 2 | — | — | — | — | — | — | 2 | 1 | 7 |

**Monthly and annual ringing totals on South Walney 1964-1989.**

| | J | F | M | A | M | J | J | A | S | O | N | D | Fg. | p. |
|---|---|---|---|---|---|---|---|---|---|---|---|---|---|---|
| 1964 | 0 | 13 | 53 | 60 | 103 | 47 | 81 | 140 | 140 | 68 | 15 | 2 | 666 | 56 |
| 1965 | 17 | 24 | 102 | 110 | 148 | 39 | 90 | 240 | 175 | 55 | 10 | 0 | 937 | 73 |
| 1966 | 5 | 5 | 69 | 201 | 76 | 74 | 35 | 287 | 187 | 217 | 21 | 9 | 1082 | 104 |
| 1967 | 4 | 1 | 47 | 87 | 89 | 22 | 7 | 217 | 96 | 50 | 15 | 1 | 594 | 42 |
| 1968 | 0 | 2 | 6 | 56 | 31 | 38 | 20 | 220 | 81 | 62 | 4 | 3 | 523 | 64 |
| 1969 | 40 | 6 | 16 | 12 | 23 | 20 | 34 | 358 | 129 | 68 | 9 | 12 | 727 | 34 |
| 1970 | 12 | 2 | 9 | 30 | 28 | 0 | 43 | 345 | 130 | 22 | 20 | 3 | 644 | 29 |
| 1971 | 4 | 1 | 6 | 64 | 44 | 61 | 0 | 204 | 171 | 58 | 48 | 21 | 682 | 32 |
| 1972 | 0 | 9 | 19 | 3 | 25 | 32 | 18 | 65 | 162 | 88 | 67 | 12 | 500 | 20 |
| 1973 | 3 | 11 | 4 | 11 | 19 | 5 | 29 | 81 | 79 | 204 | 66 | 16 | 528 | 24 |
| 1974 | 3 | 23 | 1 | 8 | 1 | 20 | 5 | 99 | 97 | 23 | 17 | 6 | 317 | 55 |
| 1975 | 2 | 3 | 2 | 16 | 9 | 10 | 8 | 136 | 44 | 57 | 37 | 8 | 332 | 27 |
| 1976 | 2 | 7 | 4 | 58 | 40 | 52 | 35 | 263 | 145 | 287 | 83 | 62 | 1038 | 17 |
| 1977 | 31 | 33 | 27 | 54 | 40 | 29 | 48 | 362 | 161 | 187 | 38 | 9 | 1019 | 57 |
| 1978 | 7 | 22 | 47 | 43 | 54 | 54 | 27 | 281 | 90 | 260 | 19 | 29 | 937 | 79 |
| 1979 | 162 | 39 | 11 | 20 | 133 | 51 | 4 | 131 | 24 | 23 | 5 | 9 | 612 | 47 |
| 1980 | 2 | 2 | 1 | 22 | 77 | 24 | 89 | 301 | 189 | 97 | 40 | 9 | 853 | 98 |
| 1981 | 10 | 9 | 41 | 86 | 55 | 19 | 41 | 366 | 153 | 287 | 89 | 65 | 1221 | 104 |
| 1982 | 15 | 5 | 26 | 72 | 74 | 48 | 104 | 243 | 113 | 111 | 65 | 22 | 899 | 133 |
| 1983 | 1 | 7 | 26 | 143 | 62 | 19 | 25 | 533 | 378 | 295 | 307 | 32 | 1828 | 88 |
| 1984 | 20 | 39 | 49 | 147 | 126 | 86 | 52 | 357 | 165 | 155 | 58 | 17 | 1271 | 84 |
| 1985 | 16 | 10 | 9 | 78 | 176 | 15 | 27 | 107 | 152 | 158 | 17 | 9 | 774 | 102 |
| 1986 | 5 | 11 | 17 | 59 | 75 | 15 | 9 | 256 | 160 | 115 | 45 | 11 | 778 | 167 |
| 1987 | 10 | 19 | 4 | 50 | 46 | 6 | 42 | 142 | 116 | 229 | 30 | 16 | 710 | 134 |
| 1988 | 4 | 3 | 25 | 81 | 57 | 3 | 10 | 103 | 294 | 441 | 87 | 3 | 1111 | 242 |
| 1989 | 0 | 1 | 59 | 106 | 126 | 25 | 52 | 166 | 658 | 114 | 46 | 0 | 1353 | 137 |

**Monthly and annual ringing totals on North Walney 1983-1989.**

| | J | F | M | A | M | J | J | A | S | O | N | D | Fg. | p. |
|---|---|---|---|---|---|---|---|---|---|---|---|---|---|---|
| 1983 | 0 | 0 | 0 | 0 | 0 | 0 | 8 | 158 | 53 | 23 | 0 | 0 | 242 | 0 |
| 1984 | 0 | 0 | 0 | 54 | 14 | 5 | 14 | 135 | 51 | 41 | 0 | 0 | 314 | 9 |
| 1985 | 0 | 2 | 2 | 23 | 54 | 13 | 1 | 2 | 0 | 0 | 1 | 1 | 99 | 6 |
| 1986 | 7 | 17 | 6 | 16 | 12 | 0 | 1 | 87 | 2 | 0 | 0 | 0 | 148 | 0 |
| 1987 | 51 | 0 | 2 | 6 | 1 | 1 | 0 | 0 | 6 | 2 | 0 | 0 | 69 | 0 |
| 1988 | 1 | 0 | 10 | 8 | 14 | 14 | 2 | 11 | 27 | 6 | 16 | 31 | 140 | 0 |
| 1989 | 3 | 0 | 0 | 0 | 3 | 0 | 0 | 0 | 0 | 0 | 0 | 1 | 7 | 0 |

Note: Fg. = Fully grown
p = pullus (nestling)

# Records Submitted to the British Birds Rarities Committee (B.B.R.C.)

**Cattle Egret,** 26th July 1964 (T. Bradshaw, E. Pithers, F. Quayle) Accepted BB 58:356

**White-throated Sparrow,** 17th June 1965 (J. Addam, Dr. R. Brown, H. Tickle) Accepted BB 59:298

**Little Bunting,** 22nd September 1965 (A. Mercer) Accepted BB 59:299

**Cory's Shearwater,** 6th August 1972 (K. Brown) Accepted BB 66:334

**Buff-breasted Sandpiper,** 5th October 1975 (J. Sheldon) Accepted BB 69:338

**Palm Warbler,** 18th May 1976 (D. Satterthwaite, J. Sheldon) Accepted to Category D BB 70:444

**King Eider,** 10th to 23rd June 1979 (M. Thom et al) Accepted BB 73:500

**Nutcracker,** 1st December 1979 (J. Deakin, T. Dean, A. and R. Normand, G. Stokes) Accepted BB 73:526

**King Eider,** 12th April to 2nd May 1980 (T. Dean et al) Accepted BB 74:463

**Tawny Pipit,** 18th October 1980 (T. Dean, A. Mackenzie) Accepted BB 74:481

**Richard's Pipit,** 8th to 10th November 1980 (T. Dean, A. Mackenzie, A. Phizacklea) Accepted BB 74:481

**Red-throated Pipit,** 12th to 14th December 1980 (T. Dean) Rejected BB 74:494

**Richard's Pipit,** 20th December 1980 to 1st February 1981 (T. Dean, R. Wimpress) Accepted BB 75:514

**Dowitcher,** 11th October 1981 (T. Dean, J. Sheldon, R. Wimpress) Rejected BB 76:529

**Tawny Pipit,** 9th August 1982 (T. Dean, L. Sanderson) Accepted BB 77:546

**Tawny Pipit,** 27th August 1982 (A. Phizacklea, D. Satterthwaite) Accepted BB 77:546

**Paddyfield Warbler,** 11th to 13th September 1982 (T. Dean, K. Parkes et al) Accepted BB 76:510

**Pallas's Warbler,** two, 13th October 1982 (T. Dean, L. Sanderson) Accepted BB 77:553

**Gyrfalcon,** 17th and 18th December 1983 (T. Dean, S. Lawson, L. Sanderson) Accepted BB 77:519

**Ring-billed Gull,** 15th and 18th April 1984 (T. Dean, J. Robinson) Accepted BB 78:555

**Bonelli's Warbler,** 7th May 1984 (T. Dean, S. Lawson, L. Sanderson) Accepted BB 78:578

**Woodchat Shrike,** 2nd to 7th June 1984 (A. Lawton, K. Parkes) Accepted BB 78:579

**Gull-billed Tern,** 24th June 1984 (S. Lawson, L. Sanderson) Rejected BB 78:587

**Crane,** 5th October 1984 (T. Dean, J. Robinson-Dean) Accepted BB 78:541

**White-rumped Sandpiper,** 7th October 1984 (J. Bhalerao, J. Dakin) Accepted BB 78:546

**Dusky Warbler,** 25th November 1984 (A. Stringer-Pratt) Rejected BB 78:588

**Black Stork** (juv), 25th October to 1st November 1985 (T. Dean, J. Robinson-Dean) Accepted BB 80:524

**Black Stork** (ad), 25th October 1985 (T. Dean, J. Robinson-Dean) Accepted BB 80:524
**Ring-billed Gull,** 31st January 1986 (T. Dean) Accepted BB 80:542
**Woodchat Shrike,** 20th to 30th May 1986 (T. Dean, J. Robinson-Dean, D. Satterthwaite) Accepted BB 80:563
**Subalpine Warbler,** 6th June 1986 (T. Dean, C. Rose) Accepted BB 80:560
**Desert Wheatear,** 15th to 21st November 1986 (G. Agar, T. Dean, I. Kinley) Accepted BB 80:557
**Greater Sand Plover,** 19th July to 5th August 1988 (T. Dean, A. Mackay, A. Phizacklea) Accepted BB 82:521
**Wilson's Phalarope,** 1st October 1989 (B. and T. Chadwick, T. Dean, C. Raven, D. Satterthwaite) Accepted BB 83:

***Pallas's Warbler at the offices***

# Records of Walney Rarities in a County Context

### First records for Cumbria

Cory's Shearwater
Sooty Shearwater
White-faced Petrel
King Eider
Greater Sand Plover
Wilson's Phalarope
Ring-billed Gull
Pallas's Sandgrouse
Tawny Pipit
Desert Wheatear
Paddyfield Warbler
Marsh Warbler
Icterine Warbler
Melodious Warbler
Subalpine Warbler
Pallas's Warbler
Bonelli's Warbler
Palm Warbler
White-throated Sparrow
Ortolan Bunting

### Second records for Cumbria

Wilson's Petrel
Cattle Egret
Black Stork
King Eider
Buff-breasted Sandpiper
Tawny Pipit
Icterine Warbler
Melodious Warbler
Pallas's Warbler
Yellow-browed Warbler
Red-breasted Flycatcher
Woodchat Shrike
Nutcracker
Ortolan Bunting
Little Bunting

### Third records for Cumbria

Black Stork
Honey Buzzard
White-rumped Sandpiper
Mediterranean Gull
Tawny Pipit
Nightingale
Icterine Warbler
Melodious Warbler
Barred Warbler
Red-breasted Flycathcer
Woodchat Shrike

### Additional records for Cumbria

Great Shearwater - 4th to 8th
Spoonbill - 8th, 11th and 14th
Gyrfalcon - 9th
Crane - 4th
Stone-curlew - 6th
Temminck's Stint - 12th
Pectoral Sandpiper - 4th
Mediterranean Gull - 6th
Sabine's Gull - 5th and 6th
Iceland Gull - 7th and 14th
Richard's Pipit - 7th, 8th, 10th, 12th, 13th, 15th.
Tawny Pipit 4th
Bluethroat - 5th
Melodious Warbler - 4th to 13th
Barred Warbler - 4th, 5th, 7th to 9th, 11th to 13th, 14th, 16th
Yellow-browed Warbler - 4th, 6th to 9th
Red-breasted Flycatcher - 4th to 8th, 9th, 12th

# References in Periodicals and Journals

**A list of papers from Bird Study (1954-1989) with some relevance to Walney.**


Jun. 1954 Loss of rings by marked Herring Gulls... R. H. Poulding

Dec. 1954 The wintering of gulls in Britain... R. A. O. Hickling

Dec. 1957 The social behaviour of gulls wintering inland ... R. A. O. Hickling

Dec. 1958 The breeding distribution of the Great Black-backed Gull in England and Wales in 1956... T. A. W. Davis

Mar. 1960 The coastal roosting of gulls in England and Wales 1955-56 ... R. A. O. Hickling

Sep. 1961 The winter status of the Lesser Black-backed Gull 1959-60 ... J. A. G. Barnes

Dec. 1961 A study of the British ringing records of the Common Tern and Arctic Tern and comparison with some foreign records ... Mrs. M. C. Radford

Mar. 1962 British ringing recoveries of the Black-headed Gull ... Mrs. M. C. Radford

Mar. 1962 Census of Black-headed Gull colonies in England and Wales ... F. C. Gribble

Mar. 1962 Census of Black-headed Gull colonies in Scotland 1958 ... Frank D. Hamilton

Jun. 1962 Difficulties in the ageing of the Herring Gull and Lesser Black-backed Gull ... M. P. Harris

Jun. 1962 Egg shell removal by the Black-headed Gull... N. Tinbergen, H. Kruuk, M. Paillette

Sep. 1962 Migration of the British Lesser Black-backed Gull as shown by ringing data ... M. P. Harris

Dec. 1962 Recoveries of ringed Great Black-backed Gulls... M. P. Harris

Jun. 1964 Aspects of autumn migration at the bird observatories 1963 ... P. Davis

Sep. 1964 Recoveries of ringed Herring Gulls... M. P. Harris

Sep. 1964 Aspects of spring migration at the bird observatories 1964 ... P. Davis

Dec. 1964 A parasitic disease in Eider Ducks... late E. A. Garden, C. Rayski and Valerie M. Thom

Jun. 1965 Aspects of passerine migration at the bird observatories, autumn 1964... P. Davis

Sep. 1965 Seasonal movements and distribution of Eider Ducks in N.E. Scotland... H. Milne

Dec. 1965 Aspects of the spring migration, 1965... P. Davis

Jun. 1967 Migration seasons of the Sylvia warblers at British bird observatories... P. Davis

Jun. 1967 The inland wintering of gulls in England, 1963 ... R. A. O. Hickling

| | | |
|---|---|---|
| Jun. | 1968 | Individual weight changes in breeding Oystercatchers ... A. J. Mercer |
| Mar. | 1969 | Grey Wagtail passage and population fluctuations in 1956-67 ... J. T. R. Sharrock |
| Mar. | 1969 | Behaviour of gulls robbing Eiders... Agnar Ingolffson |
| Dec. | 1970 | Rates and causes of increases of some British gull populations ... M. P. Harris |
| Jun. | 1971 | The predation of cultivated mussels by Eiders ... A. A. Dunthorne |
| Jun. | 1971 | Ecological adaptations of moult in some British gulls ... M. P. Harris |
| Sep. | 1971 | Seasonal movements of British terns in the Atlantic Ocean ... N. Langham |
| Dec. | 1971 | Some foods taken by waders in Morecambe Bay, Lancashire ... P. E. Davidson |
| Mar. | 1972 | Food of Turnstones in Morecambe Bay... A. J. Prater |
| Dec. | 1972 | Movements of Black-headed Gulls from colonies in England and Wales... J. J. M. Flegg and C. J. Cox |
| Mar. | 1973 | Wader populations of Morecambe Bay... John Wilson |
| Sep. | 1973 | Foods of the Oystercatcher in Morecambe Bay, Lancashire ... P. J. Dare, A. J. Mercer |
| Dec. | 1973 | Interactions between gulls and eiders in St. Andrews Bay, Fife ... O. E. Prys-Jones |
| Jun. | 1974 | The Pennine Gullery... M. E. Greenhalgh |
| Mar. | 1976 | An evaluation of the reliability of rings used on Herring and Lesser Black-backed Gulls... J. C. Coulson |
| Jun. | 1976 | A census of Black-headed Gull colonies in England and Wales in 1973... F. C. Gribble |
| Jun. | 1977 | Inland wintering of gulls in England and Wales, 1973 ... R. A. O. Hickling |
| Jun. | 1977 | Status of large gulls nesting on buildings... P. Monaghan, J. C. Coulson |
| Sep. | 1978 | Hybridization of Herring and Lesser Black-backed Gulls in Britain ... M. P. Harris, C. Morley, G. H. Green |
| Sep. | 1978 | The Ringed Plover populations of Morecambe Bay... C. Clapham |
| Sep. | 1979 | Prolonged parental care in Herring Gulls nesting in towns in eastern Scotland... W. R. P. Bourne |
| Mar. | 1980 | The significance of the Lesser Black-backed Gull to models for bird migration... R. Robin Baker |
| Jun. | 1980 | Establishment of territories in two species of gull on Walney Island, Cumbria... G. R. Hosey, F. Goodridge |
| Mar. | 1981 | Orbital ring colours of Herring Gulls in Britain... R. E. Elliott |
| Jul. | 1981 | The origins of Herring Gulls wintering inland in S.E. England... P. Stanley, T. Brough, M. R. Fletcher, N. Horton, J. B. A. Rochard |
| Jul. | 1981 | The Abbeystead and Mallowdale gull colony before control ... N. Duncan |
| Nov. | 1981 | Accuracy of nest counts at a mixed colony of Herring and Lesser Black-backed Gulls... P. N. Ferns, G. P. Mudge |

Mar. 1982 The influence of female age on breeding in the Eider... S. Baillie, H. Milne

Jul. 1982 Variation in the wing tip pattern of the Herring Gull in Britain... J. C. Coulson, P. Monaghan, J. Butterfield, N. Duncan, C. Thomas, H. Wright

Mar. 1983 The effects of culling on the Abbeystead and Mallowdale gullery ... S. Wanless, D. R. Langslow

Mar. 1983 Why do Herring Gull chicks vocalise in the shell? ... R. K. Templeton

Jul. 1983 Recent declines of Grasshopper Warblers at British observatories ... N. Riddiford

Nov. 1983 The distribution and reproduction of Ringed Plovers breeding coastally and inland in N.W. England... K. Briggs

Nov. 1984 Lesser Black-backed Gull numbers at British inland roosts in 1979/80... R. A. O. Hickling

Nov. 1984 Wintering gulls in Britain, January 1983... A. Bowes, P. Lack, M. Fletcher

Jul. 1985 Movements of British Herring Gulls... J. C. Coulson, J. Butterfield

Mar. 1986 Reproductive success and the location of the nest site in the territory of the Herring Gull... J. Graves, A. Whiten, P. Henzi

Mar. 1986 Studies on a colony of colour-ringed Herring Gulls: (I) Adult Survival rates... J. C. Coulson, J. Butterfield

Mar. 1986 Studies on a colony of colour-ringed Herring Gulls: (II) Colony occupation and feeding outside the breeding season... J. C. Coulson, J. Butterfield

Jun. 1986 The influence of food availability and competition on the use of a feeding site by Herring Gulls... P. Monaghan, N. B. Metcalfe, M. H. Hansell

Jun. 1986 Changes in the gull populations of S.W. Wales... S. J. Sutcliffe

Nov. 1988 Methods for estimating the proportions of Icelandic and British Redshanks in mixed populations wintering on British coasts...R. W. Summers, M. Nicoll, L. G. Underhill, and A. Peterson

Nov. 1988 Declines in midwinter counts of waders roosting on the Dee estuary...J. R. Mitchell, M. E. Moser and J. S. Kirby.

Nov. 1989 Ringed Plover breeding population of the United Kingdom in 1984...A. J. Prater.

## References in British Birds

1979 — Kestrel robbing Merlin...R. Freethy (Vol. 72:336)

1982 — The use of gull nests by Eiders...P. Perry (Vol. 75:360)

1984 — Goldcrest trapped in spider's web...T. Dean (Vol. 77:569)

1985 — Plastic hazards to birds...T. Dean (Vol. 78:661)

1986 — Abnormal claw lengths of Meadow Pipit...T. Dean (Vol. 79:659)

1988 — Merlin preying on Leach's Petrel...T. Dean (Vol. 81:395)

1988 — Greater Sand Plover photograph...T. Dean (Vol. 81:610)

1989 — Skylark in continuous song whilst being attacked by Merlin...T. Dean (Vol. 82:31)

1989 — Guillemot with complete dark neck-band...T. Dean (Vol. 82:271)

## Articles in Walney Bird Observatory Reports

1965 — Extract from botanical survey, 1965. . .J. Montagu B. Sc.
A list of plant-lice *(Homoptera-Aphidoidea)* collected on South Walney during August 1965. . . C. S. Wood-Baker M.Sc., Ph. D.
Walney bird adoption scheme.
The Haws Bank prehistoric site, Walney south end. . .J. G. Jackson.
Keeping up with the 'aves'. . . B. Charnley, K. Parkes, G. Pearson, C. Rose, B. Sutton.

1966 — The Walney gulleries. . . H. Gaythorpe F.S.A. (Scot.)
Prehistoric sites of the north end of Walney. . . F. Barnes B.A., F.S.A., F.L.A.
An English gull colony. . . Dr. R. G. Brown.
Results of ringing nestling Lesser Black-backed Gulls. . .J. Wilson.

1967 — Foulney Island report, 1967. . . I. Rosser.

1968 — The future of the Walney Island nature reserve . . . Prof. N. Tinbergen F.R.S.

1969 — Walney's gulls. . . B. MacRoberts, M. MacRoberts, L. C. Shaffer.

## Miscellaneous articles in journals

July 1969 — 'and seagulls crying', W. Mulligan, Lancashire Life.
February 1982 — 'Wild Walney', W. Mitchell, Cumbria.
May-June 1983 — 'Seabird city', P. Mummery, Mariner.
Spring 1983 — 'Walney's warblers', T. Dean, Birds in Cumbria.
October 1984 — 'The Isle of Walney', D. Slade, Lancashire Life.
July 1985 — 'Warden on Walney', D. Nelson, Lakescene.
October 1986 — 'A place for all seasons', M. Edwards, Birdwatching.
1987 — 'Gulls galore', M. Edwards, Cub scout annual.
June 1987 — 'Living with the seabirds', W. Mitchell, Cumbria.

## Publications on the South Walney Gull Colony

1966 J. Wilson. Results of ringing nestling lesser black-backed gulls on Walney Island. South Walney Nat. Res. and Walney Bird Obs. Ann. Rep. 3:32-37

1967 R. G. B. Brown. Species isolation between the herring gull *Larus argentatus* and lesser black-backed gull *Larus fuscus.* Ibis 109:310-317

1967 R. G. B. Brown. Breeding success and population growth in a colony of herring and lesser black-backed gulls *Larus argentatus* and *Larus fuscus.* Ibis 109:502-515

1967 R. G. B. Brown. Courtship behaviour in the lesser black-backed gull, *Larus fuscus.* Behaviour 29:122-153

1971 L. C. Shaffer. Specializations in the feeding behaviour of gulls and other birds. D. Phil. thesis, Oxford University.

1972 M. H. MacRoberts. The relationship between laying date and incubation period in herring and lesser black-backed gulls. Ibis 114:93-97

1972 B. R. MacRoberts & M. H. MacRoberts. Social stimulation of reproduction in herring and lesser black-backed gulls. Ibis 114:495-506

1973 M. H. MacRoberts. Extra-marital courting in lesser black-backed and herring gulls. Zeitschrift fur Tierpsychologie 32:62-74

1975 J. G. Galusha. Social behaviour in *Larus argentatus* and *Larus fuscus.* D. Phil. thesis, Oxford University.

1976 H. T. Porter. Species isolation in gulls. D. Phil. thesis, Oxford University.

1976 H. Kruuk. The biological function of gulls' attraction towards predators. Animal Behaviour 24:146-153

1977 N. A. M. Verbeek. Interactions between herring and lesser black-backed gulls feeding on refuse. Auk 94:726-735

1977 N. A. M. Verbeek. Age differences in the digging frequency of herring gulls on a dump. Condor 79:123-125

1977 N. A. M. Verbeek. Comparative feeding ecology of herring gulls *Larus argentatus* and lesser black-backed gulls *Larus fuscus*. Ardea 65:25-42

1977 N. A. M. Verbeek. Comparative feeding behaviour of immature and adult herring gulls. Wilson Bulletin 89:415-421

1978 J. G. Galusha & C. J. Amlaner, Jr. The effects of diurnal and tidal periodicities on the numbers and activities of herring gulls *Larus argentatus* in a colony. Ibis 120:322-328

1978 C. J. Amlaner, Jr., R. M. Sibly & R. H. McCleery. Effects of telemetry transmitter weight on breeding success in herring gulls. Biotelemetry 82:1-8

1979 C. A. Henley. Factors influencing egg loss and chick mortality in *Larus argentatus* and *Larus fuscus*. D. Phil. thesis, Oxford University.

1980 G. R. Hosey & F. Goodridge. Establishment of territories in two species of gull on Walney Island, Cumbria. Bird Study 27:73-80

1980 R. R. Baker. The significance of the lesser black-backed gull to models of bird migration. Bird Study 27:41-50

1981 V. Niebuhr. An investigation of courtship feeding in herring gulls, *Larus argentatus*. Ibis 123:218-223

1981 C. J. Amlaner, Jr. & D. J. McFarland. Sleep in the herring gull, *Larus argentatus*. Animal Behaviour 29:551-557

1983 V. Niebuhr. Feeding strategies and incubation behaviour of wild herring gulls : an experiment using operant feeding boxes. Animal Behaviour 31:708-717

1983 V. Niebuhr & D. McFarland. Nest relief behaviour in the herring gull. Animal Behaviour 31:701-707

1983 R. M. Sibly & R. H. McCleery. Increase in weight of herring gulls while feeding. Journal of Animal Ecology 52:35-50

1983 R. M. Silby & R. H. McCleery. Distribution between feeding sites of herring gulls breeding at Walney Island, UK. Journal of Animal Ecology 52:51-68

1983 C. J. Amlaner, Jr. Sleep patterns of herring gulls. D. Phil. thesis, Oxford University.

1983 N. Ball. Wariness and herring gulls. D. Phil. thesis, Oxford University.

1984 J. P. Shaffery. The development of foraging in herring gulls, *Larus argentatus*. D. Phil. thesis, Oxford University.

1985 R. M. Sibly & R. H. McCleery. Optimal decision rules for herring gulls. Animal Behaviour 33:449-465

1985 J. P. Shaffery, N. J. Ball & C. J. Amlaner, Jr. Manipulating daytime sleep in herring gulls, *Larus argentatus*. Animal Behaviour 33:566-572

1986 R. H. McCleery & R. M. Sibly. Feeding specialisation and preference in herring gull. Journal of Animal Ecology 55:245-259

# References

**Association of Natural History Societies in Cumbria 1956-1989;**
Field Naturalist; The Changing Scene; Natural History in Cumbria; Birds in Cumbria.

**Barrow Naturalists' F. C.**
Annual reports.

**Borough of Barrow-in-Furness and Sandscale Haws.**
1978, The Natural Environment of North Walney.
1980, A Study of South Walney.

**British Birds Rarities Committee**
Annual reports on rare birds in Britain.

**Carlisle Natural History Society.**
1954, Lakeland Ornithology. Thurnam, Carlisle.
1958, Lakeland Birds. Thurnam, Carlisle.

**Craggs, J. E. (Ed.)**
1982, Hilbre, the Cheshire Island. Liverpool Univ. Press.

**Cramp, S. and Simmons, K. E. L.**
1977, The Birds of the Western Palearctic, Vol.1; 1980, Vol.2; 1983, Vol.3; 1985, Vol.4; 1988, Vol.5; Oxford.

**Cullen, J. P. and Jenning, P. P.**
1980, Birds of the Isle of Man. Bridgeen, Isle of Man.

**Cumbria Naturalists' Trust/Cumbria Trust for Nature Conservation/Cumbria Wildlife Trust.**
Newsletters. 1963-1989.

**Durman, R. (Ed.)**
1976, Bird Observatories in Britain and Ireland. T. & A. D. Poyser.

**Durnford, W. A.**
1883, List of birds found in the neighbourhood of Walney Island.

**Dymond, N.**
1980, The birds of Lundy. Devon Birdwatching and Preservation Society.

**Fylde Bird Club.**
Annual reports.

**Gowland, C. H.**
Birdland.

**Hardy, E.**
1973, The Naturalist in Lakeland. David and Charles.
1979, Birdwatching in Lancashire. Dalesman.

**Harting, J. E.**
1864, The birds of Walney Island.

**Heysham Harbour Ringing and Migration Station.**
Annual reports.

**Hudson, R.**
1973, Early and late dates for summer migrants. B.T.O. Guide No. 15.

**Hutcheson, M.**
1986, Cumbrian Birds. F. Peters.

**Kirkman, F. B.**
1905, The gulls and terns of Walney Island.

**Lake District Naturalists' Trust.**
1972, Walney Island, North End.

**Lancashire and Cheshire Fauna Society.**
1950-80, Annual reports.
**MacPherson, H. A.**
Report on Pallas's Sandgrouse in the N.W. of England.
1892, A vertebrate fauna of Lakeland. David Douglas, Edinburgh.
**MacPherson, H. A. and Duckworth, W.**
1886, The Birds of Cumberland. Thurnam, Carlisle.
**MacRoberts, M. H., MacRoberts, B. R., Tinbergen, J. and Tinbergen, N.**
1971, South Walney Nature Reserve. Barrow.
**Madders, M.**
1985, Birdwatching in the Lake District.
**Mannex, P. J.**
1849, History of Westmorland with Furness and Cartmel.
**Merseyside Naturalists' Association.**
Annual reports.
**Mitchell, F. S.**
1885 and 1892, The Birds of Lancashire. John van Voorst, London.
**Mitchell, W. R. and Robson, R. W.**
1976, Lakeland Birds. Dalesman.
**Morecambe Bay Wader Ringing Group.**
Annual reports.
**Oakes, C.**
1953, The Birds of Lancashire. Oliver and Boyd, Edinburgh and London.
**Roberts, P. J.**
1985, The Birds of Bardsey. Bardsey Bird and Field Observatory.
**Riddiford, N. and Findley, P.**
1981, Seasonal movements of summer migrants. B.T.O. Guide No. 18.
**Sharrock, J. T. R.**
1973, The Natural History of Cape Clear Island. T. and A. D. Poyser.
1976, Rare birds in Britain and Ireland. T. and A. D. Poyser.
1976, The atlas of breeding birds of Britain and Ireland. T. and A. D. Poyser.
**Snow, D. W.**
1971, The status of birds in Britain and Ireland. Blackwell.
**Spencer, K. G.**
1973, The status and distribution of birds in Lancashire. Turner and Earnshaw, Burnley.
**Stokoe, R.**
1962, The birds of the Lake Counties. Thurnam, Carlisle.
**Tinbergen, N., Falkus, H. and Ennion, E.**
1970, Signals for survival. Clarendon Press, Oxford.
**Trescathric, B.**
1984, Walney, a wall in the sea. Hougenai Press.
**Walney Bird Observatory.**
Annual reports. 1965-71; 1980-89.
**West Midland Bird Club.**
Annual reports.
**Wilson, J.**
1976, The birds of Morecambe Bay. Dalesman.

THE FLORA OF WALNEY

# An Introduction to the Island and its Reserves

***Walney Geranium***

To many people, botanists and non-botanists alike, the island is associated with one particular plant — the Walney Geranium — a subspecies of Bloody Cranesbill that has a pale pink flower, *Geranium sanguineum* var. *lancastrense.* Mannex (1849) notes this "Bloody Cranesbill with a variegated flower" and his short description of the flora of the island incorporates "Sea Wormwood, Milk Thistle, Sea Starwort (Sea Aster), Isle of Man Cabbage, Sea Celandine (Yellow Horned-poppy), Danish Scurvygrass, Sea Calewort (Sea-kale), Sea Feverfew (Scentless Mayweed), Creeping Restharrow (Common Restharrow), and Sea Lungwort". Later in the century, Harting (1864) records "Burnet Rose, the Crimson Cranesbill *(Geranium sanguineum)* and a beautiful little pansy *(Viola tricolor)".* In the good old Victorian days of collecting and pressed flowers, the reports of the field outings by the Barrow Naturalists' Field Club extol the island flora and one can find references to Bittersweet, Jacob's-ladder, Lesser Meadow-rue, Burnet Rose, Sea Bindweed, Oysterplant, Bugloss, Sun Spurge, Common Hemp-nettle, Thrift, Scarlet Pimpernel, Sea-milkwort, Mugwort, Sea Wormwood, Early Forget-me-not, Sea Campion, Pennywort, English Stonecrop, White Campion, Hemlock and Hemlock Water-dropwort.

***Thrift***

How much has Walney's flora changed over the last 100 years? If we merely compare Victorian species lists with present day lists we find that many of the examples remain to this day. It is impossible to know exactly where the aforementioned collectors found their plants, but the Walney Geranium still flowers in profusion during late June and July along Biggar Bank and North Walney. Bittersweet, Sea Bindweed, Bugloss, Thrift, Scarlet Pimpernel, Sea Campion and White Campion can all be located at various sites on the island, some may have existed in greater abundance than nowadays. Certainly this is so for Oysterplant, last noted at South Walney in 1976 despite annual attempts to relocate it. Of course, the homes and gardens of the 11,000 present day inhabitants have taken over the habitat which once grew Jacob's-ladder, and where now grow Dahlias, Chrysanthemums and all sorts of 'garden centre' blooms. In Walney's history, the most rapid changes have occurred since the late 19th century with the annexation of the island as a suburb of Barrow-in-Furness. From Lenny Hill in the north to Tummer Hill Marsh in the south, the east side of the island is given over to terraced houses, council estates, private dwellings, pubs, shops, allotments and a park. On the west side of the island, from Thorney-nook in the south to Earnse Bay in the north, we have car-parks, recreational areas, school playing fields, two golf courses and a caravan site. In all that area, the Gorse bushes in the region of Sandy Gap may be the only natural reminders of what the west side of the island looked like prior to the developments of the 20th century. Refuse tips at either end of the island have changed the character of the vegetation; existing plants have been eradicated to be replaced by coarser species, but with a calcareous topsoil, who knows what species will emerge in later years. Even the nature reserves have not been free from contamination. Both have witnessed some form of industrial activity in the last 100 years. North Walney bears the scars of sand and gravel extraction, but the scars are damp and full of orchids. South Walney has seen a salt works, an enormous amount of sand and gravel extraction and bears annually the feet of thousands of gulls, the teeth of thousands of rabbits, and scores of cows and sheep, plus the odd goat or donkey. Delicate flowers do not survive well at South Walney! Of all Walney's habitats, it is the shingle ridges and saltmarshes that would probably appear little different to a time-travelling Walneyite, but even he would notice the annual creep of *Spartina* in the Channel-side bays, most dramatically Wylock Marsh.

Remains of a petrified forest are uncovered at extreme low tides off the west shore of the island. Can we link this with the vivid and extensive patches of Bluebells that are found along the road side from Biggar village to South Walney? They seem oddly naked without the customary presence of trees. Walney is almost nearly bereft of tall trees, in fact bereft of trees in general. Many of the field hedgerows from south of Ocean Road are composed of substantially sized Hawthorns — this is especially noticeable around Biggar and Rakes Lane — but apart from a small stand at Snab Point, only a handful of stunted wind-torn trees can be found beyond the refuse tip. Biggar village does have a few tall Sycamores and low Sallows can be quite plentiful in the damper areas from South Walney north, but apart from the former, it is only when one walks along the Promenade that it is necessary to raise ones' eyes skywards to see the tops of Sycamores in St. Mary's churchyard. Further north, James Dunn Park and Chairman's Walk have similar-sized Sycamores and around North Scale village, Hawthorn hedges border the fields and lanes. Only Willow Woods can be regarded as the island's arboretum. In this enclave, Sessile Oaks, Ash, Hazel, Sallow, Hawthorn and Blackthorn, have established themselves, flourished and regenerated since the end of the Second World War. Beyond the Woods, North Walney can muster a few Sallows on the Channel side of the reserve although some mis-directed tree-lovers have planted Scots Pine and European Larch.

Changes in the agricultural practices of the island have no doubt affected the indigenous vegetation. The arable fields, when the island was 'the granary of Furness', have been replaced by a pastoral system for silage meadows or grazing beef herds. Land has been drained and 'improved' and outside the nature reserves, only the pools at Snab Point, Biggar village and Moor Tarn Lane yield a freshwater flora. We should applaud the island wildfowlers, whose pond at the western end of Rakes Lane, is slowly maturing.

***Sea Campion***

*Black Stork near Wylock Marsh on 25th October 1985. This juvenile, most probably from Eastern Europe, was initially located in the Eden Valley, Cumbria on 10th September.*
(Dave Satterthwaite)

*Subalpine Warbler at South Walney Nature Reserve on 6th June 1986. This male, one of 13 in Great Britain in that year, should have been singing near the Mediterranean.*
(Dave Satterthwaite)

*Desert Wheatear at South Walney Nature Reserve on 15th November 1986. This young female, probably from North Africa, became the twenty-fourth record for Great Britain.*
(Ian Kinley)

*Greater Sand Plover near the refuse tip on 19th July 1988. More usually found in Southern Russia and east to Mongolia, this became the ninth record for Great Britain.*
(Alan Mackay)

*Yellow Horned-poppy at South Walney Nature Reserve in June. This maritime species of shingle ridges is found chiefly at the south end of the island.*
(Tim Dean)

*Heartsease Pansy at South Walney Nature Reserve in June. This dune and grassland species is abundant at both ends of the island.*
(George Higginbotham)

*Common Sea-lavender at Tummer Hill Marsh in July. An abundant species in all the island's saltmarshes.*
(Tim Dean)

*Glasswort at South Walney Nature Reserve in July. An abundant species in all the island's saltmarshes.*
(Tim Dean)

*Walney Geranium at Biggar Bank in July. Pockets of this variety can be located along Biggar Bank and at North Walney National Nature Reserve.*
(George Higginbotham)

*Sea-holly at North Walney National Nature Reserve in July. Prolific at the north end of the island but almost non-existent at the south.*
(Tim Dean)

*Portland Spurge at South Walney Nature Reserve in June. This rather local species can be found at both ends of the island but is far more numerous at the south.*
(Tim Dean)

*Sea Campion at South Walney Nature Reserve in July. A fairly abundant species on shingle throughout the length of the island.*
(Tim Dean)

*Viper's-bugloss at South Walney Nature Reserve in June. This rather local species can only be found at the south end where it is abundant.*
(George Higginbotham)

*Sea Bindweed at South Walney Nature Reserve in June. A dune species found at both ends of the island.*
(Tim Dean)

*Henbane at South Walney Nature Reserve in June. A prolific species at the south end of the island.*
(Tim Dean)

*Hound's-tongue at South Walney Nature Reserve in June. This local species can be found at both ends of the island and is abundant at the south.*
(Tim Dean)

*Northern Marsh-orchid at North Walney National Nature Reserve in June. The damp slacks at the north end are the island's only localities.*
(George Higginbotham)

*Parasol Mushroom at South Walney Nature Reserve in August. A fairly common species from July until October at both ends of the island.*
(Andre Robinson)

*Sea Aster at South Walney Nature Reserve in August. A fairly common species occurring in all the island's saltmarshes. Note the Small Tortoiseshell butterflies.*
(Tim Dean)

*Rabbit at South Walney Nature Reserve in July. Found in small numbers throughout the island except at the south end, where it is decidedly prolific.*
(Tim Dean)

*Natterjack Toad at North Walney National Nature Reserve in August. Previously found at both ends of the island and possibly throughout its length, this species now can be found solely at the north end.*
(Paul Kirkland)

*Painted Lady at South Walney Nature Reserve in August. An erratic migrant which has been recorded between early April and mid-October. This specimen is on Sea Rocket.*
(Tim Dean)

*The Cinnabar at South Walney Nature Reserve in June. This day-flying moth is far more numerous at the north end than at the south. This individual is on Common Ragwort.*
(George Higginbotham)

*Common Jellyfish* (Aurelia aurita) *at South Walney Nature Reserve in July. In some years many hundreds may be beached along the island's shores.*
(Tim Dean)

# The Flowering Plants of South Walney Nature Reserve

***Henbane***

The unsullied 19th century sand dunes at the south end, beloved by Barrow's naturalists, have not remained unsullied in the 20th century. Perhaps more than 70% of the 95 hectares has been tampered with during the course of sand and gravel extraction. Mature grey dunes are few and where once were sand dune communities, there are now shingle and cobble banks and ridges and their associated flora. The extraction of Walney sand and gravel was at its height after the Second World War when demands were met for road building and the reconstruction of the Liverpool Docks. Most left the island via the pier and flat bottomed-barge but in the 1980s lorry loads were taken to Barrow for use in the huge Trident complex, completed in 1987. Of the reserve's habitats, the saltmarshes and shingle beaches represent the least changed areas. Yet, the saltmarsh of Lighthouse Bay is in fact artificial, created during the early years of extraction, and both the bay and Haws Bed are witnessing the quite rapid advance of *Spartina*. In addition, the shingle beaches are subject to change with every storm-backed high tide, and often seeds carried by the tides have resulted in plants such as Tomato and Potato growing amongst the pebbles.

***Yellow Horned-poppy***

Another feature of later years, probably 1960 to the present day, has been the enormous amount of trampling and grazing that the region has been subjected to. The gull tenancy is a recent phenomenon, and the increase in numbers even more recent. In 1950, there were about 500 pairs of webbed feet; in 1965 there were approximately 20,000. Twenty thousand pairs of feet every day for nine months; an extra 40,000 or 50,000 young pairs of webbed feet after hatching and visualise, if you can, the corresponding dump of guano. All in all, the presence of the gulls has had a marked effect on South Walney's vegetation. Similarly, the rabbit warren, with a long pedigree, has cropped blooms and undermined the turf, and only cyclical outbreaks of myxomatosis, ensure a short-lived respite. Increased numbers of stock, both cattle and sheep, wander throughout the reserve in all months, — from May until November feeding on fresh growth and being fed silage during the intervening period. The modifying effect of the silage cannot be underestimated; the feeding areas yield lush stands of docks, nettles, Creeping Thistle, and mats of Corn Spurrey.

***Hound's-tongue***

The weed communities of the disturbed gravel areas are the lure for most of South Walney's botanically-minded visitors. However one does not need to know what a calyx is to appreciate the glorious congregations of Viper's-bugloss, Henbane, Yellow Horned-poppy, Hound's-tongue and Great Mullein. Of these species, only the poppy was mentioned by Mannex (1849); does this mean the others are recent additions? Many of the plants are useful in a herbal sense; there is certainly the possibility that the monks of Furness Abbey grew and harvested these species. Additionally, one Barrow chemist, Mr. Taylor, continued to plant and use South Walney's blossoms in the preparation of remedies. No one can deny that the members of this weed community are incredibly prolific; as soon as a patch of earth is turned over, one or more of these species will make an appearance in the following year. They are still largely confined to the eastern end of the reserve, but odd specimens of Hound's-tongue and Henbane have been located at Scar End Point. Equally breathtakingly colouful can be the coarse weeds that cover the gull colony. In early May there are carpets of ground hugging Dandelions, brilliantly yellow when the sun is at its height; less obvious are the patches of Dove's-foot Cranesbill and Common Stork's-bill, the latter occasionally having white instead of pink flowers; Wild Pansy begins to bloom, often continuing into late November. Intriguingly, the forms at South Walney are more blue than yellow, while the opposite occurs at North Walney. Later in the year, Common Nettle, Slender Thistle and Ragwort appear, the last in some years completely covering the reserve in a sea of unbroken yellow.

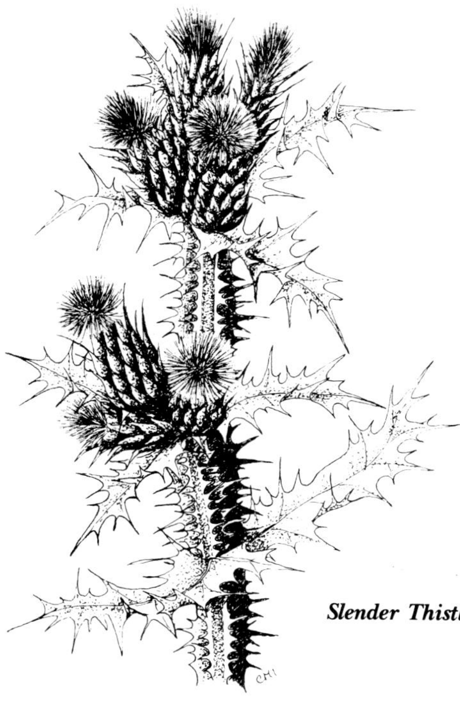

***Slender Thistle***

The comparatively untainted grey and yellow dunes near the lighthouse and groyne seem a veritable paradise, especially after a choking and claustrophobic expedition through the gull colony. The new dunes have healthy clumps of flowering Marram, without which, much of Walney's sand would be on the other side of Morecambe Bay. Amongst the Marram one can find Bittersweet and Portland Spurge; why is it that South Walney has a substantial population of Portland and no Sea Spurge, and North Walney is alive with the latter, but has little of the former? Close scrutiny of the area may also reveal a few Pyramidal Orchids, Tassel Hyacinth and Smooth Cat's-ear. The older dunes, some of them rich in lichens and mosses, produce sweet-smelling mats of Wild Thyme, carpets of Common Restharrow and Common Bird's-foot-trefoil, and dainty pink Common Centaury.

*Portland Spurge*

Danish Scurvygrass can be prolific on the more established shingle ridges during April, and is joined by Biting Stonecrop later in the season, and inconspicuous plants of Sea Sandwort. Nearer the tideline, the vagaries of the sea can change the geography and the flora overnight., In 1983, Sea Rocket and Prickly Saltwort grew in healthy clusters and the former was a popular rendezvous for Red Admirals, Painted Ladies, Graylings and even Clouded Yellows. After the winter storms of 1983 and 1984, both plants have totally disappeared from the area. Sea-holly is almost non-existent on the shingle at South Walney and yet is hugely successful between the tideline and the fore dunes at the north end.

## The Flowering Plants of North Walney National Nature Reserve

*Sea-holly*

Compared with past usage, present day North Walney, is probably going through one of its quieter patches. Admittedly 5,000 people per annum visit the reserve and old and new recreational pursuits have increased. Most come purely to appreciate or get away from it all, but abuse comes in varying degrees, from loose dogs and ponies, poaching and fire-raising, motor cycle scrambling and 'all terrain vehicles'. However, grazing cattle and sheep, continuous for many hundreds of years, ceased in 1978 and the once managed and protected rabbit warren now has few tenants. The dunes were subjected to a huge amount of use during the Second World War, the area being a training ground and shooting range, while the greater part of the north end was converted into an airfield. Sand and gravel extraction has not been confined to the south end; the North Walney site was worked by McLung until the 1970s, and the ponds in the southwest of the reserve are a permanent legacy.

***Yellow Rattle***

A very wide range of habitats occur on the reserve's 142 hectares. Over 300 species of flowering plants have been recorded and the area is undoubtedly rich, not only in quantity, but in quality as well. The visitor will normally approach the reserve via the west shore, north of Earnse Bay, and despite the almost customary presence of a refuse tip on the island, will be greeted by masses of Sea-holly, Sea Spurge and Yellow Rattle, while isolated clumps of Sea-kale, prosper on the shingle. Additionally, Yellow Horned-poppy and the uncommon Ray's Knotgrass can be located above the tideline.

Along the pond margins are Horsetails in abundance, also Marsh Willowherb and Gipsywort, while the damp surrounds are spectacular in summer with Ragged-Robin, Yellow Rattle and Kidney Vetch. Orchids are prolific, stunning in their colourful variations, and hybrids are frequent. The majority can be identified as Early Marsh or Northern Marsh. Creeping Willow and Lousewort prefer these damp areas and both species can be found over much of the southern part of the reserve. The damp slacks towards the tip of the island also hold good numbers of orchids amongst which may be Common Spotted and the all too uncommon Bee Orchid. Yellow-eyed-grass, recorded from only a handful of British sites, is evident with a small population whose ancestry may be doubtful.

***Bee Orchid***

Along the leeward side of the dunes, the Walney Geranium is plentiful, although less so than the normal form of Bloody Cranesbill. Burnet Rose and solitary spikes of Carline Thistle are equally fetching whether in spring or autumn. Carpets of Wild Pansy, generally far yellower than the South Walney blooms, compete for space with Common Restharrow and Lady's Bedstraw.

Walney's last remaining heather area, situated in the centre of the reserve, is an enclave for species that thrive on damp and dry heath. The wetter *Sphagnum* regions hold Round-leaved Sundew, Marsh Cinquefoil and Cross-leaved Heath, while Tormentil, Ling and Bell Heather are obvious on the drier tracts.

***Moonwort***

Beyond the heath, an extensive patch of bracken gives way to a few well-vegetated dune slopes. Careful searching may reveal scarce island species such as Moonwort, Adder's-tongue, Hard Fern and the rare Coralroot Orchid. In addition to the ferns mentioned above a few plants of Royal Fern survive in the heathland, where Common Cottongrass and Purple Moor Grass are abundant. Meadowsweet, Sneezewort and Purple Loosestrife are met with as one reaches the Channel-side saltmarsh, carpeted with sea-lavenders, Thrift, Sea-purslane, Annual Sea-blite and Sea Aster, at its most subtly colourful in autumn.

***Adder's-tongue***

# The Flowering Plants of Walney

The flora is based on data from the following sources:

South Walney — J. Buchanan, July 1965
M. Barratt, June-Sept. 1979
T. Dean, 1980-1989

North Walney — P. Kirkland, 1987

Snab Pools & Vickerstown Pool — Dr. M. Lock, 1978

Willow Woods — T. Dean, 1984

Additional material — P. Zaltowski, Dr. G. Halliday

The following abbreviations are used for localities mentioned in the flora:

NW — North Walney
SW — South Walney
SP — Snab Pools
VP — Vickerstown Pool
WW — Willow Woods
Wy — Wylock

## PTERIDOPHYTA

| | | |
|---|---|---|
| **EQUISETACEAE** | | |
| Equisetum arvense | Common Horsetail | NW,SP |
| fluviatile | Water Horsetail | VP |
| palustre | Marsh Horsetail | NW |
| variegatum | Variegated Horsetail | NW |
| **OSMUNDACEAE** | | |
| Osmunda regalis | Royal Fern | NW |
| **DENNSTAEDTIACEAE** | | |
| Pteridium aquilinum | Bracken | NW,SW,WW |
| **BLECHNACEAE** | | |
| Blechnum spicant | Hard Fern | NW,SW |
| **ATHYRIACEAE** | | |
| Athyrium filix-femina | Lady Fern | NW,WW |
| **ASPIDIACEAE** | | |
| Dryopteris carthusiana | Narrow Buckler-fern | NW,SW |
| dilatata | Broad Buckler-fern | NW |
| filix-mas | Male Fern | NW,SW,WW |
| **POLYPODIACEAE** | | |
| Polypodium vulgare | Common Polypody | NW,SW |
| **OPHIOGLOSSACEAE** | | |
| Botrychuim lunaria | Moonwort | NW,SW |
| Ophioglossum vulgatum | Adder's-tongue | NW |

## SPERMATOPHYTA

| | | |
|---|---|---|
| **PINACEAE** | | |
| Pinus nigra laricio | Corsican Pine | SW |
| sylvestris | Scots Pine | NW |
| **TAXACEAE** | | |
| Taxus baccata | Yew | NW,SW |

## ANGIOSPERMAE

| | | |
|---|---|---|
| **RANUNCULACEAE** | | |
| Aquilegia vulgaris | Columbine | SW |
| Ranunculus acris | Meadow Buttercup | NW,SW,WW |
| peltatus | | |
| ssp. peltatus | Water-crowfoot | NW,SP |
| bulbosus | Bulbous Buttercup | NW |
| ficaria | Lesser Celandine | NW,SW |
| flammula | Lesser Spearwort | NW,SW,SP |
| aquatilis | Pond Water-crowfoot | SP |
| repens | Creeping Buttercup | NW,SW |
| sceleratus | Celery-leaved Buttercup | SW |
| Thalictrum minus | Lesser Meadow-rue | NW |
| **PAPAVERACEAE** | | |
| Glaucium flavum | Yellow Horned-poppy | NW,SW |
| Papaver somniferum | Opium Poppy | SW |
| **FUMARIACEAE** | | |
| Fumaria officinalis | Common Fumitory | NW,SW,Wy |
| **CRUCIFERAE** | | |
| Arabidopsis thaliana | Thale Cress | NW,SW |
| Barbarea vulgaris | Winter-cress | NW |
| Brassica napus | Rape | SW |
| rapa | Wild Turnip | NW,SW |
| Cakile maritima | Sea Rocket | NW,SW |
| Capsella bursa-pastoris | Shepherd's-purse | NW,SW |
| Cardamine hirsuta | Hairy Bitter-cress | NW,SW |
| pratensis | Cuckooflower | NW,SW,WW |
| Cardaria draba | Hoary Cress | NW,SW |
| Cochlearia danica | Danish Scurvygrass | NW,SW |
| officinalis | Common Scurvygrass | NW,SW |
| Coronopus didymus | Lesser Swine-cress | NW,SW |
| Crambe maritima | Sea-kale | NW |
| Diplotaxis muralis | Annual Wall-rocket | Wy |
| tenuifolia | Perennial Wall-rocket | NW,Wy |
| Erophila verna | Common Whitlowgrass | NW,SW |
| Lepidium heterophyllum | Smith's Pepperwort | SP |
| Rorippa islandica | Marsh Yellow-cress | SW |
| nasturtium-aquaticum | Water-cress | NW,SW |
| Sinapis arvensis | Charlock | Wy |
| Sisymbrium officinale | Hedge Mustard | SW |
| orientale | Eastern Rocket | SW |

**RESEDACEAE**

| | | |
|---|---|---|
| Reseda lutea | Wild Mignonette | Wy |
| luteola | Weld | NW,SW |

**VIOLACEAE**

| | | |
|---|---|---|
| Viola canina | Heath Dog-violet | NW,SW |
| odorata | Sweet Violet | SW |
| palustris | Marsh Violet | NW |
| riviniana | Common Dog-violet | NW,SW |
| tricolor | Wild Pansy | NW,SW |

**POLYGALACEAE**

| | | |
|---|---|---|
| Polygala serpyllifolia | Heath Milkwort | NW |
| vulgaris | Common Milkwort | NW,SW |

**GUTTIFERAE**

| | | |
|---|---|---|
| Hypericum humifusum | Trailing St. John's-wort | NW,SW |
| pulchrum | Slender St. John's-wort | NW |
| tetrapterum | Square-stalked St. John's-wort | NW |

**CARYOPHYLLACEAE**

| | | |
|---|---|---|
| Arenaria serpyllifolia | Thyme-leaved Sandwort | NW,SW |
| Cerastium diffusum | Sea Mouse-ear | NW,SW |
| glomeratum | Sticky Mouse-ear | NW |
| holosteoides | Common Mouse-ear | NW,SW,WW |
| pumilum | Dwarf Mouse-ear | SW |
| semidecandrum | Little Mouse-ear | NW |
| Honkenya peploides | Sea Sandwort | NW,SW |
| Lychnis flos-cuculi | Ragged Robin | NW,WW |
| Sagina apetala | Annual Pearlwort | SW |
| maritima | Sea Pearlwort | NW |
| nodosa | Knotted Pearlwort | NW |
| procumbens | Procumbent Pearlwort | NW,SW |
| Silene alba | White Campion | SW |
| armeria | Sweet-William Catchfly | Wy |
| dioica | Red Campion | NW,SW,WW |
| maritima | Sea Campion | NW,SW |
| vulgaris | Bladder Campion | SW,SP |
| Spergula arvensis | Corn Spurrey | NW,SW |
| Spergularia marina | Lesser Sea-spurrey | SW |
| media | Greater Sea-spurrey | NW,SP |
| rubra | Sand Spurrey | SW |
| Stellaria graminea | Lesser Stitchwort | NW,SW |
| media | Common Chickweed | NW,SW,WW |

**PORTULACACEAE**

| | | |
|---|---|---|
| Montia fontana | Blinks | NW,SW |

**CHENOPODIACEAE**

| | | |
|---|---|---|
| Atriplex glabriuscula | Babington's Orache | NW,SW |
| hastata | Spear-leaved Orache | NW,SW |
| laciniata | Frosted Orache | NW,SW |

| | | |
|---|---|---|
| Atriplex littoralis | Grass-leaved Orache | NW,SW |
| patula | Common Orache | NW,SW |
| Beta vulgaris subsp. maritima | Sea Beet | NW,SW |
| Chenopodium album | Fat-hen | NW,SW |
| rubrum | Red Goosefoot | SW |
| Halimione portulacoides | Sea-purslane | NW,SW |
| Salicornia europaea | Glasswort | NW,SW |
| Salsola kali | Prickly Saltwort | NW,SW |
| Suaeda maritima | Annual Sea-blite | NW,SW |
| **MALVACEAE** | | |
| Malva neglecta | Dwarf Mallow | SW |
| sylvestris | Common Mallow | SW |
| **LINACEAE** | | |
| Linum catharticum | Fairy Flax | NW |
| Radiola linoides | Allseed | NW |
| **GERANIACEAE** | | |
| Erodium cicutarium | Common Stork's-bill | NW,SW |
| glutinosum | Sticky Stork's-bill | NW |
| Geranium dissectum | Cut-leaved Cranesbill | Wy |
| molle | Dove's-foot Cranesbill | NW,SW |
| robertianum | Herb Robert | SW,WW |
| sanguinium | Bloody Cranesbill | NW |
| var. lancastriense | Walney Geranium | NW,Biggar Bank |
| **OXALIDACEAE** | | |
| Oxalis articulata | Oxalis | SW |
| **ACERACEAE** | | |
| Acer pseudoplatanus | Sycamore | NW,SW |
| **HIPPOCASTANACEAE** | | |
| Aesculus hippocastanum | Horse-chestnut | SW |
| **AQUIFOLIACEAE** | | |
| Ilex aquifolium | Holly | SW |
| **LEGUMINOSAE** | | |
| Anthyllis vulneraria | Kidney Vetch | NW,SW |
| Genista tinctoria | Dyer's Greenweed | NW,Wy,WW,VP |
| Lathyrus pratensis | Meadow Vetchling | NW,Wy |
| Lotus corniculatus | Common Bird's-foot-trefoil | NW,SW |
| uliginosus | Greater Bird's-foot-trefoil | NW,SW,WW |
| Lupinus arboreus | Tree Lupin | NW,SW,Wy |
| Medicago lupulina | Black Medick | SW |
| Ononis repens | Common Restharrow | NW,SW |
| Ornithopus perpusillus | Bird's-foot | NW,SP |
| Trifolium arvense | Hare's-foot Clover | NW |
| campestre | Hop Trefoil | NW,SW |
| dubium | Lesser Trefoil | NW,SW |
| fragiferum | Strawberry Clover | NW |

| | | |
|---|---|---|
| Trifolium pratense | Red Clover | NW,SW,Wy |
| repens | White Clover | NW,SW |
| Ulex europaeus | Gorse | NW,SW,WW |
| Vicia angustifolia | Narrow-leaved Vetch | SW |
| cracca | Tufted Vetch | NW,SW,WW |
| lathyroides | Spring Vetch | NW |
| sepium | Bush Vetch | NW |

**ROSACEAE**

| | | |
|---|---|---|
| Agrimonia eupatoria | Agrimony | NW |
| Aphanes arvensis | Parsley-piert | SW |
| Crataegus monogyna | Hawthorn | NW,SW,WW |
| Filipendula ulmaria | Meadowsweet | NW,SW,WW |
| Malus sylvestris | Crab Apple | NW |
| Potentilla anserina | Silverweed | NW,SW,WW |
| erecta | Tormentil | NW,SW,WW,VP |
| palustris | Marsh Cinquefoil | NW,VP |
| reptans | Creeping Cinquefoil | SW |
| Prunus spinosa | Blackthorn | SW,WW |
| Rosa canina | Dog Rose | NW,SW,WW |
| pimpinellifolia | Burnet Rose | NW,SW |
| rugosa | Japanese Rose | NW |
| Rubus caesius | Dewberry | SW |
| fruticosus agg. | Bramble | NW,SW,WW |
| Sorbus aria | Common Whitebeam | NW,SW |
| aucuparia | Rowan | NW,SW |

**CRASSULACEAE**

| | | |
|---|---|---|
| Sedum acre | Biting Stonecrop | NW,SW |
| album | White Stonecrop | SW |
| anglicum | English Stonecrop | NW,SW |

**SAXIFRAGACEAE**

| | | |
|---|---|---|
| Saxifraga tridactylites | Rue-leaved Saxifrage | SW |

**GROSSULARIACEAE**

| | | |
|---|---|---|
| Ribes nigrum | Black Currant | NW |

**DROSERACEAE**

| | | |
|---|---|---|
| Drosera rotundifolia | Round-leaved Sundew | NW,SW |

**LYTHRACEAE**

| | | |
|---|---|---|
| Lythrum salicaria | Purple-loosestrife | VP |
| Peplis portula | Water-purslane | NW,SW |

**ELAEAGNACEAE**

| | | |
|---|---|---|
| Hippophae rhamnoides | Sea-buckthorn | NW,SW |

**ONAGRACEAE**

| | | |
|---|---|---|
| Epilobium angustifolium | Rosebay Willowherb | SW,WW |
| hirsutum | Greater Willowherb | NW,VP |
| palustre | Marsh Willowherb | SW |
| obscurum | Short-fruited Willowherb | SP |

| | | |
|---|---|---|
| Oenothera biennis | Common Evening-primrose | SW |
| erythrosepala | Large-flowered Evening-primrose | SW |

**HALORAGACEAE**

| | | |
|---|---|---|
| Myriophyllum spicatum | Spiked Water-milfoil | NW,SW |

**CALLITRICHACEAE**

| | | |
|---|---|---|
| Callitriche intermedia | Intermediate Water-starwort | SP |
| stagnalis | Common Water-starwort | SW |

**UMBELLIFERAE**

| | | |
|---|---|---|
| Angelica sylvestris | Wild Angelica | NW |
| Anthriscus sylvestris | Cow Parsley | NW,SW,WW |
| Apium graveolens | Wild Celery | SP |
| inundatum | Lesser Marshwort | NW,SP |
| nodiflorum | Fool's Water-cress | SW |
| Conium maculatum | Hemlock | SW |
| Daucus carota | Wild Carrot | NW |
| Eryngium maritimum | Sea-holly | NW,SW |
| Heracleum sphondylium | Hogweed | NW,SW,Wy,WW |
| Hydrocotyle vulgaris | Marsh Pennywort | NW,SW,VP |
| Oenanthe crocata | Hemlock Water-dropwort | NW,WW |
| lachenalii | Parsley Water-dropwort | NW,SW,SP |
| Pastinaca sativa | Wild Parsnip | NW,SW |
| Sanicula europaea | Sanicle | WW |
| Torilis japonica | Upright Hedge-parsley | NW,SP |

**EUPHORBIACEAE**

| | | |
|---|---|---|
| Euphorbia paralias | Sea Spurge | NW,SW |
| portlandica | Portland Spurge | NW,SW |

**POLYGONACEAE**

| | | |
|---|---|---|
| Polygonoum amphibium | Amphibious Bistort | SW |
| aviculare | Knotgrass | NW,SW |
| bistorta | Common Bistort | NW |
| convolvulus | Black-bindweed | SW |
| hydropiper | Water-pepper | SW |
| persicaria | Redshank | NW,SW |
| raii | Ray's Knotgrass | NW,SW |
| Rumex acetosa | Common Sorrel | NW,SW,WW |
| acetosella | Sheep's Sorrel | NW,SW |
| crispus | Curled Dock | NW,SW,WW |
| conglomeratus | Clustered Dock | SW |
| maritimus | Golden Dock | SW |
| obtusifolius | Broad-leaved Dock | NW,SW |

**URTICACEAE**

| | | |
|---|---|---|
| Urtica dioica | Common Nettle | NW,SW |
| urens | Small Nettle | SW |

**BETULACEAE**

| | | |
|---|---|---|
| Betula pubescens | Downy Birch | NW |

| | | |
|---|---|---|
| **CORYLACEAE** | | |
| Corylus avellana | Hazel | NW,WW |
| **FAGACEAE** | | |
| Fagus sylvatica | Beech | SW |
| Quercus petraea | Sessile Oak | NW,SW,WW |
| **SALICACEAE** | | |
| Populus alba | White Poplar | SW |
| tremula | Aspen | SW |
| Salix aurita | Eared Willow | NW |
| caprea | Goat Willow | NW,SW,WW |
| cinerea | Grey Willow | NW |
| repens repens | Creeping Willow | NW |
| repens argentea | Creeping Willow | NW |
| viminalis | Osier | NW |
| **ERICACEAE** | | |
| Calluna vulgaris | Heather | NW,SW |
| Erica cinerea | Bell Heather | NW,SW |
| tetralix | Cross-leaved Heath | NW,SW |
| **PYROLACEAE** | | |
| Pyrola rotundifolia ssp. maritima | Round-leaved Wintergreen | NW |
| **PLUMBAGINACEAE** | | |
| Armeria maritima | Thrift | NW,SW |
| Limonium humile | Lax-flowered Sea-lavender | NW,SW |
| vulgare | Common Sea-lavender | NW,SW |
| **PRIMULACEAE** | | |
| Anagallis arvensis | Scarlet Pimpernel | SW |
| Glaux maritima | Sea-milkwort | NW |
| Primula veris | Cowslip | NW |
| Samolus valerandi | Brookweed | NW |
| **OLEACEAE** | | |
| Fraxinus excelsior | Ash | WW |
| **GENTIANACEAE** | | |
| Centaurium capitatum | Tufted Centaury | SW |
| erythraea | Common Centaury | NW,SW |
| littorale | Seaside Centaury | NW |
| pulchellum | Lesser Centaury | NW |
| Gentianella campestris | Field Gentian | SW |
| **MENYANTHACEAE** | | |
| Menyanthes trifoliata | Bogbean | NW |
| **BORAGINACEAE** | | |
| Cynoglossum officinale | Hound's-tongue | NW,SW |
| Echium vulgare | Viper's-bugloss | SW |
| Lycopsis arvensis | Bugloss | SW |

| | | |
|---|---|---|
| Mertensia maritima | Oysterplant | SW |
| Myosotis arvensis | Field Forget-me-not | NW,SW |
| caespitosa | Tufted Forget-me-not | NW,SP |
| discolor | Changing Forget-me-not | NW,SW |
| ramosissima | Early Forget-me-not | NW,SW |
| scorpioides | Water Forget-me-not | NW |

**CONVOLVULACEAE**

| | | |
|---|---|---|
| Calystegia soldanella | Sea Bindweed | NW,SW |
| Convolvulus arvensis | Field Bindweed | SW |

**SOLANACEAE**

| | | |
|---|---|---|
| Hyoscyamus niger | Henbane | SW |
| Solanum dulcamara | Bittersweet | NW,SW |
| nigrum | Black Nightshade | SW |

**SCROPHULARIACEAE**

| | | |
|---|---|---|
| Euphrasia officianalis agg. | Eyebright | NW |
| Linaria vulgaris | Common Toadflax | NW,SW |
| Mimulus luteus × guttatus | Blood-drop-emlets | Biggar |
| Odontites verna | Red Bartsia | NW |
| Pedicularis sylvatica | Lousewort | NW |
| Rhinanthus minor | Yellow Rattle | NW,SW |
| Scrophularia nodosa | Common Figwort | WW |
| Verbascum thapsus | Great Mullein | SW |
| Veronica agrestis | Green Field-speedwell | Wy |
| arvensis | Wall Speedwell | NW,Wy |
| chamaedrys | Germander Speedwell | NW,SW,WW |
| officinalis | Heath Speedwell | NW,SW |
| scutellata | Marsh Speedwell | NW |
| serpyllifolia | Thyme-leaved Speedwell | NW |

**LABIATAE**

| | | |
|---|---|---|
| Ajuga reptans | Bugle | NW,WW |
| Betonica officinalis | Betony | NW |
| Galeopsis tetrahit | Common Hemp-nettle | NW,SW |
| Lamium amplexicaule | Henbit Dead-nettle | SW |
| Lycopus europaeus | Gipsywort | NW |
| Mentha arvensis | Corn Mint | NW,SW |
| × verticillata | Whorled Mint | SW |
| Prunella vulgaris | Selfheal | NW,SP |
| Stachys palustris | Marsh Woundwort | NW |
| sylvatica | Hedge Woundwort | NW |
| Thymus drucei | Wild Thyme | NW,SW |

**PLANTAGINACEAE**

| | | |
|---|---|---|
| Plantago coronopus | Buck's-horn Plantain | NW,SW |
| lanceolata | Ribwort Plantain | NW,SW,WW |
| major | Greater Plantain | NW,SW,WW |
| maritima | Sea Plantain | NW,SW |

**CAMPANULACEAE**

| | | |
|---|---|---|
| Campanula rotundifolia | Harebell | NW,SW |

| | | |
|---|---|---|
| Jasione montana | Sheep's-bit | SP |
| **RUBIACEAE** | | |
| Galium aparine | Cleavers | NW,SW,WW |
| palustre | Common Marsh-bedstraw | NW,SW,VP |
| saxatile | Heath Bedstraw | NW,SW,SP |
| verum | Lady's Bedstraw | NW,SW |
| **CAPRIFOLIACEAE** | | |
| Lonicera periclymenum | Honeysuckle | SW,WW |
| Sambucus nigra | Elder | NW,SW |
| Symphoricarpos rivularis | Snowberry | SW |
| Viburnum opulus | Guelder-rose | NW,WW |
| **VALERIANACEAE** | | |
| Valeriana officinalis | Common Valerian | SW |
| Valerianella locusta | Common Cornsalad | SW |
| **DIPSACACEAE** | | |
| Succisa pratensis | Devil's-bit Scabious | NW |
| **COMPOSITAE** | | |
| Achillea millefolium | Yarrow | NW,SW |
| ptarmica | Sneezewort | NW,SW,WW |
| Arctium lappa | Greater Burdock | SW |
| minus | Lesser Burdock | NW,SW,WW |
| minus nemorosum | Lesser Burdock | SW |
| Artemisia vulgaris | Mugwort | SW |
| maritima | Sea Wormwood | SW |
| Aster tripolium | Sea Aster | NW,SW |
| Bellis perennis | Daisy | NW,SW |
| Carlina vulgaris | Carline Thistle | NW |
| Carduus acanthoides | Welted Thistle | SW |
| tenuiflorus | Slender Thistle | SW |
| Centaurea nigra | Common Knapweed | NW,SW,WW |
| Cirsium arvense | Creeping Thistle | NW,SW,WW |
| palustre | Marsh Thistle | NW,WW |
| vulgare | Spear Thistle | NW,SW |
| Crepis capillaris | Smooth Hawk's-beard | NW,SW |
| Erigeron acer | Blue Fleabane | NW |
| Filago minima | Small Cudweed | SW |
| Gnaphalium uliginosum | Marsh Cudweed | NW,SW |
| Hieracium aurantiacum | Fox-and-cubs | SW |
| perpropinquum | Hawkweed | Wy |
| umbellatum | Hawkweed | Wy |
| pilosella | Mouse-ear Hawkweed | NW,SP |
| Hypochoeris glabra | Smooth Cat's-ear | SW |
| radicata | Cat's-ear | NW,SW |
| Inula conyza | Ploughman's-spikenard | SW |
| Leontodon autumnalis | Autumn Hawkbit | NW,SW |
| hispidus | Rough Hawkbit | NW,SW |
| taraxacoides | Lesser Hawkbit | NW,SW |

| | | |
|---|---|---|
| Leucanthemum vulgare | Oxeye Daisy | SW |
| Matricaria matricarioides | Pineappleweed | NW,SW |
| Picris echioides | Bristly Oxtongue | SW |
| Pulicaria dysenterica | Common Fleabane | NW |
| Senecio jacobaea | Common Ragwort | NW,SW,WW |
| sylvaticus | Heath Groundsel | NW,SW |
| viscosus | Sticky Groundsel | NW,SW |
| vulgaris | Groundsel | NW,SW |
| Solidago vigaurea | Goldenrod | NW |
| Sonchus arvensis | Perennial Sow-thistle | NW,SW |
| asper | Prickly Sow-thistle | NW,SW |
| oleraceus | Smooth Sow-thistle | NW,Wy |
| Taraxacum officinale | Dandelion | NW,SW |
| Tragopogon pratensis | Goat's-beard | NW |
| Tripleurospermum maritimum | | |
| ssp. maritimum | Sea Mayweed | NW |
| ssp. inordorum | Scentless Mayweed | NW,SW |
| Tussilago farfara | Colt's-foot | NW,SW,WW |

**ALISMATACEAE**

| | | |
|---|---|---|
| Alisma plantago-aquatica | Water-plantain | NW |

**HYDROCHARITACEAE**

| | | |
|---|---|---|
| Elodea canadensis | Canadian Waterweed | NW |

**JUNCAGINACEAE**

| | | |
|---|---|---|
| Triglochin maritima | Sea Arrowgrass | NW,SP |
| palustris | Marsh Arrowgrass | NW |

**ZOSTERACEAE**

| | | |
|---|---|---|
| Zostera marina | Eelgrass | SW |

**POTAMOGETONACEAE**

| | | |
|---|---|---|
| Potamogeton natans | Broad-leaved Pondweed | NW,SP |
| pectinatus | Fennel Pondweed | SW |
| polygonifolius | Bog Pondweed | NW,SP,VP |
| pusillus | Lesser Pondweed | NW |

**RUPPIACEAE**

| | | |
|---|---|---|
| Ruppia maritima | Beaked Tasselweed | Biggar |

**ZANNICHELLIACEAE**

| | | |
|---|---|---|
| Zannichellia palustris | Horned Pondweed | SP |

**LILIACEAE**

| | | |
|---|---|---|
| Endymion hispanicus | Spanish Bluebell | NW |
| non-scriptus | Bluebell | NW,SW,Wy,SP |
| Muscari comosum | Tassel Hyacinth | SW |
| atlanticum | Grape Hyacinth | SW |
| Ornithogalum pyrenaicum | Spiked Star of Bethlehem | SW |

**JUNCACEAE**

| | | |
|---|---|---|
| Juncus acutiflorus | Sharp-flowered Rush | NW,SW |
| articulatus | Jointed Rush | NW,SW,SP,VP |

| | | |
|---|---|---|
| Juncus bufonius | Toad Rush | NW,SW |
| bulbosus | Bulbous Rush | SW |
| conglomeratus | Compact Rush | VP |
| effusus | Soft Rush | NW,SW,VP |
| gerardii | Saltmarsh Rush | NW,SW |
| squarrosus | Heath Rush | NW,SW |
| subuliflorus | Compact Rush | NW,SW |
| Luzula campestris | Field Wood-rush | SW |
| multiflora | Heath Wood-rush | SW |

**AMARYLLIDACEAE**

| | | |
|---|---|---|
| Allium vineale | Wild Onion | NW |
| Narcissus sp. | Daffodil | NW |

**IRIDACEAE**

| | | |
|---|---|---|
| Crocosmia × crocosmiflora | Montbretia | NW |
| Iris pseudacorus | Yellow Iris | SW,VP |
| Sisyrinchium californicum | Yellow-eyed Grass | NW |

**ORCHIDACEAE**

| | | |
|---|---|---|
| Anacamptis pyramidalis | Pyramidal Orchid | NW,SW |
| Corallorhiza trifida | Coralroot Orchid | NW |
| Dactylorhiza fuchsii | Common Spotted-orchid | NW,WW |
| incarnata | Early Marsh-orchid | NW,WW |
| purpurella | Northern Marsh-orchid | NW |
| Epipactis palustris | Marsh Helleborine | NW |
| phyllanthes | Green-flowered Helleborine | NW |
| Gymnadenia conopsea | Fragrant Orchid | SW |
| Listera ovata | Common Twayblade | NW |
| Ophrys apifera | Bee Orchid | NW |

**LEMNACEAE**

| | | |
|---|---|---|
| Lemna minor | Common Duckweed | NW,SW,SP |
| trisulca | Ivy-leaved Duckweed | SW,SP |

**SPARGANIACEAE**

| | | |
|---|---|---|
| Sparganium emersum | Unbranched Bur-reed | NW,SP |
| erectum | Branched Bur-reed | NW |

**TYPHACEAE**

| | | |
|---|---|---|
| Typha latifolia | Bulrush | NW.VP |

**CYPERACEAE**

| | | |
|---|---|---|
| Carex arenaria | Sand Sedge | NW,SW |
| binervis | Green-ribbed Sedge | SW |
| echinata | Star Sedge | SW |
| extensa | Long-bracted Sedge | NW |
| flacca | Glaucous Sedge | NW,SW |
| hirta | Hairy Sedge | NW,SW |
| nigra | Common Sedge | NW,SW,VP |
| otrubae | False Fox-sedge | NW,SP |
| ovalis | Oval Sedge | SW,SP |
| panicea | Carnation Sedge | NW |

| | | |
|---|---|---|
| Carex pilulifera | Pill Sedge | NW |
| rostrata | Bottle Sedge | WW |
| serotina | Small-fruited Yellow-sedge | NW |
| vesicaria | Bladder Sedge | VP |
| Eleocharis multicaulis | Many-stalked Spike-rush | SW |
| palustris | Common Spike-rush | NW,SW |
| uniglumis | Slender Spike-rush | NW |
| Eriophorum angustifolium | Common Cottongrass | NW,SW |
| Scirpus fluitans | Floating Club-rush | SW |
| maritimus | Sea Club-rush | NW |
| tabernaemontani | Grey Club-rush | SW |

**GRAMINEAE**

| | | |
|---|---|---|
| Agropyron junceiforme | Sand Couch | NW,SW |
| pungens | Sea Couch | NW,SW |
| repens | Common Couch | NW,SW |
| Agrostis canina canina | Brown Bent | SW |
| canina montana | Brown Bent | SW |
| semiverticillata | Water Bent | SW |
| stolonifera | Creeping Bent | NW,SW |
| tenuis | Common Bent | NW,SW |
| Aira caryophyllea | Silver Hair-grass | SW |
| praecox | Early Hair-grass | NW,SW |
| Alopecurus geniculatus | Marsh Foxtail | NW,SW |
| myosuroides | Black-grass | SW |
| Ammophila arenaria | Marram | NW,SW |
| Anthoxanthum odoratum | Sweet Vernal-grass | NW,SW |
| Arrhenatherum elatius | False Oat-grass | NW,SW |
| Bromus mollis | Soft-brome | NW,SW |
| sterilis | Barren Brome | SW |
| Calamagrostis epigejos | Wood Small-reed | NW |
| Catapodium marinum | Sea Fern-grass | SW |
| rigidum | Fern-grass | NW,SW |
| Cynosurus cristatus | Crested Dog's-tail | SP,WW |
| Dactylis glomerata | Cock's-foot | NW,SP |
| Elymus arenarius | Lyme-grass | NW,SW |
| Deschampsia cespitosa | Tufted Hair-grass | NW |
| flexuosa | Wavy Hair-grass | NW |
| Festuca arundinacea | Tall Fescue | NW |
| ovina | Sheep's-fescue | NW,SW |
| rubra | Red Fescue | NW,SW |
| Glyceria fluitans | Floating Sweet-grass | NW,SP |
| Holcus lanatus | Yorkshire-fog | NW,SW,WW |
| mollis | Creeping Soft-grass | NW |
| Hordeum murinum | Wall Barley | NW,SW |
| Koeleria cristata | Crested Hair-grass | NW |
| Lolium perenne | Perennial Rye-grass | NW,SW |
| Molinia caerulea | Purple Moor-grass | NW |
| Nardus stricta | Mat-grass | NW,SW |
| Parapholis strigosa | Hard-grass | NW,SW |

| | | |
|---|---|---|
| Phalaris arundinacea | Reed Canary-grass | SW |
| Phleum arenarium | Sand Cat's-tail | NW |
| pratense | Timothy | SW |
| Phragmites australis | Common Reed | NW,SW,VP |
| Poa annua | Annual Meadow-grass | NW,SW |
| compressa | Flattened Meadow-grass | SW |
| pratensis | Smooth Meadow-grass | NW,SW |
| trivialis | Rough Meadow-grass | NW,SW |
| Puccinellia maritima | Common Saltmarsh-grass | NW,SW |
| Sieglingia decumbens | Heath-grass | NW,SW |
| Spartina anglica | Common Cord-grass | NW,SW |
| Vulpia bromoides | Squirreltail Fescue | NW,SP |
| membranacea | Dune Fescue | SW |

# The Mosses, Lichens and Liverworts of Walney

## Mosses at South Walney

Polytrichum commune — 1965, J. Buchanan.
    piliferum — 1965, J. Buchanan; 1982, C. Tiler.
    juniperum — 1965, J. Buchanan.

Ceratodon purpureus — 1965, J. Buchanan; 1979, M. Barratt.

Dicranella heteromella — 1965, J. Buchanan; 1982, C. Tiler.

Dicranum scoparium — 1982, C. Tiler.

Leucobryum glaucum — 1965, J. Buchanan.

Tortula ruralis subsp. ruraliformis — 1965, J. Buchanan; 1982, C. Tiler.
    muralis — 1979, M. Barratt; 1982, C. Tiler.
    subulata — 1965, J. Buchanan.

Grimmia trichophylla — 1982, C. Tiler.

Bryum caespiticium — 1982, C. Tiler.
    argenteum — 1982, C. Tiler.

Mnium hornum — 1965, J. Buchanan.

Isopterygium elegans — 1982, C. Tiler.

Hypnum cupressiforme — 1965, J. Buchanan; 1979, M. Barratt.

## Liverworts at South Walney

Calypogeia fissa — 1965, J. Buchanan.

## Lichens at South Walney

Caloplaca thallincola — 1982, C. Tiler.
Candelariella vitellina — 1982, C. Tiler.
Cladonia chlorophaea — 1986, C. Rose.
    fimbriata — 1979, M. Barratt; 1986, C. Rose.
    floerkeana — 1982, C. Tiler.
    foliacea — 1965, J. Buchanan; 1979, M. Barratt; 1982, C. Tiler.
    furcata — 1986, C. Rose.
    impexa — 1965, J. Buchanan.
    macilenta — 1965, J. Buchanan.
    pyxidata — 1982, C. Tiler; 1986, C. Rose.
    squamosa — 1965, J. Buchanan.
    tenuis — 1986, C. Rose.
    verticillata — 1986, C. Rose.

Lecanora atra — 1982, C. Tiler; 1986, C. Rose.
    dispersa — 1986, C. Rose.
    muralis — 1985, C. Rose.
    polytropa — 1986, C. Rose.

Parmelia britannica — 1986, C. Rose.
physodes — 1965, J. Buchanan.
saxatilis — 1986, C. Rose.

Peltigera canina — 1965, J. Buchanan; 1986, C. Rose.
polydactyla — 1965, J. Buchanan.

Physcia grisea — 1986, C. Rose.

Ramelina farinacea — 1986, C. Rose.
fraxinea — 1986, C. Rose.

Umbilicaria polyrrhiza — 1985, C. Rose.

Xanthoria parietina — 1985, C. Rose.
polycarpa — 1986, C. Rose.

## Mosses at North Walney

Sphagnum cuspidatum — 1982, C. Tiler.

Polytrichum formosum — 1978, NENWSH.
commune — 1982, C. Tiler; 1985, A. Orange.
piliferum — 1985, A. Orange.
juniperum — 1978, NENWSH.

Ceratodon purpureus — 1978, NENWSH; 1985, A. Orange.

Dicranium scoparium — 1978, NENWSH; 1985, A. Orange.

Encalypta streptocarpa — 1978, NENWSH.

Tortula ruralis subsp. ruraliformis — 1978, NENWSH; 1985, A. Orange.
muralis — 1978, NENWSH.
subulata — 1978, NENWSH.

Barbula fallax — 1978, NENWSH.
cylindrica — 1978, NENWSH.

Racomitrum canescens — 1978, NENWSH.

Funaria hygrometrica — 1978, NENWSH.

Pohlia nutans — 1985, A. Orange.

Bryum pseudotriquetrum — 1978, NENWSH.
argenteum — 1978, NENWSH.

Mnium hornum — 1985, A. Orange.

Plagiomnium undulatum — 1978, NENWSH.

Aulacomnium palustre — 1985, A. Orange.

Climacium dendroides — 1978, NENWSH.

Campylium stellatum — 1978, NENWSH.

Drepanocladus aduncus — 1978, NENWSH.
fluitans — 1985, A. Orange.

Calliergon cordifolium — 1978, NENWSH.
cuspidatum — 1978, NENWSH; 1985, A. Orange.

Homalothecium sericeum — 1978, NENWSH.

Brachythecium albicans — 1978, NENWSH.
rutabulum — 1978, NENWSH.

Pseudoscleropodium purum — 1978, NENWSH.

Hypnum cupressiforme — 1978, NENWSH.

## Liverworts at North Walney

Cephalozia bicuspidata — 1985, A. Orange.
Lophocolea cuspidata — 1985, A. Orange.
Pellia neesiana — 1978, NENWSH.
Anevra pinguis — 1978, NENWSH.

# The Fungi of Walney

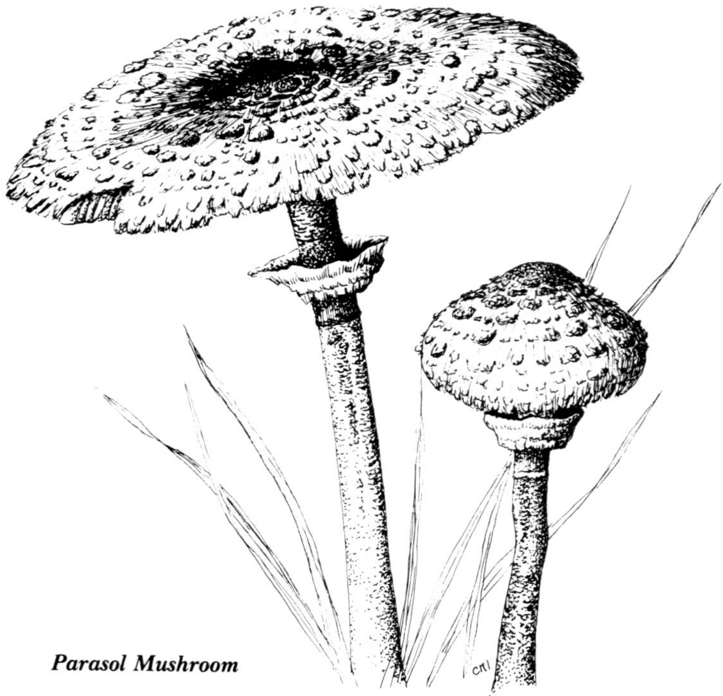

*Parasol Mushroom*

**AGARICS**

Agaricus arvensis **(Horse Mushroom).** Can be abundant throughout the island.
campestris **(Field Mushroom).** Less common than Horse Mushroom.
Amanita rubescens **(The Blusher).** A few specimens from Willow Woods.
Bolbitius vitellinus. Can be abundant at South Walney.
Calocybe carnea. Recorded once at South Walney.
gambosa **(St. George's Mushroom).** Recorded at South Walney.
Clitocybe dealbata. Abundant at both South and North Walney.
rivulosa. Abundant at both South and North Walney.
Clitopilus prunulus **(The Miller).** Specimens recorded at South Walney.
Conocybe tenera. Fairly common at South Walney.
Coprinus atramentarius **(Common Ink Cap).** Recorded at both South and North Walney.
comatus **(Lawyer's Wig).** Recorded at both South and North Walney.
niveus. A few specimens at South Walney.
picaceus **(Magpie Fungus).** Recorded once at South Walney.
plicatilis. Recorded at South Walney.
Crepidotus variabilis. Recorded at South Walney.
Cystoderma amianthinum. Recorded at South Walney.

Entoloma conferendum. Recorded at South Walney.
porphyrophaeum. Recorded at South Walney.
sericeum. Recorded at both South and North Walney.
undatum. Recorded at South Walney.
Flammulina velutipes **(Velvet Shank).** Fairly common at South Walney, growing on Tree Lupin.
Galerina hypnorum. Fairly common at South Walney.
Gymnopilus penetrans. A few examples at South Walney.
Hygrocybe conica **(Conical Wax Cap).** A few specimens at South Walney.
marchii. Recorded once at South Walney.
miniata. Recorded at South Walney.
nigrescens **(Blackening Wax Cap).** Common at both South and North Walney.
nivea **(Snowy Wax Cap).** A few examples at South Walney.
pratensis **(Meadow Wax Cap).** Recorded at South Walney.
psittacina **(Parrot Wax Cap).** Recorded at South Walney.
russocoriacea. A few specimens at South Walney.
Hygrophoropsis aurantiaca **(False Chanterelle).** Recorded once at South Walney.
Lepiota cristata. Recorded at South Walney.
excoriata. Common at South Walney.
leucothites. A few examples at South Walney.
procera **(Parasol Mushroom).** Common at both South and North Walney.
rhacodes **(Shaggy Parasol).** Recorded at South Walney.
Lepista nuda **(Wood Blewit).** Can be common at South Walney.
saevum **(Field Blewit).** Recorded at South Walney.
Lyophyllum connatum. Recorded at South Walney.
decastes. A few specimens at South Walney.
Marasmius androsaceus **(Horse-hair fungus).** Recorded at South Walney.
calopus. Recorded at South Walney.
epiphyllus. Recorded at South Walney.
oreades **(Fairy Ring Champignon).** Abundant at South Walney.
rotula. Recorded at South Walney.
Melanoleuca melaleuca. Common at South Walney.
Mycena galericulata **(Bonnet Mycena).** Recorded at South Walney.
leptocephala. Recorded at South Walney.
Omphalina fibula. Recorded at South Walney.
swartzii. Recorded at South Walney.
Paneolus foensecii. Can be abundant at both South and North Walney.
rickenii. Fairly common at South Walney.
semiovatus. Recorded at South Walney.
speciosus. Recorded at South Walney.
sphinctrinus. Fairly common at South Walney.
subbalteatus. Recorded at South Walney.
Pleurotus dryinus. Recorded from Willow Woods.
Pluteus cervinus. A few examples at South Walney.
Psathyrella conopilea. Fairly common at South Walney.
Psilocybe coprophilla. Recorded at South Walney.
semilanceata. Recorded once at South Walney.

Russula nitida. Recorded at North Walney.
Stropharia pseudocyanea. A few examples at both South and North Walney.
semiglobata. Fairly common at both South and North Walney.
Tricholoma fulvum. Recorded once at South Walney.
Tubaria furfuracea. Recorded at South Walney.
Volvariella speciosa. A few specimens at South Walney.

**JELLY FUNGI**

Dacrymyces deliquescens. Common at South Walney.
Fuligo septica flava. Common at South Walney.

**APHYLLOPHORALES**

Stereum rugosum. Recorded at South Walney.

**GASTEROMYCETES**

Bovista nigrescens. Abundant at both South and North Walney.
plumbea. Fairly common at South Walney.
Lycoperdon caelatum. Fairly common at both South and North Walney.
depressum. Fairly common at both South and North Walney.
ericetorum. Fairly common at both South and North Walney.
perlatum. Fairly common at both South and North Walney.
Phallus hadriani **(Dune Stinkhorn).** A few examples from both South and North Walney.

**ASCOMYCETES**

Auricularia auricula-judae **(Ear Fungus).** Common at South Walney.
Daldinia concentrica. Recorded at South Walney.
Nectria cinnabarina. Recorded at South Walney.

*All species recorded by M. Allison (1979) and T. Dean (1980-1989).*

**References:**


Association of Natural History Societies in Cumbria 1956-1989;Field Naturalist; The Changing Scene; Natural History in Cumbria; Birds in Cumbria.

Barrow Naturalists' Field Club. Annual reports.

Borough of Barrow-in-Furness. 1978, The Natural Environment of North Walney and Sandscale Haws.
1980, A Study of South Walney.

Clapham, A. R., Tutin, T. G. & Warburg, E. F. 1962, Flora of the British Isles. Cambridge University Press.

Cumbria Naturalists's Trust/Cumbria Trust for Nature Conservation/Cumbria Wildlife Trust. Newsletters. 1963-1989.

Dobson, F. 1981, Lichens, an illustrated guide. Richmond.

Dony, J. G., Perring, F. H. & Rob, C. M. 1980, English names of wild flowers. The Botanical Society of the British Isles.

Hardy, E. 1973, The Naturalist in Lakeland. David and Charles.

Harting, J. E. 1864, The birds of Walney Island.

Lake District Naturalists' Trust. 1972, Walney Island, North End.

Lancashire and Cheshire Fauna Society. 1950-1980. Annual reports.

Lange, M. & Hora, F. B. 1978, Mushrooms and Toadstools. Collins.

Mannex, P. J. 1849, History of Westmoreland with Furness and Cartmel.

Philips, R. 1981, Mushrooms. Pan.

Smith, A. J. E. 1980, The Moss flora of Britain and Ireland. Cambridge University Press.

Wakefield, E. M. & Dennis, R. W. G. 1981, Common British Fungi. Saiga.

Walney Bird Observatory. Annual reports, 1965-71; 1980-89.

# The Mammals of Walney

A chapter on the mammals of Walney Island is limited due to an understandable lack of records for those species that are primarily nocturnal and secretive. As such, little is known about the distribution and status of shrews, voles and mice. In addition virtually no information has been forthcoming with regard to the 'domestic pests' from the residential areas of the island. Perhaps the only indication of abundance, without recourse to a mammal trapping survey, is to note the presence and numbers of predatory birds, notably Short-eared Owls, at different times of the year and at different localities. However, no investigation has been made into the composition of their pellets, and so all we can say is that small rodents were probably in abundance. The only mammal trapping survey in recent years was performed at South Walney Nature Reserve in 1985 and 1986 by Pavlo Zaltowski and yielded a great deal of hitherto unknown information.

The larger mammals present us with little in the way of recording problems. With such a large human population on the island, incidencies of the larger species of mammal are probably not that under-recorded.

Cetacean records provide, perhaps, an indicator of the dwindling resources of the Morecambe Bay fish population and an increase in the offshore pollution of the sea. In almost every instance, sea mammals were seen far more frequently and in far larger numbers during the early years of recording. Despite the better facilities for sea-watching, provided in the 1980s, there has been only one sighting of Bottle-nosed Dolphin, one of Common Dolphin and two of Common Porpoise.

**HEDGEHOG** ***Erinaceus europaeus***

Only occasionally seen at South Walney with nine sightings since the first record of two specimens on 6th May 1973. July has produced four occurrences, September one and October two. Additionally, a corpse was found in early September 1985. North Walney has yielded three April individuals, a June sighting and two corpses in August since 1984.

Elsewhere on the island, seven road victims have been seen near Biggar since 1984, and a handful of live animals in the refuse tip and Long Rein Point areas including a youngster in August 1988. The species' status in the urban areas of Walney is not well documented except for up to nine visiting 'hogs' at a garden in French Street adjacent to James Dunn Park, Vickerstown.

**PYGMY SHREW** ***Sorex minutus***

Regularly heard at South Walney especially between April and September with a maximum of six animals on 20th August 1983. An individual was found underneath wood on 13th January 1981. Only occasionally recorded at North Walney, although it is probably present in much greater numbers than the maximum count of two on 26th June 1984.

Willow Woods held at least ten specimens on 20th April 1984. The species is probably widely distributed throughout the island and its high, thin call is commonly heard on spring walks along Rakes Lane.

**COMMON SHREW** ***Sorex araneus***

The only definite island record is of a single caught at South Walney on 10th February 1981.

**MOLE** *Talpa europaea*

At South Walney Nature Reserve, hills have not been found further south than the central marsh. Most activity has been noticed at the northern end of the reserve adjacent to the richer soils of the surrounding grazing land.
The only North Walney record is of a single animal on 25th October 1983.
Abundant hills can usually be seen in the Biggar area from which region there is a grisly record of nine dead on 11th June 1963.

**LONG-EARED BAT** *Plecotus auritus*

On 28th August 1985, one was removed from barbed wire near the South End Caravan Site and after a day in care, was able to fly off. On 27th August, it had been by-passed as a piece of typical Walney windblown litter.

**BAT SP.**

At South Walney, a small bat roosted at Coastguard's Cottages on 13th September 1982. Small bats have also been recorded at South End farm and near Willow Woods on warm evenings. More investigation with regard to specific identification and status would be desirable since there are many suitable nesting and roosting sites on the island.

**RABBIT** *Oryctolagus cuniculus*

The island holds a substantial population with greatest numbers at South Walney Nature Reserve where in peak years the colony has been estimated at 5,000 animals. It is not unusual for licenced rabbiters at South Walney to take almost 100 individuals on a day's visit in winter merely by using dogs and ferrets. This form of pest control activity seems to have little effect upon the overall numbers. Myxymatosis, on the other hand, has far greater impact and appears in three, four or five year cycles with recent outbreaks documented in 1972, 1977, 1982 and 1986. The outbreak of 1982 seemingly wiped out the colony only for it to return to peak numbers by the summer of 1983. Myxymatosis reappeared in the late spring of 1986, but the colony was again flourishing by the autumn of that year and rabbiters reported taking healthy rabbits bearing the scarring typical of diseased specimens.

The Walney population was probably farmed by the monks of Furness Abbey as early as the 12th century. Additionally, readers are referred to extracts from documents in Dalton parish church relating to rabbit farming on South Walney dated 1534 and 1613. Older Ordnance Survey maps of the area indicate "rabbit warrens" at both South Walney and at North Walney, but the latter site holds far fewer; the 200 of 15th May 1989 being totally unprecedented in recent years and possibly reflects the value of wardening.

Between 1972 and 1977, Walney Island Wildfowlers Association took 424 individuals, most of them in the area north of the refuse tip and south of Ocean Road, with 204 of them in the winter of 1973 and 1974.

**BROWN HARE** ***Lepus capensis***

The Walney Island Wildfowlers Association 'bag' totals indicated a flourishing population, for in the winter on 1976 and 1977 alone, 58 were taken. Sight records since then do not present such a healthy picture although fairly regular appearances occur throughout the rural areas of the island. At South Walney Nature Reserve peak sightings are noted in early spring with a maximum five on 12th February 1982 and four on many days. During winter, animals have been seen foraging on the tideline.

At North Walney, sightings can be daily but no more than two individuals have been recorded on any day.

**VOLE SP.**

The only records at South Walney are of single animals briefly seen on 17th September 1982 and 3rd November 1983.

**SHORT-TAILED VOLE** ***Microtus agrestis***

The only records relate to South Walney Nature Reserve where single specimens have been seen or caught on five days between May and September in the years 1981 to 1985. In addition, corpses were obtained on 9th November 1983 and 10th October 1984.

**WATER VOLE** ***Arvicola amphibius***

R. Benson (pers. comm.) reports finding a few individuals in the wet, central area of the airfield in the early 1960s.

**WOOD MOUSE** ***Sylvaemus sylvaticus***

A mammal trapping survey at South Walney Nature Reserve during 1985 indicated a far larger population than previously seen or imagined. Specimens were caught between March and November with a maximum catch of five individuals out of 12 set traps on 20th November. Additionally, four were caught on 10th April and 25th September, and three on six nights. Caught animals were marked and except for one persistent individual, all subsequent 'trapees' were newcomers.

The only sightings at North Walney involve a single on 22nd June 1985 and a corpse in late January of that year.

**BROWN RAT** ***Rattus norvegicus***

Its tenancy of the island seems to have been of long-standing. MacPherson (1892) informs us that "this rat is quite as much at home in the burrows which it has tunnelled in the hedge banks of Walney Island as in the farmers' ricks of corn."

At South Walney the species can be very abundant and provides a valuable service in clearing up the gull carcases at the end of the breeding season. This activity often takes place in broad daylight. Post breeding season behaviour is less welcome with many semi-tame specimens being seen in the vicinity of Coastguards Cottages, one even managing to enter into a resident's bread-bin. Local feeling is that the island population increased markedly after the establishment of the refuse tip at the southern end of the island. Visitors have reported the rather unnerving sight of large numbers scuttling along the South Walney tidelines at night. Surprisingly, there were no winter records at the cottages in 1986/87 and at the time of writing, the population is virtually absent with only five records from 1987 to 1989.

**HOUSE MOUSE** ***Mus musculus***

The only records are from South Walney where singles were at the Coastguards Cottages in autumn 1979, spring 1984 and spring 1987.

**RED FOX** ***Vulpes vulpes***

The species has occurred very rarely on Walney and specimens have probably reached the island from Sandscale using the low water crossing. R. Benson (pers. comm.) reports that breeding has taken place at North Walney and since 1950, his shotgun has claimed three pelts. The latest sightings were dog foxes; in early spring 1985 which were shot on the airfield on 3rd March and on 8th June 1989. At South Walney, fresh faeces were regularly seen near the offices during the winter of 1979 and 1980, while in 1989 at least two animals were seen regularly in summer.

**BADGER** ***Meles meles***

A tideline corpse was found by R. Benson on the west shore of the island in the late 1950s and a second was found at South Walney Nature Reserve on 28th September 1988. It is doubtful whether they occur in the live state on the island.

**STOAT** ***Mustela erminea***

At South Walney Nature Reserve, animals have been seen in most recent years although, after a total absence of sightings in 1983, an increase was evident in subsequent years, peaking at five specimens on 4th April 1988. The species was recorded on eight days in 1984, nine days in 1985 and 18 days in 1986 and then leapt to 60 days in 1987 — only decreasing slightly from that figure in the subsequent two years.

North Walney held singles on two days in April 1984 and on five days between January and October in 1985.

Elsewhere on the island animals have been met with in the Rakes Lane and Biggar village area.

**WEASEL** ***Mustela nivalis***

Throughout the island Weasels are recorded on far fewer occasions than Stoats. At South Walney single animals have been logged on 12 days between February and October during the years 1981 to 1989.

North Walney has produced six sightings of single specimens between March and October since 1984, with two being located on 30th May 1984.

Occasional appearances have been reported from the Rakes Lane and Biggar village region.

**AMERICAN MINK** ***Mustela vison***

Thankfully, there are only three sightings. The oyster farm at South Walney has yielded single animals on 18th December 1982 and on 26th April 1987, the latter miscreant being killed on the following day. The only other example was alive underneath a Ford Fiesta at 14, Falmouth Street, Vickerstown, on 1st September 1986.

**FERRET** ***Mustela putorius***

The species is occasionally met with at South Walney Nature Reserve, undoubtedly originating from the activities of poachers.

**OTTER** ***Lutra lutra***

R. Benson (pers. comm.) maintains that the species has occurred at North Walney in summers pursuing Mullet into the shallow waters of Scarth Channel.

**FERAL CAT** ***Felis catus***

A few specimens are regularly seen at South Walney, most probably originating from the island farms, and others perhaps being dumped as undesirables. Specimens have been seen entering rabbit burrows or emerging from the wartime gun emplacements.

**GREY SEAL** *Haliochoerus grypus*

At South Walney, singles of the species can often be seen off Hilpsford Point or in Piel Bar. Most frequent sightings have occurred in June, August and September. Days present at South Walney 1981-1989

| J | F | M | A | M | J | J | A | S | O | N | D | T |
|---|---|---|---|---|---|---|---|---|---|---|---|---|
| 10 | 12 | 5 | 4 | 7 | 20 | 10 | 25 | 42 | 24 | 9 | 7 | 175 |

The only sightings from North Walney involve two specimens on 20th December 1983 and 27th April 1989 and singles on 16th March 1984 and on four dates in 1988. Breeding does not occur on Walney; in all likelihood the species breeds on the isle of Man.

**ROE DEER** *Capreolus capreolus*

R. Benson (pers. comm.) reports that individuals were seen twice at North Walney in the 1950s, probably arriving there from Sandscale and Sowerby Woods using the low water crossing. Additionally, single animals were at Willow Woods on 6th June 1984 and 25th May 1988.

South Walney yielded an odd sequence of records with a doe at the caravan site on 10th June 1983 and a doe and fawn on the following date. On 10th July 1985 the gull colony at South Walney Nature Reserve was thrown into utter bedlam by a young Roe cantering south. On reaching the spit, it was seen to swim into Piel Channel.

**BOTTLE-NOSED DOLPHIN** ***Tursiops truncatus***

There are very few records at South Walney, the only recent sighting being 'more than nine' on 28th May 1984. Prior to this, one was 'ashore' on 8th October 1917; one on 8th October 1918 (both sightings indicating the diligence of the Home Guard); a male on 13th August 1952; and a 'small party' on 31st July 1964. Additionally, a female was off the north end on 23rd May 1924.

**COMMON DOLPHIN** ***Delphinus delphis***

At South Walney, there has been only one sighting since 1969, involving five animals moving north on 18th April 1981. Prior to 1970, 30 were seen on 14th May 1961; 19 on 31st July 1964; 'several' on 20th April and 22nd July 1965 and a single on 28th October; a small school on 18th March 1966; and six on 11th May 1969.

**KILLER WHALE** ***Orcinus orca***

R. Benson (pers. comm.) reports an individual at North Walney in 1951. At South Walney, four cruised in Piel Channel for almost one hour until the tide ebbed on 8th December 1968.

**PILOT WHALE** ***Globicephala melaena***

On 15th May 1985, an individual was observed for 30 minutes at high tide off Hilpsford Point.

**COMMON PORPOISE** ***Phocaena phocaena***

In the 1980s at South Walney there are only two records; one a corpse on 28th November 1982 and the other moving west on 18th August 1985. Prior to this, six were seen in April 1960 and 'several' on 6th October 1968. On 7th May 1963, 18 were reported off Biggar Bank, while later in the same year, on 25th and 27th August, 50 were seen in Walney Channel.

***References:***


Association of Natural History Societies in Cumbria 1956-1985. Field Naturalist; The Changing Scene; Natural History in Cumbria; Birds in Cumbria.

Barrow Naturalists' Field Club. Annual reports.

Borough of Barrow-in-Furness. 1978, The Natural Environment of North Walney and Sandscale Haws.
1980, A Study of South Walney.

Cumbria Naturalists' Trust / Cumbria Trust for Nature Conservation / Cumbria Wildlife Trust — Newsletters, 1963-1989.

Hardy, E. 1973, The Naturalist in Lakeland. David and Charles. Newton Abbot.

Lake District Naturalists' Trust. 1972, Walney Island, North End.

Lancashire and Cheshire Fauna Society. 1950-80, Annual reports.

MacPherson, H. A. 1892, A vertebrate fauna of Lakeland. David Douglas, Edinburgh.

Southern, H. N. 1965, The handbook of British Mammals. Blackwell, Oxford.

Van Den Brink, F. H. 1967, A field guide to the mammals of Britain and Europe. Collins, London.

Walney Bird Observatory. Annual reports 1965-71; 1980-89.

# The Reptiles and Amphibians of Walney

Peter Carty

Walney Island has five species of amphibian and one reptile. Its amphibian fauna resembles largely that of the mainland, but the reptile fauna is more impoverished. This is partly to do with climatic considerations but also to do with the biological barrier of the Walney Channel which has prevented the colonisation of species such as the Slow Worm *(Anguis fragilis)*, Grass Snake *(Natrix natrix)* and Adder *(Vipera berus)* which occur in varying numbers in suitable habitat just over the water. Indeed, the Slow Worm has been recorded in the gardens of Barrow-in-Furness residencies. The situation is not unlike that encountered in Ireland where most reptiles are absent due to the loss of the land connection at a time when the climate was too cold for them to occur in these latitudes. The exception is the Viviparous Lizard *(Lacerta vivipara)* which is tolerant of cooler climates and is present within the Arctic Circle.

In nature conservation terms the Natterjack Toad *(Bufo calamita)* is the most important amphibian resident on the island. Nationally it has suffered massive declines in the 20th century with more than 80% of its habitat lost or damaged. Today in Northwest England it clings to the Sefton coast near Southport and on the Cumbrian coast to the Solway Estuary.

In recent years regular surveys of the North Walney population have been conducted and have revealed a clear picture of the status of Natterjack Toads and the other amphibians present. Elsewhere on the island information is scant with the exception of South Walney Nature Reserve where very few 'herptiles' are recorded. Information is particularly lacking for the status and distribution of the Viviparous Lizard *(Lacerta vivipara)* away from the reserves.

**SMOOTH NEWT** — ***Triturus vulgaris vulgaris***

The only indication of their presence is the rather vague statement in Kirkland's 1983 report that the species was recorded at North Walney in that year. However this is in marked contrast to Sandscale Haws across Walney Channel where this species is dominant in hundreds. Additionally Palmate Newt is known from only one or two unconfirmed records at Sandscale.

**PALMATE NEWT** — ***Triturus helveticus***

According to Hardy (1973), the species bred at South Walney Nature Reserve, but since then, despite the extensive use of bottle traps in potentially suitable habitat, there has been only a single specimen near the gate pool on 15th April 1983. Kirkland (1983) is of the opinion that the South Walney pools are too polluted to sustain vertebrate life.

At North Walney the picture is markedly more healthy and the conclusion of Kirkland's 1984 report is that the reserve has a "reasonable number", adults having been caught in seven of the pools.

Elsewhere on the island the species has been reported from small pools at Mill Lane, while ponds near Willow Woods were populated in 1984. A small scale trapping programme yielded seven animals from Snab Pools in the spring of 1984 and, additionally, individuals have been seen in the Biggar village region.

**COMMON TOAD** ***Bufo bufo bufo***

The only indication of its status on the island comes from sightings at the nature reserves. South Walney's solitary record is of an individual at the gate pool on 3rd July 1980. At North Walney the picture is considerably improved. All surveys since 1978 have indicated a large and healthy population of the species. Adults are regularly seen between March and August, while vast numbers of young may be met with early in the year. A count by Cooke on 27th May 1982 indicated about one million tadpoles in just one area, while in an adjacent region, 100,000 plus of "well-grown" tadpoles were estimated. The conclusion of Kirkland's 1984 report speculates that Common Toads may be increasing at the expense of Natterjack Toads possibly due to reduced grazing at North Walney and the subsequent increase in *Salix, Ulex* and tall grasses. A mixed pair of Natterjack and Common Toad were found in 1985, while 200 corpses were counted, probably the victims of rats.

**NATTERJACK TOAD** ***Bufo calamita***

North Walney National Nature Reserve is the only modern day site for the species on the island. Annual surveys since 1983 indicate that there has been little breeding success due to adverse weather conditions in successive years (i.e. cold wet springs and mid-year droughts), fungal attacks on spawn strings, invertebrate predation, competition from Common Toads, and perhaps a certain amount of collecting. The 1985 report estimates a population of barely 100 adults, and because of the minimal recruitment in these years and perhaps their inability to increase their stocks from nearby localities on the mainland, there is obvious concern for the future of the species on the island. At South Walney, the last confirmed sighting occurred in the mid 1960s; thus its range on Walney has contracted considerably within the last 20 years and coupled with the poor success at North Walney since 1983, active conservation must be encouraged. Prior to 1983, surveys have indicated a "poor" to "good" population. Cooke's survey of 1982 estimated large numbers of Natterjack tadpoles — "certainly 1000s" in the large pool at North Walney which he describes as "perhaps the largest body of water (c. 1.2 hectares) in which Natterjacks breed in Britain". In the report summary the North Walney population was considered to be in its 100s and the assessment of metamorphic success "good".

Natterjacks are vulnerable to a variety of factors at early life stages. The spawn strings are prone to infestation by aquatic fungus. Such attacks seem to coincide with cold periods at spawning time (April and May) and these have been a feature of recent years. Spawn is also attacked by leeches — up to six leeches have been observed on a single string at North Walney.

Natterjack tadpoles are more vulnerable to invertebrate predation than the Common Frog or the Common Toad. On North Walney diving beetles and their larvae *(Dytiscus sp.)* and dragonfly larvae *(Odonata)* are noted as being voracious predators. In addition the tadpoles are poorly adapted to compete with other tadpole species and where these occur in large numbers, as is the case with the Common Toad on North Walney, Natterjack growth and development is inhibited, making them more prone to dessication if the pools dry out in late summer.

The adults are the last amphibian to emerge from hibernation in spring, waiting until dusk temperatures reach about 10°C. This ususally takes place in April and adults congregate at the breeding pools from mid-month onwards. Outside the breeding period adults are most frequently encountered amongst the yellow frontal mobile dunes and upper foreshore where they hunt at night.

**COMMON FROG** ***Rana temporaria temporaria***

Possibly, the lack of South Walney records, a single specimen on 14th May 1981, can be linked with the presence of a large gull colony and the trampling of pond edges by the resident cattle. At the other end of the scale, Poskitt's survey of 1978 indicated that the species is abundant at North Walney and counts of over 100 animals on 3rd and 10th July 1984 endorse this view.

**VIVIPAROUS LIZARD** ***Lacerta vivipara***

In recent years records have come from both ends of the island but there has been a considerable decline at South Walney since 1984. Prior to this, sightings had been fairly regular at the lighthouse and at Coastguard Cottages, the latter site providing 18 animals, including four young on 16th June 1983. Since that year, which concluded with a specimen on 1st December, records have been decidedly sparse with 1984 yielding a single on 9th January and only one since, a single on 16th May 1989.

At North Walney, individuals were seen on two dates in 1984, seven days in 1985, with a maximum of three on 6th May, on five days in 1986, with two on 9th September, two days in 1988 and three days in 1989.

There have been occasional sightings of specimens on Biggar Bank. Adults are very variable in colour, ranging from brown to green. Sometimes the latter are mistaken for Sand Lizards *(Lacerta agilis)* which do not occur north of the Sefton coast in Merseyside.

***References:***


Beebee, T. 1983, The Natterjack Toad. Oxford University Press.

Bridson, R. 1978, The Natterjack Toad. Nature Conservancy Council.

Cooke, A. and Scorgie, H. 1983, The status of commoner amphibian and reptile species endangered in Britain. Nature Conservancy Council.

Hardy, E. 1973, The Naturalist in Lakeland. David and Charles, Newton Abbot.

The Nature Conservancy Council reports 1978-1985.

Walney Bird Observatory reports 1980-1989.



***Peter Carty*** *is the National Trust warden for Sandscale Haws Nature Reserve and has worked with reptiles and amphibians on coastal nature reserves in the northwest of England for nine years.*

# The Non-Marine Invertebrate Fauna of Walney

David W. Emley

***Red Admiral***

The invertebrates of Walney, with the exception of the *lepidoptera,* have received little attention; an unfortunate, though not uncommon, state of affairs. To give a complete account of the invertebrate fauna of an island the size of Walney is more than a lifetime's work for any naturalist so the following account, which far from complete, is intended more as an overview than an exhaustive study. No single order has been studied in depth, but those species recorded include many of the commoner species likely to be encountered by the casual observer. It is hoped that the following account will provide a baseline for future recording and will encourage others to visit Walney, even if it is only en-route for the greener pastures of Sandscale to the north!

**History of Recording**

The *lepidoptera* have received better coverage than any other order, largely as a result of the work of D. W. Kydd and E. F. Hancock between 1967 and 1970 and in 1979. This has been summarized in "A Study of South Walney" and "The Natural Environment of North Walney and Sandscale Haws", hereafter referred to as SoSW and NENWSH respectively. In 1983 a mercury-vapour moth trap, based on the Robinson design, was installed at South Walney. This has been operated on a regular basis by Tim Dean but, because of the extreme weather conditions experienced at this exposed site, it has rarely been possible to operate the trap in the early spring and winter months. Nevertheless, the use of this trap has added greatly to our knowledge of the *lepidoptera* of Walney both in terms of the total number of species and their relative abundances. The use of a portable actinic moth trap of the Heath design has enabled data to be acquired from other sites on Walney resulting in a number of additions to the Island's fauna and increasing our knowledge of the distribution of the various species. Thanks are due in particular to Peter Zaltowski and to Jack and Jane Sheldon for operating this trap in their gardens in Urban Walney and Earnse Bay respectively. In all, about 160 species have been added to the list since the work of Kydd and Hancock.

If we ignore the data that remain hidden in the notebooks of visiting naturalists there appears to be, apart from my own records and those of Mr. L. S. Kelly, little available information on the *non-lepidopteran* invertebrates. Kelly published a list (Kelly 1968) of beetles caught in the Furness area which included three carabids that he found on Walney. He has since provided an excellent list of over 200 species of beetles caught by him in the 1960s, mainly in the Biggar area, most of which were additions to the Island's fauna. Mr. L. Gurr visited Walney in 1963 and provided a list of five bumblebees, all of which can still be found. A short list of beetles and two waterboatmen *(Corixidae)* found on South Walney and attributed to Dr. R. B. Angus was published in SoSW. Some of the species in this list were taken from Angus (1964, 1965). Unfortunately, during transcription, a number of typographic errors and omissions crept in and so I am grateful to Dr. Angus for providing me with photocopies of the notebook entries for his visits in 1963 and 1964. These included some species found on North and South Walney that were not included in the lists published in SoSW and NENWSH. Dr. C. S. Wood-Baker visited Walney in August 1965 and recorded a few plant lice *(Aphidoidea)*, (Wood-Baker 1965). Dr. N. L. Birkett has visited North and South Walney on a number of occasions and collected a range of insects, mainly *diptera*, a list of which he kindly provided. In addition he has published his discovery, on Walney, of two rare non-biting Chironomid midges, (Birkett 1984). Mr. P. Whitehead, who visited South Walney in July 1983, has provided a short list of insects, mainly beetles. Since 1983 I have made a number of short visits to Walney, mainly in July and September, recording insects by hand searching, sweep netting and a little pond-dipping. In 1986 a malaise trap was used in a number of sites on South Walney including gate marsh, the cottages, central marsh, and the offices. This yielded a large number of new species of *diptera* but many of the "small fry" remain to be identified. Indeed, the list tends to reflect my own interests with many orders receiving little or no attention. Most of my collecting has been done on the reserve on South Walney, but North Walney, with its greater variety of flora, should yield many more species and, apart from several moth-trapping sessions, the area know as Willow Woods has yet to be studied entomologically.

The only other invertebrate records comprise a list of spiders recorded on South Walney on 13th August 1976 by Mr. J. R. Parker of the British Arachnological Society and published in SoSW, a list of spiders and harvestmen collected on North Walney in 1985 by Mr. P. Kirkland, and a list of spiders caught in pitfall traps on South Walney in 1987 by Mr. E. E. Emmett.

**Some Major and Micro-habitats on Walney and their Invertebrates**

Wherever one goes on Walney there are invertebrates to be found. Many will undoubtedly be additions to the Island's fauna if only one had the means to identify them all! What follows is an attempt to highlight some of the more obvious and characteristic species to be found in a selection of habitats. The *lepidoptera*, especially the moths, do not figure prominently as most of our records derive from trap catches, the adults rarely being found during the day.

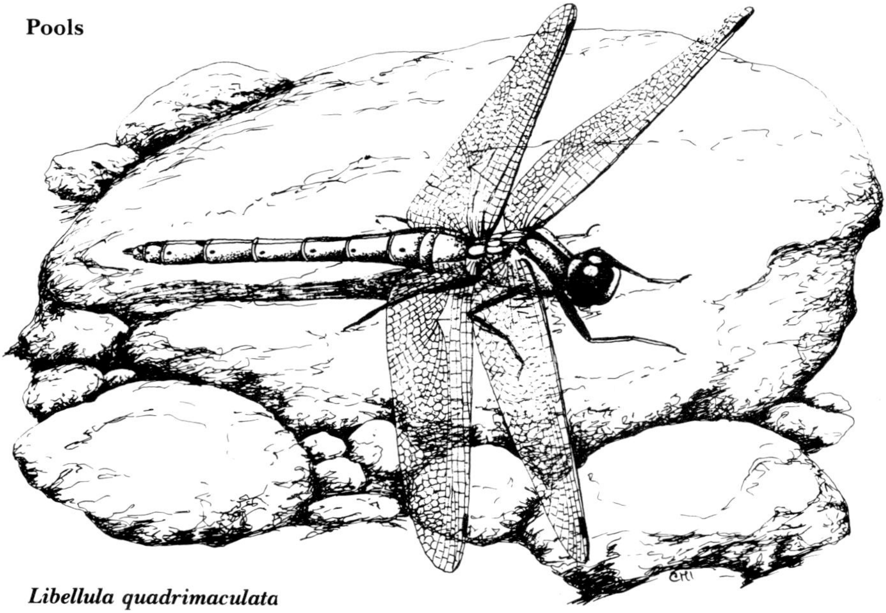

*Libellula quadrimaculata*

**North Walney:** The pools on North Walney have a rich aquatic and marginal vegetation which in turn attracts a rich insect fauna. Here we find Walney's dragonflies which include *Libellula quadrimaculata, Sympetrum striolatum* and the brown-winged *Aeshna grandis,* the latter two species being the only dragonflies to have so far been seen on the South Walney reserve. The damselflies *Ishnura elegans* and *Lestes sponsa* are particularly common.

A number of water beetles are to be found in the pools including the Great Diving Beetle *Dytiscus marginalis* and the whirligig beetle *Gyrinus substriatus.* They are accompanied by a number of species of lesser waterboatmen, the backswimmer *Notonecta obliqua* and the mayfly *Cloeon simile.* The latter species has mass emergences in spring and autumn and it is not unusual then to find them far from water.

Amongst the marginal vegetation can be found members of the *Sciomyzidae* or snail-eating flies. The adults of these strange flies have a characteristic slow gait and wings that are often mottled. The larvae are malacophagous, feeding on all types of mollusca both aquatic and terrestrial. The larvae of *Tetanocera elata,* for example, are said to feed on the mucus of slugs until their first moult after which they become predatory; a single larva having been known to kill up to ten slugs before pupating!

**South Walney:** In contrast the pools on the South Walney reserve, because of the gull colony, are quite stagnant and have little or no aquatic vegetation, resulting in an impoverished fauna compared with the pools on North Walney. The water beetles *Colymbetes fuscus, Helophorus grandis,* and *Hydrobius fuscipes,* however, favour stagnant water and are quite common both on North Walney and South Walney. Swan Pool is unusual in that it has a good growth of Spiked Water-milfoil and here we find large numbers of the lesser waterboatman *Sigara concinna;* a species prefering pools that have been enriched with organic matters such as the droppings from gulls and cattle. The damselfly *Ishnura elegans* was observed flying over this pool on one occasion.

As the pools dry out they give way to expanses of mud which in turn attracts many insects. The carabid beetle *Elaphrus riparius*, for example, can be found running over the mud by gate pool. Flies of the family *Dolichopodidae* are particularly attracted to drying mud. Ranging in size from 1·2 mm to 10·12 mm, they are to a greater or lesser extent predatory insects having a characteristic habit of appearing to walk on tip-toe, thus giving them a peering look. The majority go unnoticed by the casual observer but the metallic-green *Dolichopus ungulatus* is abundant all over South Walney in the summer months.

**Dunes**

On a walk through the dunes one often ecounters a large fly with a habit of making short, darting flights close to the ground in pursuit of other insects. This is the large robber fly *Philonicus albiceps* a member of the family *Asilidae*. The smaller, but similar-looking, robber fly *Dysmachus trigonus* is also quite common. The males of the robber fly *Thereva annulata* are particularly attractive. Being covered in silver-blue hairs they give the impression of blue flashes as they dart about the dunes. Their larvae, which live beneath the sand, can inflict a very painful bite. The closely related *Thereva nobilitata*, which is larger and all brown rather than silvery-grey, is common throughout Walney.

The base of the dunes is a particularly good place in which to find insects, especially beetles and ants. They are deposited here by the wind and, because of the unstable nature of the dune face, are unable to climb back. These hapless insects fall prey to a group of predatory insects; the solitary wasps. These wasps do not kill their prey but anaesthetize it and take it to a prepared cell where an egg is then laid. The prey thus provides fresh food for the larva when it hatches. The most noticeable solitary wasps on North Walney are the black-and-yellow *Mellinus arvensis* and *Crabro cribarius*, the males of the latter having extraordinary flanges on their fore-tibias. Both are frequently to be seen on umbellifers. *Oxybelus uniglumis*, a black-and-white banded species, can be found in small colonies on North and South Walney where it digs small burrows in the more stable parts of the dune face.

Amongst the beetles that you find in the dunes, one of the most distinctive is the large black carabid *Broscus cephalotes*. It hides in a burrow in the sand, ready to pounce on passing prey and is unusual amongst carabids in having perfectly smooth elytra or wing-cases. There are two weevils that are often found in the dunes by casual observers. One is the all-black *Otiorhynchus atroapterous* which feeds on grasses, and the other is a very large species, (up to 15 mm), *Cleonus piger* that feeds on thistles. The chafer *Euchlora dubia*, with its green head and thorax and orange elytra is a not uncommon sight in the dunes.

Walney's rarest insect to date was first discovered on Sandscale by Dr. N. L. Birkett who later found it in the dunes of North Walney. It is the non-biting chironomid midge *Dicrodentipes pallidicornis*. At the time of its discovery the only known site for it was Basra in the Persian Gulf!

**Dune Heath**

The dune heath that once covered South Walney is now largely confined to North Walney. In late summer the expanse of purple heather is a great attraction to insects, especially the bees and hoverflies. Here too we can find, either as the adult or more commonly the larva, three of Walney's most spectacular moths; the Emperor, Oak Eggar and Fox. All fly during the day or at dusk, but an Emperor was attracted to a moth trap in Willow Woods in late April.

On the edge of the heath one finds damper areas that are covered with willow bushes. Here, in late June/July, occurs an entomological spectacular; the mass emergence of White Satin Moths *Leucoma salicis.* They can be so numerous that the bushes appear to be covered with blobs of cotton wool.

***White Satin Moth***

**Tide-line**

The shore, being submerged regularly, is a hostile environment. However, a number of insects live in the region just above the high tide line. Under pebbles on the seaward shore one can find the carabid beetle *Bembidion pallidepenne,* while on the clayey shore of the estuary can be found the carabids *Agonum marginatum* and *Pogonus chalceus* together with the very common carabid *Dicheirotrichus gustavi. Ligia oceanica,* our largest and most primitive woodlouse, can be found under stones just above the high tide line at the edge of the saltmarsh.

A narrow strand of drying seaweed is to be found on the seaward shore of South Walney, thickening a little towards the groyne in the summer and autumn. This seaweed is frequented by a large number of flies, amongst the commonest of which are the small black bristly coelopid *Coelopa frigida* and the powdery-grey anthomyiid *Fucellia tergina.*

In the areas that are only occasionally flooded, gull valley for example, there is an accumulation of driftwood and other rubbish which is used to advantage by many invertebrates. Beneath this one finds a number of xerophilic carabid beetles, especially species of *Calathus, Agonum* and *Harpalus.* Here too you can also find the two large Devil's coach-horse beetles *Staphylinus ater* and *Staphylinus olens,* both of which can inflict a painful bite on the unwary!

Probably the most numerous insect to be found under the rubbish on the highest of high tide lines is the earwig *Forficula auricularia,* occurring sometimes in hundreds beneath a single piece of wood. It is often accompanied by the common woodlouse *Porcellio scaber*. While most of the invertebrates use the driftwood for shelter one, the beetle *Nacerdes melanura*, actually feeds on the driftwood itself in its larval stage and hence its distribution is strictly confined to coastal areas. The rather sandy turf is ideally siuted to nesting ants. *Lasius niger* and *Myrmica rubra* being particularly abundant beneath driftwood and stones.

**Carrion**

A visitor to the gull colony on South Walney at the height of the breeding season cannot help but be aware of the number of dead and dying gulls. The corpses, in their varying states of decay, attract a range of carrion-feeding insects. The most obvious and numerous of these are the greenbottle flies *Lucilia caesar* and *Lucilia sericata*. The adult flies lay their eggs around wounds or natural openings on the corpse and on hatching the larvae enter the body cavity and proceed to digest the flesh. The number of larvae can be so great that the corpse appears to move! Another green fly that is attracted to carrion, and which is not uncommon on South Walney, is *Cynomya mortuorum*. It differs from the two aforementioned species in being noticeably larger and by having a yellowish face and cheeks.

Whilst the corpses are still fresh, they are visited by the Histerid beetle *Saprinus cuspidatus*. These small, shiny, black beetles, are particularly noticeable in more open situations where they resemble small black pills scattered over and around the corpse. Another, more familiar, carrion beetle is *Nicrophorus investigator*. This well-known black beetle, with orange patches on the elytra or wing-cases, frequently occurs in the moth trap. Once the corpse has dried out it then becomes attractive to beetles such as *Dermestes murinus* and *Omosita colon*, both of which specialize in feeding on dried skin and bone.

**Dung**

The dung from sheep and cattle that graze South Walney attracts its own specialist fauna. The insects most often seen by visitors are those that visit dung simply to lay their eggs in it. One of the most obvious of these is the muscid fly *Mesembrina meridiana*, a large black fly with orange bases to the wings and an orange face, often to be seen resting on walls and fence posts. The golden-yellow males of the well-known Yellow Dung Fly *Scathophaga stercoraria* are a common and familiar sight on fresh cow pats. Less noticeable, but occurring sometimes in large numbers, particularly on fresh cow pats, are flies belonging to the family *Sepsidae*. These small, black, ant-like flies, which are generally less than 5 mm long, have a characteristic habit of waving their wings as they walk. *Sepsis cynipsea*, with a black tip to an otherwise clear wing, is the most common member of the family on Walney. In heavily cow-trodden areas *Themira superba*, with its remarkable fan of bristles at the tip of its abdomen, is particularly common. Sepsids are usually accompanied by even smaller flies belonging to the family *Sphaeroceridae* or lesser dung flies of which *Copromyza atra* is one of the commonest members.

Break open the dung and you find a completely new group of insects, mainly beetles. The most obvious of these are the familiar dung beetles, chiefly belonging to the genus *Aphodius*. The red and black *Aphodius fimetarius* is a particularly common species. Occasionally there are mass flights of dung beetles, especially in the spring and autumn and it is not unusual then to find them floating in puddles or caught in the moth trap. *Aphodius rufipes* is, in fact, a regular visitor to the moth trap. Living alongside are smaller beetles of the family *Hydrophilidae,* an essentially aquatic beetle family. This is not surprising as fresh dung is a very liquid medium! The beetles, most of which belong to the genus *Cercyon,* are very small and rather rounded, *Cercyon melanocephalus,* a red and black species, being one of the commonest. They are accompanied by staphylinid or rove beetles, a particularly difficult group of beetles to identify.

**Ragwort**

The large, yellow expanse of Ragwort *Senecio jacobaea* is a noticeable feature of South Walney in the summer and autumn. Whilst there are a number of insects that include Ragwort as part of their diet, there are a few that feed almost exclusively on it. The best-known of these is the orange-and-black striped larvae of the Cinnabar Moth *Tyria jacobaeae.* A puzzling observation is that while the larvae are to be found along the road from South Walney to Barrow, they are rarely seen on the reserve itself. The larvae are said to be distasteful to birds so it is unlikely that the gulls prey on them. Another species of moth that feeds on Ragwort is the small black-and-white mottled tortrix, *Cochylis atricapitana.* This is an interesting species because the larvae from the two broods feed on different parts of the plant. The small, yellow chrysomelid beetle *Longitarsus jacobaeae* also feeds on Ragwort and is to be found most infrequently in the flower heads.

The flowers of the Ragwort attract many species of insects both during the day and night. Daytime visitors include the familiar hoverflies, of which *Eristalis arbusivus* is worthy of note. This species, which is very local inland, was only described in the 1930s. However in some coastal sites, including South Walney, it can be amongst the most numerous of hoverflies, especially in the damper areas such as the *Juncus* marsh by gate pool. However, because of its similarity to the commoner *Eristalis arbustorum,* it is probably overlooked. Another notable visitor to Ragwort flowers is the coastal hoverfly *Eristalis aeneus* which is not uncommon on Walney. Amongst the moths, the day-flying pyralids *Udea lutealis* and Mother-of-Pearl *Notarcha ruralis* are particularly common on Ragwort flowers and it is not unusual to see Antler moths *Cerapteryx graminis* on the flower heads during the day. At night the flowers can attract many more species of moth.

## The species lists

In the list of lepidoptera I have given details of the flight periods of the adult and distribution, together with an assessment of relative abundance. This has been based, in the case of nocturnal species, on the numbers of each species caught by moth trap since 1983. However, it is well-known that not all species are equally attracted to light and that some species have cycles of abundance. These comments can therefore only be taken as a rough guide. I have also given, based on published data (Skinner, 1984 and Emmet, 1979) details of the probable food-plant of the larvae. The initials of the recorder and date are given for records that are additions to the work of Kydd and Hancock in SoSW and NENWSH. The numbers preceding each species are those used in the checklist of Bradley and Fletcher, 1986.

This amount of detail does not, unfortunately, exist for the remaining invertebrate orders. Instead I have given, when known, details of the date and location/habitat of capture, together with the recorder's initials and the date of the sighting (when this constitutes the only record). Records with no initials are my own.

Throughout the species account South Walney (SW) and North Walney (NW) refer to the area covered by the reserves unless stated otherwise, (UW) to Urban Walney, (EB) to Earnse Bay, (LRP) to Long Rein Point and (WW) to Willow Woods.

**Initials of collectors/recorders other than myself are as follows:**

| | | | | | |
|---|---|---|---|---|---|
| RBA | RB Angus | LSK | LS Kelly | J&JS | J &J Sheldon |
| NLB | NL Birkett | PK | P Kirkland | BS | B Skinner |
| TO'C | TO'Connor | CMcC | C McCarty | PW | P Whitehead |
| TD | T Dean | JRP | JR Parker | CSW-B | CS Wood-Baker |
| EEE | EE Emmett | LHS | LH Sanderson | PZ | P Zaltowski |

**The nomenclature used is as follows:**

Arachnida: Merrett, Locket & Millidge (1985)
Coleoptera: Pope (1977)
Dermaptera, Hemiptera, Orthoptera and Trichoptera: Kloet & Hincks (1964)
Diptera: Kloet & Hincks (1975)
Ephemeroptera: Elliot & Humpesch (1983)
Isopoda: Sutton (1972)
Lepidoptera: Bradley & Fletcher (1986)
Neuroptera: Barnard (1978)
Odonata: Hammond (1977)
Opiliones: Sankey & Savory (1974)

**Acknowledgements**

With the exception of most of the lepidoptera, voucher specimens, of all but the most common insects caught by myself, have been retained for future reference. I am very grateful to Messrs. D. W. Kydd, E. A. Hancock, C. W. Plant and R. G. Warren for identifying most of the micro-lepidoptera, to Messrs. C. Johnson and M. Waterhouse for checking the identification of difficult coleoptera, to Messrs. M. Bloxham and D. M. Ackland for checking critical diptera and to Dr. S. Judd for checking the Heteroptera. I am particularly grateful to Dr. N. L. Birkett and to Messrs. D. W. Kydd and E. A. Hancock for their comments on the species lists and to Mr. G. Halfpenny for his criticism of the text.

# LEPIDOPTERA

## HEPIALIDAE

14 *Hepialus humuli* (Linn.) — **Ghost Moth :** 6/6-25/7: on the roots of grasses, docks, Nettle etc. Reported from NW, scarce on SW.

15 *Hepialus sylvina* (Linn.) — **Orange Swift :** on roots of herbaceous plants. One on Urban Walney 7/8/86 (PZ).

18 *Hepialus fusconebulosa* (DeG.) — **Map-winged Swift :** on roots of herbaceous plants. One EB 15/7/87 (J&JS).

## ZYGAENIDAE

### Zygaeninae

169 *Zygaena filipendulae* (Linn.) — **Six-spot Burnet :** 15/6-10/8: on Bird's-foot-trefoil, the adults are day-fliers. Common-abundant on SW, abundant on NW.

171 *Zygaena lonicerae* (Schev.) — **Narrow-bordered 5-spot Burnet :** 10/7-20/7: on species of *Lotus,* trefoils and vetches; adults are day-flying. Scarce on NW.

## LYONETIIDAE

### Cemiostominae

260 *Leucoptera malifoliella* (Costa) — mines Hawthorn, Apple, Pear etc. One in Rakes Lane 30/6/87 (DWE).

## CHOREUTIDAE

385 *Anthophila fabriciana* (Linn.) : on Nettle. One on SW 1/9/85 (TD).

## GLYPHIPTERIGIDAE

397 *Glyphipterix thrasonella* (Scop.) : on rushes. One on NW 3/7/87 (DWE).

## YPONOMEUTIDAE

### Argyresthiinae

412 *Agyresthia pygmaeella* (D. & S.) : in buds and catkins of Sallow. One on NW 3/7/87 (DWE).

### Yponomeutinae

424 *Yponomeuta evonymella* (Linn.) : the larvae feed on Bird Cherry which has yet to be recorded on the island. One on SW 1/8/83 (DWE).

426 *Yponomeuta malinellus* (Zell.) : on Apple. A member of a complex group, but one showing features of this species in UW 4/8/87 (PZ).

### Plutellinae

453 *Ypsolopha dentella* (Fabr.) : larvae on Honeysuckle. One on SW 10/8/87 (TD).

## ELACHISTIDAE

597 *Elachista atricomella* (Stt.) : in leaves and stem of Cock's-foot. One on SW.

610 *Elachista argentella* (Cl.) : on grasses. One on NW 1/7/87 (DWE).

## OECOPHORIDAE

### Oecophorinae

647 *Hofmannophila pseudospretella* (Stt.) : 23/6-15/10. A common house moth, the larvae feeding on dried plants, wool, skins, seeds, etc. On SW.

648 *Endrosis sarcitrella* (Linn.) : 31/5-30/8. Another common house moth that feeds on dried plants, wool etc. On SW

658 *Carcina quercana* (Fabr.) : on Oak. One in UW 10/8/87 (PZ).

### Chimabachinae

663 *Diurnea fagella* (D. & S.) : larvae on Oak, Birch. Common in WW in April.

**Depressariinae**

672 *Depressaria pastinacella* (Dup.) : on Hogweed. Recorded on SW.

677 *Depressaria douglasella* (Stt.) : on Wild Carrot and Wild Parsnip. One on SW in 1985 (TD).

688 *Agonopterix heracliana* (Linn.) : on flowers and seeds of Hogweed. One on SW 26/8/85 (TD).

689 *Agonopterix ciliella* (Stt.) : larvae feed on Hogweed, Angelica, Wild Carrot etc. One on SW 12/10/85 (TD).

695 *Agonopterix alstromeriana* (Cl.) : on Hemlock. One in Urban Walney in 1984 (T.O'C). Last recorded by Ellis (1890).

706 *Agonopterix nervosa* (Haw.) : on Gorse and Dyer's Greenweed. One on SW 1/8/83 (DWE).

## GELICHIIDAE

**Gelichiinae**

829 *Caryocolum marmoreum* (Haw.) : on Common Mouse-ear. One on SW 31/7/85 (TD).

843 *Aproaerema anthyllidella* (Hb.) : on Kidney Vetch, trefoils. One on NW in 1979 (NLB).

## BLASTOBASIDAE

873 *Blastobasis lignea* (Wals.) : on conifers. Recorded on SW.

## SCYTHRIDIDAE

915 *Scythris picaepennis* (Haw.) : larvae on Bird's-foot Trefoil. Recorded on NW and SW.

## TORTRICIDAE

**Cochylininae**

937 *Agapeta hamana* (Linn.) : 23/7-31/7. On roots of *Carduus* spp. and other thistles. On SW, UW.

946 *Aethes rubigana* (Treit.) : on burdocks. One on SW 15/7/86 (DWE).

947 *Aethes smeathmanniana* (Fabr.) : on Yarrow and knapweeds. One on SW 24/7/85 (TD).

950 *Aethes francillana* (Fabr.) : on Wild Carrot. One on SW 4/7/87 (DWE/TD) is a new vice-county record.

956 *Cochylidia implicitana* (Wocke) : on mayweeds, and Golden-rod. Noted on SW, and NW.

965 *Cochylis hybridella* (Hb.) : on Bristly Ox-Tongue. One on SW in 1985 (TD).

966 *Cochylis atricapitana* (Steph.) : 16/6-4/7. A common species on Common Ragwort. Found on SW.

**Tortricinae**

970 *Pandemis cerasana* (Hb.) : on a variety of trees and shrubs. One on SW 20/6/88 (TD).

972 *Pandemis heparana* (D. & S.) : A common species feeding on a wide variety of plants throughout summer.

977 *Archips podana* (Scop.) : on a variety of trees. One in UW 21/7/87 (PZ).

981 *Archips rosana* (Linn.) : on a variety of plants. One on SW 22/7/85 (TD).

993 *Clepsis spectrana* (Treit.) : larvae on a wide range of plants. Common on SW.

1010 *Ditula angustiorana* (Haw.) : on various plants. Recorded on SW.

1019 *Cnephasia conspersana* (Dougl.) : A mainly coastal species feeding on a range of *Compositae.* Found on SW and NW in July.
1033 *Tortrix viridana* (Linn.) : A sometimes abundant species in oakwoods. Found on NW 26/6.
1037 *Croesia holmiana* (Linn.) : on a variety of shrubs. One in UW 22/7/87 (PZ).
1042 *Acleris rhombana* (D. & S.) : on various trees and shrubs. SW 1986 (TD).
1048 *Acleris variegana* (D. & S.) : mainly on *Rosaceae* and Bramble, Hawthorn, Blackthorn, Apple, etc. On SW 31/7/85 (TD).
1053 *Acleris hastiana* (Linn.) : Larvae feed on willows. Found throughout.

**Olethreutinae**

1063 *Celypha striana* (D. & S.) : on Dandelion. Found on SW.
1067 *Celypha cespitana* (Hb.) : larvae feed on a variety of low plants. One on NW 15/7/86 (DWE).
1076 *Olethreutes lacunana* (D. & S.) : the larvae feed between spun leaves or in leaves and young shoots of a variety of plants. On SW and NW in August.
1082 *Hedya pruniana* (Hb.) : on *Prunus* spp. On Long Rein Point 29/6/87 (DWE).
1083 *Hedya dimidioalba* (Retz.) : on Hawthorn and *Prunus* spp. On SW and UW in June.
1087 *Orthotaenia undulana* (D. & S.) : on a variety of trees and shrubs. On SW and Long Rein Point in June 1987.
1089 *Apotomis semifasciana* (Haw.) : larvae on willows. One on SW 24/7/85 (TD).
1110 *Bactra furfurana* (Haw.) : on Club Rush or Compact Rush. On NW 3/7/87 (DWE).
1111 *Bactra lancealana* (Hb.) : on rushes and club-rushes. On NW 1/7/87 (DWE).
1147 *Epinotia cruciana* (Linn.) : on willows. On NW 3/7/87 (DWE).
1159 *Rhopobota naevana* (Hb.) : larvae polyphagous, especially on Blackthorn. One on SW 1/9/85 (TD).
1163 *Zeiraphera ratzeburgiana* (Ratz.) : a pinewood species. One on SW 1/8/83 (DWE) was probably a vagrant.
1174 *Epiblema cynosbatella* (Linn.) : feeding on roses and Bramble. One on SW 1/8/83 (DWE).
1175 *Epiblema uddmanniana* (Linn) : larvae on Bramble. One on SW 20/6/88 (TD).
1178 *Epiblema roborana* (D. & S.) : larvae on roses. One on SW 22/6/88 (TD).
1183 *Epiblema foenella* (Linn.) : on the roots of Mugwort. One on SW 24/7/85 (DWE).
1184 *Epiblema scutulana* (D. & S.) : on thistles. Found on NW, Rakes Lane and Long Rein Point.
1184a *Epiblema cirsiana* (Zell.) : larvae on thistles. Found on NW 3/6/76 (EFH/DWK).
1197 *Eucosma campoliliana* (D. & S.) : on Common Ragwort. Common on SW in July.
1200 *Eucosma hohenwartiana* (D. & S.) : on Knapweed. One on SW 2/7/87 (TD/DWE).
1201 *Eucosma cana* (Haw.) : on thistles. One on NW 3/7/87 (DWE).
1232 *Pammene populana* (Fabr.) : on willows. Found on NW (NLB).
1272 *Cydia aurana* (Fabr.) : on Hogweed. Adults common on NW on flower heads of foodplant.

## PYRALIDAE

**Crambinae**

1293 *Chrysoteuchia culmella* (Linn.) : common grass feeder throughout.
1294 *Crambus pascuella* (Linn.) : common grass moth on SW.
1302 *Crambus perlella* (Scop.) : a common grass moth on SW.
1304 *Agriphila straminella* (D. & S.) : on grasses, very common on SW.

1305 *Agriphila tristella* (D. & S.) : on grasses, very common on SW.
1307 *Agriphila latistria* (Haw.) : on various grasses. On NW (NLB).
1309 *Agriphila geniculea* (Haw.) : grass moth of dry pasture and particularly sandhills. One on NW 6/9/85 (TD).
1313 *Catoptria pinella* (Linn.) : a local grass moth, chiefly in heathy woods and on boggy ground. Found on SW 11/8/85, possibly a vagrant.

**Scopariinae**

1333 *Scoparia pyralella* (D. & S.) : larvae feed on decaying plant material and possibly on roots of ragworts. Found on SW and NW in July.
1334 *Scoparia ambigualis* (Treit.) : larvae are thought to feed on moss. Common on SW.
1341 *Eudonia lineola* (Curt.) : local coastal species. Larvae feed on lichens scarce on SW in July.
1342 *Eudonia angustea* (Curt.) : larvae feed on moss. On SW in September.
1344 *Eudonia mercurella* (Linn.) : common species, the larvae feeding in moss. On SW July.

**Nymphulinae**

1345 *Elophila nymphaeata* (Linn.) : — **Brown China-mark** : larvae are aquatic, feeding on pondweeds etc. Common on SW and NW in July.
1348 *Parapoynx stratiotata* (Linn.) : larvae on pondweeds. One on SW in 1985 (TD).
1350 *Nymphula stagnata* (Don.) — **Beautiful China-mark** : larvae on pondweeds. Around pools on NW in July (DWE).

**Evergestinae**

1356 *Evergestis forficalis* (Linn.) — **Garden Pebble** : Larvae on *Cruciferae.* Found throughout but scarce on SW.
1358 *Evergestis pallidata* (Hufn.) : larvae on various crucifers. One on SW 17/7/89 (TD).

**Pyraustinae**

1376 *Eurrhypara hortulata* (Linn.) — **Small Magpie** : larvae feed on Nettle mainly. Common throughout.
1378 *Phlyctaenia coronata* (Hufn.) : on Elder. One in UW 20/7/87 (PZ).
1386 *Obsibotys fuscalis* (D. & S.) : on Yellow-rattle. One on NW 3/7/87 (DWE) and in UW (PZ).
1388 *Udea lutealis* (Hb.) : adults readily disturbed from flowers during daytime. Larvae on a wide range of low plants. Very common on SW and NW.
1390 *Udea prunalis* (D. & S.) : on a range of low plants. Common on SW.
1395 *Udea ferrugalis* (Hb.) : An erratic migrant. Recorded on SW.
1398 *Nomophila noctuella* (D. & S.) — **Rush Veneer** : an erratic migrant species on SW.
1405 *Pleuroptya ruralis* (Scop.) — **Mother of Pearl** : readily disturbed during daytime, especially from Nettle — its foodplant. Common on SW.

**Pyralinae**

1415 *Orthopygia glaucinalis* (Linn.) : on decaying vegetable matter. One on SW 14/7/86 (TD). A probable migrant species, last recorded by Ellis (1890).
1428 *Aphomia sociella* (Linn.) — **Bee Moth** : in nests of wasps and bumble-bees. One on SW 13/7/87 (TD).

**Phycitinae**

1432 *Anerastia lotella* (Hb.) : larvae on various coastal grasses. Recorded on NW (NLB).
1480 *Homoeosoma nebulella* (D. & S.) : larvae on Spear Thistle and Ragwort. One on SW in 1983 (TD).

1483 *Phycitodes binaevella* (Hb.) : on various thistles. Recorded on SW.
1484 *Phycitodes saxicola* (Vaugh.) : immature stages unknown. Recorded on SW.

## PTEROPHORIDAE

### Platyptiliinae

1501 *Platyptilia gonodactyla* (D. & S.) : the larvae feed on Colt's-foot. Recorded on SW
1504 *Platyptilia pallidactyla* (Haw.) : on Yarrow. One on Long Rein Point 29/6/87 (DWF
1509 *Stenoptilia pterodactyla* (Linn.) : larvae on Germander Speedwell. On SW 26/6/8 and at NW.

### Pterophorinae

1513 *Pterophorus pentadactyla* (Linn.) : larvae feed on bindweeds. Recorded on SW.

## HESPERIIDAE

### Hesperiinae

1531 *Ochlodes venata* (Brem. & Grey) — **Large Skipper** : 5/6-31/7. On various grasses. Or on SW 8/6/83, scarce on NW.

### Pyrginae

1532 *Erynnis tages* (Linn.) — **Dingy Skipper** : an inconspicuous species and therefo possibly under-recorded, the larvae feeding on Bird's-foot-trefoil. Rare on S and NW in May.

## PIERIDAE

### Coliadinae

1545 *Colias croceus* (Geoffr.) — **Clouded Yellow** : An erratic migrant with a maximum seven on SW on 9/8/83.

### Pierinae

1549 *Pieris brassicae* (Linn.) — **Large White** : 4/5-24/9. A familiar pest species; the larv feeding on species of *Cruciferae.* Found throughout; common — abundant o SW, scarce — common on NW.
1550 *Pieris rapae* (Linn.) — **Small White** : 21/4-17/10. a pest species, the larvae o *Cruciferae.* Found throughout; abundant on SW, common — abundant on NV
1551 *Pieris napi* (Linn.) — **Green-veined White** : 17/4-30/9. Another *Cruciferae* feede Found throughout; abundant on SW, common on NW.

## LYCAENIDAE

### Lycaeninae

1561 *Lycaena phlaeas* (Linn.) — **Small Copper** : 12/5-21/10. Larvae feed on dock Common throughout.
1574 *Polyommatus icarus* (Rott.) —**Common Blue** : 12/5-15/9. Larvae feed on Bird's-foo trefoil. Common throughout.

## NYMPHALIDAE

1590 *Vanessa atalanta* (Linn.) — **Red Admiral** : 5/5-15/11. A common migrant an transient resident, feeding on Nettle. A maximum of 120 on SW 19/8/84.

1591 *Cynthia cardui* (Linn.) — **Painted Lady** : 2/4-21/10. A well-known erratic migrant. Larvae feed primarily on thistles. A maximum on 80 on SW 9/8/83.

1593 *Aglais urticae* (Linn.) — **Small Tortoiseshell** : 18/2-27/11. A ubiquitous species that feeds on Nettle. Adults hibernate so could be found in any month.

1597 *Inachis io* (Linn.) — **The Peacock** : 16/4-10/9. A well-known species that feeds on Nettle. Adults hibernate. Uncommon on NW, rare on SW.

1601 *Boloria euphrosyne* (Linn.) — **Pearl-bordered Fritillary** : on Dog Violet. One on NW 25/6/86 (PK).

1607 *Argynnis aglaja* (Linn.) — **Dark Green Fritillary** : larvae feed on Heath Dog Violet. Scarce on NW in July.

## SATYRIDAE

1615 *Lasiommata megera* (Linn.) — **The Wall** 18/5-25/9. Feeds on Annual Meadow Grass. Common throughout.

1621 *Hipparchia semele* (Linn.) — **The Grayling** : 3/7-16/9. A species, typical of open and often rough ground. The larvae feed on grasses. Common on NW, SW.

1625 *Pyronia tithonus* (Linn.) — **The Gatekeeper** : 5/7-10/8. A species of open grassy areas that is on the edge of its range here. The larvae feed on grasses. Rare on SW and NW.

1626 *Maniola jurtina* (Linn.) — **Meadow Brown** : 14/5-5/9. One of Walney's commonest butterflies. The larvae feed on a range of grasses.

1627 *Coenonympha pamphilus* (Linn.) — **Small Heath** : 15/5-28/9. A grassland species, feeding on a variety of grasses. Noted in WW, rare on SW, abundant on NW.

***Small Heath***

## LASIOCAMPIDAE

1636 *Lasiocampa trifolii* (D. & S.) — **Grass Eggar** : larvae feed on various grasses heathers, and Bramble. Larvae recorded on NW in 1923.

1637 *Lasiocampa quercus quercus* (Linn.) — **Oak Eggar** : larvae on a range of plants Uncommon on sandy heath on NW in July.

1638 *Macrothylacia rubi* (Linn.) — **Fox Moth** : on heathers and Bramble. Common on heathy parts of NW in July.

1640 *Philudoria potatoria* (Linn.) — **The Drinker** : 29/6-31/8. On various grasses and reeds. Common throughout.

## SATURNIIDAE

1643 *Saturnia pavonia* (Linn.) —**Emperor Moth** : 25/4-15/5. Larvae feed on various plant including heathers and Bramble. Rare on NW, one at light in WW 25/4/8 (TD/DWE).

## DREPANIDAE

1651 *Cilix glaucata* (Scop.) — **Chinese Character** : larvae on Hawthorn. Rare on SW in August.

## THYATIRIDAE

1653 *Habrosyne pyritoides* (Hufn.) —**Buff Arches** : on Bramble. One on SW 7/7/84 (TD)

## GEOMETRIDAE

### Geometrinae

1665 *Pseudoterpna pruinata* (Hufn.) —**Grass Emerald** : 4/7-17/8. On Gorse and Dyer' Greenweed. Found throughout; uncommon on SW.

1669 *Hemithea aestivaria* (Hb.) — **Common Emerald** : 7/7-26/8. Larvae feed on variou trees and shrubs. One in UW (PZ), scarce on SW.

### Sterrhinae

1689 *Scopula marginepunctata* (Goeze) — **Mullein Wave** : 19/8-23/8. Mainly coastal feeding on Mugwort, plantains and Yarrow. Scarce on SW.

1690 *Scopula imitaria* (Hb.) — **Small Blood-vein** : larvae on various plants. One on SW 17/7/87 (TD).

1693 *Scopula floslactata* (Haw.) —**Cream Wave** : larvae on Dandelion, Knotgrass etc. One at UW 18/6/88 and at EB.

1702 *Idaea biselata* (Hufn.) — **Small Fan-footed Wave** : 13/7-16/8. On a variety o herbaceous plants. Noted in UW and WW; scarce on SW.

1708 *Idaea dimidiata* (Hufn.) — **Single-dotted Wave** : 29/6-8/8. Larvae feed on Cow Parsley. Scarce on SW.

1713 *Idaea aversata* (Linn.) — **Riband Wave** : 3/7-20/8. Larvae feed on various low plants On NW and UW; scarce on SW.

1716 *Rhodometra sacraria* (Linn.) — **The Vestal** : 1/8-8/10. An uncommon and erratic migrant the maximum recorded being nine on 1/10/85.

### Larentiinae

1718 *Phibalapteryx virgata* (Hufn.) — **Oblique-striped** : A mainly coastal species, the larvae feeding on Lady's Bedstraw. No post-1980 records.

1719 *Orthonama vittata* (Borkh.) — **Oblique Carpet** : 26/6-30/9. A marshland species feeding on various species of bedstraw. Scarce on SW.

1722 *Xanthorhoe designata* (Hufn.) — **Flame Carpet** : 18/7-27/8. A hedgerow species feeding on various crucifers. One in UW, rare on SW.

1724 *Xanthorhoe spadicearia* (D. & S.) — **Red Twin-spot Carpet** : larvae on bedstraws. One on NW 10/8/87 (BS) and one on SW 1/8/83 (DWE).

1725 *Xanthorhoe ferrugata* (Cl.) — **Dark-barred Twin-spot Carpet** : 26/4-12/9. On various low plants. Found throughout; common on SW.

1727 *Xanthorhoe montanata* (D. & S.) — **Silver-ground Carpet** : 7/6-5/7. On various low plants. Scarce on SW, common elsewhere.

1728 *Xanthorhoe fluctuata* (Linn.) — **Garden Carpet** : 26/4-28/9. On a variety of crucifers. Recorded EB and UW; common SW.

1732 *Scotopteryx chenopodiata* (Linn.) — **Shaded Broad-bar** : 31/7-31/8. A day-flying species, larvae on species of vetch and trefoil. Recorded throughout; common SW.

1734 *Scotopteryx luridata* (Hufn.) — **July Belle** : 17/6-15/7. On Gorse. Noted in July on NW and LRP; scarce on SW.

1738 *Epirrhoe alternata* (Mull.) — **Common Carpet** : 18/6-27/8. On species of *Galium*. Noted on LRP, UW and WW; common on SW.

1742 *Camptogramma bilineata* (Linn.) — **Yellow Shell** : 6/6-12/9. Sometimes abundant throughout Walney, the larvae feeding on various low plants.

1745 *Larentia clavaria* (Haw.) — **The Mallow** : larvae feed on mallows. Singles on SW and UW in September 1986. First county records since Ellis (1890).

1746 *Anticlea badiata* (D. & S.) — **Shoulder Stripe** : larvae on roses. Scarce in April WW and LRP.

1749 *Pelurga comitata* (Linn.) — **Dark Spinach** : 15/7-20/8. A waste ground species that feeds on goosefoot and orache. Rare on SW, EB.

1750 *Lampropteryx suffumata* (D. & S.) — **Water Carpet** : Larvae on Common Cleavers. Common WW and LRP in April.

1752 *Cosmorhoe ocellata* (Linn.) — **Purple Bar** : 26/5-24/9. On various species of bedstraw. Noted at NW and EB; rare on SW.

1754 *Eulithis prunata* (Linn.) — **The Phoenix** : on currants. One in UW 9/8/86 (PZ).

1755 *Eulithis testata* (Linn.) — **The Chevron** : 11/8-12/9. On species of willows and Birch. Noted in WW, uncommon on SW.

1757 *Eulithis mellinata* (Fabr.) — **The Spinach** : on species of currant. One in UW; rare on SW.

1758 *Eulithis pyraliata* (D. & S.) — **Barred Straw** : On various species of bedstraw. Two on SW 25/7/85 (TD).

1759 *Ecliptopera silaceata* (D. & S.) — **Small Phoenix** : larvae on willowherb. One on SW 30/7/89 (TD).

1760 *Chloroclysta siterata* (Hufn.) — **Red-green Carpet** : woodland species on Oak and Rowan, possibly drifted to SW by wind. No post-1980 records.

1761 *Chloroclysta miata* (Linn.) — **Autumn Green Carpet** : on a variety of trees. One on SW 26/9/86 (TD).

1762 *Chloroclysta citrata* (Linn.) — **Dark Marbled Carpet** : on willows and Birch. Recorded on SW but no post-1980 records.

1764 *Chloroclysta truncata* (Hufn.) — **Common Marbled Carpet** : 17/6-3/10. On a variety of plants. Noted in UW; scarce on SW.

1765 *Cidaria fulvata* (Forst.) — **Barred Yellow** : 21/7-7/8. On roses. Recorded in UW and WW; scarce on SW.

1768 *Thera obeliscata* (Hb.) — **Grey Pine Carpet** : 8/7-17/9. On various conifers. Rare on SW.

1769 *Thera variata* (D. & S.) — **Spruce Carpet** : on Norway Spruce and various other species of *Picea*. Only two post-1980 records; on SW 16/9/84 and 22/9/89.

1773 *Electrophaes corylata* (Thunb.) — **Broken-barred Carpet** : on various trees. One in UW 5/6/87 (PZ).

1775 *Colostygia multistrigaria* (Haw.) — **Mottled Grey** : on various species of bedstraw. One on SW 18/4/87 is the only post-1980 record.

1777 *Hydriomena furcata* (Thunb.) — **July Highflyer** : 14/7-24/8. Feeds on willows and heathers. Reported from WW and UW; uncommon on SW.

1789 *Rheumaptera undulata* (Linn.) — **Scallop Shell** : On willows. Reported from NW but no post-1980 records.

1790 *Triphosa dubitata* (Linn.) — **The Tissue** : on Blackthorn. One in WW 27/4/87 (DWE/TD).

1803 *Perizoma alchemillata* (Linn.) — **Small Rivulet** : 19/6-17/7. Feeds on hemp-nettle. Reported from LRP and UW; rare on SW.

1804 *Perizoma bifasciata* (Haw.) — **Barred Rivulet** : on seeds of Red Bartsia. One in Chairman's Walk, Urban Walney 30/8/86 (LHS), also at EB. An uncommon county record.

1807 *Perizoma albulata* (D. & S.) — **Grass Rivulet** : 18/6-3/7. Found only on NW where its foodplant, Yellow Rattle, is common.

1808 *Perizoma flavofasciata* (Thunb.) — **Sandy Carpet** : 20/6-26/7. On seed pods of Red Campion. Noted on NW and LRP; rare-scarce on SW.

1809 *Perizoma didymata* (Linn.) — **Twin-spot Carpet** : on various low plants. Singles seen at EB and Rakes Lane in June 1987.

1811 *Eupithecia tenuiata* (Hb.) — **Slender Pug** : feeds on Sallow catkins. A female in UW 21/7/87 (PZ).

1816 *Eupithecia linariata* (D. & S.) — **Toadflax Pug** : on Common Toadflax. Reported from UW; one on SW 16/9/85.

1817 *Eupithecia pulchellata* (Steph.) — **Foxglove Pug** : 16/5-24/7. On flowers of Foxglove. Caught in UW; rare on SW.

1823 *Eupithecia venosata* (Fabr.) — **Netted Pug** : on ripening seed-pods of Sea Campion. One post-1980 record; SW 15/7/83 (DWE).

1825 *Eupithecia centaureata* (D. & S.) — **Lime-speck Pug** : 9/6-13/9. On a wide variety of herbaceous plants. Found throughout; common on SW.

1830 *Eupithecia absinthiata* (Cl.) — **Wormwood Pug** : 7/6-24/7. On flowers of Mugwort, Ragwort, Yarrow etc. Found in WW, common on SW.

1831 *Eupithecia goosensiata* (Mab.) — **Ling Pug** : 24/7-13/8. On heathers. Scarce on SW.

1834 *Eupithecia vulgata* (Haw.) — **Common Pug** : 17/6-25/6. On a variety of plants. One caught in UW; scarce on SW.

1837 *Eupithecia subfuscata* (Haw.) — **Grey Pug** : On a variety of plants. One on SW 17/6/85 (TD).

1838 *Eupithecia icterata* (Vill.) — **Tawny-speckled Pug** : 7/7-18/9. On flowers and leaves of Yarrow. Reported from UW; uncommon on SW.

1839 *Eupithecia succenturiata* (Linn.) — **Bordered Pug** : on leaves of Mugwort. Found in EB; one on SW 16/7/83. A rare species in the county.

1846 *Eupithecia nanata* (Hb.) — **Narrow-winged Pug** : a characteristic species of heathland, the larvae feeding on flowers of heather. Noted in July on NW; scarce on SW.

1851 *Eupithecia virgaureata* (Doubl.) — **Golden-rod Pug** : larvae on Golden-rod and Ragwort. One on SW 20/5/89 (TD).

1852 *Eupithecia abbreviata* (Steph.) — **Brindled Pug** : on Oak. One in WW 27/4/87 (DWE/TD).

1858 *Chloroclystis v-ata* (Haw.) — **V-Pug** : on flowers of a wide variety of plants. Found in WW; scarce on SW.

1860 *Chloroclystis rectangulata* (Linn.) — **Green Pug** : larvae probably on Blackthorn. One at UW 28/6/88 (PZ).

1862 *Gymnoscelis rufifasciata* (Haw.) — **Double-striped Pug** : 18/4-27/7. On a variety of plants. Recorded in WW and LRP; scarce on SW.

1867 *Aplocera plagiata* (Linn.) — **Treble-bar** : 10/6-1/10. On various species of St. John's-wort. Reported from UW; uncommon on SW.

1876 *Hydrelia flammeolaria* (Hufn.) — **Small Yellow Wave** : probably feeds on Alder. One at EB 15/7/87 (J&JS).

1881 *Trichopteryx carpinata* (Borkh.) — **Early Tooth-striped** : On Honeysuckle, Sallow and Birch. Several in WW 25/4/87 (DWE/TD).

**Ennominae**

1884 *Abraxas grossulariata* (Linn.) — **The Magpie** 7/7-28/8. On currants and other plants. Found throughout; rare on SW.

1887 *Lomaspilis marginata* (Linn.) — **Clouded Border** : 12/6-17/8. On willows. Reported from NW and LRP; rare on SW.

1894 *Semiothisa clathrata* (Linn.) — **Latticed Heath** : 19/6-19/8. On various species of trefoil. Found throughout; rare-scarce on SW.

1902 *Petrophora chlorosata* (Scop.) — **Brown Silver-line** : 24/5-1/7. One of the few species to feed on Bracken. Found on LRP; scarce on SW.

1906 *Opisthograptis luteolata* (Linn.) — **Brimstone Moth** : 9/5-16/9. On a variety of trees and shrubs. Found throughout; scarce on SW.

1907 *Epione repandaria* (Hufn.) — **Bordered Beauty** : larvae on willows. One in Chairman's Walk, Urban Walney 25/7/86 (LHS).

1913 *Ennomos alniaria* (Linn.) — **Canary-shouldered Thorn** : 24/8-21/9. On a variety of trees. Found in UW; scarce on SW.

1915 *Ennomos erosaria* (D. & S.) — **September Thorn** : on Oak, Birch etc. One in UW 14/9/86 (PZ).

1917 *Selenia dentaria* (Fabr.) — **Early Thorn** : 24/4-23/8. On a variety of trees. Found throughout; scarce on SW.

1919 *Selenia tetralunaria* (Hufn.) — **Purple Thorn** : larvae on a variety of deciduous trees. One at UW 15/4/89 (PZ).

1920 *Odontopera bidentata* (Cl.) — **Scalloped Hazel** : on a variety of deciduous and coniferous trees. Recorded in May/June on NW and UW; scarce on SW.

1921 *Crocallis elinguarua* (Linn.) — **Scalloped Oak** : 22/7-23/8. On most deciduous trees and shrubs. Found throughout; scarce on SW.

1922 *Ourapteryx sambucaria* (Linn.) — **Swallow-tailed Moth** : on Ivy and a variety of trees and shrubs. Reported from UW and WW; scarce on SW.

1923 *Colotois pennaria* (Hb.) — **Feathered Thorn** : On various trees and shrubs. Recorded on SW but no post-1980 records.

1931 *Biston betularia* (Linn.) — **Peppered Moth** : 19/6-26/7. On a wide variety of plants. Scarce-uncommon on SW.

1934 *Agriopis marginaria* (Fabr.) — **Dotted Border** : larvae on a variety of deciduous trees. One at EB 16/3/89 (J&JS).

1935 *Erannis defoliaria* (Cl.) — **Mottled Umber** : larvae on a variety of deciduous trees. One at EB 21/11/87 (J&JS) and at SW.

1937 *Peribatodes rhomboidaria* (D. & S.) — **Willow Beauty** : 5/7-12/9. On a wide variety of plants. Found in UW; scarce-uncommon on SW.

1941 *Alcis repandata* (Linn.) — **Mottled Beauty** : 15/6-11/8. On a variety of trees and shrubs. Scarce on SW.

1947 *Ectropis bistortata* (Goeze) — **The Engrailed** : larvae on various trees. One on SW 27/4/87 (DWE)).

1951 *Aethalura punctulata* (D. & S.) — **Grey Birch** : mainly on Birch; a spring woodland species. Found on NW; scarce on SW.

1952 *Ematurga atomaria* (Linn.) — **Common Heath** : on heathers and trefoils. Seen in summer on NW; rare on SW.

1954 *Bupalus piniaria* (Linn.) — **Bordered White** : larvae are a serious pest of Scots Pine and other *Pinus* species. One at EB; one post-1980 record on SW.

1955 *Cabera pusaria* (Linn.) — **Common White Wave** : larvae on a range of trees and shrubs. One on SW 15/7/87 (TD).

1956 *Cabera exanthemata* (Scop.) — **Common Wave** : 29/6-31/7. Larvae on willows. Reported on NW.

1961 *Campaea margaritata* (Linn.) — **Light Emerald** : larvae on a variety of deciduous trees. One on SW 26/6/88 (TD).

1964 *Gnophos obscuratus* (D. & S.) — **The Annulet** : on a variety of low plants. One in UW 12/8/86 (PZ).

## SPHINGIDAE

### Sphinginae

1972 *Agrius convolvuli* (Linn.) — **Convolvulus Hawk-moth** : an uncommon and erratic migrant. One on SW 17/6/83 (TD).

1980 *Smerinthus ocellata* (Linn.) — **Eyed Hawk-moth** : 19/6-16/7. On various willows. Reported from NW and WW; scarce on SW.

1981 *Laothoe populi* (Linn.) — **Poplar Hawk-moth** : 28/5-16/7. On species of willow and poplar. Found on NW and UW; scarce on SW.

### Macroglossinae

1984 *Macroglossum stellatarum* (Linn.) — **Humming-bird Hawk-moth** : 18/8-3/10. An uncommon and erratic migrant. Reported from NW and SW.

1987 *Hyles galii* (Rott.) — **Bedstraw Hawk-moth** : An uncommon migrant. One on SW 24/7/87 (TD).

1991 *Deilephila elpenor* (Linn.) — **Elephant Hawk-moth** : 19/6-6/7. The larvae, that feed mainly on willowherbs and bedstraws, are better known than the adult. Seen on NW, scarce on SW.

1992 *Deilephila porcellus* (Linn.) — **Small Elephant Hawk-moth** : 19/5-7/7. Mainly on species of bedstraw. Reported from NW and UW; scarce on SW.

## NOTODONTIDAE

1994 *Phalera bucephala* (Linn.) — **Buff-tip** : on a wide variety of deciduous trees and shrubs. Reported from NW, SW and EB.

1995 *Cerura vinula* (Linn.) — **Puss Moth** :18/5-14/6. Larvae, which feed of poplars and willows, are better known than the adults. Seen on NW; scarce on SW.

2003 *Eligmodonta ziczac* (Linn.) — **Pebble Prominent** : 27/4-8/8. On willows and poplars. Recorded on NW and UW; rare on SW.

2008 *Ptilodon capucina* (Linn.) — **Coxcomb Prominent** : larvae on a variety of deciduous trees. One on SW 8/6/88 (TD).

2020 *Diloba caeruleocephala* (Linn.) — **Figure of Eight** : 28/9-21/10. Mainly on Hawthorn. Reported from UW; scarce on SW.

## LYMANTRIIDAE

2027 *Dicallomera fascelina* (Linn.) — **Dark Tusssock** : coastal and moorland species, the larvae feeding on a variety of plants. Only reported from NW and EB.

2030 *Euproctis similis* (Fuess.) — **Yellow-tail** : 20/7-30/8. On Hawthorn, willows and many other trees. Found throughout; scarce on SW.

2031 *Leucoma salicis* (Linn.) — **White Satin Moth** : 2/7-26/7. On willows and poplars. Scarce on SW, abundant on NW.

## ARCTIIDAE

### Lithosiinae

2050 *Eilema lurideola* (Zinck.) — **Common Footman** : 25/6-21/7. On various lichens. Seen at EB; uncommon on SW.

### Arctiinae

2057 *Arctia caja* (Linn.) — **Garden Tiger** : 30/6-30/8. On a wide variety of plants. Found throughout; common on SW.

2060 *Spilosoma lubricipeda* (Linn.) — **White Ermine** : 9/5-26/7. On a variety of wild plants. Reported from UW and EB; uncommon — common on SW.

2061 *Spilosoma luteum* (Hufn.) — **Buff Ermine** : 22/5-25/7. On a variety of wild plants. Recorded at EB and UW; common on SW.

2063 *Diaphora mendica* (Cl.) — **Muslin Moth** : larvae on docks, plantains and chickweeds. One at EB 18/5/89 (J&JS).

2064 *Phragmatobia fuliginosa* (Linn.) — **Ruby Tiger** : 24/5-17/8. On docks, Dandelion and other herbaceous plants. Occurs throughout, scarce on SW.

2069 *Tyria jacobaeae* (Linn.) — **The Cinnabar** : 10/5-10/7. On Common Ragwort and Common Groundsel; the adults are day-flying. Reported from NW, scarce on SW.

## NOLIDAE

2077 *Nola cucullatella* (Linn.) — **Short-cloaked Moth** : larvae on Hawthorn and Blackthorn. One on SW 23/7/89 (TD).

2078 *Nola confusalis* (H.-S.) — **Least Black Arches** : on Oak. Two in WW 27/4/87 (DWE/TD).

## NOCTUIDAE

### Noctuinae

2081 *Euxoa tritici* (Linn.) — **White-line Dart** : 12/6-9/10. A typical coastal and heathland species exhibiting a wide variety of forms. Feeds on a variety of plants. Found throughout, abundant on SW.

2082 *Euxoa nigricans* (Linn.) — **Garden Dart** : 19/7-10/9. Larvae on a wide variety of wild and cultivated plants. Found throughout, scarce on SW.

2083 *Euxoa cursoria* (Hufn.) — **Coast Dart** : 20/7-3/10. A coastal species feeding on roots of oraches and Prickly Saltwort. Uncommon on SW.

2085 *Agrotis vestigialis* (Hufn.) — **Archer's Dart** : 13/6-30/9. Typically coastal species on various grasses. Common throughout.

2087 *Agrotis segetum* (D. & S.) — **Turnip Moth** : 27/5-3/10. A cutworm pest on roots of vegetables and other plants. Recorded in UW, scarce on SW.

2089 *Agrotis exclamationis* (Linn.) — **Heart & Dart** : 24/5-8/9. On a wide variety of plants. Abundant throughout.

2090 *Agriotis trux* (Hb.) — **Crescent Dart** : larvae on a variety of low plants. One at EB 21/7/89 (J&JS) and at SW.

2091 *Agrotis ipsilon* (Hufn.) — **Dark Sword-grass** : 23/5-17/10. Migrant and temporary resident. Recorded throughout, scarce on SW.

2092 *Agrotis puta* (Hb.) — **Shuttle-shaped Dart** : 18/5-12/10. On knotweeds, docks, Dandelion etc. Recorded in UW, uncommon on SW.

2093 *Agrotis ripae* (Hb.) — **Sand Dart** : 8/6-22/7. A typical coastal species, the larvae feeding on various sandhill plants. Scarce on SW.

2098 *Axylia putris* (Linn.) — **The Flame** : 28/5-9/8. On a wide variety of low plants. Recorded in UW, uncommon on SW.

2099 *Ochropleura praecox* (Linn.) — **Portland Moth** : coastal and heathland species feeding on various sandhill plants. Recorded throughout but adults rare on SW.

2102 *Ochropleura plecta* (Linn.) — **Flame Shoulder** : 20/5-5/10 on plantains, docks and many other plants. Recorded in UW, uncommon — common on SW.

2104 *Standfussiana lucernea* (Linn.) — **Northern Rustic** : A mainly coastal species on various grasses and herbaceous plants. Singles in UW and on SW in August 1987.

2105 *Rhyacia simulans* (Hufn.) — **Dotted Rustic** : 7/9-20/9. Foodplant unknown. A species that is undergoing an expansion of range. Scarce on SW.

2107 *Noctua pronuba* (Linn.) — **Large Yellow Underwing** : 23/5-16/10. A pest species feeding on a wide range of plants and grasses. Abundant throughout.

2109 *Noctua comes* (Hb.) — **Lesser Yellow Underwing** : 24/6-3/10. On a wide variety of plants and shrubs. Common throughout.

2110 *Noctua fimbriata* (Schreb.) — **Broad-bordered Yellow Underwing** : on a variety of plants. One on SW 22/7/87.

2111 *Noctua janthina* (D. & S.) — **Lesser Broad-bordered Yellow Underwing** : 15/7-1/9. On a variety of plants. Found throughout, scarce on SW.

2112 *Noctua interjecta* (Hb.) — **Least Yellow Underwing** : 17/7-25/8. On various grasses and herbaceous plants. Found throughout, scarce on SW.

2117 *Paradiarsia glareosa* (Esp.) — **Autumnal Rustic** : 11/9-16/9. An autumnal species on a variety of plants and grasses. Recorded at EB, scarce on SW.

2118 *Lycophotia porphyrea* (D. & S.) — **True Lover's Knot** : July — August. A mainly heathland species that feeds on heathers. Scarce on SW, common on NW.

2120 *Diarsia mendica* (Fabr.) — **Ingrailed Clay** : 10/6-28/8. Feeds on a variety of plants. Found throughout, uncommon on SW.

2123 *Diarsia rubi* (View.) — **Small Square-spot** : 20/5-16/10. On a variety of plants. Found throughout, abundant on SW.

2126 *Xestia c-nigrum* (Linn.) — **Setaceous Hebrew Character** : 10/6-14/10. On Nettle. Recorded in UW, scarce on SW.

2128 *Xestia triangulum* (Hufn.) — **Double Square-spot** : On a variety of plants and shrubs. One found in UW, rare on SW.

2130 *Xestia baja* (D. & S.) — **Dotted Clay** : 9/7-10/8. On a variety of plants and trees. Recorded throughout, scarce on SW.

2133 *Xestia sexstrigata* (Haw.) — **Six-striped Rustic** : 31/7-7/9. On various plants. Recorded throughout, uncommon on SW.

2134 *Xestia xanthographa* (D. & S.) — **Square-spot Rustic** : 3/8-28/9. On grasses and low plants. Found throughout, scarce on SW.

2136 *Naenia typica* (Linn.) — **The Gothic** : 2/7-7/7. On a variety of plants. Reported from EB and UW, scarce on SW.

2139 *Cerastis rubricosa* (D. & S.) — **Red Chestnut** : feeds on a variety of plants. Found in early spring at EB and LRP, scarce on SW.

2145 *Discestra trifolii* (Hufn.) — **The Nutmeg** : 11/5-30/9. Mainly on species of goosefoot and orache. Found throughout, common on SW.

2147 *Hada nana* (Hufn.) — **The Shears** : 29/5-19/7. On hawkweeds, Dandelion and Colt's-foot. Scarce on SW.

2152 *Sideridis albicolon* (Hb.) — **White Colon** : 22/5-13/8. Coastal and heathland species on a variety of plants. Scarce on SW.

2154 *Mamestra brassicae* (Linn.) — **Cabbage Moth** : 24/5-2/9. Pest species on various species of *Brassica.* Reported from EB and UW, uncommon — common on SW.

2155 *Melanchra persicariae* (Linn.) — **Dot Moth** : 14/6-23/8. On a variety of wild and cultivated plants. Found in UW, scarce on SW.

2158 *Lacanobia thalassina* (Hufn.) — **Pale-shouldered Brocade** : 14/5-3/7. On Hawthorn, Broom and other shrubs. Rare on SW.

2159 *Lacanobia suasa* (D. & S.) — **Dog's Tooth** : 18/5-6/8. A saltmarsh, wasteland and moorland species on herbaceous plants. Uncommon on SW.

2160 *Lacanobia oleracea* (Linn.) — **Bright-line Brown-eye** : 27/4-22/9. Larvae feed on a variety of plants. Found throughout, common on SW.

2163 *Ceramica pisi* (Linn.) — **Broom Moth** : 5/6-24/7. On a wide variety of plants. Found throughout, scarce on SW.

2164 *Hecatera bicolorata* (Hufn.) — **Broad-barred White** ; 5/6-4/8. Mainly on species of *Hieracium.* Scarce on SW.

2166 *Hadena rivularis* (Fabr.) — **The Campion** : On Ragged Robin and various species of campion. Only three post-1980 records all on SW.

2167 *Hadena perplexa perplexa* (D. & S.) — **Tawny Shears** : 21/5-12/9. Larvae on species of campion. Found in WW, scarce on SW.

2171 *Hadena confusa* (Hufn.) — **Marbled Coronet** : 22/5-16/7. A variable species on campions. Uncommon on SW.

2173 *Hadena bicruris* (Hufn.) — **The Lychnis** : 17/5-24/8. On Ragged Robin and species of campion. Found in UW, uncommon — common on SW.

2176 *Cerapteryx graminis* (Linn.) — **Antler Moth** : 4/7-10/9. On fescues and other grasses. Adults often found during the day on Common Ragwort. Found throughout, common on SW.

2177 *Tholera cespitis* (D. & S.) — **Hedge Rustic** : 31/7-28/9. On various grasses. Occurs throughout; uncommon — common on SW.

2178 *Tholera decimalis* (Poda) — **Feathered Gothic** : 23/8-27/9. On various grasses. Uncommon — common on SW.

2179 *Panolis flammea* (D. & S.) — **Pine Beauty** : a pest species on various conifers. Rare on SW in spring.

2186 *Orthosia gracilis* (D. & S.) — **Powdered Quaker** : a spring species on a variety of plants. Caught in WW and LRP, rare on SW.

2187 *Orthosis stabilis* (D. & S.) — **Common Quaker** : a spring species on willows and other trees. Scarce on SW, abundant WW, LRP.

2188 *Orthosia incerta* (Hufn.) — **Clouded Drab** : on a variety of plants; scarce SW, LRP in spring.

2190 *Orthosia gothica* (Linn.) — **Hebrew Character** : larvae on a variety of plants. A spring species, scarce on SW, common WW and LRP.

2192 *Mythimna conigera* (D. & S.) — **Brown-line Bright-eye** : 5/7-10/8. Larvae on various grasses. Recorded from EB, scarce on SW.

2193 *Mythimna ferrago* (Fabr.) — **The Clay** : 19/6-4/8. On various grasses and other low plants. Found throughout, uncommon on SW.

2197 *Mythimna straminea* (Treit.) — **Southern Wainscot** : larvae on Reed Canary-grass. Singles on SW 24/8/86 and 2/8/87 are, apart from one on Sandscale in 1946, the most northerly records for this species.

2198 *Mythimna impura* (Hb.) — **Smoky Wainscot** : 29/6-16/10. On a variety of grasses. Occurs throughout, common on SW.

2199 *Mythimna pallens* (Linn.) — **Common Wainscot** : 4/7-18/9. Larvae feed on a variety of grasses. Reported from EB, uncommon — common on SW.

2201 *Mythimna litoralis* (Curt.) — **Shore Wainscot** : 24/6-9/8. Coastal species feeding on Marram. Found on NW, uncommon on SW.

*Shore Wainscot*

2205 *Mythimna comma* (Hb.) — **Shoulder-striped Wainscot** : 24/5-9/8. On Cock's-foot and other grasses. Recorded from UW, uncommon — common on SW.

**Cuculliinae**

2214 *Cucullia chamomillae* (D. & S.) — **Chamomile Shark** : 18/5-23/5. On flowers of Pineappleweed, Scentless Mayweed etc. Found throughout, scarce on SW.

2216 *Cucullia umbratica* (Linn.) — **The Shark** : 22/5-8/8. On various species of sow-thistle. Uncommon on SW.

2221 *Cucullia verbasci* (Linn.) — **The Mullein** : 23/4-9/5. On leaves of mullein. Scarce on SW.

2231 *Aporophyla lutulenta lunenburgensis* (D. & S.) — **Northern Deep-brown Dart** : Larvae mostly on heather. One on SW 29/9/87 (TD) is the first Furness record.

2232 *Aporophyla nigra* (Haw.) — **Black Rustic** : 30/9-8/10. On various low plants. Rare on SW.

2233 *Lithomoia solidaginis* (Hb.) — **Golden-rod Brindle** : on a variety of plants such as heathers, Birch. A typical moorland species and probably wind-blown. One on SW 18/8/84 (TD).

2241 *Xylena vetusta* (Hb.) — **Red Sword-grass** : 15/4-12/9. On a variety of low plants. Scarce on SW.

2243 *Xylocampa areola* (Esp.) — **Early Grey** : on Honeysuckle. One in WW 25/4/87 (DWE/TD).

2245 *Allophyes oxyacanthae* (Linn.) — **Green-brindled Crescent** : 28/9-21/10. On Hawthorn and Blackthorn. Found in UW, rare on SW.

2250 *Blepharita adusta* (Esp.) — **Dark Brocade** : 26/5-10/7. Larvae on a variety of plants and grasses. Rare on SW.

2254 *Antitype chi* (Linn.) — **Grey Chi** : 2/8-27/8. On a variety of low plants. Recorded in UW, scarce on SW.

2255 *Eumichtis lichenea* (Hb.) — **Feathered Ranunculus** : 19/8-16/10. Larvae feed on a variety of plants. More frequent on coast than inland. Reported from EB and UW, uncommon — common on SW.

2258 *Conistra vaccinii* (Linn.) — **The Chestnut** : 2/10-5/10. On Oak, Birch and other trees. Occurs at EB, scarce on SW.

2262 *Agrochola circellaris* (Hufn.) — **The Brick** : On poplar and Ash. One on SW 26/9/85 (TD).

2263 *Agrochola lota* (Cl.) — **Red-line Quaker** : 13/9-16/10. On willows. Recorded in UW, scarce on SW.

2267 *Agrochola lychnidis* (D. & S.) — **Beaded Chestnut** : 10/9-6/10. On grasses and low plants. Reported from EB, scarce on SW.

2270 *Omphaloscelis lunosa* (Haw.) — **Lunar Underwing** : 4/8-12/10. On grasses. Occurs throughout, uncommon — common on SW.

2273 *Xanthia togata* (Esp.) — **Pink-barred Sallow** : 27/8-21/9. Feeds on willow catkins at first, followed by low plants. Caught in UW, scarce on SW.

2274 *Xanthia icteritia* (Hufn.) — **The Sallow** : 17/8-26/9. Feeds on willow catkins at first followed by low plants. Found in UW, scarce on SW.

2275 *Xanthia gilvago* (D. & S.) — **Dusky-lemon Sallow** : an autumnal species on the seeds of species of elm. One on SW 16/9/84 (TD).

**Acronictinae**

2280 *Acronicta leporina* (Linn.) — **The Miller** : Larvae mainly on Birch. Recorded on SW but no post-1980 records.

2284 *Acronicta psi* (Linn.) — **Grey Dagger** : 6/7-22/9. Larvae on many trees. Impossible to separate from Dark Dagger *A. tridens* (D. & S.) without dissection. Rare on SW.

2293 *Cryphia domestica* (Hufn.) — **Marbled Beauty** : 30/6-11/8. Larvae feed on lichens. Occurs in UW, uncommon — common on SW.

**Amphipyrinae**

2298 *Amphipyra berbera* ssp. *svenssoni* (Fletch.) — **Svensson's Copper Underwing** : on a variety of trees. One on SW 24/8/84 (TD).

2299 *Amphipyra tragopogonis* (Cl.) — **Mouse Moth** : 8/7-11/10. On a variety of low plants. Occurs throughout, common on SW where often found in observation hides.

2302 *Rusina ferruginea* (Esp.) — **Brown Rustic** : 4/6-2/8. Larvae on low plants. Uncommon on SW.

2303 *Thalpophila matura* (Hufn.) — **Straw Underwing** : 16/7-9/8. Larvae feed on various grasses. Occurs throughout, uncommon on SW.

2305 *Euplexia lucipara* (Linn.) — **Small Angle Shades** : 11/6-15/7. Larvae on ferns as well as various low plants and trees. Caught in UW, scarce on SW.

2306 *Phlogophora meticulosa* (Linn.) — **Angle Shades** : 26/4-29/10. Adults hibernate so could be found in any month, larvae feed on a variety of plants. Found in UW, common on SW.

2313 *Enargia paleacea* (Esp.) — **Angle-striped Sallow** : as a resident it is a moth of mature birch woodland, but occurs as a migrant. One at EB, one on SW 13/10/84.

2318 *Cosmia trapezina* (Linn.) — **The Dun-bar** : 25/7-23/8. Larvae feed on a variety of trees but are unusual in being carnivorous as well. Found in WW, scarce on SW.

2321 *Apamea monoglypha* (Hufn.) — **Dark Arches** : 11/6-30/9. The larvae feed on grasses. Found throughout, abundant on SW.

2322 *Apamea lithoxylaea* (D. & S.) — **Light Arches** : 4/7-16/8. Larvae feed on grasses. Occurs throughout, uncommon on SW.

2326 *Apamea crenata* (Hufn.) — **Clouded-bordered Brindle** : 23/5-4/8. Larvae on grasses. Recorded in UW, scarce on SW.

2330 *Apamea remissa* (Hb.) — **Dusky Brocade** : 10/6-24/7. Larvae feed on seeds and leaves of grasses. Caught in UW, uncommon on SW.

2331 *Apamea unanimis* (Hb.) — **Small Clouded Brindle** : larvae on various grasses. On SW 2/7/86 (TD) and EB, UW.

2334 *Apamea sordens* (Hufn.) — **Rustic Shoulder-knot** : 23/5-29/6. Larvae on grasses. Reported from UW, scarce on SW.

2336 *Apamea ophiogramma* (Esp.) — **Double Lobed** : larvae on Reed Canary-grass and Reed Sweet-grass. One on SW 8/8/84.

2337 *Oligia strigilis* (Linn.) — **Marbled Minor** : 28/5-10/7. Larvae on grasses. In UW, uncommon on SW.

2338 *Oligia versicolor* (Borkh.) — **Rufous Minor** : probably feeds on grasses. One in UW 15/7/87 (PZ) was a new county record. Several caught subsequently on SW.

2339 *Oligia latruncula* (D. & S.) — **Tawny Marbled Minor** : 12/6-7/7. Larvae on various grasses. On UW, uncommon on SW.

2340 *Oligia fasciuncula* (Haw.) — **Middle-barred Minor** : 7/6-26/7. Larvae feed on grasses. Occurs throughout, common on SW.

2341 *Mesoligia furuncula* (D. & S.) — **Cloaked Minor** : 7/7-31/8. On various grasses. Found throughout, uncommon on SW.

2342 *Mesoligia literosa* (Haw.) — **Rosy Minor** : 21/7-12/9. On a variety of grasses. Occurs throughout, common on SW.

2343 *Mesapamea secalis* (Linn.) — **Common Rustic** : 4/7-1/10. Larvae feed on grasses. Found throughout, abundant on SW.

2343a *Mesapamea secalella* (Remm.) — **Remm's Rustic** : This species has only recently been separated from *M. secalis.* As yet there is no way of separating the two on external characters but it has been suggested that they are equally common. Whilst the presence of this species has been confirmed (SW 29/7/86), without dissecting specimens, the records for *M. secalis* must be combined with those of *M. secalella.*

2344 *Photedes capitiuncula* (Treit.) — **Least Minor** : a local species, the larvae feeding on Glaucous Sedge. One on SW 20/7/84 (TD).

2345 *Photedes minima* (Haw.) — **Small Dotted Buff** : 4/7-9/9. Larvae on Wavy and Tufted Hair-grasses. Rare on SW.

2350 *Photedes pygmina* (Haw.) — **Small Wainscot** : 5/8-18/10. Larvae on various sedges, rushes and grasses. Found at EB, uncommon on SW.

2353 *Luperina testacea* (D. & S.) — **Flounced Rustic** : 13/6-3/10. Larvae on grasses. Occurs at UW and EB, abundant on SW.

2357 *Amphipoea lucens* (Freyer) — **Large Ear** : larvae on moorland grasses. Recorded on SW, no post-1980 records.

2360 *Amphipoea oculea* (Linn.) — **Ear Moth** : 23/7-26/9. Larvae on grasses. Occurs throughout, uncommon — common on SW.

2361 *Hydraecia micacea* (Esp.) — **Rosy Rustic** : 22/7-15/10. Larvae on low plants. In UW, common on SW.

2364 *Gortyna flavago* (D. & S.) — **Frosted Orange** : 9/8-13/10. The larvae feed on stems of burdocks, Foxglove, various thistles etc. Common on SW.

2368 *Celaena leucostigma* (Hb.) — **The Crescent** : 15/7-8/10. A species of damp habitats. Larvae feed on Yellow Flag and some sedges. Reported from EB and UW, common on SW.

2369 *Nonagria typhae* (Thunb.) — **Bulrush Wainscot** : larvae feed in stems of Reed Mace. One on SW 20/8/84.

2375 *Rhizedra lutosa* (Hb.) — **Large Wainscot** : 13/9-13/10. Larvae feed on *Phragmites.* Scarce on SW.

2377 *Arenostola phragmitidis* (Hb.) — **Fen Wainscot** : a reed bed species feeding on *Phragmites*. Recorded on SW but no post-1980 records.

2380 *Charanyca trigrammica* (Hufn.) — **Treble Lines** : larvae on various plants. Recorded on SW pre-1980 and once since, 24/5/89.

2381 *Hoplodrina alsines* (Brahm) — **The Uncertain** : 19/7-9/8. Difficult to separate from *H. blanda*. Larvae feed on low plants. Occurs throughout, scarce on SW.

2382 *Hoplodrina blanda* (D. & S.) — **The Rustic** : 12/6-25/8. On low plants. Occurs throughout, scarce on SW.

2385 *Spodoptera exigua* (Hb.) — **Small Mottled Willow** : migrant species. One on SW 12/10/86 (TD).

2387 *Caradrina morpheus* (Hufn.) — **Mottled Rustic** : 28/5-8/9. Larvae feed on low plants. Recorded at EB and UW, uncommon on SW.

2389 *Caradrina clavipalpis* (Scop.) — **Pale Mottled Willow** : 20/6-26/9. Larvae on seeds of plantains, grasses, peas, etc. In UW, scarce on SW.

2391 *Chilodes maritimus* (Tausch.) — **Silky Wainscot** : larvae forage in old reed stems. One on SW 4/8/86 (TD).

2394 *Stilbia anomala* (Haw.) — **The Anomalous** : larvae on hair-grass. One at EB 6/9/89 and at UW.

**Heliothinae**

2399 *Pyrrhia umbra* (Hufn.) — **Bordered Sallow** : larvae on Restharrow. Rare at SW, one on NW on Hogweed July 1987 (DWE).

2403 *Heliothis peltigera* (D. & S.) — **Bordered Straw** : a rare and erratic migrant. Recorded on SW but no post-1980 records.

**Acontiinae**

2412 *Eustrotia uncula* (Cl.) — **Silver Hook** : moth of boggy or marshy areas, larvae feeding of grasses and sedges. Common on NW where easily disturbed during daytime in June/July.

**Plusiinae**

2434 *Diachrysia chrysitis* (Linn.) — **Burnished Brass** : 16/6-22/9. Larvae on Nettle. Occurs throughout, common on SW.

2439 *Plusia festucae* (Linn.) — **Gold Spot** : 19/6-8/10. A moth of damp habitats, feeding on grasses and marshland plants. Occurs on NW, common on SW.

2441 *Autographa gamma* (Linn.) — **Silver Y** : 19/5-17/11. A transient resident and common (sometimes abundant on migration). Found throughout.

2442 *Autographa pulchrina* (Haw.) — **Beautiful Golden Y** : 11/6-30/7. Larvae feed on various low plants. Recorded in UW, rare on SW.

2443 *Autographa jota* (Linn.) — **Plain Golden Y** : larvae on various low plants. Caught in UW, rare on SW.

2444 *Autographa bractea* (D. & S.) — **Golden Spangle** : larvae on various low plants. Caught in UW, one on SW 24/7/86 (TD).

2449 *Abrostola trigemina* (Werneb.) — **Dark Spectacle** : 16/6-20/8. On Nettle. Found on NW, scarce on SW.

2450 *Abrostola triplasia* (Linn.) — **The Spectacle** : 19/5-24/9. Larvae feed on Nettle. Caught in UW, common on SW.

**Catocalinae**

2462 *Callistege mi* (Cl.) — **Mother Shipton** : 5/6-25/6. A day-flying grassland species, the larvae on trefoils. Occurs on NW, rare — scarce on SW.

### Ophiderinae

2469 *Scoliopteryx libatrix* (Linn.) — **The Herald** : 21/4-8/8. Larvae on willows, poplars etc. Overwinters as adult so could be found in any month of year. Reported from UW and WW, scarce on SW.

2474 *Rivula sericealis* (Scop.) — **Straw Dot** : larvae on grasses. One on SW 14/7/87 (TD).

### Hypeninae

2477 *Hypena proboscidalis* (Linn.) — **The Snout** : 15/7-7/8. Larvae feed on Nettle. Occurs in UW, scarce on SW.

2484 *Schrankia costaestrigalis* (Steph.) — **Pinion-streaked Snout** : Moth of marshy areas. Larvae not known in the wild. Two on SW 17/6 and 18/6/84 (TD).

# COLEOPTERA

## CARABIDAE (ground beetles)

### Cicindelinae

*Cicindela campestris* (Linn.) : in dunes on NW in 1950s (LSK).

### Carabinae

*Abax parallelepipedus* (P&M) : (LSK).
*Acupalpus meridianus* (Linn.) : (LSK).
*Agonum albipes* (Fabr.) : common under stones and driftwood on SW.
*Agonum dorsale* (Pont.) : (LSK).
*Agonum fuliginosum* (Pz.) : one in out-building on SW 9/9/85.
*Agonum marginatum* (Linn.) : under stones on muddy shore and in *Juncus* tussocks on SW.
*Agonum muelleri* (Herbst.) : (LSK).
*Agonum thoreyi* (Dej.) : in *Juncus* tussocks on SW 16/9/86.
*Amara aenea* (Deg.) : common in dunes on SW.
*Amara anthobia* (Villa) : SW, 2/7/60 (LSK).
*Amara familiaris* (Duft.) : under stones on SW.
*Amara fulva* (Mull.) : on bare sandy ground on SW.
*Amara lucida* (Duft.) : under driftwood on the Spit, SW 17/9/86.
*Amara ovata* (Fabr.) : (LSK).
*Amara plebeja* (Gyll.) : (LSK).
*Amara spreta* (Dej.) : Biggar area, 28/5/60 (LSK).
*Amara tibialis* (Pk.) : under stones on sandy turf on SW.
*Asaphidion flavipes* (Linn.) : (LSK).
*Bembidion biguttatum* (Fabr.) : (LSK).
*Bembidion femoratum* (Sturm) : (LSK).
*Bembidion harpaloides* (Serv.) : (LSK).
*Bembidion lampros* (Herbst) : (LSK).
*Bembidion lunulatum* (Four.) : NW (LSK).
*Bembidion pallidipenne* (Ill.) : common under stones and driftwood on the beach of SW. A coastal species
*Bembidion tetracolum* (Say) : recorded on NW on 1/7/64 (RBA) and on beach on SW 7/9/85.
*Bradycellus sharpi* (Joy) : (LSK).

*Bradycellus verbasci* (Duft.) : (LSK).
*Broscus cephalotes* (Linn.) : large sand dune species found on both reserves.
*Calathus erratus* (Sahl.) : under driftwood on sandy turf on NW.
*Calathus fuscipes* (Goeze) : common under stones and driftwood on sandy turf on SW.
*Calathus melanocephalus* (Linn.) : Biggar 2/7/60 (LSK), under driftwood and stones on SW.
*Calathus mollis* (Marsh.) : on dry sandy ground on both NW and SW.
*Carabus violacea* (Linn.) : one in Willow Woods 27/4/87.
*Clivina fossor* (Linn.) : (LSK).
*Cychrus* ssp. *rostratus* (Linn.) : (LSK).
*Dicheirotrichus gustavi* (Crot.) : common on clayey ground above high tide line on SW.
*Dromius notatus* (Step.) : SW 11/6/67 (LSK).
*Dyschirus globosus* (Herbst) : (LSK).
*Dyschirus salinus* (Sch.) : NW (LSK).
*Dyschirus thoracicus* (Rossi) : NW (LSK).
*Elaphrus riparius* (Linn.) : common on mud around gate pool, SW.
*Harpalus affinis* (Schr.) : common under stones and driftwood on SW.
*Harpalus latus* (Linn.) : (LSK).
*Harpalus rufipes* (Deg.) : very common under stones and driftwood on SW.
*Leistus fulvibarbis* (Dej.) : (LSK).
*Loricera pilicornis* (Fabr.) : by gate pool, SW 22/7/83 (PW).
*Metabletus foveatus* (Four.) : under stones on the beach SW 15/9/86.
*Nebria brevicollis* (Fabr.) : (LSK).
*Nebria salina* (F&L.) : under stones on the spit, SW 17/9/86.
*Notiophilus aquaticus* (Linn.) : one in dunes by groyne hide, SW 2/9/85.
*Notiophilus biguttatus* (Fabr.) : (LSK).
*Notiophilus palustris* (Duft.) : (LSK).
*Pogonus chalceus* (Marsh.) : common under stones on muddy shore on SW and also on NW amongst tidal refuse.
*Pterostichus diligens* (Sturm) : (LSK).
*Pterostichus madidus* (Fabr.) : (LSK).
*Pterostichus melanarius* (Ill.) : (LSK).
*Pterostichus niger* (Schall.) : (LSK).
*Pterostichus nigrita* (Pk.) : attracted to light in Willow Woods 25/4/87.
*Pterostichus strenuus* (Pz.) : (LSK.)
*Trechus obtusus* (Erich.) : (LSK).
*Trechus quadristriatus* (Schr.) : on bare ground by the offices on SW.

## **HALIPLIDAE** (crawling water beetles)

*Haliplus confinis* (Step.) : in ponds on NW in 1976 (NLB).
*Haliplus lineolatus* (Mann.) : in ponds on NW in 1976 (NLB).
*Haliplus ruficollis* (Deg.) : (LSK).

## **NOTERIDAE**

*Noterus clavicornis* (Deg.) : one on NW in August 1962 (RBA).

## DYTISCIDAE (predacious diving beetles)

### Laccophilinae

*Laccophilus minutus* (Linn.) : (LSK).

### Hydroporinae

*Coelambus impressopunctatus* (Sch.) : by gate pool 27/4/86.
*Hyphydrus ovatus* (Linn.) : in ponds on NW 29/4/87.
*Hygrotus inaequalis* (Fabr.) : in ponds on NW 16/7/86.
*Hydroporus erythrocephalus* (Linn.) : in pond on SW 1/7/64 (RBA).
*Hydroporus gyllenhali* (Schi.) : in pond on SW 1/7/64 (RBA).
*Hydroporus memnonius* (Nic.) : (LSK).
*Hydroporus nigrita* (Fabr.) : (LSK).
*Hydroporus planus* (Fabr.) : in pond on SW 1/7/64 (RBA).
*Hydroporus pubescens* (Gyll.) : in pond on SW 1/7/64 (RBA).
*Hydroporus tessellatus* (Drap.) : (LSK).
*Stictonectes lepidus* (Ol.) : in ponds on NW (RBA).

### Colymbetinae

*Agabus bipustulatus* (Linn.) : in ponds on SW 1/7/64 (RBA) and on NW (CMcC).
*Agabus chalconatus* (Pz.) : (LSK).
*Agabus nebulosus* (Forst.) : (LSK).
*Colymbetes fuscus* (Linn.) : stagnant water species, found on NW and SW.
*Copelatus haemorrhoidalis* (Fabr.) : common in pond on SW 1/7/64 (RBA).
*Ilybius ater* (Deg.) : (LSK).
*Ilybius fuliginosus* (Fabr.) : (LSK).
*Ilybius subaeneus* (Er.) : a dead specimen on dunes of NW 1960-63 (RBA).

### Dytiscinae

*Acilius sulcatus* (Linn.) : found in ponds on NW (LSK).
*Dytiscus marginalis* (Linn.) : found in pond on NW in 1986. A stagnant water species.
*Dytiscus semisulcatus* (Mull.) : found in ponds on NW (LSK). A stagnant water species.

## GYRINIDAE (whirligig beetles)

### Gyrininae

*Gyrinus caspius* (Mene.) : (LSK).
*Gyrinus substriatus* (Step.) : common in ponds on NW.

## HYDROPHILIDAE (water scavenger beetles)

### Helophorinae

*Helophorus aequalis* (Thom.) : edge of gate pool 26/4/87.
*Helophorus brevipalpis* (Bedel) : in pond on SW 1/7/64 (RBA).
*Helophorus flavipes* (Fabr.) : in cow dung on SW 7/9/85, also found on NW by (RBA).
*Helophorus grandis* (Ill.) : muddy pool in elderberry grove SW, 25/4/87.
*Helophorus minutus* (Fabr.) : (LSK).
*Helophorus porculus* (Bedel) : (LSK).

### Sphaeridiinae

*Cercyon atomarius* (Fabr.) : (LSK).
*Cercyon haemorrhoidalis* (Fabr.) : common in cow dung on SW.
*Cercyon littoralis* (Gyll.) : (LSK).
*Cercyon melanocephalus* (Linn.) : common in dung on SW.
*Cercyon pygmaeus* (Ill.) : in cow dung on SW 26/4/87.
*Coelostoma orbiculare* (Fabr.) : (LSK).
*Cryptopleurum minutum* (Fabr.) : (LSK).
*Sphaeridium bipustulatum* (Fabr.) : common in cow dung on SW.
*Sphaeridium scarabaeoides* (Linn.) : (LSK).

### Hydrophilinae

*Cymbiodyta marginella* (Fabr.) : in pond on SW 1/7/64 (RBA).
*Enochrus bicolor* (Fabr.) : on drying mud of stagnant pond on SW July 1986.
*Hydrobius fuscipes* (Linn.) : common stagnant water species on SW.
*Laccobius minutus* (Linn.) : in pool on NW 29/4/87.
*Laccobius striatulus* (Fabr.) : (LSK).

## HISTERIDAE

### Saprininae

*Hypocaccus rugiceps* (Duft.) : in sand dunes on NW 1/7/64 (RBA).
*Saprinus cuspidatus* (Ihssen) : This species can only be separated from *S. semistriatus* (Scr.) by examination of the genitalia of the males. All the specimens examined by myself have proved to be this species.

### Tribalinae

*Onthophilus striatus* (Forst.) : in cow dung on SW 27/4/87.

### Histerinae

*Hister striola* (Sahl.) : (LSK).
*Hister unicolor* (Linn.) : (LSK).
*Paralister purpurascens* (Herbst) : recorded on SW 8/6/63 (RBA).

## HYDRAENIDAE

*Ochthebius auriculatus* (Rey) : abundant on saltings of NW 1960-63 (RBA).
*Ochthebius marinus* (Pk.) : three on saltings of NW 1960-63 (RBA).

## PTILIIDAE (featherwing beetles)

*Acrotrichis fascicularis* (Herbst) : (LSK).
*Acrotrichis montandoni* (Allibert) : (LSK).
*Acrotrichis thoracica* (Waltl) : (LSK).
*Ptenidium nitidum* (Heer) : (LSK).
*Ptenidium pusillum* (Gyll.) : (LSK).

## LEIODIDAE

### Catopinae

*Catops chrysomeloides* (Pz.) : (LSK).
*Catops grandicollis* (Eric.) : (LSK).

*Catops tristis* (Pz.) : (LSK).
*Choleva agilis* (Ill.) : (LSK).
*Nargus velox* (Spence) : (LSK).
*Ptomophagus subvillosus* (Goeze) : (LSK).

## SILPHIDAE (carrion beetles)

*Necrodes littoralis* (Linn.) : on dead gull, NW 21/4/55 (LSK).
*Nicrophorus humator* (Gled.) : on dead oystercatcher, NW 21/4/55 (LSK), in moth trap on SW 26/4/87.
*Nicrophorus investigator* (Zett.) a common burying beetle on SW. Caught regularly in moth trap.
*Silpha atrata* (Linn.) : (LSK).
*Silpha tristis* (Ill.) : NW 1/7/64 (RBA).
*Thanatophilus rugosus* (Linn.) : near gull corpse on shingle beach SW 23/7/85.

## STAPHYLINIDAE (rove beetles)

### Proteinae

*Megathrus depressus* (Pk.) : (LSK).
*Proteinus ovalis* (Steph.) : (LSK).

### Omaliinae

*Acidota crenata* (Fab.) : on dunes (LSK).
*Phyllodrepa floralis* (Pk.) : (LSK).
*Omalium laeviusculum* (Gyll.) : (LSK).

### Oxytelinae

*Anotylus complanatus* (Erich.) : (LSK).
*Anotylus maritimus* (Thom) : (LSK).
*Anotylus rugosus* (Fab.) : (LSK).
*Anotylus tetracarinatus* (Block) : (LSK).
*Bledius fuscipes* (Rye) : (LSK).
*Bledius opacus* (Block) : (LSK).
*Bledius spectabilis* (Kraatz) : (LSK).
*Bledius subniger* (Schn.) : (LSK).
*Platystethus arenarius* (Four.) : (LSK).
*Oxytelus lagueatus* (Marsh) : (LSK).

### Steninae

*Stenus boops* (Ljungh) : (LSK).
*Stenus canaliculatus* (Gyll.) : (LSK).
*Stenus cicindeloides* (Schaller) : (LSK).
*Stenus clavicornis* (Scop) : (LSK).
*Stenus exiguus* (Erich) : (LSK).
*Stenus formicetorum* (Mann.) : in *Juncus* tussock, SW 16/9/86. An uncommon species with a southern distribution.
*Stenus guttula* (Muller) : (LSK).
*Stenus juno* (Pk.) : in *Juncus* tussocks, SW 16/9/86.
*Stenus nitidiusculus* (Steph.) : (LSK).
*Stenus ossium* (Steph.) : (LSK).
*Stenus similis* (Herbst) : (LSK).

**Paederinae**
*Lathrobium brunnipes* (Fab.) : (LSK).
*Lathrobium elongatum* (Linn.) : (LSK).
*Lathrobium multipunctum* (Grav.) : (LSK).
*Rugilus orbiculatus* (Pk.) : (LSK).
*Rugilus rufipes* (Germ.) : (LSK).

**Staphylininae**
*Cafius xantholoma* (Grav.) : (LSK).
*Creophilus maxillosus* (Linn.) : SW 27/5/63 (RBA).
*Gabrius bishopi* (Sharp) : (LSK).
*Gabrius piliger* (Mulsant & Rey) : (LSK).
*Gyrohypnus punctulatus* (Pk.) : (LSK).
*Othius laeviusculus* (Steph.) : (LSK).
*Phacophallus parampunctus* (Gyll.) : (LSK).
*Philonthus addendus* (Sharp) : (LSK).
*Philonthus albipes* (Grav.) : (LSK).
*Philonthus cognatus* (Steph.) : (LSK).
*Philonthus cruentatus* (Gmelin) : (LSK).
*Philonthus decorus* (Grav.) : (LSK).
*Philonthus laminatus* (Creut.) : common on fresh gull corpses on SW.
*Philonthus marginatus* (Strom) : (LSK).
*Philonthus politus* (Linn.) : (LSK).
*Philonthus splendens* (Fab.) : (LSK).
*Philonthus succicola* (Thom.) : (LSK).
*Philonthus umbratilis* (Grav.) : (LSK).
*Philonthus varius* (Gyll.) : (LSK).
*Quedius aridulus* (Jansson) : (LSK).
*Quedius cinctus* (Pk.) : (LSK).
*Quedius fuliginosus* (Grav.) : (LSK).
*Quedius lateralis* (Grav.) : (LSK).
*Quedius molochinus* (Grav.) : (LSK).
*Quedius semiaeneus* (Steph.) : (LSK).
*Quedius semiobscurus* (Marsh) : (LSK).
*Quedius tristis* (Grav.) : (LSK).
*Staphylinus ater* (Grav.) : under driftwood on NW and SW.
*Staphylinus melanarius* (Heer) : under driftwood on the spit, SW 17/9/86.
*Staphylinus nero* (Faldermann) : (LSK).
*Staphylinus olens* (Mull.) : under driftwood on SW 23/7/85.
*Xantholinus glabratus* (Grav.) : on mud by gate pool and under driftwood on the Spit.
*Xantholinus linearis* (Ol.) : (LSK).

**Tachyporinae**
*Sepedophilus littoreus* (Linn.) : (LSK).
*Sepedophilus marshami* (Steph.) : (LSK).
*Sepedophilus nigripennis* (Steph.) : in *Juncus* tussocks, SW 16/9/86.
*Tachyporus chrysomelinus* (Linn.) : common in vegetable matter throughout Walney.
*Tachyporus hypnorum* (Fab.) : (LSK).
*Tachyporus nitidulus* (Fab.) : (LSK).
*Tachyporus obtusus* (Linn.) : (LSK).

*Tachyporus pusillus* (Grav.) : in *Juncus* tussocks, SW 16/9/86.
*Tachinus marginalis* (Fab.) : (LSK).
*Tachinus signatus* (Grav.) : (LSK).
*Tachinus subterraneus* (Linn.) : (LSK).

### Aleocharinae

*Aleochara bipustulata* (Linn.) : (LSK).
*Aleochara curtula* (Goeze) : (LSK).
*Aleochara grisea* (Kraatz) : (LSK).
*Aleochara intricata* (Mann.) : (LSK).
*Aleochara lanuginosa* (Grav.) : (LSK).
*Aleochara villosa* (Mann.) : (LSK).
*Atheta vestita* (Grav.) : (LSK).
*Calodera aethiops* (Grav.) : (LSK).
*Cordalia obscura* (Grav.) : (LSK).
*Crataraea suturalis* (Mann.) : (LSK).
*Drusilla canaliculata* (Fab.) : (LSK).
*Falagria caesa* (Erich.) : (LSK).
*Gyrophaena affinis* (Steph.) : (LSK).
*Mniusa incrassata* (Mulsant & Rey) : (LSK).
*Ocalea badia* (Erich.) : (LSK).
*Ocyusa maura* (Erich.) : (LSK).
*Oxypoda elogatula* (Aube) : (LSK).
*Phytosus balticus* (Kraatz) : (LSK).

## GEOTRUPIDAE (dor beetles)

*Geotrupes spiniger* (Marsh.) : found in dunes on SW 13/9/85.
*Geotrupes stercorarius* (Linn.) : (LSK).
*Geotrupes stercorosus* (Scriba) : (LSK).
*Geotrupes vernalis* (Linn.) : under gull corpse on NW 1/7/64 (RBA).

## SCARABAEIDAE (dung beetles & chafers)

### Aphodiinae

*Aegialia arenaria* (Fabr.) : a local sand dune species. Found on NW and SW 10/9/85.
*Aphodius ater* (Deg.) : recorded in cow dung on SW 26/4/87.
*Aphodius contaminatus* (Herbst) : abundant in sheep dung on SW 7/9/85.
*Aphodius fimetarius* (Linn.) : under stone on SW 15/7/85.
*Aphodius foetens* (Fab.) : (LSK).
*Aphodius granarius* (Linn.) : common in puddles following mass emergence on SW; 31/7/85.
*Aphodius ictericus* (Laich.) : a southern species found in moth trap on SW 24/7/85.
*Aphodius paykulli* (Bedel) : (LSK).
*Aphodius plagiatus* (Linn.) : (LSK).
*Aphodius prodromus* (Brahm) : (LSK).
*Aphodius rufipes* (Linn.) : occurs frequently in moth trap on SW.
*Aphodius rufus* (Moll) : a local species. One in moth trap on SW 21/7/85.
*Aphodius sphacelatus* (Pz.) : (LSK).
*Colobopterus erraticus* (Linn.) : (LSK).
*Colobopterus fossor* (Linn.) : in cow dung on SW 21/4/87.
*Colobopterus haemorrhoidalis* (Linn.) : caught in moth trap on SW 7/9/85.

**Melolonthinae**

*Hoplia philanthus* (Fuessly) : found in dunes on NW 1960-63 (RBA).
*Melolontha melolontha* (Linn.) : (LSK).
*Serica brunnea* (Linn.) : (LSK).

**Rutelinae**

*Euchlora dubia* (Scop.) : a distinctive coastal chafer found in dunes on NW and SW.

## SCIRTIDAE

*Microcara testacea* (Linn.) : common in the *Juncus* around gate pool on SW.

## BYRRHIDAE (pill beetles)

*Simplocaria semistriata* (Fab.) : (LSK).
*Syncalypta striatopunctata* (Steff.) : (LSK).

## HETEROCERIDAE

*Heterocerus fusculus* (Kiesenwetter) : (LSK).

## DRYOPIDAE

*Dryops ernesti* (des Gozis) : (LSK).
*Dryops luridus* (Erich.) : (LSK).

## ELATERIDAE (click beetles)

**Agrypninae**

*Agrypnus murinus* (Linn.) : on NW 15/7/86.

**Athoinae**

*Athous haemorrhoidalis* (Fabr.) : common in grassy areas on SW.

**Elaterinae**

*Agriotes lineatus* (Linn.) : attracted to light in Willow Woods 25/4/87.

## CANTHARIDAE (soldier beetles)

*Cantharis livida* (Linn.) : common on NW 16/7/85.
*Cantharis nigra* (Deg.) : common on SW 16/7/85.
*Cantharis nigricans* (Muller) : (LSK)
*Cantharis pallida* (Goeze) : (LSK).
*Cantharis rustica* (Fall.) : (LSK).
*Rhagonycha femoralis* (Brulle) : (LSK).
*Rhagonycha fulva* (Scop.) : abundant throughout Walney in summer.

## LAMPYRIDAE (glow-worms)

*Lampyris noctiluca* (Linn.) : One in Wylock Marsh area, July 1986 (TD).

## DERMESTIDAE (hide beetles)

*Attagenus pellio* (Linn.) : (LSK).
*Dermestes murinus* (Linn.) : in dunes on SW 10/9/85. Feeds on dried carcasses.

## ANOBIIDAE

*Anobium punctatum* (Degeer) : (LSK).

## PTINIDAE (spider beetles)

### Ptininae

*Niptus hololeucus* (Faldermann) : (LSK).
*Ptinus fur* (Linn.) : (LSK).
*Ptinus lichenum* (Marsham) : (LSK).
*Ptinus tectus* (Boieldieu) : (LSK).

## MELYRIDAE

### Dasytinae

*Psilothrix viridicoeruleus* (Four.) : on west shore of SW, near Biggar 4/6/60 (LSK).

## NITIDULIDAE

### Cateretinae

*Brachypterus glaber* (Step.) : numerous on nettle and in flower heads of Common Ragwort on SW.
*Brachypterus urticae* (Fab.) : on nettle (LSK).

### Carpophilinae

*Epuraea aestiva* (Linn.) : SW 2/7/60 (LSK).
*Epuraea melina* (Erich.) : (LSK).
*Meligethes aeneus* (Fab.) : (LSK).
*Meligethes obscurus* (Erich.) : (LSK).
*Meligethes viridescens* (Fsb.) : (LSK).

### Nitidulinae

*Omosita colon* (Linn.) : very common in corpses on SW, especially dried ones.
*Omosita discoidea* (Fab.) : (LSK).

## SILVANIDAE

### Silvaninae

*Oryzaephilus surinamensis* (Linn.) : (LSK).

## CRYPTOPHAGIDAE

### Cryptophaginae

*Antherophagus pallens* (Linn.) : common in flowers of Spear Thistle on SW.
*Cryptophagus cellaris* (Scopoli) : (LSK).
*Cryptophagus pilosus* (Gyll.) : (LSK).
*Cryptophagus pubescens* (Sturm) : (LSK).
*Micrambe vini* (Pz.) : on SW 15/7/85.

### Atomariinae

*Atomaria apicalis* (Erich.) : (LSK).
*Atomaria atricapilla* (Step.) : in grass/*Juncus* tussocks, SW 16/9/86.
*Atomaria lewisi* (Reitter) : (LSK).
*Ephistemus globulus* (Pk.) : in grass/*Juncus* tussocks, SW 16/9/86.

## BYTURIDAE

*Byturus tomentosus* (Degeer) : (LSK).

## COCCINELLIDAE (ladybirds)

### Epilachninae

*Subcoccinella vigintiquattuorpunctata* (Linn.) : on NW 1960-63 (RBA).

### Coccinellinae

*Adalia bipunctata* (Linn.) : a ubiquitous species.
*Adonia variegata* (Goeze) : found on NW 1960-63 (RBA).
*Anatis ocellata* (Linn.) : (LSK).
*Chilocorus bipustulatus* (Linn.) : NW 1/7/64 (RBA).
*Coccidula rufa* (Herbst) : a marshland species found in *Juncus* by gate pool and pools off Rakes Lane.
*Coccinella septempunctata* (Linn.) : a ubiquitous ladybird.
*Coccinella undecimpunctata* (Linn.) : a saltmarsh species found on SW 10/9/85.
*Rhyzobius litura* (Fabr.) : found on nettle on SW 14/7/85.
*Scymnus frontalis* (Fab.) : (LSK).
*Tytthaspis sedecimpunctata* (Linn.) : edge of saltmarsh on LRP 15/9/86.

## LATHRIDIIDAE (mould beetles)

### Lathridiinae

*Aridius nodifer* (West.) : very common on SW.
*Deinerella elongata* (Curtis) : (LSK).
*Stephostethus lardarius* (Degeer) : (LSK).

### Corticariinae

*Corticaria crenulata* (Gyll.) : under stones on the beach, SW 15/9/86.
*Corticaria elongata* (Gyll.) : (LSK).
*Corticaria impressa* (Olivier) : (LSK).
*Corticarina fuscula* (Gyll.) : generally distributed in grass tussocks, SW 16/9/86.
*Cortinicara gibbosa* (Herbst) : common on SW.

## MYCETOPHAGIDAE

*Typhaea stercorea* (Linn.) : (LSK).

## TENEBRIONIDAE (darkling beetles)

### Pedininae

*Phylan gibbus* (Fabr.) : common coastal species, found under driftwood on NW and SW.

### Opatrinae

*Melanimon tibialis* (Fabr.) : a coastal species on SW 2/7/60 (LSK) and on the dunes of NW 16/7/85.

## SCRAPTIIDAE

*Anaspis frontalis* (Linn.) : (LSK).
*Anaspis rufilabris* (Gyll.) : (LSK).

## OEDEMERIDAE

*Nacerdes melanura* (Linn.) : occurs in timber on the shore of SW; a coastal species.

## CHRYSOMELIDAE (leaf beetles)

### Criocerinae

*Oulema melanopa* (Linn.) : (LSK)

### Chrysomelinae

*Chrysolina polita* (Linn.) : (LSK).
*Gastrophysa polygoni* (Linn.) : on SW 8/6/63 (RBA).
*Hydrothassa glabra* (Herbst) : (LSK).
*Phaedon armoraciae* (Linn.) : common on SW.
*Phaedon concinnus* (Steph.) : (LSK).
*Phyllodecta laticollis* (Suffrian) : (LSK).
*Phyllodecta vitellinae* (Linn.) : common on willow on NW 17/7/86.
*Prasocuris junci* (Brahm) : (LSK).

### Galerucinae

*Lochmaea suturalis* (Th.) : on sandy heath, NW 27/4/87.
*Lochmaea caprea* (Linn.) : common on willow on NW 10/9/86.

### Halticinae

*Chaetocnema concinna* (Marsham) : (LSK).
*Chalcoides aurea* (Four.) : common on willow on NW 17/7/86.
*Crepidodera transversa* (Marsh.) : common on Common Ragwort, SW 10/9/85.
*Longitarsus jacobaeae* (Water.) : common on Common Ragwort, SW 7/9/85.
*Longitarsus rubiginosus* (Foud.) : one caught by offices, SW 14/7/86.
*Phyllotreta undulata* (Kutschera) : (LSK).

### Cassidinae

*Cassida rubiginosa* (Mull.) : on shore of NW in 1950s (LSK), one found along Rakes Lane 15/9/86.

## ATTELABIDAE

*Deporaus betulae* (Linn.) : (LSK).

## APIONIDAE (weevils)

### Apioninae

*Apion confluens* (Kirby) : under driftwood on sandy turf, SW 9/9/86.
*Apion carduorum* (Kirby) : found in grass on SW 7/9/85.
*Apion fuscirostre* (Fab.) : (LSK).
*Apion hydrolapathi* (Marsham) : (LSK).
*Apion loti* (Kirby) : on Restharrow on NW 1960-63 (RBA).
*Apion nigritarse* (Kirby) : (LSK).
*Apion punctigerum* (Pk.) : (LSK).
*Apion rufirostre* (Fab.) : (LSK).

## CURCULIONIDAE (Weevils).

### Otiorhynchinae

*Otiorhynchus atroapterus* (Deg.) : common weevil in dunes of NW where it feeds on grasses.
*Otiorhynchus ovatus* (Linn.) : (LSK).
*Otiorhynchus singularis* (Linn.) : (LSK).
*Phyllobius argentatus* (Linn.) : common, on Hawthorn on NW 16/7/85.
*Phyllobius maculicornis* (Germar) : (LSK).
*Phyllobius oblongus* (Linn.) : (LSK).
*Phyllobius pyri* (Linn.) : abundant on Creeping Willow on NW, 27/4/87.
*Phyllobius roboretanus* (Gredler) : (LSK).

### Brachyderinae

*Barypeithes araneiformis* (Schrank) : (LSK).
*Cneorhinus plumbeus* (Marsham) : (LSK).
*Philopedon plagiatus* (Scha.) : common coastal weevil, found on NW and SW.

### Sitoninae

*Sitona griseus* (Fabr.) : recorded on NW 1960-63 (RBA).
*Sitona hispidulus* (Fab.) : (LSK).
*Sitona lepidus* (Gyll.) : (LSK).
*Sitona lineatus* (Linn.) : recorded on NW 1960-63 (RBA); a common species.
*Sitona sulcifrons* (Thunberg) : (LSK).

### Cleoninae

*Cleonus piger* (Scop.) : in dunes on NW (NLB) and in dunes of SW 10/9/85.

### Hyperinae

*Hypera arator* (Linn.) : (LSK).
*Hypera plantaginis* (Degeer) : (LSK).
*Hypera postica* (Gyll.) : (LSK).

### Rhynchophorinae

*Sitophilus granarius* (Linn.) : (LSK).

### Ceuthorhynchinae

*Ceutorhynchus erysimi* (Fabr.) : on SW 27/4/87.
*Ceutorhynchus pollinarius* (Forst.) : found on nettle, SW 10/9/85.
*Rhinoncus castor* (Fab.) : (LSK).
*Rhinoncus pericarpius* (Linn.) : found on the mud by gate pool 14/7/85.

### Anthonominae

*Anthonomus rubi* (Herbst) : in grass tussock, SW 16/9/86.

# DIPTERA

## TIPULIDAE (craneflies)

### Tipulinae

*Tipula paludosa* (Mg.) : abundant on SW.

## **PSYCHODIDAE** (owl or sewage midges)

**Psychodinae**

*Clytocerus ocellaris* (Mg.) : common in central marsh, SW.

## **CHAOBORIDAE**

*Chaoborus flavicans* (Mg.) : pools on NW (NLB).

## **CULICIDAE** (mosquitoes)

**Culicinae**

*Culex pipiens* (Linn.) : in out-buildings on SW.

## **CHIRONOMIDAE** (non-biting midges)

**Tanypodinae**

*Psectrotanypus varius* (Fabr.) : on NW (NLB).

**Orthocladiinae**

*Isocladius pilitarsis* (Zett.) : SW, 1/7/67 (NLB).
*Isocladius sylvestris* (Fabr.) : NW (NLB).
*Halocladius braunsi* (Goet.) : SW, 1/7/67. A new species to England (NLB).
*Psectrocladius obvious* (Walk.) : NW, 10/7/78 (NLB).

**Chironominae**

*Dicrodentipes pallidicornis* (Goet.) : in dunes on NW, 10/8/78 (NLB).
*Microtndipes pedellus* (Deg.) : NW (NLB).
*Tanytarsus debilis* (Mg.) : NW (NLB).

## **SIMULIIDAE** (black flies)

*Simulium ornatum* (Mg.) : one at light in Willow Woods 25/4/87.

## **ANISOPODIDAE**

**Anisopodinae**

*Sylvicola punctatus* (Fabr.) : at light in Willow Woods 25/4/87, common on SW.

## **BIBIONIDAE**

*Bibio johannis* (Linn.) : abundant all over Walney in late April.
*Dilophus febrilis* (Linn.) : common throughout, especially in late autumn.

## **STRATIOMYIDAE** (soldier flies)

**Beridinae**

*Beris vallata* (Forst.) : not common on SW.

**Clitellariinae**

*Nemotelus fraternus* (Lw.) : common in *Phragmites* beds on NW and Creephaw Marsh.
*Nemotelus notatus* (Zett.) : on NW 24/7/84 (NLB).
*Nemotelus uliginosus* (Linn.) : common in *Phragmites* of Creephaw Marsh.

**Sarginae**

*Chloromyia formosa* (Scop.) : abundant throughout.

## RHAGIONIDAE (snipe flies)

**Chrysopilinae**

*Chrysopilus cristatus* (Fabr.) : common in damper areas throughout.

**Rhagioninae**

*Rhagio scolopaceus* (Linn.) : common throughout.
*Rhagio tringarius* (Linn.) : one by pool on NW 11/9/86.

## TABANIDAE (horse flies)

**Tabaninae**

*Haematopota pluvialis* (Linn.) : the ubiquitous cleg. Especially common in the damper areas.

## ASILIDAE (robber flies)

*Dysmachus trigonus* (Mg.) : common in dunes on NW and SW.
*Machimus cingulatus* (Fabr.) : one behind cottages, SW 11/9/86.
*Philonicus albiceps* (Mg.) : common in dunes of NW and SW.

## THEREVIDAE (stiletto flies)

*Thereva annulata* (Fabr.) : common in dunes throughout.
*Thereva bipunctata* (Mg.) : common in dunes but more strictly coastal than the following species.
*Thereva nobilitata* (Fabr.) : very common throughout.

## BOMBYLIIDAE (bee flies)

**Exoprosopinae**

*Villa modesta* (Mg.) : not uncommon on SW in the summer.

## EMPIDIDAE

**Tachydrominae**

*Platypalpus nigritarsis* (Fall.) : NW (NLB).
*Platypalpus notatus* (Mg.) : NW (NLB).
*Platypalpus pallidiventris* (Mg.) : common on SW.
*Platypalpus strigifrons* (Par.) : one in marram on SW, 8/9/87.
*Tachydromia aemula* (Lw.) : one on SW in grass behind gate marsh, 12/9/87.
*Tachypeza nubila* (Mg.) : NW (NLB).

**Empidinae**

*Empis punctata* (Mg.) : common on SW.
*Empis livida* (Linn.) : common on SW.
*Empis stercorea* (Linn.) : common on NW and LRP.
*Empis tessallata* (Linn.) : common in hedgerows at Snab and Long Rein Point.
*Hilara lundbecki* (Frey) : NW 1/7/67 (NLB), SW 28/4/87.
*Rhamphomyia subcinerascens* (Coll.) : one at light in Willow Woods 27/4/87.
*Rhamphomyia variabilis* (Fall.) : NW (NLB).

## DOLICHOPODIDAE

### Dolichopodinae

*Dolichopus clavipes* (Hal.) : generally distributed on SW in July.
*Dolichopus diadema* (Hal.) : one by the offices on SW 15/7/86.
*Dolichopus griseipennis* (Stann.) : common on SW, edge of saltmarsh on NW.
*Dolichopus nitidus* (Fall.) : one by offices on SW 15/7/85.
*Dolichopus nubilus* (Mg.) : found in damp areas on NW and SW in July.
*Dolichopus pennatus* (Mg.) : on NW 8/7/80 (NLB).
*Dolichopus plumipes* (Scop.) : generally distributed on SW in July.
*Dolichopus sabinus* (Hal.) : by the cottages on SW 14/7/86. A coastal species.
*Dolichopus ungulatus* (Linn.) : very common throughout.
*Hercostomus cupreus* (Fall.) : edge of saltmarsh on NW 1/7/87.
*Hercostomus germanus* (Weid.) : on NW 24/7/84 (NLB).
*Hercostomus nigripennis* (Fall.) : on NW 24/7/84 (NLB).
*Poecilobothrus nobilitatus* (Linn.) : SW, Wylock Marsh and Rakes Lane. At northern limit of its range.

### Hydrophorinae

*Hydrophorus oceanus* (Macq.) : NW 24/7/84 (NLB), in marram on SW 29/6/87.

### Medeterinae

*Medetera jacula* (Fall.) : in marram on SW 29/6/87.
*Medetera petrophiloides* (Par.) : NW 26/7/79 (NLB).
*Medetera truncorum* (Mg.) : by pools on SW in July 1986.

### Rhaphiinae

*Machaerium maritimae* (Hal.) : common SW and Snab, a coastal species.
*Syntormon pallipes* (Fabr.) : cottages and central marsh on SW.

### Diaphorinae

*Argyra perplexa* (Becker) : one in central marsh, SW 9/9/87.
*Chrysotus cilipes* (Mg.) : by side of pool on SW 17/7/86.

### Campsicneminae

*Campsicnemus armatus* (Zett.) : one behind gate marsh, SW 12/9/87.
*Campsicnemus scambus* (Fall.) : NW (NLB).
*Sympycnus desoutteri* (Par.) : NW (NLB), common on SW.

## LONCHOPTERIDAE (pointed-wing flies)

*Lonchoptera lutea* (Pz.) : common throughout, especially in grass and *Juncus* tussocks.

## PIPUNCULIDAE

### Chalarinae

*Verrallia aucta* (Fall.) : one on NW 3/7/87.

## SYRPHIDAE (hover-flies)

### Syrphinae

*Chrysotoxum festivum* (Linn.) : one on SW 7/9/85 and one on NW in September 1986.
*Episyrphus balteatus* (Deg.) : very common throughout.

*Leucozona lucorum* (Linn.) : one on NW July 1986 (PK).
*Melanostoma mellinum* (Linn.) : common in grassy areas throughout.
*Melanostoma scalare* (Fabr.) : common in grassy areas throughout.
*Meliscaeva cinctella* (Zett.) : one by the offices on SW 16/7/86.
*Metasyrphus corollae* (Fabr.) : common throughout.
*Metasyrphus luniger* (Mg.) : common throughout.
*Platycheirus albimanus* (Fabr.) : common in grassy areas throughout.
*Platycheirus clypeatus* (Mg.) : common throughout.
*Platycheirus fulviventris* (Macq.) : one on NW 3/7/87.
*Platycheirus immarginatus* (Zett.) : NW (NLB).
*Platycheirus manicatus* (Mg.) : common throughout, especially in damper areas.
*Platycheirus peltatus* (Mg.) : common in damp areas on SW.
*Platycheirus scutatus* (Mg.) : common in damp areas on SW.
*Pyrophaena granditarsa* (Forst.) : occurs on SW in *Juncus* of gate marsh.
*Pyrophaena rosarum* (Fabr.) : one by pool on NW 3/7/87.
*Scaeva pyrastri* (Linn.) : common throughout.
*Sphaerophoria menthastri* (Linn.) : frequent throughout.
*Sphaerophoria philanthus* (Mg.) : one on NW 3/7/87.
*Sphaerophoria rueppellii* (Weid.) : one on NW 1/7/87.
*Sphaerophoria scripta* (Linn.) : common throughout.
*Sphaerophoria taeniata* (Mg.) : NW (NLB).
*Syrphus ribesii* (Linn.) : extremely common throughout.
*Syrphus vitripennis* (Mg.) : common throughout.
*Xanthogramma pedissequum* (Harr.) : several found around the pools on NW in July 1986.

**Milesiinae**

*Cheilosia albitarsis* (Mg.) : common along hedgerows on Long Rein Point.
*Cheilosia bergenstammi* (Beck.) : on NW (NLB) and in gate marsh on SW.
*Cheilosia illustrata* (Harr.) : common on umbellifers on NW.
*Eristalinus aeneus* (Scop.) : common throughout; a coastal species.
*Eristalinus sepulchralis* (Linn.) ; common in the damper areas throughout.
*Eristalis abusivus* (Coll.) : commonest *Eristalis* in the damper areas of SW in 1986.
*Eristalis arbustorum* (Linn.) : common throughout.
*Eristalis horticola* (Deg.) : on SW in September 1986.
*Eristalis intricarius* (Linn.) : common throughout.
*Eristalis pertinax* (Scop.) : one of the commonest hoverflies on Walney.
*Eristalis tenax* (Linn.) : common throughout; the familiar Drone Fly.
*Helophilus hybridus* (Lw.) : not uncommon in the damper areas throughout.
*Helophilus pendulus* (Linn.) : common throughout.
*Lejogaster metallina* (Fabr.) : not uncommon in gate marsh, SW and Wylock Marsh.
*Neoascia podagrica* (Fabr.) : one in Rakes Lane 15/9/86.
*Parhelophilus versicolor* (Fabr.) : one on umbels by pool on NW 3/7/87.
*Pipiza noctiluca* (Linn.) : one on NW 15/7/86. Identifications of members of this genus can only be tentative at present.
*Rhingia campestris* (Mg.) : common throughout.
*Sericomyia silentis* (Harr.) : one on SW in September 1986, probably a vagrant.
*Syritta pipiens* (Linn.) : common throughout.
*Tropidia scita* (Harr.) : two in marshy area on Long Rein Point 29/6/87.
*Trichopsomyia flavitarsis* (Mg.) : not uncommon by marshy pools on NW in July.
*Volucella pellucens* (Linn.) : one on SW in September 1983.

## TEPHRITIDAE (gall flies)

### Trypetinae

*Xyphosia miliaria* (Schr.) : found commonly throughout Walney on Spear Thistle.

### Urophorinae

*Urophora jaceana* (Her.) : a pair found on Knapweed on NW 16/7/85.

## PSILIDAE

### Loxocerinae

*Psila rosae* (Fabr.) : common around gate marsh, SW.

## CHAMAEMYIIDAE

### Chamaemyiinae

*Chamaemyia flavipalpis* (Hal.) : in dunes on NW 10/9/85.

## COELOPIDAE (kelp flies)

*Coelopa frigida* (Fabr.) : common on SW, especially on seaweed by groyne hide.

## HELEOMYZIDAE

### Suilliinae

*Neoleria inscripta* (Mg.) : one on a gull corpse on SW 10/9/87.
*Trixoscelis obscurella* (Fall.) : one by offices, SW 15/7/86. A coastal species.

## SEPSIDAE

*Nemopoda nitidula* (Fall.) : generally distributed on SW. Several were found on a gull corpse.
*Sepsis cynipsea* (Linn.) : commonest Sepsid, often found in large numbers on fresh dung.
*Sepsis flavimana* (Mg.) : one in central marsh, SW 14/9/86.
*Sepsis fulgens* (Mg.) : found on SW 7/9/85.
*Themira annulipes* (Mg.) : common on SW.
*Themira leachi* (Mg.) : in central marsh, SW 9/9/87.
*Themira lucida* (Stae.) : one by offices, SW 13/7/86.
*Themira minor* (Hal.) : generally distributed on SW.
*Themira putris* (Linn.) : on SW by offices and on cow-trodden ground by the cottages.
*Themira superba* (Hal.) : on SW by offices and common on cow-trodden ground by cottages.

## SCIOMYZIDAE (snail-eating flies)

### Sciomyzinae

*Knutsonia albiseta* (Scop.) : common around the edges of pools on NW.
*Phenbellia cinerella* (Fall.) : in marram by lighthouse 29/6/87.
*Tetanocera elata* (Fabr.) : common around the edges of pools on NW.
*Tetanocera robusta* (Lw.) : one on SW behind gate marsh 12/9/87.

## SPHAEROCERIDAE (lesser dung flies)

*Copromyza atra* (Mg.) : common around fresh cow dung on SW.
*Copromyza equina* (Fall.) : one on SW in *Juncus* tussock behind cottages 29/11/86.
*Leptocera acutangula* (Zett.) : frequent around fresh cow dung on SW.

## PIOPHILIDAE (cheese skippers)

*Piophila varipes* (Mg.) : common in central marsh, SW. Often found on carrion.
*Piophila vulgaris* (Fall.) : on gull corpse on SW 10/9/87.

## OPOMYZIDAE

*Geomyza balachowskyi* (Mesn.) : one by the cottages, SW 18/9/86.
*Opomyza germinationis* (Linn.) : common throughout and is frequently found in the moth trap on SW.

## DROSOPHILIDAE

### Drosophilinae

*Scaptomyza flava* (Fall.) : on seaweed by groyne hide, SW 8/9/87.
*Scaptomyza pallida* (Fabr.) : on SW in central marsh and gate marsh in September.

## TACHINIDAE (parasite flies)

### Tachininae

*Pelatachina tibialis* (Fall.) : one on Long Rein Point 27/6/87.
*Thelaira nigripes* (Fabr.) : a common species in the autumn on SW.
*Voria ruralis* (Fall.) : one on bramble by offices, SW 13/9/87.

### Goniinae

*Exorista larvarum* (Linn.) : one bred from a larva of the Drinker Moth *Philudoria potatoria,* collected on NW on 28/7/78 (NLB).
*Gonia ornata* (Mg.) : common in dunes in late April.
*Ocytata pallipes* (Fall.) : one on bramble by offices, SW 13/9/87.
*Phryxe vulgaris* (Fall.) : one found on SW 11/9/85.
*Siphona cristata* (Fabr.) : not uncommon on SW.
*Siphona geniculata* (Deg.) : not uncommon on SW.

## SARCOPHAGIDAE (flesh flies)

### Miltogramminae

*Senotainia conica* (Fall.) : one by offices, SW 15/7/86.

### Sarcophaginae

*Sarcophaga carnaria* (Linn.) : one by cottages, SW 14/7/86.
*Sarcophaga dissimilis* (Mg.) : one by groyne hide, SW 16/9/86.
*Sarcophaga subvicina* (Roh.) : one on bramble by offices, SW 13/9/87.

## CALLIPHORIDAE (blow-flies)

### Calliphorinae

*Bellardia pusilla* (Mg.) : not uncommon on SW and NW.
*Calliphora vicina* (R-D.) : common throughout.

*Calliphora vomitoria* (Linn.) : the ubiquitous bluebottle.
*Cynomya mortuorum* (Linn.) : frequent throughout.
*Lucilia caesar* (Linn.) : common throughout and abundant in the gull colony on SW where its larvae are one of the main carrion feeders.
*Lucilia illustris* (Mg.) : one on bramble by offices, SW 13/9/87.
*Lucilia sericata* (Mg.) : common throughout, especially in the gull colony on SW.

## SCATHOPHAGIDAE (dung flies)

### Scathophaginae

*Ceratinostoma ostiorum* (Curt.) : one on the saltmarsh in Lighthouse Bay, SW 16/9/86.
*Norellisoma spinimanum* (Fall.) : one by offices, SW 8/9/87.
*Scathophaga litorea* (Fall.) : common in dunes on SW, also Long Rein Point.
*Scathophaga stercoraria* (Linn.) : the ubiquitous dung fly.

## ANTHOMYIIDAE

*Fucellia tergina* (Zett.) : abundant on seaweed on SW.
*Delia albula* (Fall.) : in dunes on SW 15/9/86.
*Pegomyia bicolor* (Hoff.) : one on SW in central marsh 14/9/86.

## FANNIIDAE

*Fannia armata* (Mg.) : one on SW 14/7/86.
*Fannia canicularis* (Linn.) : common inside the cottages on SW in autumn; the Lesser House Fly.

## MUSCIDAE

### Muscinae

*Hydrotaea cinerea* (R-D.) : one found by the offices on SW 13/7/86.
*Hydrotaea dentipes* (Fabr.) : common on SW.
*Hydrotaea irritans* (Fall.) : common on SW.
*Hydrotaea occulta* (Mg.) : one in central marsh, SW 10/9/87.
*Drymeia hamata* (Fall.) : one by cottages on SW 14/7/86.
*Mesembrina meridiana* (Linn.) : common throughout.
*Morellia aenescens* (R-D.) : common on SW.
*Morellia hortorum* (Fall.) : common on SW.
*Musca autumnalis* (Deg.) : found commonly on SW by gate pool and the cottages.
*Muscina pabulorum* (Fall.) : one on SW 7/9/85.
*Ophyra leucostoma* (Weid.) : found commonly on SW in July.
*Polietes lardarius* (Fabr.) : common in central marsh, SW.

### Phaoniinae

*Helina allotalla* (Mg.) : one on SW in central marsh 16/7/86.
*Helina duplicata* (Mg.) : found commonly in central marsh, SW.
*Helina impuncta* (Fall.) : in central marsh, SW 11/9/86.
*Helina laetifica* (Des.) : in marram on SW and in hedgerow on Long Rein Point; September 1987.
*Phaonia basalis* (Zett.) : one in hedgerow along Long Rein Point 10/9/87.
*Phaonia errans* (Mg.) : common in central marsh, SW in September.

*Phaonia incana* (Weid.) : common around gate pool, SW in July.
*Phaonia perdita* (Mg.) : common on SW in July.

#### Mydaeinae

*Hebecnema umbratica* (Mg.) : found on SW 7/9/85.
*Myospila meditabunda* (Fabr.) : found on SW 10/9/85, 14/7/86.
*Graphomya maculata* (Scop.) : found commonly on umbellifers throughout.
*Mydaea urbana* (Mg.) : one in hedgerow along Long Rein Point 10/9/87.

#### Limnophorinae

*Villeneuvia aestuum* (Vill.) : common by the offices on SW.
*Lispe caesia* (Mg.) : not uncommon in dunes on NW.
*Lispe tentaculata* (Deg.) : on NW (NLB).

#### Coenosiinae

*Coenosia verralli* (Collin.) : one in Marram by Lighthouse on SW 8/9/87.
*Coenosia tricolor* (Zett.) : not uncommon on SW in September.
*Dexiopsis lacteipennis* (Zett.) : one in central marsh, SW 9/9/87.

#### Stomoxyinae

*Haematobosca stimulans* (Mg.) : one in Rakes Lane 15/9/86. A parasite of cattle.
*Stomoxys calcitrans* (Linn.) : SW 23/7/83 (PW.) A parasite of cattle.

### **HIPPOBOSCIDAE** (flat flies)

#### Ornithomyinae

*Ornithomyia fringillina* (Curt.) : one found on a juvenile Linnet.

## **DERMAPTERA** (earwigs)

### FORFICULIDAE

#### Forficulinae

*Forficula auricularia* (Linn.) : the common earwig, abundant throughout.

## **EPHEMEROPTERA** (mayflies)

### BAETIDAE

*Cloeon simile* (Eaton) : common on NW in spring and autumn.

## **HEMIPTERA** (HETEROPTERA)

### LYGAEIDAE

#### Rhyparochrominae

*Stygnocoris fuligineus* (Geoff.) : under driftwood in gull meadow, SW 9/9/86.
*Scolopostethus affinis* (Schill.) : under driftwood in gull meadow, SW 9/9/86.

### **NABIDAE** (damsel bugs)

#### Nabinae

*Stalia major* (Costa) : under driftwood in gull meadow, SW 9/9/86.

## MIRIDAE (capsid bugs)

### Orthotylinae

*Heterotoma planicornis* (Pallas) : generally distributed on SW.
*Orthotylus marginalis* (Reut.) : in grass on NW 17/7/86.

### Mirinae

*Calocoris norvegicus* (Gm.) : common throughout.
*Capsus ater* (Linn.) : found in grass by Wylock Marsh in July 1986.

## NOTONECTIDAE (backswimmers)

*Notonecta obliqua* (Gallen) : one in pool on NW 29/4/87.
*Notonecta viridis* (Del.) : one in a weedy pool off Rakes Lane 16/9/86.

## PLEIDAE

*Plea leachi* (McG.) : common in weedy pool off Rakes Lane 16/9/86.

## CORIXIDAE (lesser water-boatmen)

### Corixinae

*Cymatia bonsdorffi* (Sahl.) : in pool on NW 29/4/87.
*Callicorixa praeusta* (Fieb.) : pool off Rakes Lane 16/9/86, on NW 29/4/87.
*Corixa panzeri/affinis* : a female in pool on NW 11/9/86.
*Corixa punctata* (Ill.) : common in swan pool, SW 14/9/86.
*Sigara concinna* (Fieb.) : central marsh SW, especially common in swan pool.
*Sigara distincta* (Fieb.) : in pools on NW 11/9/86.
*Sigara dorsalis* (Leach) : pool on NW 29/4/87.
*Sigara lateralis* (Leach) : pools in central marsh, SW 13/9/86.

# HEMIPTERA (HOMOPTERA)

## CERCOPIDAE (froghopper bugs)

### Cercopinae

*Philaenus spumarius* (Linn.) : abundant throughout.

## CICADELLIDAE (leafhopper bugs)

### Aphrodinae

*Aphrodes bicinctus* (Schr.) : on SW 10/9/85.

## CHAITOPHORIDAE

### Siphinae

*Sipha glyceriae* (Kalt.) : central marsh, SW on grasses and *Juncus* 14/8/65 (CSW-B).

## APHIDIDAE (aphids or plant lice)

### Aphidinae

*Aphis fabae* (Scop.) : eastern shoreline of SW on Annual Sea-blite, 19/8/65 (CSW-B).
*Rhopalosiphum padi* (Linn.) : one caught in flight on SW, 10/8/65 (CSW-B).

**Myzinae**

*Brachycaudus klugkisti* (Born.) : eastern shoreline, SW on Red Campion, 18/8/65 (CSW-B).
*Capitophorus hippophaes* (Walk.) : central marsh, SW on Spear Thistle 19/8/65 (CSW-B).
*Ericaphis ericae* (Born.) : eastern mud-flats, SW on Cross-leaved Heath, 12/8/65 (CSW-B).
*Hyperomyzus lactucae* (Linn.) : dense colony in the SW dunes on Perennial Sow-thistle 19/8/65 (CSW-B).
*Myzus ascalonicus* (Don.) : near the lighthouse, SW on Common Mouse-ear, 22/8/65 (CSW-B).
*Myzus certus* (Walk.) : east coast and dunes, SW on Wild Pansy 9/8/65 (CSW-B).

**Macrosiphinae**

*Acyrthosiphon auctus* (Walk.) : eastern shoreline of SW on Annual Sea-blite (CSW-B).
*Acyrthosiphon malvae geranii* (Mos.) : on Stork's-bill seaward of the dunes on SW 11/8/65 (CSW-B).
*Acyrthosiphon pisum* (Harr.) : numerous on seaward edge of east coast dunes, SW; on Restharrow, 11/8/65 (CSW-B).
*Dactynotus cirsii* (Linn.): central marsh, SW on Spear Thistle 14/8/65 (CSW-B).
*Metopolophium dirhodum* (Walk.) : SW, on the eastern mud-flats on Annual Sea-blite 8/8/65 (CSW-B).

## HYMENOPTERA (ACULEATA)

### CHRYSIDIDAE (ruby-tailed wasps)

**Chrysidinae**

*Omalus auratus* (Linn.) : occurs on brambles all over SW.

### FORMICIDAE (ants)

**Myrmicinae**

*Myrmica rubra* (Linn.) : found under driftwood in gull meadow, SW 14/7/85.
*Myrmica ruginodis* (Nyl.) : a mass emergence occurred on SW 11/9/85.
*Myrmica scabrinodis* (Nyl.) : under driftwood in gull meadow, SW.

**Formicinae**

*Lasius flavus* (Fabr.) : common on sandy turf on NW, also on Long Rein Point.
*Lasius niger* (Linn.) : commmon on sandy turf on SW.

### POMPILIDAE (spider-hunting wasps)

**Pompilinae**

*Episyron rufipes* (Linn.) : along wall by gate pool, SW 15/7/85.
*Pompilius cinereus* (Fab.) : in dunes on NW 11/9/86.

### EUMENIDAE (potter wasps)

*Gymnomerus laevipes* (Schuck.) : on brambles, SW 15/7/85.
*Ancistrocerus scoticus* (Curt.) : common throughout in July.

### SPHECIDAE (solitary or digger wasps)

**Crabroninae**

*Crabro cribrarius* (Linn.) : common on umbellifers on NW.

*Crabro peltarius* (Schreber) : common on umbellifers on NW.
*Crossocerus megacephalus* (Ross.) : common in the dunes of SW in July.
*Crossocerus wesmaeli* (van der L.) : common in the dunes of NW and SW in September.
*Oxybelus uniglumis* (Linn.) : small colonies in the dunes of NW and SW.

**Pemphredoninae**

*Pemphredon inornata* (Say) : found by the offices on SW in July.
*Pemphredon lethifer* (Schuck.) : found on bramble on SW in July.

**Mellininae**

*Mellinus arvensis* (Linn.) : common in the dunes of NW, especially in the autumn.

### COLLETIDAE

**Colletinae**

*Colletes succinctus* (Linn.) : one on the heather of NW 10/9/86.

### HALICTIDAE

**Halictinae**

*Lasioglossum laevigatum* (Kirby) : in the dunes on NW 11/9/86.

### MEGACHILIDAE

**Megachilinae**

*Megachile circumcincta* (Kirby) : one found on NW 15/7/86.

### APIDAE (bumblebees)

**Bombinae**

*Bombus lapidarius* (Linn.) : common throughout.
*Bombus lucorum* (Linn.) : common throughout.
*Bombus muscorum* (Linn.) : not uncommon on SW in September. A coastal species.
*Bombus pascuorum* (Scop.) : common throughout.
*Bombus pratorum* (Linn.) : one on Long Rein Point 10/9/87.
*Bombus terrestris* (Linn.) : common throughout.
*Psithyrus barbutellus* (Kirby) : one found in Rakes Lane 15/9/86. Said to breed in the nests of *Bombus hortorum* (Linn.) though this species was not found.
*Psithyrus bohemicus* (Seidl) : on the heather of NW 10/9/86. Breeds in the nests of *Bombus lucorum.*

**Apininae**

*Apis mellifera* (Linn.) : common throughout; the well-known Honeybee.

## MEGALOPTERA (alder flies)

### SIALIDAE

*Sialis lutaria* (Linn.) : common around pools on NW 29/4/87.

# NEUROPTERA (lacewings)

## CHRYSOPIDAE

*Chrysopa carnea* (Step.) : common throughout, hibernates as an adult.
*Chrysopa perla v. prasina* (Linn.) : one found on NW on 17/7/86.

# ODONATA (dragonflies and damselflies)

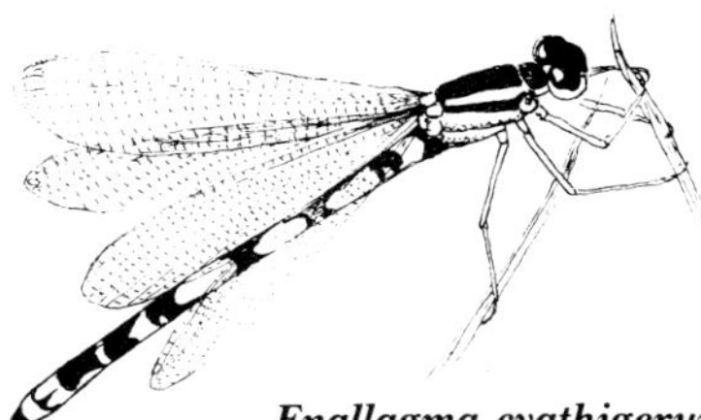

***Enallagma cyathigerum***

## COENAGRIIDAE

*Enallagma cyathigerum* (Charp.) : common on NW.
*Ishnura elegans* (van der L.) : common on NW and Snab Pools, seen once on reserve on SW.
*Pyrrhosoma nymphula* (Sulzer) : common on NW.

## LESTIDAE

*Lestes sponsa* (Hans.) : common on NW.

## AESHNIDAE

*Aeshna grandis* (Linn.) : common on NW and seen once on the reserve on SW.
*Aeshna juncea* (Linn.) : several sightings on NW in September and October (CMcC).

## CORDULEGASTERIDAE

*Cordulegaster boltonii* : one on NW 22/5/88 (TD).

## LIBELLULIDAE

*Libellula quadrimaculata* (Linn.) : not uncommon on NW.
*Sympetrum striolatum* (Charp.) : common on NW and several seen by the pools in Rakes Lane. One seen flying along the beach on the SW reserve in September 1986.

# ORTHOPTERA (grasshoppers)

## TETRIGIDAE

### Tetriginae

*Tetrix undulata* (Sow.) : one on NW 3/7/87; the common groundhopper.

## ACRIDIDAE

### Truxalinae

*Omocestus viridulus* (Linn.) : common throughout.
*Chorthippus brunneus* (Thun.) : common throughout.

# **TRICHOPTERA** (caddis flies)

## LIMNEPHILIDAE

### Limnephilinae

*Grammotaulius atomarius* (Fabr.) : common in moth trap by cottages, SW.
*Limnephilus affinis* (Curtis) : on SW around gate pool and in moth trap by cottages.
*Limnephilus lunatus* (Curtis) : in moth trap by cottages, SW in summer.
*Limnephilus luridus* (Curtis) : in moth trap by cottages, SW in summer.
*Limnephilus marmoratus* (Curtis) : on SW around gate pool 9/9/85.
*Limnephilus sparsus* (Curtis) : in moth trap by cottages, SW in summer.
*Limnephilus vittatus* (Fabr.) : in moth trap by cottages, SW in summer.

## LEPTOCERIDAE

*Triaenodes bicolor* (Curtis) : common by pools on NW 3/7/87.

# Invertebrates other than Insects

# **ISOPODA** (woodlice)

## LIGIIDAE

*Ligia oceanica* (Linn.) : common under stones on tide line on Long Rein Point.

## PORCELLIONIDAE

*Porcellio scaber* (Lat.) : abundant under driftwood on SW.

# **ARACHNIDA** (spiders)

## GNAPHOSIDAE

*Drassodes cupreus* (Black.) : By lighthouse on SW September 1987 (EEE).
*Drassodes pubescens* (Thorell) : NW 1985 (PK).
*Drassyllus lutetianus* (L.Koch) : SW 13/8/76 (JRP).

## CLUBIONIDAE

*Clubiona terrestris* (Westring) : NW 1985 (PK).

## THOMISIDAE

*Xysticus cristatus* (Clerck) : SW 13/8/76 (JRP) and September 1987 (EEE).

## PHILODROMIDAE

*Philodromus cespitum* (Walckenaer) : NW 1985 (PK).
*Tibellus oblongus* (Walckenaer) : SW 13/8/76 (JRP) and September 1987 (EEE)

## SALTICIDAE

*Euophrys frontalis* (Walckenaer) : NW 1985 (PK), SW (in Hardy, 1973).

## LYCOSIDAE

*Alopecosa pulverulenta* (Clerck) : By lighthouse on SW September 1987 (EEE).
*Arctosa perita* (Latreille) : SW 13/8/76 (JRP).
*Pardosa agricola* (Thorell) : SW 13/8/76 (JRP).
*Pardosa amentata* (Clerck) : central marsh, SW September 1987 (EEE).
*Pardosa monticola* (Clerck) : NW 1985 (PK).
*Pardosa nigriceps* (Thorell) : SW 13/8/76 (JRP), NW 1985 (PK).
*Pardosa pullata* (Clerck) : SW 13/8/76 (JRP), NW 1985 (PK).
*Pardosa purbeckensis* (Cambridge) : NW 1985 (PK).
*Pirata piraticus* (Clerck) : NW 1985 (PK).
*Trochosa ruricola* (DeG.) : central marsh, SW September 1987 (EEE).
*Xerolycosa miniata* (L. Koch) : by lighthouse on SW September 1987 (EEE).

## AGELENIDAE

*Tegenaria atrica* (C.L.Koch) : SW (in Hardy, 1973).

## THERIDIIDAE

*Enoplognatha ovata* (Clerck) : SW 13/8/76 (JRP).
*Theridion bimaculatum* (Linn.) : SW 13/8/76 (JRP).

## TETRAGNATHIDAE

*Pachygnatha clercki* (Sundevall) : SW 13/8/76 (JRP) and September 1987 (EEE).
*Tetragnatha extensa* (Linn.) : NW 1985 (PK).

## ARANEIDAE

*Agalenatea redii* (Scopoli) : NW 1985 (PK).
*Araneus diadematus* (Clerck) : SW 13/8/76 (JRP), NW 1985 (PK).
*Araneus quadratus* (Clerck) : NW 1985 (PK).
*Larinioides cornutus* (Clerck) : NW 1985 (PK).

## LINYPHIIDAE

*Diplocephalus permixtus* (Cambridge) : SW 13/8/76 (JRP).
*Erigone arctica* (White) : SW September 1987 (EEE).
*Erigone dentipalpis* (Wider) : SW 13/8/76 (JRP).
*Erigone longipalpis* (Sundevall) : SW 13/8/76 (JRP).
*Lepthyphantes tenuis* (Blackwall) : SW 13/8/76 (JRP).

*Leptorhoptrum robustum* (Westring) : SW 13/8/76 (JRP).
*Microlinyphia impigra* (Cambridge) : NW 1985 (PK).
*Oedothorax apicatus* (Blackwall) : SW September 1987 (EEE).
*Oedothorax fuscus* (Blackwall) : SW 13/8/76 (JRP).
*Oedothorax retusus* (Westring) : SW 13/8/76 (JRP).
*Tiso vagans* (Blackwall) : SW 13/8/76 (JRP).
*Tapinopa longidens* (Wider) : SW 13/8/76 (JRP).

## OPILIONES (harvestmen)

### NEMASTOMATIDAE

*Nemastoma bimaculatum* (Fabr.) : NW 1985 (PK).

### PHALANGIIDAE

*Mitopus morio* (Fabr.) : NW 1985 (PK).
*Opilio saxatilis* (C.L.Koch) : NW 1985 (PK).
*Phalangium opilio* (Linn.) : SW September 1987 (EEE).
*Platybunus triangularis* (Herbst) : NW 1985 (PK), SW September 1987 (EEE).

**References:**


**Angus, R. B.,** 1964. Some Coleoptera from Cumberland, Westmorland and the northern part of Lancashire. *Entomologist's Monthly Magazine.* 100:61-69.

**Angus, R. B.,** 1965. Further Coleoptera from Cumberland, Westmorland and the northern part of Lancashire. *Entomologist's Monthly Magazine.* 101:4-9.

**Barnard, P. C.,** 1978. A Check-list of British Neuroptera with Taxonomic Notes. *Entomologist's Gazette.* 29:165-176.

**Birkett, N. L.,** 1984. Some unusual brackish water Chironomids (Diptera) from Cumbria. *Entomologist's Gazette.* 35:197-198.

**Bradley, J. D. and Fletcher, D. S.,** 1986. *An Indexed List of British Butterflies and Moths.* Kedleston Press.

**Bradley, J. D., Tremewan, W. G. & Smith, A.,** 1973. *British Tortricoid Moths.* Ray Society.

**Colyer, C. N. & Hammond, C. O.,** 1968. *Flies of the British Isles.* 2nd edition. Warne.

**Ellis, J. V.,** 1890. *The Lepidopterous fauna of Lancashire and Cheshire.*

**Emmet, A. M.** Editor, 1979. *A Field Guide to the Smaller British Lepidoptera.* Brit. Ent. Nat. Hist. Soc.

**Fitton, M. G.** et al, 1978. A Check-list of British Insects (2nd. Ed.), pt. 4 Hymenoptera. *Handbk. Ident. Br. Insects* 11(4): 1-159.

**Goater, B.,** 1986. *British Pyralid Moths, a Guide to their Identification.* Harley Books.

**Hammond, C. O.,** 1977, *The Dragonflies of Great Britain and Ireland.* Curwen.

**Harde, K. W. & Hammond, P. M.** (Editor)., 1984. *A Field Guide in Colour to Beetles.* Octopus.

**Hardy, E.,** 1973. *The Naturalist in Lakeland.* David & Charles.

**Heath, J.** (Editor), 1976-. *The Moths and Butterflies of Great Britain and Ireland.* Vols 1, 2, 9, 10. Curwen and Harley Books.

**Joy, N. H.,** 1932. *A Practical Handbook of British Beetles.* Witherby.

**Kelly, L. S.,** 1968. *Field Naturalist.* 13: parts 1-3.

**Kloet, G. S. and Hincks, W. D.,** 1964. A Check-list of British Insects (2nd Ed.), pt. 1 Small Orders and Hemiptera. *Handbk. Ident. Br. Insects.* 11(1):1-119.

**Kloet, G. S. and Hincks, W. D.,** 1975. A Check-list of British Insects (2nd Ed.), pt. 5 Diptera and Siphonaptera. *Handbk. Ident. Br. Insects* 11(5):1-139.

**Merrett, P., Lockett, G. H., and Millidge, A. F.,** 1985. A check list of British Spiders. *Bulletin British Arachnological Society.* 6(9).

**NENWSH,** 1978. *The Natural Environment of North Walney and Sandscale Haws.* Borough of Barrow-in-Furness.

**Pope, R. D.,** 1977. A Check-list of British Insects (2nd Ed.), pt. 3 Coleoptera and Strepsiptera. *Handbk. Ident. Br. Insects* 11(3): 1-105.

**Rozkosny, R.,** 1984. The Sciomyzidae (Diptera) of Fennoscandia and Denmark. *Fauna Entomologica Scandinavica* 14: 1-224.

**Sankey, J. H. D., and Savory, T. H.,** 1974. *British Harvestmen.* Linnean Societv of London.

**Skinner, B.,** 1984. *Colour Identification Guide to Moths of the British Isles (Macrolepidoptera).* Viking.

**SoSW,** 1980. *A Study of South Walney.* Borough of Barrow-in-Furness.

**Stubbs, A & Chandler, P.** (Editors), 1978. A Dipterist's Handbook. *Amateur Entomologist* 15: 1-255.

**Stubbs, A. E. and Falk, S. J.,** 1983, *British Hoverflies.* Brit. Ent. Nat. Hist. Soc.

**Sutton, S. L.,** 1972. *Woodlice.* Ginn & Co.

**Wood-Baker, C. S.,** 1965. A List of Plant-lice (Homoptera-Aphidoidea) collected on South Walney during 1965. *South Walney Nature Reserve & Walney Bird Observatory Annual Report* No. 2.

***David Emley** works at Keele University and has been entomologically active for the last twenty years both in lecturing and research.*

# The Marine Invertebrate Fauna of Walney

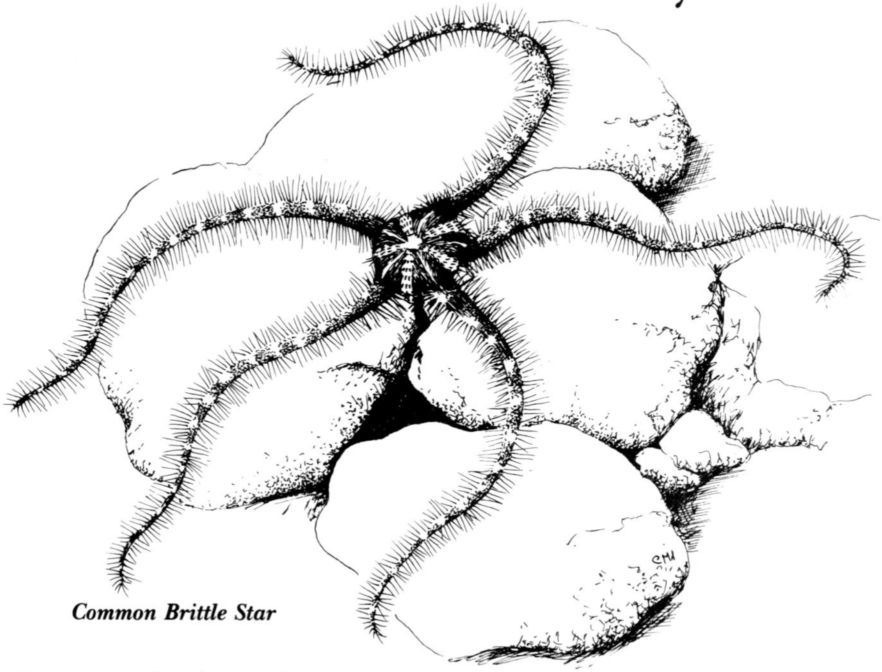


***Common Brittle Star***

**Protozoa** — Single-celled Animals.
*Noctiluca scintillans* — occasional, T. Dean.

**Porifera** — Sponges.
*Grantia compressa* — **(Purse Sponge),** 1980, F. Robinson.
*Halichondria panicea* — **(Breadcrumb Sponge),** 1980, F. Robinson.
*Spongelia fragilis* — 1888, Barrow Naturalists' F.C.

**Coelenterata** — Hydroids, Sea Anenomes, Jellyfish.
*Tubularia indivisa* — 1888, Barrow Naturalists' F.C.
*Campanularia verticillata* — 1888, Barrow Naturalists' F.C.
*Obelia geniculata* — 1888, Barrow Naturalists' F.C.
*Sertularia sp.* — **(Sea Oak),** 1980, F. Robinson.
*argentea* — 1888, Barrow Naturalists' F.C.
*Chrysaora hyoscella* — many beached 1985, T. Dean.
*Aurelia aurita* — many beached 1985, T. Dean.
*Rhizostoma octopus* — many beached 1985, T. Dean.
*Alcyonium digitatum* — **(Dead Man's Fingers),** 1973, E. Hardy.
*Actinea equina* — **(Beadlet Anenome),** 1888, Barrow Naturalists' F.C.; 1980, F. Robinson.
*Tealia felina* — **(Dahlia Wartlet),** 1888, Barrow Naturalists' F.C.; 1980, F. Robinson.

*Metridium senile* — 1888, Barrow Naturalists' F.C.
*Pleurobranchia pileus* — **(Sea Gooseberry),** 1980, T. Dean.

**Annelida —** Segmented Worms.
*Aphrodite sp.* — **(Sea Mouse),** 1980, F. Robinson.
*Eulalia viridis* — 1980, F. Robinson.
*Nereis pelagica* — 1980, T. Dean.
*diversicolor* — **(Rag Worm),** 1980, T. Dean.
*virens* — **(King Rag Worm),** 1980, T. Dean.
*Spiophanes bombyx* — 1973, E. Hardy.
*Pygospio elegans* — 1973, E. Hardy.
*Cirratulid sp.* — 1980, F. Robinson.
*Arenicola marina* — **(Lug Worm),** 1980, T. Dean.
*Sabellaria alveloata* — **(Honeycomb Worm),** 1980, F. Robinson.
*Lanice conchilega* — **(Sand Mason Worm),** 1980, F. Robinson.
*Pomatoceros sp.* — 1980, F. Robinson.
*Spirorbis sp.* — 1980, F. Robinson.

**Arthropoda —** Crabs, Shrimps, Copepods.
*Lepas fascicularis* — **(Buoy making Barnacle),** beached November 1982, T. Dean.
*Balanus balanoides* — **(Common Barnacle),** 1973, E. Hardy; 1980, F. Robinson.
*Elminius modestus* — **(Australasian Barnacle),** 1973, E. Hardy.
*Ligia oceanica* — **(Sea Slater),** 1980, F. Robinson.
*Gammarus sp.* — **(Sand Hopper),** 1980, F. Robinson.
*Pandalus montagui* — 1973, E. Hardy.
*Leander serratus* — **(Common Prawn),** 1980, F. Robinson.
*Crangon vulgaris* — **(Common Brown Shrimp),** 1973 E. Hardy.
*Homarus gammarus* — **(Lobster),** 1980, T. Dean.
*Porcellana sp.* — **(Porcelain Crab),** 1973, E. Hardy.
*Eupagurus bernardus* — **(Hermit Crab),** 1980, F. Robinson.
*Portunus puber* — **(Velvet Crab),** 1888, Barrow Naturalists' F.C.
*Carcinus maenas* — **(Shore Crab),** 1980, F. Robinson.
*Cancer pagurus* — **(Edible Crab),** 1980, F. Robinson.
*Hyas araneus* — **(Spider Crab),** 1973, E. Hardy.
*coarctatus* — 1973, E. Hardy.

**Ectoprocta —** Polyzoa, Sea Mats.
*Scrupocellaria reptans* — 1888, Barrow Naturalists' F.C.
*Bicellaria plumosa* — 1888, Barrow Naturalists' F.C.
*Flustra foliocea* — **(Hornwrack),** 1888, Barrow Naturalists' F.C.
*Membranipora membranacea* — 1888, Barrow Naturalists' F.C.
*Electra pilosa* — 1888, Barrow Naturalists' F.C.
*Crisia eburnea* — 1888, Barrow Naturalists' F.C.

**Echinodermata —** Starfish, Brittle Stars, Sea Urchins.
*Asterias rubens* — **(Common Starfish),** 1888, Barrow Naturalists' F.C.; 1980, F. Robinson.
*Solaster papposus* — **(Common Sun Star),** 1888, Barrow Naturalists' F.C.
*Henricia sp.* — **(Scarlet Starfish),** 1888, Barrow Naturalists' F.C.
*Ophiothrix fragilis* — **(Common Brittle Star),** 1888, Barrow Naturalists' F.C.; 8000 beached, 1973, E. Hardy.
*Psammechinus miliaris* — 1973, E. Hardy.

**Chordata** — Sea Squirts.
*Botryllus schlosseri* — **(Star Sea Squirt),** 1980, F. Robinson.
*Ascidiella aspersa* — 1973, E. Hardy.
*Ciona intestinalis* — 1973, E. Hardy.

***Spider Crab, Sand Mason Worm and Fucus serratus***

***References:***


Barrow Naturalists' Field Club. 1879-80, 1888 Annual reports.

Eales, N. B. 1967, The littoral fauna of the British Isles. Cambridge University Press, Cambridge.

Hardy, E. 1973, The Naturalist in Lakeland. David and Charles, Newton Abbot.

Robinson, F. 1980, The littoral fauna of Walney Island.

# The Non-Marine Mollusca of Walney

***Brown-lipped Snail***

*Cochlicopa lubrica* **(Slippery Snail).** Recorded at North Walney, 1988 (D. Coward).

*Arion ater* **(Black Slug).** Recorded at South and North Walney, 1984 (T. Dean).

*Vitrina pellucida* **(Pellucid Snail).** Present at South Walney, 1964 (P. Braithwaite), and 1984 (T. Dean).

*Oxychilus alliarus* **(Garlic Snail).** Recorded at South Walney, 1984 (T. Dean).

*Candidula intersecta* **(Wrinkled Snail).** Present at South Walney, 1963 and 1964 (P. Braithwaite); also 1984 (T. Dean). Recorded at North Walney, 1988 (D. Coward).

*Trichia hispida* **(Hairy Snail).** Present at South Walney, 1988 (T. Dean).

*Ponentina subvirescens.* Recorded at North Walney, 1988 (D. Coward), at the northern edge of its range.

*Cepaea nemoralis* **(Brown-lipped Snail).** Recorded at South and North Walney, 1984 (T. Dean).

*Cepaea hortensis* **(Garden Snail).** Present at South Walney, 1984 (T. Dean). Common on North Walney, 1984 (P. Kirkland).

*Helix aspersa* **(Common Snail).** Recorded at South and North Walney, 1983 (T. Dean).

***References:***

Garnett, M. and Milne, M. 1967, Lakeland Molluscs. Carlisle Natural History Society, Thurnam, Carlise.

# The Marine Mollusca of Walney

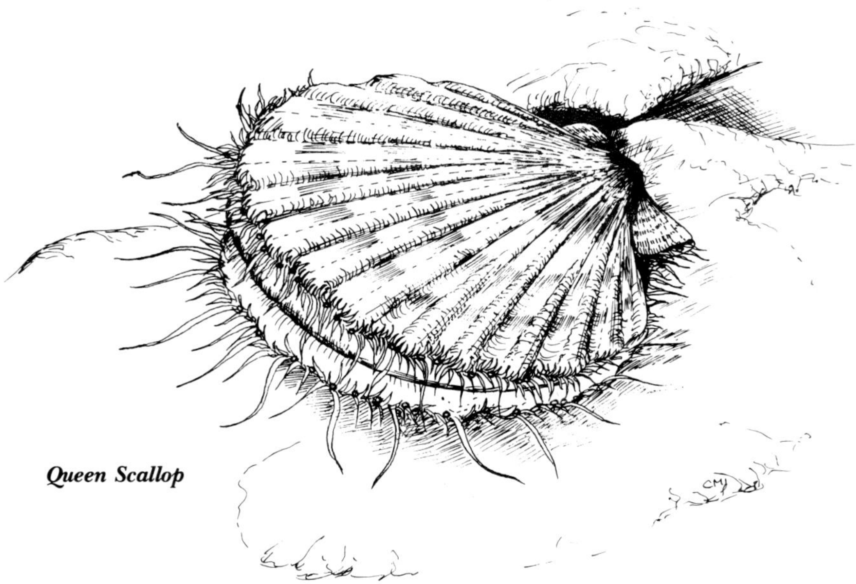

*Queen Scallop*

*Lepidopleurus asellus* **(Grey Mail-shell).** Rare, under boulders Earnse Point, 16th September 1951 (G.W.P.).

*Tonicella rubra* **(Red Mail-shell).** Rare, under boulders Earnse Point, 16th September 1951 (G.W.P.).

*Lepidochitona cinereus* **(Bordered Mail-shell).** Abundant, under boulders, 16th September 1951 (G.W.P.).

*Patella vulgata* **(Common Limpet).** Abundant, on boulders between Earnse Point and Hollow Scar, 6th September 1950 (G.W.P.). Dead shells, South Walney, 23rd August 1977 (Lord).

*Patina pellucida* **(Blue-rayed Limpet).** On *'Laminariae'* between Earnse Point and Hollow Scar, 4th September 1950 (G.W.P.).

*Calliostoma zizyphinum* **(Common Top-shell).** Dead shells between Mill Scar and Hollow Scar, 4th September 1950 (G.W.P.). Dead shells, South Walney, 23rd August 1977 (Lord).

*Gibbula magus* **(Painted Top-shell).** One, South Walney, 23rd August 1977 (Lord).

*Gibbula cineraria* **(Grey Top-shell).** On boulders and seaweed, Tummer Hill Scar, 8th September 1949. Plentiful on boulders and seaweed, Hollow Scar, 4th September 1950 (G.W.P.). Several dead shells, South Walney, 23rd August 1977 (Lord).

*Gibbula umbilicalis* **(Flat Top-shell).** Scarce, on boulders, Hollow Scar, 4th September 1950 (G.W.P.).

*Littorina littorea* **(Common Winkle).** Abundant, 27th August 1950 (G.W.P.). Dead shells, South Walney, 23rd August 1977 (Lord).

*Littorina saxatilis* **(Rough Winkle).** Common (G.W.P.).

*Littorina saxatilis tenebrosa.* Plentiful, Tummer Hill Marsh, 22nd July 1956 (G.W.P.).

*Littorina saxatilis rudis.* Plentiful, 4th September 1950 (G.W.P.).

*Littorina littoralis* **(Flat Winkle).** Abundant among *'Fucus vesiculosus'*, 6th September 1950 (G.W.P.). Dead shells, South Walney, 23rd August 1977 (Lord).

*Hydrobia ulvae* **(Laver Spire-shell).** Abundant, Tummer Hill Marsh, 22nd July 1956 (G.W.P.).

*Turritella communis* **(Auger-shell).** Recorded, 6th September 1950 (G.W.P.).

*Capulus ungaricus* **(Hungarian Cap).** One recently dead shell, Earnse Point, 16th September 1951. Two fresh shells between Earnse Point and North Scar, 12th September 1957 (G.W.P.).

*Aporrhais pes-pelicani* **(Pelican's-foot).** Present between Earnse Point and Hollow Scar, 6th September 1950, and between Earnse Point and North Scar, 12th September 1957 (G.W.P.).

*Natica catena* **(Large Necklace-shell).** Present, North Scar, 12th September 1957 (G.W.P.).

*Natica poliana* **(Common Necklace-shell).** Present, North Scar, 12th September 1957 (G.W.P.).

*Trivia monacha* **(European Cowry).** Dead shells cast on shore, Earnse Point, 16th September 1951 (G.W.P.). A fresh shell at South Walney, 23rd August 1977 (Lord).

*Velutina velutina* **(Velvet-shell).** One fresh shell at South Walney, 23rd August 1977 (Lord).

*Nucella lapillus* **(Dog-whelk).** Abundant, Earnse Point to Hilpsford Scar. Large specimens at Tummer Hill Scar, 8th September 1949 (G.W.P.).

*Ocenabra erinacea* **(Sting-whelk).** Dead shells, South Walney, 23rd August 1977 (Lord).

*Colus gracilis* **(Slender Spindle-shell).** Dead shells plentiful between Earnse Point and Hollow Scar, 16th September 1951 (G.W.P.).

*Neptunea antiqua* **(Red Whelk).** Dead shells abundant between Earnse Point and Hollow Scar, 4th September 1950 (G.W.P.).

*Buccinum undatum* **(Common Whelk).** Recorded in 1864 by Harting. Present, Earnse Point, 16th September 1951 (G.W.P.). Dead shells, South Walney, 23rd August 1977 (Lord).

*Tricla lignaria* **(Canoe-shell).** Present, North Scar, 12th September 1957 (G.W.P.).

*Nucula turgida* **(Shining Nut-shell).** One valve, South Walney, 23rd August 1977 (Lord).

*Glycymeris glycymeris* **(Dog-cockle).** Dredged from Morecambe Bay 1921 (Hopwood).

*Anomia ephippium* **(Saddle-oyster).** Dead shell at South Walney, 23rd August 1977 (Lord).

*Monia patelliformis* **(Ribbed Saddle-oyster).** Morecambe Bay, May 1893 (Specimen in Liverpool Museum).

*Mytilus edulis* **(Common Mussel).** Abundant between Earnse Point and Cross Dyke Scar, 6th September 1950 (G.W.P.). Dead shells, South Walney, 23rd August 1977 (Lord).

*Modiolus modiolus* **(Horse Mussel).** A fragment at South Walney, 23rd August 1977 (Lord).

*Modiolus barbatus* **(Bearded Horse Mussel).** Fairly common, Morecambe Bay, 1921 (Hopwood).

*Ostrea edulis* **(Common Oyster).** Dead shells between Earnse Point and Hollow Scar, 4th September 1950 (G.W.P.). Old valves, South Walney, 23rd August 1977 (Lord).

*Chlamys varia* **(Variegated Scallop).** Dead shells, Earnse Point to Hollow Scar, 4th September 1950 (G.W.P.). Several old valves at South Walney, 23rd August 1977 (Lord).

*Chlamys varia purpurea.* Earnse Point, 16th September 1951 (G.W.P.).

*Chlamys opercularis* **(Queen Scallop).** Fairly common, Morecambe Bay, 1921 (Hopwood). Dead shells plentiful between Earnse Point and Hollow Scar, 4th September 1950 (G.W.P.). Fresh valves at South Walney, 23rd August 1977 (Lord).

*Cyprina islandica* **(Iceland Cyprina).** Rare, Morecambe Bay, 1921 (Hopwood). Dead shells plentiful, North Scar, 12th September 1957 (G.W.P.).

*Cardium echinatum* **(Prickly Cockle).** Frequent, Morecambe Bay, 1921 (Hopwood). Dead shells common between Earnse Point and Hollow Scar 4th September 1950. Living specimens cast ashore between Earnse Point and North Scar, 12th September 1957 (G.W.P.). Present at South Walney, 23rd August 1977 (Lord).

*Cardium edule* **(Common Cockle).** Recorded by Harting in 1864, abundant.

*Dosina exoleta* **(Rayed Artemis).** Recorded, Morecambe Bay, 1921 (Hopwood).

*Dosina lupinus* **(Smooth Artemis).** Recorded, Morecambe Bay, 1921 (Hopwood). Living specimens cast ashore between Earnse Point and North Scar, 12th September 1957 (G.W.P.).

*Venus ovata* **(Oval venus).** Morecambe Bay, 1892 (specimens in Liverpool Museum).

*Venus striatula* **(Striped Venus).** Not common, Morecambe Bay, 1921 (Hopwood). Recorded North Scar, 12th September 1957 (G.W.P.). Dead shell, South Walney, 23rd August 1977 (Lord).

*Venerupis rhomboides* **(Banded Carpet-shell).** Rather rare, Morecambe Bay, 1921 (Hopwood). Dead shells, Earnse Point to Hollow Scar, 4th September 1950 (G.W.P.).

*Venerupis pullastra* **(Pullet Carpet-shell).** Recorded, Morecambe Bay, 1921 (Hopwood). Dead shells plentiful between Earnse Point and Hollow Scar, 4th September 1950 (G.W.P.). Dead shells, South Walney, 23rd August 1977 (Lord).

*Donax vittatus* **(Banded Wedge-shell).** Common, Earnse Point to Hollow Scar, 12th September 1957 (G.W.P.).

*Tellina tenuis* **(Thin Tellin).** Fine specimens common, Earnse Point to North Scar, 12th September 1957 (G.W.P.).

*Tellina crassa* **(Blunt Tellin).** Morecambe Bay, 1891 and 1893 (specimens in Liverpool Museum).

*Macoma balthica* **(Baltic Tellin).** Fresh pairs, South Walney, 23rd August 1977 (Lord).

*Abra alba* **(White Furrow-shell).** Living specimens cast ashore between Earnse Point and Hollow Scar, 12th September 1957 (G.W.P.).

*Ensis ensis* **(Sword Razor).** Common, Morecambe Bay, 1921 (Hopwood).

*Ensis arcuatus.* A fresh specimen, South Walney, 23rd August 1977 (Lord).

*Ensis siliqua* **(Pod Razor).** Morecambe Bay 1892 (specimens in Liverpool Museum). Recorded, North End, 18th September 1951 (G.W.P.).

*Mactra corallina cinerea* **(Rayed Trough-shell).** Recorded, North Scar, 12th September 1957 (G.W.P.).

*Spisula elliptica* **(Elliptical Trough-shell).** Present, Earnse Point to North Scar, 12th September 1957 (G.W.P.).

*Spisula solida* **(Thick Trough-shell).** Living specimens cast ashore between Earnse Point and North Scar, 12th September 1957 (G.W.P.). Dead shell, South Walney, 23rd August 1977 (Lord).

*Lutraria lutraria* **(Common Otter-shell).** Common, Morecambe Bay (Brooks).

*Mya truncata* **(Blunt Gaper).** Common, Morecambe Bay, 1921 (Hopwood). Several valves, South Walney, 23rd August 1977 (Lord).

*Barnea candida* **(White Piddock).** Dead shells between Earnse Point and North Scar, 12th September 1957 (G.W.P.).

*Alloteuthis subulata.* Recorded, Morecambe Bay, 1921 (Hopwood). One stranded alive, west shore, June 1959 (Walkden).

*Loligo forbesi* **(Common Squid).** Present, Morecambe Bay, 1886 (Darbishire), 1921 (Hopwood). Walkden considers it common off the west coast of Walney, in Walney Channel and in Morecambe Bay. Large numbers stranded alive September and October 1959, the coastline apparently 'saturated'.

*Sepia officinalis* **(Common Cuttle).** Dredged from Morecambe Bay, 1921 (Hopwood). Walkden considers it quite common in the area.

*Sepia atlantica* **(Little Cuttle).** Walkden reports it as fairly common off the west coast of the island and in Morecambe Bay.

***References:***

Garnett, M. and Milne, M. 1967, Lakeland Molluscs. Carlisle Natural History Society, Thurnam, Carlisle.

Hardy, E. 1973, The Naturalist in Lakeland. David and Charles. Newton Abbot.

Harting, J. E. 1864, The birds of Walney Island.

Lord. 1977, List of shells collected at South Walney.

McMillan, N. 1962, The Marine Mollusca of Lancashire and Cheshire. Lancashire and Cheshire Fauna Society.

Robinson, F. 1983, The littoral fauna of Walney Island.

# The Fish of Walney

***Red Mullet***

**Sea Lamprey** *(Petromyzon marinus).* Infrequent in Morecambe Bay (MacPherson 1892).

**Basking Shark** *(Cetorhinus maximus).* During summer one or two pass the island Walkden (1962). Singles were seen off South Walney on 5th and 29th July 1964, and in Lighthouse Bay on 14th September 1985. Also reported off Sandy Gap on 20th September 1985.

**Thresher** *(Alopias vulpinus).* Reported from the Duddon Estuary (Walkden 1962).

**Tope** *(Galeorhinus galeus).* All authors refer to its commonness. Price (1982) states that it is common from mid-April until migration in October.

**Blue Shark** *(Prionace glauca).* Walkden (1962) reports two instances from Walney Channel; a single on 4th June 1959, and two specimens on 7th.

**Lesser Spotted Dogfish** *(Scyliorhinus caniculus).* Although MacPherson (1892) regards it as unknown in shallow waters, Walkden (1962) considers it ubiquitous in the Irish Sea.

**Monkfish** *(Squattina squattina).* Recorded in Walney Channel (Walkden 1962).

**Thornback Ray** *(Raja clavata).* All authors regard it as fairly common.

**Starry Ray** *(Raja radiata).* A specimen was taken on 4th July 1964 (Walkden 1972).

**Spotted Ray** *(Raja montagui).* Walkden (1962) describes it as rare.

**Cuckoo Ray** *(Raja naevus).* Some are caught in the Piel area, but mainly off the west coast of Walney (Walkden 1962).

**Skate** *(Raja batis).* Both MacPherson (1892) and Walkden (1962) consider it common. Price (1982) states that although once frequent, the species is now rare.

**Herring** *(Clupea harengus).* Both MacPherson (1892) and Walkden (1962) report its abundance.

**Sprat** *(Sprattus sprattus)*. Both MacPherson (1892) and Walkden (1962) consider it plentiful.

**Trout** *(Salmo trutta)*. Although MacPherson (1892) states it as common, Price (1982) informs us that it is not often caught.

**Smelt** *(Osmerus eperlanus)*. MacPherson (1892) maintains that the species moves into the Bay in autumn, and Walkden (1962) cites an old record of Herdman and Dawson (1902), "taken in Barrow Channel".

**Common Eel** *(Anguilla anguilla)*. Walkden (1962) and Price (1982) refer to it as widely distributed.

**Conger Eel** *(Conger conger)*, MacPherson (1892) describes it as 'often taken', Walkden (1962) as 'abundant', and Price (1982) as 'fairly common'. Walkden (1972) reports a specimen of 100-120 lbs. taken off Walney.

**Garfish** *(Belone belone)*. Walkden (1962) cites E. Wheeler of Walney lighthouse who reports that the species is occasionally taken.

**Broad-nosed Pipefish** *(Syngnathus typhle)*. Not common, although can be found off the west shore (Walkden 1962).

**Nilsson's Pipefish** *(Syngnathus rostellatus)*. Walkden (1962) is of the opinion that closer examination would reveal the species as common.

**Great Pipefish** *(Syngnathus acus)*. Fairly common off the west shore (Walkden 1962).

**Snake Pipefish** *(Entelurus aequoreus)*. Rare in the Barrow/Walney area (Walkden 1962).

**Worm Pipefish** *(Nerophis lumbriciformis)*. There are only two records, one taken by Walkden from Walney Channel on 30th August 1960 (Walkden 1962), and the other from Roa Island on 14th August 1968 (Walkden 1972).

**Sea-horse** *(Hippocampus hippocampus)*. According to Walkden (1962), the species was widely distributed in small numbers in the Walney/Barrow area up to 1930, but was now rarely found.

**Cod** *(Gadus morrhua)*. All authors consider it widely distributed and common.

**Haddock** *(Melanogrammus aeglefinus)*. Walkden (1962) states that the species is subject to periods of great abundance which alternate with periods of scarcity.

**Bib** *(Trisopterus luscus)*. Not common in the area; Walkden (1962) can only report small shoals.

**Poor-cod** *(Trisopterus minutus)*. Rare in the Barrow area (Walkden 1962).

**Whiting** *(Merlangius merlangus)*. MacPherson (1892) states that a few are taken in Morecambe Bay, while Walkden (1962) describes it as abundant in sandy estuaries. Price (1982) refers to it as one of few fish taken during winter.

**Norway Pout** *(Trisopterus esmarkii)*. Walkden (1962) reports it from the inshore waters of Morecambe Bay, while Price (1982) informs us that it is caught from May to June.

**Pollack** *(Pollachius pollachius)*. Although described by Walkden (1962) as uncommon in the area, it is now caught with increasing frequency according to Price (1982).

**Saithe** *(Pollachius virens)*. MacPherson (1892) refers to it as common although Walkden (1962) maintains that it is uncommon and occurs only in small numbers. Price (1982) mentions its increasing regularity.

**Greater Forkbeard** *(Phycis blennioides).* Walkden (1962) cites Johnstone (1910) who reports it from Walney.

**Three-bearded Rockling** *(Gaidropsarus vulgaris).* MacPherson (1892) records a few, Walkden (1962) considers that it may be commoner than expected, and Price (1982) states it is very common.

**Five-bearded Rockling** *(Ciliata mustela).* Described as very common in the area Walkden (1962).

**Bass** *(Dicentrarchus labrax).* All authors consider it to be regular and at times abundant in the region between April and November.

**Red Mullet** *(Mullus surmuletus).* According to Walkden (1962) it is well known to the fishermen of Morecambe Bay.

**Red Sea Bream** *(Pagellus bogaraveo).* Walkden (1962) cites Herdman and Dawson (1902) who record it as frequently taken in Morecambe Bay.

**Cuckoo Wrasse** *(Labrus mixtus).* Although Walkden (1962) regards it as rare, he also suggests that it is increasing in the area.

**Corkwing** *(Creilabrus melops).* Rare, but odd specimens are taken in the region of Piel (Walkden 1962).

**Greater Sand-eel** *(Hyperoplus lanceolatus).* Recorded from Morecambe Bay and the Furness region (Walkden 1962).

**Sand-eel** *(Ammodytes tobianus).* Abundant (Walkden 1962).

**Lesser Weever** *(Trachinus vipera).* Abundant and widely distributed (Walkden 1962).

**Dragonet** *(Callionymus lyra).* Abundant in shallow waters (Walkden 1962).

**Thick-lipped Mullet** *(Crenimugil labrosus).* Walkden (1962) and Price (1982) consider it to be extremely common around Walney between May and early November.

**Mackerel** *(Scomber scombrus).* MacPherson (1892) and Walkden (1962) reckon it to be widespread, and common in Walney Channel prior to industrial pollution. Price (1982) maintains it is abundant between June and October.

**Tunny** *(Thunnus thynnus).* Walkden (1962) records a single specimen of 200 lbs. off Scarth Channel in 1929.

**Shanny** *(Blennius pholius).* Very common in Walney Channel (Walkden 1962).

**Butterfish** *(Pholis gunnellus).* Walkden (1962) and Price (1982) regard it as widely distributed and often found under stones near low water.

**Sand Goby** *(Gobius minutus).* Walkden (1962) considers it to be probably common in the area.

**Common Goby** *(Pomatoschistus microps).* Walkden (1962) believes it to be as common as the Sand Goby.

**Transparent Goby** *(Aphia minuta).* Walkden (1962) cites Herdman and Dawson (1902) who regard it as occasional in Walney Channel.

**Grey Gurnard** *(Eutrigla gurnardus).* Widely distributed (Walkden 1962).

**Tub Gurnard** *(Trigla lucerna).* Walkden (1962) cites Herdman and Dawson (1902) who recorded it from Walney Channel.

**Red Gurnard** *(Aspitrigla cuculus).* Frequently taken (Walkden 1962).

**Father Lasher** *(Myoxocephalus scorpius)*. Common on mussel scars (Walkden 1962).

**Norway Bullhead** *(Taurulus lilljeborgi)*. Very common (Price 1982).

**Sea Scorpion** *(Taurulus bubalis)*. Walkden (1962) cites Herdman and Dawson (1902) who recorded it from Walney Channel.

**Pogge** *(Agonus cataphractus)*. Considered by Walkden (1962) to be abundant, Price (1982) regards it as rare.

**Lumpsucker** *(Cyclopterus lumpus)*. Walkden (1962) cites E. Wheeler of Walney lighthouse who reports it as plentiful at times. Price (1982) states that it is found in pools on the west shore of the island.

**Sea Snail** *(Liparis liparis)*. Widely distributed (Walkden 1962).

**Montagu's Sea Snail** *(Liparis montagui)*. Widely distributed (Walkden 1962).

**Three-spined Stickleback** *(Gasterosteus aculeatus)*. Prolific in Barrow docks and Walney (Walkden 1962).

**Sea Stickleback** *(Spinachia spinachia)*. Seen in Walney Channel (Walkden 1962).

**Turbot** *(Scophthalmus maximus)*. All authors agree that it is scarce and rarely taken.

**Brill** *(Scophthalmus rhombus)*. MacPherson (1892) considers it to be plentiful in some seasons. Walkden (1962) and Price (1982) assert that it is taken less frequently now.

**Topknot** *(Zeugopterus punctatus)*. Rare, but odd specimens (Walkden 1962).

**Dab** *(Limanda limanda)*. Described by Walkden (1962) as "the most prolific fish in the Walney area". Very common (Price 1982).

**Plaice** *(Pleuronectes platessa)*. All authors reckon it to be abundant.

**Flounder** *(Platichthys flesus)*. Regarded as abundant by all authors.

**Lemon Sole** *(Microstomus kitt)*. Recorded from the area (Walkden 1962).

**Sole** *(Solea solea)*. Fairly abundant (Walkden 1962).

**Solenette** *(Buglossidium luteum)*. Not common (Walkden 1962).

**Angler** *(Lophius piscatorius)*. Walkden (1962) regards it as fairly common, while according to Price (1982), it is rarely caught.

***References:***


Hardy, E. 1973, The Naturalist in Lakeland. David and Charles. Newton Abbot.

MacPherson, H. A. 1892, A vertebrate fauna of Lakeland. David Douglas, Edinburgh.

Price, G. 1982, Furness beach and boat fishing. Barrow Printing Co. Ltd.

Walkden, R. 1962, Lancashire and Cheshire Fauna Society. September 1962 and 1972.

# The Seaweeds of South Walney

Dr. Charles Rose

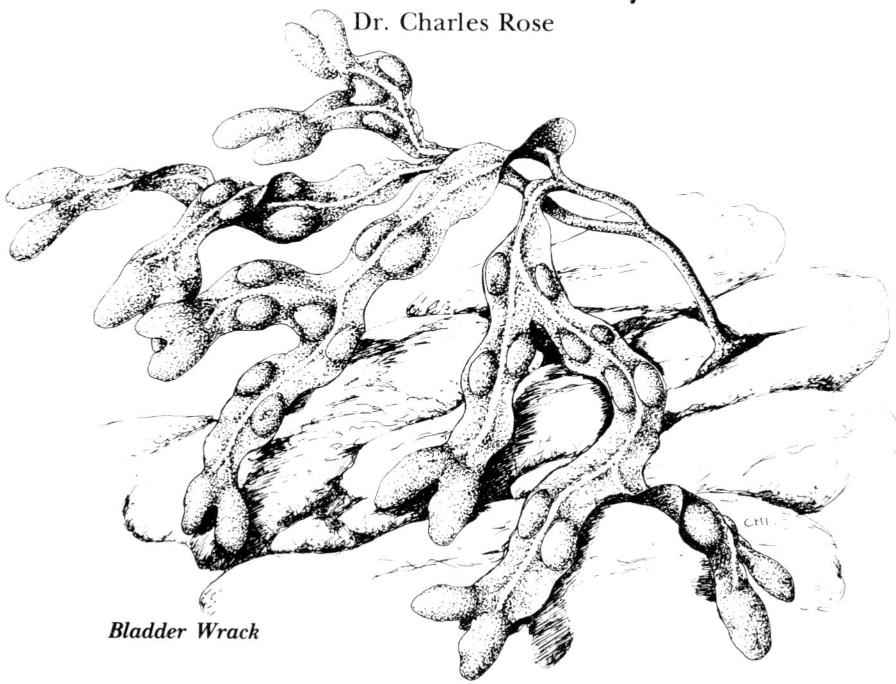


***Bladder Wrack***

During a visit to South Walney Nature Reserve, the intertidal flora will be, by no means, obvious to the casual observer. Seaweeds are seldom consciously noticed by the layman, even when they occur in profusion, and on South Walney, the sparsity of algal distribution gives the initial impression that the shores are devoid of any plant life. There are coastal habitats around Britain where seaweeds are found in spectacular amounts, with great specific variety, mainly where the coastal geology is of a rocky nature. However, the reserve's shores consist of gently sloping, sandy middle and lower zones, with the highest levels of the beaches being covered with smoothly rounded pebbles. Almost without exception, seaweeds need to be anchored in a particular location for their survival for various reasons. They are normally attached by means of a 'root system' known as a holdfast, which has no conventional root functions of mineral and water absorption but acts merely, as the nature suggests, to anchor the plant to the substratum. Obviously, therefore, some solid object needs to be adhered to, such as rock-outcrops, or man-made objects. A tour of the reserve's shores will reveal that such attachment points are small in number and size. The extent of a rocky outcrop with its attendant covering of larger seaweeds e.g. *Fucus vesiculosus*, can have an effect on the species diversity of an area, as the bigger seaweeds will protect the smaller, more delicate species around their bases from the elements at low tide, and from wave action when immersed. Shelter from such exposure is also afforded by rock pools, but on South Walney's shores, very few of these exist also.

The attachment of seaweeds occurs when microscopic spores, released into the sea by mature plants, come into contact with solid objects. These spores consist of no more than a few cells, and initial adhesion is fairly tenuous, by means of a layer of mucus.

On a pebbly shore we are all familiar with the constant movement of the stones as the waves break and ebb; indeed this is how the pebbles attain their smooth rounded shapes. Obviously any microscopic seaweed plantlet may be scraped off the pebble's surface at this stage, and as a consequence the only seaweeds to be found on pebbly shores are relatively scarce, microscopic encrusting algae (e.g. *Lithophyllum*).

There are several advantages for seaweeds to be fixed in one position. Some are to do with the need for proximity to other plants for reproduction purposes, but the main reasons for immobilisation are concerned with the plants' energy requirements. Like most land plants, seaweeds depend on the process of photosynthesis to produce 'food', this in turn being dependent on light. The depth to which seaweeds are found growing, and to some extent their profusion, depends mainly on the depth to which light will penetrate the seawater. In Britain, the maximum penetration depth (or photic zone) is approximately 20 metres in areas where the water is clear. Where, as is the case around Walney's shores, there is suspended sand and mud, the depth of the photic zone is reduced, as is the amount of light reaching any particular level within the zone. The light-filtering and scattering effects of the water and suspended solids also changes the spectral quality of the light reaching the seaweeds, with progressively less of the shorter wavelengths being present the deeper the penetration. Plants near to the water surface make use of light of a similar quality as land plants do, and the green chlorophylls are the predominant absorbing pigments. The deepest growing seaweeds receive mainly light in the red end of the spectrum and are consequently red in colour. In between these zones, brown seaweeds tend to predominate.

Zonation on the shore is complicated by other factors, such as each species tolerance to exposure to the air at low tide, and the availability of suitable attachment sites. It is not surprising therefore, that on South Walney with its lack of solid substrata and its muddied waters, that the biomass of seaweeds present is small, and the specific variety reduced compared with rocky coastal areas with clear waters.

## List of Species

### *Chlorophyceae*

*Enteromorpha compressa* — (C. Rose, 1985)
*Enteromorpha intestinalis* — (F. Robinson, 1980; C. Rose, 1985)
*Enteromorpha minima* — (C. Rose, 1985)
*Ulva lactuca* — (F. Robinson, 1980; C. Rose, 1985)
*Cladophora restangularis* — (E. Hodgson, 1876)
*Cladophora rupestris* — (C. Rose, 1985)
*Cladophora utriculosa* — (E. Hodgson, 1876)
*Cladophora glaucescens* — (Barrow Naturalists' F.C. 1879-80)
*Bryopsis hypnoides* — (E. Hodgson, 1876)

***Phaeophyceae***

*Ectocarpus fasciculatus* — (C. Rose, 1985)
*Mesogloia Griffithsiana* — (C. Rose, 1985)
*Desmarestia aculeata* — (E. Hodgson, 1876; C. Rose, 1985)
*Punctaria plantaginea* — (C. Rose, 1985)
*Punctaria latifolia* — (Barrow Naturalists' F.C. 1879-80)
*Cladostephus spongiosus* — (C. Rose, 1985)
*Stypocaulon scoparium* — (E. Hodgson, 1876)
*Chorda fylum* — (C. Rose, 1985)
*Laminaria saccharina* — (F. Robinson, 1980; C. Rose, 1985)
*Laminaria digitata* — (F. Robinson, 1980)
*Saccorhiza bulbosa* — (C. Rose, 1985)
*Alaria esculenta* — (F. Robinson, 1980)
*Dictyota dichotoma* — (E. Hodgson, 1876)
*Fucus spiralis* — (C. Rose, 1985)
*Fucus vesiculosus* — (F. Robinson, 1980; C. Rose, 1985)
*Fucus serratus* — (E. Hodgson, 1876; F. Robinson, 1980; C. Rose, 1985)
*Ascophyllum nodosum* — (F. Robinson, 1980; C. Rose, 1985)

***Rhodophyceae***

*Porphyra umbilicalis* — (C. Rose, 1985)
*Polyides rotundus* — (E. Hodgson, 1876; F. Robinson, 1980; C. Rose, 1985)
*Lithophyllum incrustans* — (C. Rose, 1985)
*Corallina officinalis* — (E. Hodgson, 1876; T. Dean, 1983)
*Delesseria sanguinea* — (E. Hodgson, 1876)
*Membranoptera alata* — (E. Hodgson, 1876)
*Hypoglossum Woodwardii* — (E. Hodgson, 1876)
*Phycodrys rubens* — (E. Hodgson, 1876; C. Rose, 1985)
*Cryptopleura ramosum* — (Barrow Naturalists' F.C. 1879-80)
*Rhodomela subfusca* — (E. Hodgson, 1876)
*Rhodomela lycopodiodes* — (E. Hodgson, 1876)
*Laurencia obtusa* — (E. Hodgson, 1876)
*Laurencia pinnatifida* — (E. Hodgson, 1876)
*Polysiphonia urceolata* — (E. Hodgson, 1876)
*Polysiphonia var. formosa* — (E. Hodgson, 1876)
*Polysiphonia fastigata* — (E. Hodgson, 1876; C. Rose, 1985)
*Polysiphonia elongata* — (E. Hodgson, 1876)
*Polysiphonia fibrillosa* — (E. Hodgson, 1876)
*Polysiphonia violaceae* — (E. Hodgson, 1876)
*Polysiphonia nigrescens* — (C. Rose, 1985)
*Polysiphonia var. affinus* — (Barrow Naturalists' F.C. 1879-80)
*Brongniartella byssoides* — (E. Hodgson, 1876)
*Griffithsia flosculosa* — (C. Rose, 1985)
*Rhodochorton floridulum* — (C. Rose, 1985)
*Antithamnion plumula* — (E. Hodgson, 1876)
*Ceramium diaphanum* — (Barrow Naturalists' F.C. 1879-80; C. Rose, 1985)
*Ceramium botrycarpum* — (Barrow Naturalists' F.C. 1879-80)
*Ceramium rubrum* — (C. Rose, 1985)
*Ceramium flabelligerum* — (Barrow Naturalists' F.C. 1879-80)

*Microcladia glandulosa* — (Barrow Naturalists' F.C. 1879-80)
*Chondrus crispus* — (C. Rose, 1985)
*Gigartina stellata* — (Barrow Naturalists' F.C. 1879-80; C. Rose, 1985)
*Phyllophora epiphylla* — (E. Hodgson, 1876)
*Ahnfeltia plicata* — (Barrow Naturalists' F.C. 1879-80)
*Gracilaria confervoides* — (C. Rose, 1985)
*Calliblepharis ciliata* — (Barrow Naturalists' F.C. 1879-80)
*Calliblepharis lanceolata* — (E. Hodgson, 1876)
*Rhodymenia palmata* — (C. Rose, 1985)
*Lomentaria articulata* — (E. Hodgson, 1876)
*Champia parvula* — (E. Hodgson, 1876)
*Chylocadia kaliformis* — (E. Hodgson, 1876)
*Plocamium coccineum* — (E. Hodgson, 1876)

## Survey areas.

### 1) Hilpsford to Sea hide.

On this seaward shore the upper pebbly area of the beach supports no seaweeds. Immediately below this zone the sandy shore also has very few examples. the most obvious species is *Porphyra umbilicalis,* a transient red seaweed that resembles pieces of wet, black plastic attached to pebbles embedded in the sand. In the past this species has been collected from Walney and sent to South Wales, to be the main constituent of laver bread. At the junction of the pebbles and the sand, in moist depressions, the almost microscopic, strap-like green seaweed *Enteromorpha minina,* forms small vivid green patches. At extremely low tides a walk further down the beach will reveal a greater diversity of species, on and around an old shipwreck, the only good solid attachment point for seaweeds in this area. A variety of larger species can be found here e.g. *Fucus* sp., *Laminaria saccharina* and *Palmaria palmata.* The greens are less common at this depth but a healthy amount of *Enteromorphas* and *Ulva lactuca* are present adhering to the wreck and surrounding stones. This area is sheltered by a large ridge of mud and stones on the seaward side with the result that a few of the more delicate species grow e.g. several species of filamentous *Ceramium, Polysiphonia* and *Cladophora* and the leaf-like *Phycodrys* and *Punctaria.* Also the adjacent sand has large stones buried in it allowing the fastening of larger seaweeds e.g. *Chorda, Gracilaria* and the large leathery *Laminaria.*

### 2) Sea hide to the groyne.

The rest of the western shore is of a similar make-up but with fewer embedded stones in the lower shore and with a greater degree of exposure to wave action. Consequently, virtually the only species to be found is the encrusting *Lithophyllum,* which appears as a pinkish/red stain on some pebbles.

The concrete groyne at the southeast point of the reserve provides the only real adhesion site. Smaller reds, browns and greens are afforded some protection by crevices in the concrete and a reasonable growth of *Fucus.* Species diversity is probably prevented by strong tidal currents and a high degree of exposure. One rather interesting *rhodopycean* to be found around the groyne is one of the British seaweeds that has no conventional attachment organ. *Rhodochorton floridulum* is a microscopic sand-binder that can only be found by gently crushing lumps of sand which are anchored to the sheltered sides and crevices of the groyne.

### 3) The spit.

The shore on the seaward side of the spit differs from the west shore as it is more steeply sloping and is less exposed to wave action. There are a few man-made structures where similar seaweeds to those growing at the groyne can be found, particularly on an old concrete light base, where a cover of *Fucus* grows. The edible *Chondrus crispus* and the similar *Polyides rotundus* can easily be found on the middle levels of the shore, and at extreme low tides the edge of deep water (Haws Hole) is exposed and reveals a fairly extensive deep-water bed of such species as *Laminaria, Mesogloia* and *Sacchoriza.*

### 4) Lighthouse Bay.

Because this area is a gently sloping bay with a large amount of saltmarsh, the intertidal region consists of either higher plants or smooth sandy mud below the pebbly shore. This and the length of exposure to the air between tides makes this area particularly poor for seaweeds. The only exception is the tract of the upper middle shore at the northeast point, where embedded stones support a small amount of species already listed.

### 5) The pier.

The old sand and gravel works pier is the largest solid structure to be found on South Walney's beaches and it holds the only seaweed community that has members normally met with on the upper shore. *Ascophyllum nodosum,* a large brown, can be seen hanging from the pitch-pine struts. None of these plants are of any great age (determined by counting the number of air bladders on a strap), and there is not a large amount of this or any other species present. This is probably due to competition for space with animal life e.g. barnacles and mussels, which contest with seaweeds in areas where conditions are not ideal for seaweed growth, caused here by low light conditions of the very muddied waters. Another seaweed present on the pier which is typical of the zone, is *Polysiphonia fastigiata* which grows on the *Ascophyllum* plants, partially parasitically.

### 6) The pier to the boundary wall (Haws Bed).

Following the shore westwards from the pier, the only apparent seaweed is *Fucus vesiculosus* attached to stones embedded at the top of the main channel. However, at the junction of the muddy sand and the upper shore pebbles, a green band of closely adhering *Enteromorpha* is found, which on closer examination proves to consist of three delicate species *Enteromorpha compressa, Enteromorpha clathrata* and *Enteromorpha minima.*

One small spot of prolific seaweed growth on this shore is where an outfall emerges on to the beach from the gravel pools inland. The almost constant flow of seawater has created a depression in the sand, always full of aerated water. Within this pool are a variety of delicate greens and reds, and the surrounding structure of the outfall supports mainly *Fucus vesiculosus.*

### 7) The gravel pools.

In the centre of the reserve there exists a fairly extensive system of gravel pools which have connection with the open sea by means of a sluice. This results in the pools being capable of supporting seaweed growth. Some exchange of water between the pools and the sea occurs with each tidal cycle, but dilution of the salinity will occur due to the effects of rainfall, causing the pools to vary in salinity, as occurs in an estuarine situation. Similar effects occur commonly on the seashore in rock pools which are also subject to dilution by rain; the gravel pools, however, differ in their vast expanse and depth, and their construction of sand and gravel.

*Enteromorpha ramulosa,* normally found between the tide marks, grows near the sluice, the source of the sea-water. *Enteromorpha compressa* and *Entermorpha intestinalis,* both typical of estuarine or brackish waters, can be found further into the pool system. During the spring and summer months, the surfaces of the connecting canals can be covered by floating *Enteromorpha intestinalis.* This is caused by the plant's tubular construction becoming inflated with oxygen produced in photosynthesis, its appearance giving rise to its specific Latin name.

## Species Lists for specific locations.

### 1) Hilpsford to Sea hide

| | |
|---|---|
| ***Chlorophyceae*** | *Enteromorpha compressa*<br>*Enteromorpha intestinalis*<br>*Enteromorpha minima*<br>*Ulva lactuca*<br>*Cladophora rupestris* |
| ***Phaeophyceae*** | *Ectocarpus fasciculatus*<br>*Desmerestia aculeata*<br>*Punctaria plantaginea*<br>*Chorda filum*<br>*Laminaria saccharina*<br>*Fucus spiralis*<br>*Fucus vesiculosus*<br>*Fucus serratus* |
| ***Rhodophyceae*** | *Porphyra umbilicalis*<br>*Lithophyllum incrustans*<br>*Phycodrys rubens*<br>*Polysiphonia nigrescens*<br>*Griffithsia flosculosa*<br>*Ceramium diaphanum*<br>*Ceramium rubrum*<br>*Ceramium sp.*<br>*Gracilaria confervoides*<br>*Rhodymenia palmata* |

### 2) Sea hide to the groyne

| | |
|---|---|
| ***Chlorophyceae*** | *Enteromorpha intestinalis*<br>*Enteromorpha minima*<br>*Ulva lactuca* |

| | |
|---|---|
| ***Phaeophyceae*** | *Ectocarpus fasciculatus*<br>*Cladostephus spongiosus*<br>*Fucus vesiculosus* |
| ***Rhodophyceae*** | *Porphyra umbilicalis*<br>*Lithophyllum incrustans*<br>*Rhodochorton floridulum*<br>*Ceramium diaphanum*<br>*Chondrus crispus*<br>*Rhodymenia palmata* |

**3) The spit**

| | |
|---|---|
| ***Chlorophyceae*** | *Enteromorpha compressa*<br>*Enteromorpha intestinalis*<br>*Enteromorpha minima*<br>*Ulva lactuca*<br>*Cladophora rupestris* |
| ***Phaeophyceae*** | *Ectocarpus fasciculatus*<br>*Mesogloia Griffithsiana*<br>*Desmerestia aculeata*<br>*Sacchoriza bulbosa*<br>*Fucus spiralis*<br>*Fucus vesiculosus* |
| ***Rhodophyceae*** | *Porphyra umbilicalis*<br>*Polyides rotundus*<br>*Rhodochorton floridulum*<br>*Ceramium rubrum*<br>*Ceramium sp.*<br>*Chondrus crispus* |

**4) Lighthouse Bay**

| | |
|---|---|
| ***Chlorophyceae*** | *Enteromorpha compressa*<br>*Enteromorpha minima* |
| ***Phaeophyceae*** | *Fucus spiralis*<br>*Fucus vesiculosus* |
| ***Rhodophyceae*** | *Porphyra umbilicalis* |

**5) The pier**

| | |
|---|---|
| ***Phaeophyceae*** | *Fucus spiralis*<br>*Fucus vesiculosus*<br>*Ascophyllum nodosum* |
| ***Rhodophyceae*** | *Polysiphonia fastigiata*<br>*Chondrus crispus*<br>*Gigartina stellata* |

### 6) The pier to the boundary wall (Haws Bed)

| | |
|---|---|
| ***Chlorophyceae*** | *Enteromorpha clathrata*<br>*Enteromorpha compressa*<br>*Enteromorpha intestinalis*<br>*Enteromorpha minima*<br>*Ulva lactuca* |
| ***Phaeophyceae*** | *Fucus vesiculosus* |
| ***Rhodophyceae*** | *Polysiphonia nigrescens*<br>*Ceramium diaphanum*<br>*Ceramium rubrum* |

### 7) The gravel pools

| | |
|---|---|
| ***Chlorophyceae*** | *Enteromorpha ramulosa*<br>*Enteromorpha compressa*<br>*Enteromorpha intestinalis* |

***References:***


Barrow Naturalists' Field Club. 1879-80 Annual report.

Hodgson, E. 1876, Barrow Naturalists' F.C.

Newton, L. 1931, A handbook of British seaweeds. British Museum of Natural History, London.

Robinson, F. 1980, The littoral fauna of Walney Island.



***Charles Rose*** *studied botany at Swansea University and researched into the effects of marine pollution on seaweeds for his doctorate.*

# The Phytoplankton of South Walney's Saline Pools

*Adenoides eludens* — April 1985, K. Thompson.
*Biddulphia alternans* — May, June 1984, K. Thompson.
*Chaetoceros debilis* — June 1985, K. Thompson.
*Chaetoceros socialis* — July, August 1983; October 1984; October 1985, K. Thompson.

*Coscinodiscus granii* — November 1983; June, October 1985, K. Thompson.
*Coscinodiscus eccentricus* — June 1983; August, October 1985, K. Thompson.
*Eucampias zoodiacus* — August, October, November 1983, K. Thompson.
*Gonyaulax tamerensis* — July 1983; September 1985, K. Thompson.
*Gymnodinium incolouratum* or *vitiligo* — March to June, December 1983; January to June 1984; April, May, November, December 1985; February, March, May, August, September 1986, K. Thompson.

*Gymnodinium splendens* — November, December 1986, K. Thompson.
*Gyrodinium aureoleum* — May, July 1983; January to May, August 1984; June 1985, K. Thompson.

*Katodinium rotundatum* — March 1983; August 1986, K. Thompson.
*Melosira juergensii* — April 1984; May 1985, K. Thompson.
*Navicula sp.* — July 1983; April, May 1984, K. Thompson.
*Nitzschia closterium* — March, August, October to December 1983; April, May, August, October 1984; April to October 1985; February, March, June to September 1986, K. Thompson.

*Nitzschia delicatissima* — August 1984, K. Thompson.
*Oliscodiscus valvolarea* — May to July 1983, K. Thompson.
*Oxyrrhis marina* — April, May, August, November 1983; June, July 1984; April, June, July, October 1985, K. Thompson.

*Parasitische euglena* — March, April, June, July, November, December 1983; January, February, April, May, July, August, October 1984; April to July, November, December 1985; February to July, September 1986, K. Thompson.

*Peridinium sp.* — November 1983, K. Thompson.
*Pyramimonas sp.* — May 1983, K. Thompson.
*Rhizosolenia delicatula* — July, November 1983; August to October 1984; April, July, October 1985; August 1986, K. Thompson.

*Skeletonema sp.* — March to May 1983; July 1985, K. Thompson.

***References:***


Dodge, J. D. 1982, Marine Dinoflagellates of the British Isles. H.M.S.O. London.
Dreves, G. 1974, Marines Phytoplankton. G. Thieme Verlag, Stuttgart.
Parke, M. and Dixon, P. S. 1976, Check-list of British Marine Algae. Journal of marine biology.
Sykes, J. B. 1981, An illustrated guide to the Diatoms of British coastal plankton. Field Studies Council, Invicta Press, Kent.